Heidegger and the Emergence of the Question of Being

Also Available From Bloomsbury

Bloomsbury Studies in Continental Philosophy presents cutting-edge scholarship in the field of modern European thought. The wholly original arguments, perspectives and research findings in titles in this series make it an important and stimulating resource for students and academics from across the discipline.

Adorno's Concept of Life, Alastair Morgan
Adorno's Poetics of Critique, Steven Helmling
Badiou and Derrida, Antonio Calcagno
Badiou, Marion and St Paul, Adam Miller
Being and Number in Heidegger's Thought, Michael Roubach
Crisis in Continental Philosophy, Robert Piercey
Deleuze and Guattari, Fadi Abou-Rihan
Deleuze and Guattari's Philosophy of History, Jay Lampert
Deleuze and the Genesis of Representation, Joe Hughes
Derrida, Simon Morgan Wortham
Derrida and Disinterest, Sean Gaston
Derrida: Ethics Under Erasure, Nicole Anderson
Domestication of Derrida, Lorenzo Fabbri
Encountering Derrida, Simon Morgan Wortham
Foucault's Heidegger, Timothy Rayner
Foucault's Legacy, C.G. Prado
Gabriel Marcel's Ethics of Hope, Jill Graper Hernandez
Gadamer and the Question of the Divine, Walter Lammi
Gilles Deleuze, Constantin V. Boundas
Heidegger and a Metaphysics of Feeling, Sharin N. Elkholy
Heidegger and Authenticity, Mahon O'Brien
Heidegger and Happiness, Matthew King
Heidegger and Philosophical Atheology, Peter S. Dillard
Heidegger and the Place of Ethics, Michael Lewis
Heidegger Beyond Deconstruction, Michael Lewis
Heidegger, Politics and Climate Change, Ruth Irwin
Heidegger's Early Philosophy, James Luchte
In the Shadow of Phenomenology, Stephen H. Watson
Irony of Heidegger, Andrew Haas
Kant, Deleuze and Architectonics, Edward Willatt
Merleau-Ponty's Phenomenology, Kirk M. Besmer

Merleau-Ponty's Existential Phenomenology and the Realization of Philosophy,
Bryan A. Smyth
Michel Henry, Jeffrey Hanson
Nietzsche and the Anglo-Saxon Tradition, Louise Mabille
Nietzsche's Ethical Theory, Craig Dove
Nietzsche's Thus Spoke Zarathustra, James Luchte
Phenomenology, Institution and History, Stephen H. Watson
Ricoeur and Lacan, Karl Simms
Sartre's Phenomenology, David Reisman
Simultaneity and Delay, Jay Lampert
Thinking Between Deleuze and Kant, Edward Willatt
Who's Afraid of Deleuze and Guattari?, Gregg Lambert
Žižek and Heidegger, Thomas Brockelman

Forthcoming in this series:

Philosophy, Sophistry, Antiphilosophy: Badiou's Dispute with Lyotard,
Matthew R. McLennan
Heidegger, History and the Holocaust, Mahon O'Brien
Desire in Ashes: Deconstruction, Psychoanalysis, Philosophy, Simon Morgan Wortham

Heidegger and the Emergence of the Question of Being

Jesús Adrián Escudero

Translated by Juan Pablo Hernández Betancur

Bloomsbury Academic
An imprint of Bloomsbury Publishing Plc

B L O O M S B U R Y
LONDON · OXFORD · NEW YORK · NEW DELHI · SYDNEY

Bloomsbury Academic
An imprint of Bloomsbury Publishing Plc

50 Bedford Square
London
WC1B 3DP
UK

1385 Broadway
New York
NY 10018
USA

www.bloomsbury.com

BLOOMSBURY and the Diana logo are trademarks of Bloomsbury Publishing Plc

First published 2015
Paperback edition first published 2016

© Jesús Adrián Escudero, original edition published in Spanish by
Herder Editorial S.L., Barcelona, Spain 2010

English language translation © Juan Pablo Hernández Betancur 2015

Jesús Adrián Escudero has asserted his right under the Copyright, Designs and
Patents Act, 1988, to be identified as the Author of this work.

All rights reserved. No part of this publication may be reproduced or transmitted
in any form or by any means, electronic or mechanical, including photocopying,
recording, or any information storage or retrieval system, without prior
permission in writing from the publishers.

No responsibility for loss caused to any individual or organization acting on or
refraining from action as a result of the material in this publication can be
accepted by Bloomsbury or the author.

British Library Cataloguing-in-Publication Data
A catalogue record for this book is available from the British Library.

ISBN: HB: 978-1-47251-180-5
PB: 978-1-47429-944-2
ePDF: 978-1-47250-514-9
ePub: 978-1-47250-740-2

Library of Congress Cataloging-in-Publication Data
A catalog record for this book is available from the Library of Congress.

Series: Bloomsbury Studies in Continental Philosophy

Typeset by RefineCatch Limited, Bungay, Suffolk

Contents

Acknowledgements		ix
Abbreviations		xi
1	Introduction	1
2	Historical and Intellectual Context	13
3	The Hidden Root of Being in Heidegger's Early Writings	21
4	From the Being of Factual Life to the Meaning of Being as Such	40
5	Development and Methodological Presuppositions of the Hermeneutic Phenomenology	86
	Conclusion	149
Notes		153
Bibliography		173
Index		198

Acknowledgements

This book is a shortened version of a book written in Spanish and published by Herder publishers under the title *Heidegger y la genealogía de la pregunta por el ser. Una articulación temática y metodológica de su obra temprana* (2010). It is the result of several years of research on Heidegger's early work, which began with a research stay during the winter semester, 1999–2000, at Freiburg University. During this time, and under close supervision by Friedrich-Wilhelm von Herrmann, I finished writing my doctoral dissertation on the young Heidegger. Since then, I have edited and translated several of Heidegger's writings and lecture courses, and published a number of papers on his work and thought. All that work is now gathered in this book. I thank the publishers of *Analecta Husserliana, Anales del Seminario de Metafísica, Dianoia, Eidos, Enrahonar, Gatherings, The Heidegger Circle Annual, Heidegger Studien, Pensamiento, Phainomena, Philosophisches Jahrbuch, Philosophy Today, Signos Filosóficos, Revista de Filosofía* and *Taula* and *Quaderns de Pensament Thémata* for giving me their permission to use part of the material they published for the composition of this book.

I owe to my wife the spiritual strength necessary to undertake a work such as this. She supported and encouraged me during the many hours we shared at our office. Without her perseverance and love I would still be working on the preliminaries of this book. I cannot forget to mention my son, who despite his youth has had to put up with my constant travels and research stays. This book is a way of giving back to them some of the many hours together I have robbed them of and of showing them my gratefulness for their support.

Among the numerous persons that have followed closely the elaboration of this book I would like to mention professors Raúl Gabás Pallás (Universidad Autónoma de Barcelona), Friedrich-Wilhelm von Herrmann (Albert Ludwig University of Freiburg) and Franco Volpi (Università degli Studi di Padova).

I have been able to discuss many aspects of this monograph with my close friend, colleague and former professor, Raúl Gabás Pallás. His wide-ranging view of the history of philosophy and his knowledge of Heidegger's work have allowed me to understand better Heidegger's philosophy and to frame it in the context of his discussions with other philosophers.

Since the aforementioned research stay at Freiburg University, I have been able to continue discussing the complex process that led Heidegger to the elaboration of hermeneutic phenomenology with Professor Friedrich-Wilhelm von Herrmann. His exhaustive knowledge of Husserl's work and his thorough assistance during my reading of Heidegger's early work have been extremely helpful for disentangling the so-called hermeneutic transformation of phenomenology. I want to express here my gratitude for his advice and encouragement during the last several years.

Likewise, I would like to thank the late professor Franco Volpi, who lost his life in 2009 in a tragic accident. The memories of him and his friendship will continue to accompany all of those who, like me, were lucky enough to meet him. He has left us a marvelous philosophical legacy. His numerous publications and editions in relation to Heidegger are an obligatory reference for any researcher in the field of Heidegger studies. From here I say to Franco: *Danke, mein lieber Iron-Freund!*

Among the colleagues with whom I have been able to discuss different parts of this book I would like to mention Ángel Xolocotzi, Arturo Leyte, Alejandro Vigo, Francisco de Lara, Jean-François Courtine, Jean Grondin, Peter Trawny, Ramón Rodríguez, Richard Capobianco and Richard Polt.

I would also like to mention that part of this work was written in the University of Padova, where I spent the spring of 2008 as an invited professor. This was possible thanks to Franco Volpi's help and a grant from the Agència de Gestió d'Ajuts Universitaris i de Recerca de la Generalitat de Catalunya that was part of the programme 'Beques per a estades de recerca fora de Catalunya' (BE1 2008). The research supporting this book was partially undertaken as part of the research projects 'Guía de lectura de Ser y tiempo de Martin Heidegger' (HUM 2005-05965) and 'El vocabulario filosófico de Martin Heidegger' (FFI 2009-13187 FISO), funded by Spain's Ministry of Science and Innovation. During the complex process of revision of the English translation I have enjoyed the Fellowship for Advanced Researchers granted by the Humboldt Foundation (2012–2014). Finally, I would like to thank the publisher of the Spanish version, Raimund Herder, who kindly conferred the translation rights on Bloomsbury.

Abbreviations

Texts of Heidegger

Volumes of the *Gesamtausgabe*

GA 1	*Frühe Schriften*
GA 2	*Sein und Zeit*
GA 9	*Wegmarken*
GA 13	*Aus der Erfahrung des Denkens*
GA 15	*Seminare*
GA 16	*Reden und andere Zeugnisse eines Lebensweges*
GA 17	*Einführung in die phänomenologische Forschung*
GA 18	*Grundbegriffe der aristotelischen Philosophie*
GA 19	*Plato: Sophistes*
GA 20	*Prolegomena zur Geschichte des Zeitbegriffes*
GA 21	*Logik. Die Frage nach der Wahrheit*
GA 22	*Grundbegriffe der antiken Philosophie*
GA 23	*Geschichte der Philosophie von Thomas von Aquin bis Kant*
GA 24	*Die Grundprobleme der Phänomenologie*
GA 25	*Phänomenologische Interpretation von Kants Kritik der reinen Vernunft*
GA 26	*Metaphysische Anfangsgründe der Logik*
GA 27	*Einleitung in die Philosophie*
GA 28	*Der deutsche Idealismus*
GA 29/30	*Die Grundbegriffe der Metaphysik. Welt – Endlichkeit – Einsamkeit*
GA 31	*Vom Wesen der menschlichen Freiheit*
GA 33	*Aristoteles*, Metaphysik θ, *1–3*
	Von Wesen und Wirklichkeit der Kraft
GA 42	*Schelling. Vom Wesen der menschlichen Freiheit*

GA 49	*Die Metaphysik des deutschen Idealismus*
GA 56/57	*Zur Bestimmung der Philosophie*
GA 58	*Grundprobleme der Phänomenologie*
GA 59	*Phänomenologie der Anschauung und des Ausdruckes*
GA 60	*Phänomenologie des religiösen Lebens*
GA 61	*Phänomenologische Interpretationen zu Aristoteles. Einführung in die phänomenologische Forschung*
GA 62	*Phänomenologische Interpretationen ausgewählter Abhandlungen des Aristoteles zu Ontologie und Logik*
GA 63	*Ontologie. Hermeneutik der Faktizität*
GA 64	*Der Begriff der Zeit (Abhandlung 1924)*
GA 66	*Besinnung*

Other Heideggerian texts

AKJ	*Anmerkungen zu Karl Jaspers' Psychologie der Weltanschauungen*
BH	*Brief über den Humanismus*
BZ	*Der Begriff der Zeit (Vortrag 1924)*
KPM	*Kant und das Problem der Metaphysik*
KV	*Kasseler Vorträge*
NB	*Phänomenologische Interpretationen zu Aristoteles. Anzeige der hermeneutischen Situation (Natorp-Bericht)*
SuZ	*Sein und Zeit*
US	*Unterwegs zur Sprache*
VS	*Vier Seminare*
WM?	*Was ist Metaphysik?*
ZSD	*Zur Sache des Denkens*

English abbreviations

BCAP	*Basic Concepts of Aristotelian Philosophy*
BP	*The Basic Problems of Phenomenology*
BT	*Being and Time*
CKJ	*Comments on Karl Jaspers' Pyschology of Worldviews*

HCT	*History of the Concept of Time*
HF	*Ontology. The Hermeneutics of Facticity*
IP	*Idea of Philosophy*
IPR	*Introduction to Phenomenological Research*
KNS	*Kriegsnotsemester (The Idea of Philosophy and the Problem of Worldview)*
LQT	*Logic. The Question of Truth*
MWP	*My Way to Phenomenology*
OWL	*On the Way to Language*
PIA	*Phenomenological Interpretations of Aristotle*
PS	*Plato's Sophist*
PRL	*The Phenomenology of Religious Life*
WM?	*What is Metaphysics?*

Other authors

Augustine

Conf.	*Confessions*

Aristotle

De an.	*On the Soul*
Nic. Eth.	*Nichomachean Ethics*
Phy.	*Physics*
Met.	*Metaphysics*
Pol.	*Politics*
Rhet.	*Rhetoric*

Husserl

HU III/1	*Ideen zu einer reinen Phänomenologie und phänomenologischen Philosophie*. First book
HU XVIII	*Logische Untersuchungen*. First volume: *Prolegomena zur reinen Logik*
HU XIX/1	*Logische Untersuchungen*. Second volume/Book one: *Untersuchungen zur Phänomenologie und Theorie der Erkenntnis*

HU XIX/2	*Logische Untersuchungen.* Second volume/Book two: *Untersuchungen zur Phänomenologie und Theorie der Erkenntnis*
HU XI	*Analysen zur passiven Synthesis*
HU XVII	*Formale und transzendentale Logik*
HU XXXI	*Aktive Synthesen*

English abbreviations of Husserl's works

Ideas	*Ideas*
Log. Inv.	*Logical Investigations*

Paul

Cor.	*Letters to Corinthians*
Heb.	*Letters to Hebrews*
Gal.	*Letters to Galatians*
Rom.	*Letters to Romans*
Thess.	*Letters to Thessalonians*

1

Introduction

Being is the ether in which man breathes. Without this ether, he would descend to the mere beast and his whole activity to the breeding of beasts.

Martin Heidegger

Schelling. Vom Wesen der menschlichen Freiheit[1]

Every great philosopher thinks only one single thought, as Heidegger liked to say in his classes. At this point, there is no novelty in saying that what characterized Heidegger's thinking is the question about the meaning of being. Heidegger himself confirmed this in several autobiographical comments. However, as the first lecture courses of Heidegger's early period come to light, seeing how the horizon of that question is delineated in the context of a rich interplay of philosophical superpositions, an interplay that in one way or another seeks to travel the path that goes from human life to the question of being, is something that can still awaken the interest of the readers of *Being and Time*. The young Heidegger's thinking moved across that track, constantly coming back to the steps taken by the philosophical tradition in order to reach a primordial understanding of human existence. During his first years as a PhD student, Heidegger began his philosophical journey, moving between the rigour of Catholic theology and the systematic character of neo-Kantianism, the prevailing school of thought in German universities at the beginning of the twentieth century. But it was a long time before Heidegger moved away from that intellectual environment, so formal and far removed from the matters of real life. During the post-war period Heidegger began to dive into the sources of the mediaeval mystics and Paul's epistles, and into Augustine's writings and Luther's work. All these within the framework of a philosophical quest into the ontological constitution of human life and a precocious discovery of Husserl's phenomenology, with its ability to get to the root of things themselves. Despite the deep differences between his own work and Husserl's transcendental phenomenology, the latter continued to be a constant companion of Heidegger's thinking throughout, as did Dilthey's hermeneutics and, above all, Aristotle's practical philosophy. These are, without a doubt, three names that are crucial to understanding the philosophical and academic itinerary of a young Heidegger determined to rethink the meaning of being in a fully radical way.

Now what is the leading thread of Heidegger's thought? When did his early philosophical programme begin to crystallize? How did he reinterpret Husserlian phenomenology in a hermeneutic key? What role do thinkers such as Aristotle, Kant, Dilthey and Husserl play in this period? What was the intellectual environment in which Heidegger's thinking moved during the 1920s? These are some of the questions I want to address in this work. I will draw on the rich textual evidence that is available nowadays and maintain a constant dialogue with the main inquiries into the subject published in the last two decades.

The question regarding the being of factical life as the leading thread of the young Heidegger's thinking

What does being mean? This is the question that Heidegger asked himself over and over again from his years as a student up until the end of his life.[2] To be sure, the problem of being is the central subject matter of his thought, the topic that articulates all his philosophical endeavours and delineates the horizon upon which one must approach each aspect of his work. *Being and Time* starts off with the firm purpose of 'working out the question about the meaning of *being* and to do so concretely' (SuZ 1/ BT, xxiv, italics in the original).[3] But what do we really understand by being? Why is it so important and necessary to formulate once again the question about its meaning? The only way to reach an adequate answer to these questions is by considering Heidegger's discussion of the philosophical tradition. For the main culprit of the systematic forgetfulness into which this fundamental question has fallen is the blind and uncritical acceptance of the meaning of being handed down by the tradition. Even the modern philosophy of subjectivity has contributed to make this hermeneutic situation of forgetfulness even more acute. This is why it is so imperative to undertake a radical reformulation of the question of being, a reformulation that reaches back to the origins of Greek philosophy.

It was Aristotle who, drawing on Parmenides, formulated the question What is a being? Or more exactly, What are beings *qua* beings? However, this way of formulating the question deploys a determinate *way* of understanding the meaning of being on the basis of beings. By 'beings' is understood everything that is. In this sense, stones, plants, animals and human beings are beings. When we define beings as that which *is*, we define them on the basis of a previous understanding of something else.

> What then is philosophy supposed to concern itself with if not with beings, with that which is, as well as with the whole of what is? [...] What can there be apart from nature, history, God, space, number? We say of each of these, even though in a different sense, that it *is*. We call it a being. In relating to it, whether theoretically or practically, we are comporting ourselves towards a being. [...] In the end, something is given, which *must* be given, if we are to be able to make beings accessible to us as beings, and comport ourselves towards them; something which, to be sure, is not, but which must be given, if we are to experience and understand something like beings at all. We are able to grasp beings as such, as beings, only

when we understand something like *being*. If we did not understand, even though at first roughly and without conceptual comprehension, what actuality signifies, then the actual would remain hidden from us. [...] We must understand being so that we may be able to be given over to a world that *is*, so that we can exist in it and be our own Dasein itself as a being. We must be able to understand actuality *before* all factual experience of actual beings. This understanding of actuality or of being in the widest sense as over against the experience of beings is in a certain sense *earlier* than the experience of beings.

GA 24, 13–14/BP, 11–12, italics in the original

This fundamental and irreducible level of reality, which transcends all that is immediately given, is called 'being'.

Now is it possible to reach a representation of something like being? Any attempt to do so leaves us in a state of perplexity. Heidegger's philosophy revolves precisely around the recognition that being cannot be thematized, that is to say, that it is not an object one can study in order to enunciate the list of its properties. Being is not *a being*, and therefore it cannot be the object of a representation. There is an insurmountable ontological difference between being and beings. By the same token, being cannot be defined. So we need to turn to the pre-understanding we always have of being. For this reason, the only alternative is to show being on the basis of the aforementioned ontological experience. For being is always in some way given with every particular being. Being provides the comprehension that is present in all comportment towards beings. But comporting towards beings is a distinctive possibility of a particular type of beings, namely, we ourselves, human beings, Dasein. In this way, the particular being that asks about being becomes the object of the question.

And how are we to understand human being in its relation to being? As *zoon logon echon, animale rationale*, spirit, subject, self-consciousness? Heidegger rejects all these conceptions of human being because they ground the different ways of access to things exclusively in perception and reason. In other words, these conceptions understand the reality of all existent things exclusively through the prism of theory. Heidegger reproaches the ancient and modern philosophical traditions for not having distinguished in a clear way between the essence of things and the essence of human being, to the point that in these traditions human being was categorially understood as something existent out there in front of the subject. Heidegger's innovative proposal is to understand human being as characterized by care (*Sorge*). This conception puts the accent on the primarily practical relation that the finite, historical and temporal human being has with what is real. From this perspective, Dasein is understood as thrown projection (*geworfener Entwurf*) and not as a being that is rationally transparent, sovereign and autonomous. This new conception of the human 'subject' is what sets Heidegger apart from the philosophical tradition. Existence and the possibility of understanding being belong to Dasein's nature. In this understanding of being that is intrinsic to Dasein, we find a place for the manifestation of being. In this manner, the question of being refers to human being in an immediate and unavoidable way. The question can be tackled only from within the intimate relation of co-belonging that holds between being and Dasein.

> Dasein is a being that does not simply occur among other beings. Rather it is ontically distinguished by the fact that in its being this being is concerned *about* its very being. Thus it is constitutive of the being of Dasein to have, in its very being, a relation to being to this being. And this in turn means that Dasein understands itself in its being some way and with some explicitness. *Understanding of being is itself a determination of being of Dasein.*
>
> SuZ, 12, italics in the original/BT, 11

Recognizing this fact enables us to see that Dasein has a privileged mode of access to being.

In the end, what makes it possible that in our everyday and pre-philosophical comportments we are able to distinguish, without difficulty, among tools, artefacts, natural objects, states of affairs and contexts of action is the fact that we are always moving within a non-thematic previous comprehension of their respective modes of being. Heidegger calls this pre-understanding of the open character of being in general 'there' (*Da*). This is why human being is named 'being-there', 'Dasein'.[4] For in its factical and concrete existence (*Da*), being (*Sein*) manifests itself. Human being is *there*, in the openness of the world, but it is there as the *there* of being, as the ontic place where being reveals itself, as the privileged being where being comes to light.[5] But while this *there* manifests itself in varying ways according to the situation and interests of each human being, the question of being concerns the unified meaning of all those multiple modalities of being. 'Meaning' means here the transcendental horizon upon which we understand, in each case, the being of beings. This nexus between the meaning of being and Dasein is decisive when it comes to formulating correctly the fundamental question of being. If the meaning of being in general is somehow 'given' in the understanding of being that belongs to the existent Dasein, it is necessary, first of all, to carry out a preliminary analysis of the ontological constitution of Dasein.

In this manner, one might affirm that the question that really defines the young Heidegger's thought is the question regarding the meaning of the being of human life. Human life and its prior understanding of being are the arteries that nourish Heidegger's early work. The abundant references that mark this prolific stage of his output offer a reliable picture of the genealogy of this question and of the different methodological requirements he considered in order to work it out in a sound way. In this sense, Heidegger's early work is articulated along two axes. On the one hand, there is a *thematic axis* that revolves around a systematic analysis of the ontological structures of Dasein. This analysis is the starting point and the leading thread of the question of being in general. On the other hand, we have a *methodological axis* that rests on the destruction of the history of metaphysics and a hermeneutic transformation of phenomenology (see Adrián 2001a, 93–117, 2008, 11–21). This is why the methodological aspect of the problem became so important for Heidegger. The way the analysis of factical life is carried out determines the very conception of philosophy that is at play. Within this framework, Heidegger's hermeneutic phenomenology must be understood as an attempt to articulate in a conceptual way the understanding that life has of itself. But in order to accomplish this task it is necessary first to perforate the sediments of the metaphysical tradition that cover up the real roots of life. And, no doubt, Heidegger was a genius of destruction, one capable of bringing to light the real modes of being of human existence.

These two axes are clearly laid out in what one may consider the young Heidegger's first programmatic text, *Phenomenological Interpretations of Aristotle*, also known as *Natorp Report*, from 1922. The publication of the first Freiburg lecture courses has come to confirm the conjecture that Heidegger's philosophical programme was conceived during these years, and at the same time provides very valuable documentary material for the reconstruction of the genesis of *Being and Time*.[6] The textual evidence that is currently available allows us to appreciate how in his 1919 post-war course *The Idea of Philosophy and the Problem of Worldview*, Heidegger began to lay out the master lines of his thinking. This means that by this time he was taking a critical stance towards his scholastic background and his neo-Kantian training, at the same time beginning to incorporate in his work some aspects of Dilthey's influential philosophy and, more importantly, drawing on the consequences of his rediscovery of Aristotle and qualifying his critique of Husserl's phenomenology. During these years Heidegger concentrated his energies toward offering a dynamic interpretation of life. The philosophical categories that he uses to scrutinize the movement of life give some hints about how human existence unfolds in a temporal way according to its limited possibilities. The aim is not to categorize, nor, thereby, to stop the flux of life, but rather to open up a horizon of appropriation. Only in this way, by recovering the primordial roots of human life, does it become possible to reach an authentic understanding of its being. Interpreting the being of Dasein is a taxing task that cannot be satisfied by capturing life in a theoretical net made out of fixed conceptual schemes and by projecting it upon a reassuring worldview.

The young Heidegger devoted several years of work to this task, during which, as is well known, he did not publish at all.[7] The twelve years of silence that span from 1915 to 1927 should be thought of as a period of lonely work in a philosophical laboratory, that is to say, as a slow and solid preparation towards formulating the question about the meaning of being. During Heidegger's early period, the starting point of the question is the being of factical life, whereas in the later work the question is formulated from the point of view of the event of appropriation (*Ereignis*). In other words, Heidegger works out the question of being from two different perspectives: on the one hand, from the point of view of fundamental ontology, on the other, from the point of view of the thinking of the historical event of being. The former is realized in *Being and Time* (1927), the latter in *Contributions to Philosophy* (1936–1938).

In my view, and against some commentators that see *Being and Time* as a failure,[8] Heidegger does not formulate two different questions but *one and the same* from two different standpoints: that of fundamental ontology (*fundamentalontologie Perspektive*) and that of the history of being (*seinsgeschichtliche Perspektive*). The relation between these two standpoints is made clear in Heidegger's famous letter to William Richardson: 'the distinction you make between "Heidegger I" and "Heidegger II" is justified only on the condition that this is kept constantly in mind: only by way of what [Heidegger] I has thought does one gain access to what is to-be-thought by [Heidegger] II'. In fact, the proposal of 'Heidegger I', his fundamental ontology, can only be fully appreciated from the standpoint of the *Ereignis*, opened up by 'Heidegger II'. To put it another way, the path of the question of being expounded in *Being and Time* is a necessary part of a trajectory that leads towards the distinct formulation of the question offered in *Contributions to Philosophy*. The mythologized *Kehre*, 'the turn', must be understood as a turn of a screw rather than as a change in direction that opens the door to poetry, to the critique of technology, to mysticism and to art. This turn is, to some extent, already prefigured in the development of *Being and Time*. The decisive modification is the abandonment of the horizontal-transcendental perspective proper to fundamental ontology. But the central thought is still present in the historical-ontological perspective, though in a more primordial and radical way. For that reason, it might be more adequate to speak about one single Heidegger, a Heidegger that never ceased to formulate the fundamental philosophical problem, i.e. the question of being in its double movement of concealment and unconcealment, givenness and refusal.

In a short retrospective reflection about his own philosophical development entitled *Mein bisheriger Weg*, 'My Path Up to the Present', composed between 1937 and 1938, and which makes reference to his doctoral dissertation, his early Freiburg courses and his early lectures on Aristotle and Husserl, Heidegger acknowledges that *Being and Time* was the first attempt at thinking through the question about the meaning of being in depth, from the point of view of an ontology of human life: 'This ontology was not conceived as a "regional" treatise on the question about human being, but as laying out the foundations for the question about *beings* as such – and at the same time, it was conceived as a confrontation with the beginning of Western metaphysics, which starts with the Greeks' (GA 66, 413; italics and quotation marks in the original). Heidegger's efforts in the ten years that followed the publication of *Being and Time* show how difficult it was for him to think the truth of being and its relation to Dasein in a completely new and more primordial way, namely, that of the onto-historical perspective, that is, within the framework of the history of being. Heidegger's work is to be understood as a trajectory, as the somewhat trite *motto* that serves as a heading for the *Gesamtausgabe* indicates: *Wege, nicht Werke!* ('Pathways, not works!'). This does not mean that Heidegger's pathway is the result of a methodological decision or that it has well demarcated stages that can be reconstructed a posteriori. Rather, it means that Heidegger recognizes that philosophy, with its unfathomable interrogative capacity, is essentially itinerant. By asking the most fundamental questions, philosophy, particularly that of the great thinkers such as Plato, Aristotle, Descartes, Kant, Hegel, Nietzsche and Heidegger, transforms our way of seeing things and so opens up a new perspective on the world.

The young Heidegger's lecture courses and manuscripts: a new textual basis

The publication of the totality of the lecture courses the young Heidegger gave during his first period as a lecturer in Freiburg (1919–1923) and his subsequent appointment as a extraordinary professor in Marburg (1924–1928) opens up a new perspective on this stage of the development of his thought and provides new textual evidence for the study of the complex genesis of *Being and Time* (1927). Furthermore, this wealth of information has come hand in hand with an enormous production of critical literature devoted to the analysis of the process of gestation and maturation of the young

Heidegger's philosophical programme. This has made it possible to fill up an important gap for the exegesis of Heidegger's work. From the seventies up to the beginning of the publication of the aforementioned material this gap could only be partially filled through the study of fragmentary and ambivalent autobiographical allusions, the texts it was known Heidegger read during his formative years, the compilation of the testimonies of his friends and students, his correspondence with colleagues and some monographs by other authors written in collaboration with Heidegger himself.[9]

The publication of a big part of this material in the *Gesamtausgabe* makes it possible to outline the genealogy of Heidegger's thinking in a precise way.[10] Likewise, this edition has contributed to awaken the interest of scholars, and as a consequence, fecund interpretations of the pathways – to use Heidegger's expression – that his philosophical endeavours follow have been made available. All this has generated a whole research field on the interplay between the different philosophical influences at work in this early stage of Heidegger's intellectual and academic development: from neo-Kantianism, theology and vitalism, to ontology, hermeneutics and phenomenology.[11]

These lecture courses provide evidence that *Being and Time* did not come out of nowhere. They allow us to see how this work is the result of ten years of a hard intellectual effort to systematically build up the edifice of a philosophical project whose foundation is the quest for an answer to the question regarding the meaning of being. The new textual sources allow us to reconstruct, faithfully and accurately, Heidegger's complex early philosophical itinerary, and argue for the continuity between his first lecture courses and the composition of *Being and Time*. Heidegger himself corroborates this fact at different points in his life. In a well-known footnote from *Being and Time*, which takes us back to Heidegger's initial period in Freiburg, he asserts the uniformity of his investigations since the end of World War I: 'The author would like to remark that he has repeatedly communicated the analysis of the surrounding world and the "hermeneutic of the facticity" of Da-sein in general in his lecture courses ever since the winter semester of 1919–1920' (SuZ, 72/BT, 72, quotation marks in the original). Some years later, in *On the Way to Language*, Heidegger adds: 'as far as I remember, I used for the first time the name [hermeneutics of facticity] in a course during the summer of 1923. By that time I started the drafts of *Being and Time*' (US, 95). These references contest the monolithic picture that prevailed across a wide spectrum of the scholarship of the sixties, seventies and eighties, on which *Being and Time* was regarded as something of a sudden event, as a magnificent work that came out of nowhere, just as Athena emerged out of Zeus's head. This misconception was partly due to the fact that scholars did not have access to the original sources of the lecture courses and that the published material was not considered from the perspective of the initial philosophical programme.[12] As a result, Heidegger was seen as a converted theologian, an existential philosopher, or an advocator of nihilism.[13]

All these autobiographical reminiscences, now backed by the publication of the early lecture courses, evince the undeniable continuity of Heidegger's reflections prior to the publication of *Being and Time*. Thematically speaking, these reflections always lead to the question regarding the meaning of factical life; methodologically, they consist in a hermeneutic reinterpretation of phenomenology. As Heidegger puts it in his autobiographical essay *My Way to Phenomenology*:

As I myself practiced phenomenological seeing, teaching and learning in Husserl's proximity after 1919 and at the same time tried out a transformed understanding of Aristotle in a seminar, my interest leaned anew toward the *Logical Investigations*, above all the sixth investigation in the first edition. The distinction which is worked out there between sensuous and categorial intuition revealed itself to me in its scope for the determination of the 'manifold meaning of being'

ZSD, 86/MWP, 78

It is therefore appropriate to say that Heidegger had an early philosophical programme, a programme clearly articulated in terms of a unitary topic and a well-defined methodological strategy, and that this programme established the path towards *Being and Time*.

In this manner, I distance myself from the two interpretations of Heidegger's early work that prevailed up until recently. The first one takes its lead from Kisiel's monumental research. By going through Heidegger's correspondence and different university archives, Kisiel made an invaluable amount of documentary work available for researchers of Heidegger's philosophy that wanted to delineate the genesis of *Being and Time*. However, and leaving aside the undeniable merits of Kisiel's work, I think that his way of approaching the lecture courses that precede *Being and Time* has two flaws. On the one hand, as a result of his interest in clarifying Heidegger's philosophical itinerary, Kisiel provides what is essentially a historical and genetic account. To a large extent, Kisiel's work is limited to summing up the content of the lecture courses, offers a classification of influences, records the presence, absence and transformation of certain concepts, and thus provides great tools for specifying the coincidence and divergence between Heidegger's philosophy in this period and *Being and Time*. No doubt it is still important to engage in this kind of endeavour, but nowadays it is also necessary to complement it with a systematic understanding of the lecture courses of the early years. On the other hand, Kisiel's excessively compartmental way of seeing the evolution of the young Heidegger's thinking leads him to portray Heidegger as if the philosophical stages he went through were independent from each other. From neo-Kantianism and scholastics to vitalism and phenomenology, all these views become, on Kisiel's account, different steps of an evolution whose pinnacle is the encounter with Aristotelian philosophy. At this point, Heidegger's thought undergoes an abrupt ontological turn that stands unconnected to the main problems he addressed in the preceding years (cf. Kisiel 1986/87, 119, 1993, 3, 16). In my view, this type of interpretation is mistaken. One must not ignore the fact that in his doctoral dissertation, from 1913, Heidegger already suggests that it is necessary to delineate the sphere of being in terms of the different modes of reality (cf. GA 1, 186-187). In the conclusion Heidegger composed in 1916 for the publication of his *Habilitationsschrifft* on Duns Scotus this ontological stance is reinforced. Here Heidegger sets out to understand the true reality and the real truth (GA 1, 400). This can be seen as the announcement of the question regarding the ontological meaning of life, which Heidegger started to elaborate in detail in 1919 within the framework of a primordial science of life and of a hermeneutic transformation of phenomenology. As mentioned, without the methodological foundations provided by the hermeneutic phenomenology Heidegger developed during the first term after the war, it would have been impossible for him to uncover the being of life and to frame it as the topic of a phenomenological ontology.

The second line of interpretation, led by Gadamer, construes the earlier Freiburg lecture courses on the basis of the later Heidegger's philosophy of the event of the history of being, as if the turn of Heidegger's thinking, the *Kehre*, were nothing but a return to the 'to world' (*welten*) and the 'appropriation' (*Ereignis*) he discusses in 1919. Gadamer goes as far as to assert that the 'to world' is a preparation for 'the turn before the turn' (Gadamer 1987c, 423).[14] This interpretation, however, overlooks the aim of these early lecture courses, namely, to pave the way, methodologically speaking, for a hermeneutic-phenomenological analysis of the structures of human life. As we will see, the expressions 'to world' and 'to eventuate' refer exactly to what Heidegger calls 'significance' in *Being and Time*'s analysis of the world, rather than to the impersonal event of appropriation of being that reveals itself in the thrown projection in which human being dwells. The point is, then, not to focus exclusively on the terminology and its transformations. Heidegger's lexicon can only be understood in the context of application. Interpreting only the nomenclature poses the risk of losing sight of the matter itself.

What is then the appropriate way of framing and assessing these early lecture courses? Heidegger himself gives us an answer in a letter dated Todtnauberg, 20 August 1927 to Karl Löwith. Here Heidegger states that ontology can only be founded in an ontic way and recalls that by the time he was writing *Being and Time*:

> The problem of facticity was still as present as it was during the beginning of my career in Freiburg [...] It was not a coincidence that I studied Duns Scotus, the Middle Ages and then Aristotle [...] The notion of formal indication, the critique of the traditional doctrine of the a priori, the formalization and other similar topics are still present to me, even though I do not mention them. Besides, it is clear that I do not take interest in my philosophical evolution, but when it comes to that, this evolution cannot be recomposed on the basis of a superficial assessment of the lecture courses. This type of hurried assessment that looks backward and forward forgets the central perspectives and impulses.
>
> In Papenfuss and Pöggeler 1990–1991, 36–37

We should not limit ourselves to undertaking an external reconstruction of Heidegger's thought that does not take into account its premises and its aim. This aim, which guides the present work, revolves around the question regarding being.

The number of monographs that follow this criterion of internal coherence in Heidegger's early output is considerable. Each of these works focuses on a specific aspect of Heidegger's early work: the phenomenon of life, the hermeneutic turn of phenomenology, the formal indication, Heidegger's appropriation of Aristotelian philosophy, the development of the hermeneutics of facticity, and so on. My aim is, however, to offer a global view of Heidegger's work, a view that integrates the different contributions of the earlier university courses within the framework of what one may call a genealogical interpretation of the first writings and lecture courses. In other words, this interpretation seeks to delineate the thematic and methodological threads of the young Heidegger's philosophical programme. Naturally, attempting to articulate in a comprehensive and unitary way Heidegger's early work does not invalidate or put into question another type of investigation, namely, that which, rather than focusing on the genealogy, addresses the philosophical problems the young Heidegger discusses. Topics such as his novel conception of philosophy as hermeneutic phenomenology, the problem of philosophical conceptuality, the notion of interpretation, the destruction of metaphysics, the importance of the method and its meaning for any philosophical inquiry, and so on, are all fundamental issues that continue to have a central role in contemporary debates.[15]

How can we secure the appropriate way of undertaking a genealogical interpretation? If we start by admitting that every interpretation responds to certain specific questions, we have no choice but to be faithful to the fundamental question of the author. This question takes the form of a problem that can be elaborated in a philosophical programme. Heidegger spelled out his project in a completely clear way: 'Our aim in the following treatise is to work out the question of the meaning of *being*' (SuZ, 1/BT, xxiv, italics in the original). The elaboration of this problem was long and complex, with Heidegger spending several years discussing Kant, Rickert, Aristotle and Husserl. In this way, and provided one keeps in sight the immovable aim of Heidegger's thinking, his early lecture courses provide an excellent access to *Being and Time*'s ontological project.

The present book approaches the thematic richness of this period of Heidegger's intellectual life with the purpose of providing a coherent and unitary interpretation of his early work. In contrast to some authors for whom the lecture courses constitute an autonomous body of work, more or less unconnected to *Being and Time*'s ontological platform, I hold that the horizon of the question of being is present in Heidegger's thinking from the outset. At the beginning, this is so only in a latent manner. Thus, when in his doctoral dissertation (1913) and in his *Habilitationsschrift* (1915) Heidegger addresses the question regarding the primordial field of givenness that makes logical judgements and the encounter with entities possible, a shift towards the pre-ontological comprehension of human life is insinuated. From the post-war semester of 1919 onwards, human life as a topic and the problem of the type of access we can have to it become the core of his philosophical project. On the basis of a thorough analysis of the ontological structures of human life, Heidegger opens up the doors that are to grant him access to the meaning of being. My claim is that the explicit thematization of the question of being is only possible once the question is asked as to the conditions of possibility of the openness of a world that is always already symbolically structured. This question is discernible in a tenuous way in Heidegger's first publications, which concern the existence of a trans-logical horizon of meaning (1912–1916), but is profusely elaborated within the framework of a phenomenological ontology of human existence in the early Freiburg courses (1919–1923). It is only by embracing a methodological assumption regarding the hermeneutic transformation of phenomenology, and by establishing Dasein as the thematic ground of the inquiry, that Heidegger is able to tackle the question of being in a solid way in his Marburg lecture courses (1914–1928).

I will trace the problem of being back to Heidegger's first writings in order to show the different ways in which he lays out the main subject of his philosophy. I will do this as part of an internal reconstruction of Heidegger's thinking. It will become apparent that Heidegger constantly engaged in discussion with the philosophical currents of his time: first, neo-Kantianism and neo-scholasticism, then Protestant theology and hermeneutics, and finally neo-Aristotelianism and phenomenology. After bridging the gaps with all these tendencies, a genuine reformulation of the meaning of being became possible. Reformulating the meaning of being consisted, for Heidegger, in taking up once again a question that he had to put aside when he first read Franz Brentano's *On the Manifold Meaning of Being According to Aristotle*, because at the time he lacked the methodological resources and a solid starting point from which to face it. Without the hermeneutic revision of phenomenology and the ontology of human life, the edifice of fundamental ontology would have crumbled like a god with feet of clay, for these two elements are what makes it possible to unfold the question of being.

Thematic structure

In accordance with this general perspective, the present work is structured in the following way.

First, I will lay out the general features of the historical, social and intellectual context of the young Heidegger's thought, and briefly outline his philosophical itinerary in order to gain a panoramic view of the topics and problems his early work addresses.

Second, I will show how the problem of being is already present in his first writings from 1912 to 1916. We can find the hidden root of the problem of being in Heidegger's attempt at grounding logic on trans-logical bases, in his abandonment of the primacy of the transcendental subject as the foundation of knowledge, and in his increasing interest in the horizon of the manifestation of what is given prior to any act of knowledge.

Third, I will break down the thematic core of his early philosophical programme in terms of the phenomenon of human life. In the beginning, Heidegger devotes his philosophical investigations to analysing the factical experience of life in authors such as Pablo, Augustine, Eckhart, Luther and Schleiermacher. Before long, his interest starts to shift towards Aristotle's practical philosophy. The ontological interpretation of these authors' work leads Heidegger to discover an array of primordially practical modes of existence, which will become an important component of his hermeneutics of factical life.

Heidegger finds in the historical paradigm of primitive Christian religiosity an initial manifestation of factical life (1919–1921). This paradigm, however, is soon replaced by his rediscovery of Aristotle (1922–1924). Thus, his analysis of intellectual virtues in *Nichomachean Ethics* offers a wide variety of comportments that Husserl, in his project of philosophy as strict science, never took into consideration. Finally, for a number of reasons, Heidegger's interpretations of Husserl's phenomenology and Aristotle's practical philosophy become less important in his work in favour of a reading of Kant's work aimed at studying the relation between the 'I think' and time within the framework of the analysis of Dasein's primordial temporality.

Fourth, I will explain the *methodological problems* Heidegger faces in his early Freiburg lecture courses of 1919 in order to gain access to the primary sphere of factical life. This task leads him to put into question Husserl's reflective phenomenology and, at the same time, to reformulate phenomenology in hermeneutical terms. I start with a preliminary clarification of the idea of philosophy understood, first, as a primordial science of life, and second, as hermeneutics of facticity. Next, I explain the stages of the development of Heidegger's phenomenological hermeneutics and contrast them with the methodological principles of Husserl's reflective phenomenology.

Finally, I explain how the phenomenological ontology that is coming into fruition during the early twenties presupposes the ontological difference.

2

Historical and Intellectual Context

Historical context: from Bismarck to Weimar Germany

The historical and social situation of Germany between the late nineteenth century and the first third of the twentieth century had very particular characteristics. In contrast to England, which had opted early on for an economic model based on industrial development and exports, Bismarck's Germany was torn between the power still held by landowners (the so-called *Junkers*) and the emergent force of an industrial bourgeois class that attracted many immigrants from the East. For this reason, one of the main goals of the German reformers was to suppress the power of the *Junker*, a decadent class, and limit the excessive weight of army officials, in order to promote industrial development, which was perceived as the real engine for change. However, there is no doubt that Germany became a centralized nation-state under Bismarck's political leadership; a state that had an efficient administrative team, as well as a strong body of army officials, the latter due to the imposition of compulsory military service. At the same time, borders were opened, taxes to imports established, a robust rail network was built and urbanization was promoted; in other words, the government adopted a number of measures demanded by an unstoppable process of industrialization.[1]

Evidently, during this time, Germany was heavily influenced by positivism, which puts all its trust in reason as the fundamental vector of human progress. A good part of the optimism in reason that characterizes the mentality of the nineteenth century was due to the scientific achievements of the time and their application to rail, navigation and chemical industries, to name but a few. However, working-class movements and labour unions quickly revealed the dark side of capitalism: exploitation of children and women, pockets of poverty, hygiene crises, analphabetism, overcrowding of the working class in the suburbs of the main industrial cities, and so on. As society became aware of these hidden realities, confidence in capitalism started to wane, on the part both of the bourgeoisie and the working class, at this point disillusioned with the unfulfilled promises of change. Lack of confidence turned, first, into pessimism with the advent of World War I (1914–1917), and then into fear with the return of the ghost of militarism (in 1912 in Russia, 1920 in Hungary, 1922 in Italy, Spain and Bulgaria). For a while, the Weimar Republic fuelled new hope in democracy, but this hope was later frustrated as the National Socialist Party rose to power (1933). In the face of this, doubts about the ideal of progress and of human rationality increased, mistrust of political discourse started to grow, the impression that thought was powerless to change reality strengthened, and an attitude of rejection of all ideology became entrenched in society. At the same time, the growing inflation of the twenties, which caused the savings of the middle class to evaporate, the fact that the cost of war drowned the German economy, the resistance to reforms on the part of the army and the more traditionalist groups, the unprecedented increase in unemployment and the 1929 crash weakened the Republic to the point where increasingly nationalist discourses found a fertile soil. In this context, criticizing and unveiling a reality covered up by ideology and tradition became the first task of philosophy and, therefore, of social sciences.

Intellectual context

During his first years as a professor at Freiburg University, between 1919 and 1923, Heidegger was a restless and nonconformist thinker immersed in the project of providing philosophy with a new meaning. His constant and fruitful investigations into the neo-Kantian theory of knowledge, the theological tradition, different vitalist currents, Dilthey's hermeneutics, and, above all, Husserl's phenomenology and Aristotle's practical philosophy, manifest the efforts of someone who passionately pursues the possibility of endowing life and philosophy with a meaning capable of surpassing the thick walls of the academic world, someone who avidly seeks to shake off the yoke of a determinist view of human being. The young Heidegger was not indifferent to the expressionist pathos that pervaded the cultural environment of post-war Germany. Alarmed by the threat of a rigid determinism, artists, writers, sociologists, anthropologists, historians and philosophers raised their voices in unison against positivist optimism in reason and sought to give back to thought the freedom and dignity it had enjoyed a century earlier. It was within this context that a whole new constellation of intellectuals of different kinds came to the scene, a constellation that marked the spirit of the time: Kirchner, Kandinsky, Klee and Klimt in painting; Mahler and Schönberg in music; Dilthey, Husserl, Cassirer, Jaspers, Scheler and Heidegger in philosophy; Brecht, Hofmannsthal, Mann, Rilke and George in literature; Ehrenfels, Jung, Weininger and Freud in psychology; Gropius, Loos and Wagner in architecture; Ranke, Troeltsch and Meinecke in history; Planck, Mach, von Weizsäcker, Heisenberg, Bohr and Einstein in science; Weber, Simmel, Spengler and Mannheim in sociology. All these intellectual figures had to face the problem of how to capture the immediacy of human experience within a fragmented social reality that was completely devoid of value.

In all the aforementioned disciplines took place what Lukács characterized, quite graphically, as 'an assault on reason'; that is to say, the endeavour of putting into question ideological indecision, criticizing the massive use of propaganda, unveiling the indoctrination of society, denouncing the emergence of totalitarian views, nurturing mistrust of all political discourse and bringing to the surface the poverty pockets created by ferocious capitalist ethics. It is not surprising then that within this context questions arose regarding the ideological distortion of reality, information manipulation, propaganda strategies, the role of intellectuals and existential uprooting. All this amounted to a crude diagnosis of reality, one already anticipated by Nietzsche, when in his *Untimely Meditations* he described the German cultural situation as under the domain of professors, technocrats, the army and civil servants. As Nietzsche put it, it is not possible to be, simultaneously, a man of action and an intellectual, without undermining the dignity of each way of life. This idea was later restated by Max Weber in *Science as a Vocation* (1919) and by Oswald Spengler in *The Decline of the West* (1922), to name just a couple of works from the period in question that Heidegger knew by heart.[2] No doubt, Spengler's book was deeply influential for a whole generation of intellectuals, thinkers and artists in post-war Germany. According to Spengler's diagnosis, the West was atomized and disseminated by the triumph of the sciences, and thus lacked a collective and national spirit (*Volksgeist*). This explained, in part, why German society was able to unite with such strength in the face of adversities, particularly the draconian economic sanctions imposed with the Versailles Peace Treaty, as John Keynes showed clearly in his *The Economic Consequences of the Peace* (1919).

The young Heidegger's thinking evolved in this environment of intellectual unease, existential inhospitality and spiritual anxiety, characteristic of the age of the twilight of the idols. One can find different portraits of this fragmented society, with its lack of heroes, in works such as *The Man Without Qualities*, by Robert Musil, *The Magic Mountain*, by Thomas Mann, *Ulysses*, by James Joyce, *The Metamorphosis*, by Franz Kafka and, in a graphical way, in Edward Munch's *The Scream* and Robert Wiene's film, *The Cabinet of Dr Caligari*. In this sense, Heidegger's *magnum opus, Being and Time*, can be read as a philosophical novel of formation, which, as for other novels of the period, reflects on the meaning of human life in a science-dominated age and makes visible human beings' subjection to powerful forces that suppress them, make them small, and manipulate them to the point of making them lose sight of the meaning of their own existence. *Being and Time* presents us with Dasein as the protagonist of a three-act narrative structure. First, Dasein is comfortably settled in the certainties of everyday life. Dasein knows how to move pragmatically and efficiently in accordance with collectively recognized norms of conduct, shares a horizon of values and expectations with other people and feels that society guarantees its safety. In the second act, this familiar world in which Dasein feels at home is abruptly disrupted, causing confusion and perplexity in a being that for the first time finds itself overcome by angst, unable to respond to the world, to get a hold on it, cast adrift in an unknown ocean. Finally, Dasein becomes aware of its erratic situation, faces its own thrownness and resolves to take back control over its existence by projecting an authentic way of living, a way that unfolds in constant struggle with the fatal inertia that threatens to bring Dasein back into the anonymous traps of everyday life.

It is therefore not surprising that in the face of such a bleak panorama of German society, questions spontaneously arose regarding, in one way or another, the meaning of human existence: what to do as a member of a drifting society? How to escape a technical rationality that calculates all variables of human existence, eliminates all trace of individuality and subjugates each person's will to the causal order of sciences? The human spirit felt imprisoned and mistrusted the positivist discourse that purported to create an ideal society and govern the course of history in a purely rational manner. Life needed to break through false conceptions of the world. It became necessary to turn one's gaze to reality, look deep into its true mystery and live according to its essence. In a letter dated 1 May 1919, Heidegger confided to Elisabeth Blochmann that: '[t]he new life we want for ourselves, or that wants in ourselves, has renounced to be universal, that is, inauthentic, flat and superficial; its sole possession is originality, not what is contrived and made-up, but the evidence of total intuition' (in Heidegger and Blochmann 1989). For this reason, it was urgent to face the tortuous question of how to capture the immediacy of lived experience in a language that traditionally tended to dissect the complexity of human reality and to store it in the compartments of logic. Heidegger's stance regarding this type of procedure was unequivocal: it is necessary to break with traditional language, to distrust the metaphysical conceptual edifice, to make fluid categories with which to analyse the phenomenon of life, and, in sum, to practise a constant hermeneutics of suspicion in order to give back to individuals their capacity to think and to act.

It is clear that, as a young professor, Heidegger was able to translate in a masterly way this generalized feeling of incipient decadence to the university classrooms. In spite of the fact he did not publish during the first years of his intense teaching career, his fame as a professor fully committed to philosophy quickly spread across Germany. As a result, the word of a new star of German philosophy began to circulate, making of Heidegger something of a hidden king that awakened the interest and fascination of disciples as renowned nowadays as Karl Löwith, Hans-Georg Gadamer, Hannah Arendt, Walter Bröcker, Max Horkheimer, Hans Jonas, Herbert Marcuse, etc. (see Arendt 1969, 893–903; Gadamer 1977, 15ff.). Not to mention the friendships Heidegger built with important intellectual figures like Paul Natorp, Nicolai Hartmann, Paul Friedländer, Rudolf Bultmann and Karl Jaspers. With the latter, Heidegger shared an implicit agreement about the necessity of renewing the archaic German academic institutions and of reformulating the chief problems of philosophy. Both philosophers felt the call to open a new path for the discipline, brandishing the flag of protest and expressing their discontent with the informal and popular philosophical talks and discussions organized in coffee shops and other venues at the time.[3] For them, philosophy was to subvert the prevailing conceptions and aim at the core of things themselves. Living in a philosophical manner was to be willing to run the necessary risks and think against predetermined norms.

Charismatic thinkers, capable of renovating the old structures of thought and action were needed. The young Heidegger embraced this call and already in his first 1919 lectures took up the challenge of developing a new conception of philosophy. 'We are standing', Heidegger said in a tone filled with expressionist pathos, 'at the methodological cross-roads which will decide on the very life or death of philosophy' (GA, 56/57, 62/IP, 53). This is one of the more decisive moments in Heidegger's life, both on a personal and on a philosophical level. On the one hand, his breakup with Catholicism came to a point of no return with his Protestant marriage to Elfride Petri;[4] on the other, clear symptoms that he was distancing himself from his solid theological and post-Kantian training and shifting towards a hermeneutics of factical life begin to become visible. In this respect, Karl Löwith sharply underscores the existential aspect of Heidegger's character: 'By education a Jesuit, he became Protestant out of indignation, a Scholastic dogmatist in his training and an existential pragmatist through experience, a theologian by tradition and an atheist as a researcher' (Löwith 1986, 45). Different faces of a person attempting to apprehend a phenomenon as mysterious, elusive and confusing as human existence is in all its bare facticity. Deciphering such a phenomenon determined to a large extent Heidegger's philosophical itinerary.

The young Heidegger's philosophical itinerary

During the period that immediately followed World War I, Karl Barth's and Rudolf Bultmann's work consolidated theology's dissociation from liberal theology, Ernst Cassirer's philosophy of symbolic forms weakened the foundational impulse of neo-Kantianism, and a new constellation of philosophers such as Max Scheler, Karl Jaspers and Martin Heidegger, among others, came on the scene under the banner of phenomenology and existentialism. What characterized this new generation of thinkers was their critical stance towards neo-Kantian methodologicism, a stance that reached its peak in the phenomenological school with the rejection of the priority of science in favour of a radical affirmation of the experience of factical life. During his first years as a professor in Freiburg University, that is to say, from 1919 to 1923, Heidegger started to develop a deeply original intellectual outlook in which the theological tradition, neo-Kantianism, hermeneutics, several forms of the philosophy of life, and above all Aristotle's practical philosophy and Husserl's phenomenology, all came together in a tense yet fruitful way.

From this point of view, one could say that the young Heidegger's philosophical programme was basically established in his first Freiburg lecture courses. The publication of his lectures from this period provides us with a better understanding of, and allows us to reconstruct with more precision, his early philosophical itinerary. These lecture courses are *The Idea of Philosophy and the Problem of Worldview*, from the post-war semester of 1919, *Phenomenology and Transcendental Philosophy of Value*, from the summer semester of the same year, *The Basic Problems of Phenomenology*, from the winter semester, 1919–1920, and *Phenomenology of Intuition and Expression*, from the summer semester of 1920. By the same token, two writings from this period, *Comments on Karl Jaspers' Psychology of Worldviews* (1919–1921) and the so-called *Natorp-Bericht* (1922), are very useful to illustrate and support the claim that there is an essential continuity in the young Heidegger's thinking, at least up until the publication of *Being and Time*. This should break the spell of the idea that the latter is a master work without history. The availability of all this new textual evidence has awakened the interest of scholars focused on the young Heidegger's thought, a fact reflected by the myriad of recently published investigations on the subject.[5]

It is my contention that the early Freiburg lecture courses (1919–1923), as well as the Marburg ones (1924–1928), do not constitute an independent period of Heidegger's thinking, as Figal, Gander and Gadamer, among others, argue; nor do they fall into different stages of an evolution, as defended by Pöggeler and Kisiel. In my view, these lecture courses must be read in light of *Being and Time*, that is, as one unitary pathway leading to this major work. Heidegger himself makes this clear in his retrospective piece, *My Way to Phenomenology*:

Thus I was brought to the path of the question of Being, illumined by the phenomenological attitude, again made uneasy in a different way than previously by the questions prompted by Brentano's dissertation. But the path of questioning became longer than I suspected. It demanded many stops, detours and wrong paths. What the first lectures in Freiburg and then in Marburg attempted shows the path only indirectly.

ZSD 87/MWP, 79–80

In this respect, Ángel Xolocotzi is right in claiming that 'Gadamer's and Figal's "evolutionist interpretation", as well as Pöggeler's and Kisiel's "pluralist interpretation" analyse the first lecture courses independently of *Being and Time*: both lines of interpretation see the lecture courses as a finished work rather than as the result of "being on the way"' (Xolocotzi 2004, 36). It is thus necessary to underscore once again the necessity of interpreting the early lecture courses within the framework of a philosophical programme that begins to take form during the early twenties and is fully delineated in *Being and Time*: the question regarding the meaning of being.

Broadly speaking, the lecture courses with which Heidegger began his academic activity in the post-war period aimed at elaborating a new conception of philosophy, a conception that does not put the phenomenon of life in the straitjacket of the standards of scientific knowledge. A very noticeable 'existentialist' tone is characteristic of a good part of Heidegger's early work. The question that comes up over and over again is how it is possible to apprehend, in an authentic way, the phenomenon of life without resorting to the instruments of the philosophical tradition with their objectifying tendencies. The answer is unequivocal: it is necessary to curtail the primacy of the theoretical attitude and to suspend the ideal of knowledge pervasive in philosophical reflection from Descartes to Husserl, an ideal borrowed from physics and mathematics. The result of the slow and systematic inspection of the true ontological structures of human life is reflected in the different and recurrent analyses of the ontological framework of human existence that Heidegger developed during the twenties. Thus, in 1919 Heidegger talks about the idea of a primordial science of life, in 1922 about the phenomenological ontology of factical life, in 1923 about the hermeneutics of facticity, in 1927 about the existential analytics of Dasein and in 1928 about a metaphysics of Dasein. The central concern around which the young Heidegger's philosophical endeavours revolved up until the publication of *Being and Time* was to show, in a phenomenological sense, the different modes of being of Dasein, so as to apprehend the meaning of being within the horizon of historicity and temporality.

Heidegger was moved – perhaps even more that he would be willing to admit – by this willingness to uncover the reality of life, the core that puts the edifice of philosophy in motion. Schopenhauer showed that the will is the real ground of reason; Kierkegaard made it clear that abstract thinking sacrifices concrete existence in favour of absolute truth; Marx discovered that economy moves the spirit; Nietzsche and Freud exposed the instincts lying under culture. What about Heidegger? He penetrated into the potentiality of life, the real source of worldviews. Heidegger constantly insists that one should not philosophize *about* life but *from* it. And life is falling into emptiness and no longer has a metaphysical hold; it has to be embraced with all its risks and enigmas, because those who want to understand themselves have to clarify their own situation. Rather than establishing a system about life or pointing to a new reality, the goal must be to think life and its history as the sea one is already navigating. Everybody lives in history, but many do not realize it. Others know their time is historical but do not live according to this.

In sum, one could say that the question that concerned the early Heidegger's thinking was the question regarding the meaning of factical life. The syllabus Heidegger wrote in 1922 as part of his application for a place as titular professor in the University of Gottingen bears witness to this: '[T]he investigations that support all the work behind my lecture courses aim at developing a systematic ontological-phenomenological interpretation of the fundamental problem of factical life' (GA 16, 44).[6]

Human life and its comprehension of being are the axes that articulate most of Heidegger's early work. The kaleidoscope of philosophical references that characterizes this prolific stage offers a rather faithful picture of the genealogy of that question and of the methodological requirements necessary to reach a successful answer to it. In this way, Heidegger's attempt at apprehending the primordial reality of human life involved two crucial decisions.

The first decision is *methodological* and led Heidegger, as early as in the lecture courses of 1919, to dismantle the history of metaphysics and to transform Husserl's phenomenology in a hermeneutical manner. This decision refers to the fact that Heidegger's philosophical method progresses in two fundamental moments: a destructive and a constructive one. The former reveals philosophy's intricate conceptual map and brings the phenomenon of life back to its primordial state. The latter proposes a formal analysis of the diverse ways in which life is realized in its process of historical gestation. Without these two moments, venturing into the enterprise of giving a categorial articulation of the field of the immediate givenness of factical life and of its ontological nature would be in vain.

The second decision is *thematic* and led, also in the first Freiburg years, to a systematic analysis of the ontological structures of human life. The question regarding the meaning of the being of a-theoretical and unreflective life was Heidegger's point of departure and the leading thread towards the question of being in general. One can see how, on the basis of this decision, and once the methodology for the phenomenological hermeneutics of Dasein is completed, the question of being starts to gradually gain in importance, beginning with the Marburg lectures (1924–1927), and reaching a peak in *Being and Time*, where it is the central theme. The gradual publication of the first Freiburg and the Marburg lecture courses confirms that the young Heidegger's philosophical programme began to form in those years.

Having put into context Heidegger's early work and expounded the leading thread of his philosophical itinerary, I turn, in the next chapter, to explain in detail these two axes. However, it will be necessary first to show how the hidden root of being is already manifest in his first academic writings, namely, *Theory of Judgment in Psychologism*, from 1913, and his *Habilitationsschrift*, *The Theory of Categories and Meaning in Duns Scotus*, from 1915. It is worth noticing, however, that addressing the question of being requires both the thematic and the methodological aspects, which develop simultaneously from the Freiburg lecture courses onwards. So it is not as if Heidegger analysed the structures of factical life first and then turned to develop the hermeneutic-phenomenological method. For the discovery and analysis of those structures requires the method. Nor is it as if the hermeneutic transformation of phenomenology came first, because this transformation was the direct result of appreciating the necessity to find a method different to Husserl's and adequate to the task of capturing the meaning of life. The subject matter and the method cannot be separated. In fact, the method is determined by the matter itself, namely, factical life. Given the requirements of a lineal exposition, I present first the thematic aspect and then the methodological one. But it is crucial to bear in mind that for Heidegger both aspects are part of one and the same problem, and consequently he worked them out at the same time.

3

The Hidden Root of Being in Heidegger's Early Writings

During the first years of his academic training, Heidegger devoted himself to a careful reading of Husserl's *Logical Investigations* and the study of logic and mathematics in the framework of neo-Kantianism, the prevailing school of thought in German universities at the beginning of the twentieth century. Between 1912 and 1916, Heidegger published several works that discuss in different manners the main logical theories of the time. His early interest in this subject is noticeable in his first papers, 'The Problem of Reality in Modern Philosophy' (1912) and 'New Research on Logic' (1912), continues to develop in his doctoral dissertation, *Theory of Judgement in Psychologism*, from 1913, and his *Habilitationschrifft, The Theory of Categories and Meaning in Duns Scotus*, from 1915,[1] and is still apparent in some of Marburg lecture courses (1924-1928).[2] And yet, Heidegger's work is frequently deemed anti-scientific and irrationalistic, particularly since the early 1950s, when, in *What is Called Thinking?* (1952), he claimed, quite provocatively, that 'science does not think'. Since then, scientists and philosophers who felt attacked by that statement considered Heidegger antagonistic to science.

In light of Heidegger's interest in the meaning of science, apparent in his lecture courses and conferences, it is necessary to put into question the idea that he was hostile to science. One should not forget that after finishing his theological training (1909–1911), he took courses on physics and mathematics (1911–1913) at the University of Freiburg. By the same token, from 1947 Heidegger entered into a thoughtful dialogue with Medard Boss and psychiatry. Unpublished sources show that by 1928 Heidegger was in contact with psychiatrist Ludwig Binswanger, who found in Heidegger's phenomenology a novel way of approaching human being. Additionally, during the winter semester of 1927-1928, Heidegger organized an academic group with faculty from the departments of natural science, mathematics and medicine. The title that was associated with the group was '*Die Bedrohung der Wissenschaft*' ('The Threat of Science'). In 1934, Heidegger gave a talk entitled '*Die Notwendigkeit der Wissenschaft*' ('The Need of Science'). And in autumn the next year, in his Todtnauberg cabin, he met for the very first time with two eminent scientists of the time, Werner Heisenberg, who won the Physics Nobel Prize in 1932, and Victor Weizsäcker, uncle of Carl Friedrich von Weizsäcker, who by that time was twenty-four years old and also attended the meeting. This was the beginning of Heidegger's relationship with these physicists, a relationship that became even closer from the fifties onwards, due to the preparation of the conference '*Die Künste in der Zeit der Wissenschaft*', organized by Clemens von

Podewils, and which took place in Munich in 1953. Subsequently, Carl Friedrich von Weizsäcker visited Heidegger several times during the sixties with his students (see Neske 1977, 240ff). All these examples should suffice to make manifest Heidegger's interest in the meaning of science. It is not the case, as it is frequently held, that he despised science. Rather, he was critical of the fact that science was not thoughtful enough with regard to itself.[3]

Given this reductive and simplistic image of Heidegger as anti-scientific, it becomes necessary to clarify his early stance towards logic and show how the results of his investigations made it necessary for him to inquire into the conditions of possibility of scientific knowledge. These conditions are not anchored any longer in transcendental subjectivity, nor are they found by means of an epistemological query. Rather, in order to search for them, one has to look into the meaningful contexts in which human life moves. This inquiry is not interested in the knowing subject as much as in the horizon of manifestation that is given with priority to any act of knowledge.

Having this in mind, the present chapter is structured as follows. First, I examine, in a preliminary manner, the nature of logic in the context of the debate with psychologism, and discuss the emergence of an initial and fundamental ontological difference, namely, the one between psychic and logical realities. Second, having showed that logical reality is irreducible to psychic reality, I show how the question arises as to the relation between the logical dimension of meaning and the being of beings, that is to say, the question of how is it possible to go from the domain of the ideal to that of reality and vice versa. Answering this question involves facing the highest and ultimate task of philosophy: to elaborate a doctrine of categories capable of grasping the structure of the realm of being and its different modes of reality. This puts Heidegger, for the first time, as he acknowledges in the preface to the first edition of his *Frühe Schriften*, in front of two problems he would never abandon in the future: 'the problem of the categories, the question of being, as the doctrine of meanings, the question regarding language' (GA 1, 55).[4] At the end of his *Habilitationsschrift*, Heidegger gives a metaphysical answer to the question of how is it possible, in general, that meaning be valid in relation to objects. His idea is that it is not possible to see logic in all its dimensions in abstraction from the trans-logical horizon in which it is grounded. In this regard, Emil Lask and his principle of the material determination of form come to centre stage. Third, I explain how this solution allowed the young Heidegger to free himself from the epistemological conception of the subject and thus open up the path towards a temporal and dynamic comprehension of human life, which, in these early works, is understood as 'living spirit'. This is the preamble to the primordial science of life that starts to develop in the early Freiburg lecture courses.

The nature of logic

The definition and domain of logic

The first volume of Husserl's *Logical Investigations*, published in 1900 with the title *Prolegomena to Pure Logic*[5] is considered one of the more serious and systematic philosophical attempts at restoring the specificity of logic in the face of the prevalent psychologism of the last years of the nineteenth century. Heidegger himself acknowledged in his lecture course from the winter 1925-1926, *Logic. The Question of Truth*, that Husserl's work 'was the first book to shake up present-day logic again and to advance its productive possibilities' (GA 21, 24/LQT, 19). With pure logic, philosophy secures an exclusive domain of inquiry for itself, one that is independent of psychology and natural sciences. Before establishing the ideal conditions of knowledge, it is necessary to purify logical laws from any psychologistic residue. Similarly, if the place of logic is by nature an ideal sphere of thought, it becomes necessary to clarify the differences between logical and psychological laws. As Husserl points out, 'the psychologistic logicians ignore the fundamental, essential, never-to-be-bridged gulf between ideal and real laws, between normative and causal necessity, between logical and real grounds' (HU XVIII, 79–80/Log. Inv. 1, 104). Husserl hints at the existence of non-psychological laws, that is, purely logical laws of thinking. The universality and absolute necessity of ideal laws is what distinguishes them from empirical laws, contingent and relative as they are. Psychological descriptions of thought processes are a necessary but not sufficient condition of logic. Psychological factors do not suffice when formulating the laws that make correct scientific knowledge possible. Thinking is a psychic process, but at the same time is governed by universal logical laws that cannot be derived from the factual nature of thought. The task of pure logic is to investigate these universal laws. In other words, the purpose of pure logic is to develop a universal theory of deductive formal systems that prescribe the conditions of scientific knowledge. Logic is not an empirical science that operates by means of inductive generalizations but a purely formal one. Its subject matter is abstract entities, and it should seek to formulate extra-temporal laws of correspondence and a priori conditions of logical consistency and evidence (cf. HUA XVIII, 28/Log. Inv., 71).

For Heidegger, however, the question regarding logic is inseparable from the problem of being. As Courtine notes, Heidegger's earliest writings as a student and doctoral candidate, dated between 1912 and 1916, focus on the domain of logic, particularly on the problem of the validity of judgements, understood as the first level of manifestation of being (Courtine 1996b, 13–18).[6] The question of being remains, by this time, implicit and opaque. It starts to come to light only during the initial stages of the phenomenology of life that Heidegger undertook in the first lecture courses of the twenties. It is worth keeping in mind that the question regarding being is directed to clarifying the *meaning* of being. This puts us in the domain of judgement, truth and the categorial apprehension of being. This becomes apparent in the early paper 'New Research on Logic' (1912). Heidegger states the aim of the paper in the first line: to offer a critical reflection on the very principles of logic (GA 1, 17). After taking stock of the latest research on the field of logic, and considering Husserl's, Frege's and Russell's contributions, Heidegger argues that the fundamental question of what is logic is still unsolved: 'this question puts us before a problem whose solution can only be expected in the future' (GA 1, 18). This is a problem that, following Emil Lask, belongs to philosophical logic.

In contrast with traditional logic and its excessive theoretical orientation, philosophical logic has a more radical purpose: 'to ask for what is true in an primordial and proper sense' (GA 1, 12). This means going back towards the logical comportment of asserting and judging, and looking for the fundamental ontological structures that remain veiled to traditional logic. Heidegger asks himself how logical content, that is to say, meaning, relates to acts of thought and perhaps also to the thinking being that we, humans, are. In fact, Heidegger states in *Being and Time* that 'the "logic" of *logos* is rooted in the existential analytic of Da-sein' (SuZ, 160/BT, 155; quotation marks in the original). This is exactly the task that Heidegger undertakes in his first works and which comes to completion in the Freiburg courses with a radical affirmation of the primordial value of human life. However, Heidegger has not yet arrived at this point in his earliest analyses and reflections. Here, the sphere of validity of pure logic, which resists the danger of relativization characteristic of biology and psychology, is the domain where the transcendent value of human life and the objective reality of spirit can be located. The latter cannot be a mere mental product. With this, the young Heidegger places himself in a philosophical framework that aims at avoiding both falling into materialism and rising up to subjective idealism.

What are the tasks and problems that, according to the young Heidegger, belong to philosophical logic? To begin with, philosophical logic is not a new discipline as much as the actualization of the *telos* that characterizes the history of logic (Mohanty 1988, 113–115). Now, how can we undertake the study of philosophical logic? Are we supposed to establish what philosophy is first, in order to apply the resulting concept to logic? Or, on the contrary, should we begin with traditional logic, facing its main problems in a way that leads us to philosophy? Heidegger takes the second path. In his opinion, there is no doubt we already have some historical understanding of logic. On the basis of this fore-conception we can interrogate logic in order to make its philosophical potentiality emerge. So what is the thread that takes us from traditional logic to philosophical logic? For Heidegger, the answer is judgement, and in particular its intentional and predicative structure, as well as its truth value and realm of validity. But how is this predicative structure to be understood? What is predication and what is its role in a theory of judgement? What is it about the structure of judgement that allows for the double possibility of being either true or false? What kind of relation holds between truth and judgement? Is truth a property of judgement? Also, if there is a distinction between theoretical and practical truth, which of them holds the primary meaning of truth? And what is the metaphysical foundation of logic? A whole battery of questions for which the young Heidegger would progressively find answers as his thought evolved.

The refutation of psychologism: the ontological difference between the ideal being of logical beings and the real being of psychic beings

Around the year 1900, natural sciences, together with positivism, materialism and pragmatism, seemed to have cornered philosophy. The sense of triumph that pervaded the sciences stemmed from the increasingly precise knowledge and technical mastering of nature that had been achieved. The predominant method of scientific research drew on observation, hypothesis formulation and verification. The philosophical question *par excellence*, 'What is this?', was replaced by the patently instrumentalist question, 'How does this work?'. Faith in progress reduced all human spiritual activity to mere brain functions. In this context, from 1830, idealism ceased to be the dominant philosophical current in Germany. The reasons for this were, on the one hand, that Hegelian idealism was considered closely linked to Prussian authoritarianism, and on the other, that scientific research seemed to show that philosophy of nature clashed with empirical evidence. In this way, a new philosophical tradition arose, a tradition that sought to face philosophical problems from a more scientific standpoint. It was within the framework of this philosophical naturalism that the term 'psychologism' entered the scene. For this standpoint, the rules of thought are the laws of nature. Logic is conceived as a science that *describes* certain metal processes, rather than as a *normative* science regarding the principles of thought. In other words, this view overlooks the fact that that logic says how we should think in favour of the idea that it describes, in an empirical way, how we actually think.

The strategy of reasoning that characterized natural sciences was extrapolated to the domain of human sciences in general and psychology in particular. The functional analysis of the psyche searched for laws that explained the transformation of physiological stimuli, identified regular structures of association of mental representations, and ultimately discovered the logical principles of thought itself. Despite the strength that philosophical naturalism had between 1830 and 1870, this view had detractors, namely, thinkers that challenged the idea that the philosophical tradition would be swallowed by natural sciences. By the end of the nineteenth century and at the beginning of the twentieth, this rejection of philosophical naturalism, and particularly psychologism, had become common currency among the neo-Kantians from Marburg and Baden universities. Also, even though Brentano and Husserl started their philosophical careers by embracing naturalism, they ended up rectifying their views on logic.[7] In different ways, all these thinkers claimed that thinking, insofar as it is a mental process, is a real existence, whereas the logical content of thought is an ideal one. What characterizes psychologism is that it confuses both domains, and so confines thought to the relativity of different mental acts.

Husserl's refutation of psychologism

In the first part of the *Logical Investigations*, that is, *Prolegomena to Pure Logic* (1900), Husserl decries the relativist consequences of psychologism. As mentioned, however, he started his philosophical career under the then prevailing influence of this perspective. For him, logical laws were inductive, that is, laws governing facts of consciousness that rested on habit. By the time Husserl wrote his *Philosophy of Arithmetic* in 1891, he conceived the world as a construct whose building blocks were psychic acts. The world was mental rather than real. Nothing could be asserted regarding the real world, the world where things are and relate to each other, because knowledge was limited to psychic phenomena, that is to say, knowledge does not regard things but only the representation of things.[8] Soon enough, however, Husserl realized that he was victim of a widely spread philosophical illness. In the preface to *Logical Investigations*, Husserl confides, quoting Goethe, that 'there is nothing to which one is more severe than the errors that one has just abandoned' (HU XVIII, 7/Log. Inv. 1, 43). In this way, from 1900 onwards, Husserl firmly opposed any theory that claimed that reason depends on something that is not rational, something relative to the psychic constitution of human being, something linked to mental processes. This type of view, which Husserl gathered under the heading 'psychologism', would become the target of a severe critique.

Husserl lays bare the prejudices that characterize the psychologistic attitude, the main one being the confusion between a psychic act and its content. The advocator of psychologism regards the terms 'proposition', 'judgement', 'proof', 'truth' and so on as psychic phenomena. Should this be the case, Husserl argued, mathematics would have to be considered a branch of psychology. But no matter the extent to which mathematical concepts have a psychological origin, the laws they allow us to formulate do not depend on the psychic constitution of human beings. Counting 'one, two, three' is obviously a concrete psychic act that takes place in time and space, here and now. But the numbers 1, 2 and 3 present to us a non-empirical content over and beyond the factual and temporal psychic act that gives it expression. Arithmetics directs us to ideal unities such as 1, 2, 3 and not to the simply act of counting. The same goes for logic: one thing is the act in which I assert the principle of identity, and a very different thing is the principle itself, which is the requirement of universality and necessity (*cf.* HU XVIII, 170–182/Log. Inv. 1, 178–188).

Husserl insists that it is necessary to distinguish between the particular psychic act of thinking (what he latter calls '*noesis*') and the objective content of thought (the latter called '*noema*'). Take a simple mathematical proposition, say, $2 \times 2 = 4$. The content expresses an ideal and objective necessity, which is, as such, independent of the real act of thinking that content. The truth of this proposition is not governed by the factual thinking of *a* psyche. Rather, it must govern the factual thinking of *any* psyche. If *noesis* and *noema* are different things, where does the sameness of the latter come from? The identity of *noema* cannot derive from the mind, but from the ideal object itself. Here, what is at stake is absolute and a priori validity, and this does not stem from thought but from the object of thought. When I assert a true proposition, I assert its ideal essence, valid for all cases and eternally. Truth is either absolute or is no truth at all. This is Husserl's response to those who embraced psychologism. They wanted to make truth relative and dependent on the human being that thinks it. But truth is unitary and identical, 'it does not hang somewhere in the void, but is a case of validity in the timeless realm of Ideas' (HU XVIII, 136/Log. Inv. 1, 149). From the psychologistic point of view, human beings are completely bounded by the factual conditions in which they come to existence. Husserl, on the contrary, strives to show that human beings are not a mundane fact but the place of reason and truth, that is to say, they are transcendental subjectivity.

Heidegger's stance towards psychologism

Heidegger thought psychologism was not a trivial philosophical topic. His reasons were, first, that it had a strong presence in the philosophical discussions of his time, and second, that it proved to have a tremendous recovering capacity in the face of the various neo-Kantian and phenomenological criticisms of which it was the target. As he put it, 'as soon as one approaches the *special problems* of logic and tries to reach a sound solution, it becomes manifest the extent to which the psychologistic way of thinking prevails, and how entangled and multifarious are the paths that pure logic has to travel' (GA 1, 64, italics in the original). As a matter of fact, the exposition of several logical theories Heidegger offers in his doctoral dissertation aims not so much at refuting psychologism as at showing the extent to which the theories of judgement one finds in the works of Wilhelm Wundt, Franz Brentano, Theodor Lipps and Heinrich Meier have psychologistic vestiges.

Now, what aspects of Husserl's dispute with psychologism does Heidegger incorporate in his own proposal? Basically two: the understanding of the diversity of regions of being, and intentionality as the fundamental structure of psychic phenomena. For the defender of psychologism, things are known 'outside', whereas psychic processes are known 'inside', that is, in consciousness. Heidegger subscribes to the Husserlian conclusion that logical-mathematical laws are not inductive but a priori, that their necessity is not merely psychological in nature but objective. The mistake of psychologism rests in ignoring that intentionality is the fundamental property of consciousness. Also, the difference between ideal being and real being makes it clear that there are at least these two regions of being. This difference is crucial for defending the validity ambitions of logic against psychologistic relativization. Developing a theory of pure logic requires elaborating a doctrine of the categories that articulate the realm of being in its different senses. Only in this way 'will one be able to approach epistemological problems and give structure to the domain of "being" in its different modes of reality' (GA 1, 186; quotation marks in the original).

In the paper 'New Research on Logic' (1912) Heidegger claims that 'once one acknowledges the theoretical sterility of psychologism, the distinction between psychic act and logical content becomes crucial, the distinction between the real occurrence of thinking, which takes place in time, and the extra-temporal sense, identical to itself and ideal; briefly, the distinction between what "is" and what has "validity"' (GA 1, 22; quotation marks in the original). For psychologism, actual psychic reality is the source of the validity of thought. In consequence, the truth of judgements also depends on psychic dispositions which might vary on different particular occasions. What might be true relative to a certain type of psychic disposition might be false relative to another one. As mentioned, Husserl contested this view by forcefully arguing that the fundamental principles of thinking were not real but ideal laws, that truth was not relative but absolute, that it constitutes an ideal unity which contrasts with the plurality of individuals and real or actual lived experiences (*Erleben*).[9] Among all the different modes of being, psychologism recognizes only one, namely, the real being of psychic lived experiences. In contrast, Husserl clearly distinguished between ideal and real being.

Heidegger's ontology also locates the sphere of logical sense in an autonomous domain, distinct from the domain of the spatio-temporal reality of the psychic acts of judging and the physical world those judgements are about. In this respect, Heidegger even goes as far as to say that 'logic is built on an ontological background' (GA 1, 50). The young Heidegger insists on the *ontological difference* between the a-temporal validity of sense and the spatio-temporal existence of psycho-physic beings. Along the lines of Henri Bergson's account, Heidegger describes the here and now of the act of judging in terms of the fluctuating stream of consciousness (cf. GA 1, 170). This is an activity in which ever-changing psychic acts follow each other in a particular duration and in which 'the same psychic situation can never be repeated' (GA 1, 205). By contrast, the sense or meaning of a judgement is a-temporal, identical to itself and ideal; it is 'an "ecstatic" phenomenon located over and beyond all evolution and transformation, and for this reason it does not comes to be, but rather, has validity' (GA 1, 179; quotation marks in the original). Meaning is not affected by the time of its physical correlate. Moreover, it remains constant amidst the incessant flow of the psyche.

Heidegger illustrates the ideal nature of meaning in his 1913 doctoral dissertation with the assertion 'the book cover is yellow'. One might assert this judgement while giving a lecture, remembering a book, comparing its colour to that of other book covers or answering a student's question. More examples can be given, but in all these acts of asserting, remembering, comparing and answering – which are different modifications of consciousness – remains 'a constant factor in each act of judging; at each moment I mean: "the book cover is yellow"' (GA 1, 167–168). The circumstances in which I say 'the book cover is yellow' may vary, but the meaning of the judgement remains the same. The ideality of meaning cannot change according to psychological circumstances, that is to say, it is not possible that it is subject to the temporal, real and subjective nature of psychic acts. Otherwise, it would be impossible to iterate that meaning. The fact that it is possible to express the same meaning in different acts should actually be sufficient reason to refute psychologism and its confusion of ideality and reality. The truth of the judgement 'In 1992, the Olympic Games were celebrated in Barcelona' remains constant whether I utter that assertion today or tomorrow, whether I utter it in Barcelona or in New York, whether it is uttered by me or by a TV presenter.

Irrespective of the fact that meaning occurs in temporal experiences, or even in a cultural worldview, there are two different ontological spheres. One has to suspend all temporal elements and subject them to an eidetic reduction so that the a-temporal meaning of historical facts emerges:

> Even though the religious, political and, in the narrowest sense, cultural moments of an epoch are indispensable for the comprehension of the genesis and historical conditioning of a philosophy, it is possible [in philosophical analysis] to make abstraction of all these moments in the name of purely philosophical interest. *Time*, understood as a *historical* category, is *suspended*. [...] The history of philosophy maintains an essential relation to philosophy if and only if it stops being history, science of facts, and projects itself onto pure philosophical systematics.
>
> GA 1, 196–197, italics and quotation marks in the original

The static character of logic enters into a tense relation with a reality that is temporal, dynamic and changing. Heidegger explores this topic through an example that would become very important for his later philosophy: the problem of 'nothingness'. Initially, he approaches the problem in terms of the phenomenon of negation in the act of judgement. We can say that 'the book cover is not yellow'. This 'not' means that a certain particular property we are referring to is not given, that is, that the yellowness of the cover is lacking. On the basis of this lack that the 'not' denotes we can extract a 'nothingness', a thing that is nothing but an object of thought, something that can only be present in the act of judgement and not in reality. In the conference 'What is Metaphysics?' from 1929, Heidegger encapsulated the history of metaphysics in the experience of 'nothingness'. The 'nothingness' locates the whole world of beings in a questionable and anguishing state of mystery. No doubt the young Heidegger knew this state of mind, but he did not incorporate it in his philosophy at this stage. He still breathed in the neo-Kantian academic atmosphere and abided by the principle that judgements are the sole locus of 'nothingness' and therefore that 'nothingness' had no place in reality.

In Heidegger's approach to impersonal judgement, that is, sentences without a grammatical subject,[10] it becomes manifest how far the young doctoral candidate is from the anguishing aspects of reality. We say, for instance, 'it thunders'.[11] 'What does this mean? Do I mean a property, a momentary state that refers to a mysterious 'it' (*es*), or does the judgement have a completely different meaning?' (GA 1, 185). Who or what is this 'it' that thunders? Heidegger picks out the example of the impersonal judgement 'it rumbles' (*es kracht*) and writes:

> If, for instance, during a maneuver my friend and I rush to reach a battery that quickly advances in firing position, and, when we hear the bang I say to him: 'hurry up, it rumbles already,' then what rumbles is completely determinate. The meaning of the judgment is defined by the rumbling, by its production (now) at that precise moment.
>
> GA 1, 186

Doesn't this hint at the being-uncovered of beings, at *aletheia* understood as the prior condition of predicative truth?

The analysis of impersonal judgements shows that neither psychological investigations nor determining the meaning of words can express the content of judgements. In order to do this, it is first necessary to know and understand the context of action. This brought Heidegger to the topic of the life-world, which he began to study prolifically and with great intensity from his 1919 lecture courses onwards. It is clear that in the period in which Heidegger wrote his first serious academic works, namely, *Theory of Judgement in Psychologism*, from 1913, and *The Theory of Categories and Meaning in Duns Scotus*, from 1915, he distanced himself from mathematical logic, which was closely linked to propositional calculus, and began to lean towards a philosophical logic that locates the foundation of logic in the living substrate of human existence.[12] Nevertheless, he resisted the widespread fascination for the topic of the life-world and finished his doctoral dissertation hinting at the necessity of developing a philosophical logic that is capable of working out the structure of the different aspects of being.

To sum up, even though the young Heidegger adopted a clear and explicit anti-psychologistic stance very much in line with neo-Kantianism and phenomenology, he openly complained about the adoption of an excessively formalistic approach to logic. Pure logic has nothing to do with psychology insofar as the latter naturalizes consciousness and logical laws. By equating logical laws and empirical laws, psychologism locates the question regarding the object of logic in the wrong terrain: that of the genesis of thought in the context of mental operations. At the same time, the young Heidegger distanced himself from the formal rigorousness of formal logic and realized that this discipline was incapable of guaranteeing its own foundation within the sphere of validity. It is at this point that Emil Lask's reflection on the existence of a trans-logical horizon becomes particularly relevant.

Towards philosophical logic

The trans-logical horizon of judgement: Lask and the principle of the material determination of form

In the history of philosophy, Emil Lask's work has been overshadowed by that of such notable neo-Kantians as Hermann Cohen, Heinrich Rickert, Wilhelm Windelband and Ernst Cassirer. Heidegger, however, acknowledged the importance of Lask at different moments of his career.[13] The problem both thinkers share is how to capture the multiplicity of what is given in the unity of thought. In other words, how to go from the indeterminacy of matter to the determination of form?[14] This was a recurrent issue for all those philosophers who, by going back to Kant, intended to escape from the claws of the pervasive irrationalism of the philosophy of the mid-nineteenth century. In this sense, Lask's posture was terribly suggestive in Heidegger's eyes, and offered him a possible way of solving the problem of the validity and grounding of logic.[15] As Heidegger himself says in the conclusion he wrote for the published version of his *Habilitationsschrift*, '[...] it is not possible to see logic and its problems in all its dimensions without taking into account the trans-logical context in which they originate' (GA 1, 405). In a letter to Rickert, dated 27 January 1917, Heidegger asserts that pure logic 'is an extreme, a violent covering up of the living spirit' (Heidegger and Rickert 2002, 38). Thus, the point is not to restore transcendental logic, but to acknowledge the possibility of philosophy as such, and particularly of philosophy's capacity to capture as rich and diverse a phenomenon as life is.

Keeping this in mind, it is easier to appreciate the reason the young Heidegger had for advocating a form of critical realism along the lines of Oswald Külpe's, and for accusing the multiple idealist views defended since Berkeley's time of losing touch with reality.[16] Similarly, the widespread vitalist doctrines of the time came under attack by those who saw them as a form of irrationalism. In contrast to the prevailing academic tendency of the time, Emil Lask does not equate irrationalism to the purely non-rational or a-logical. In his book, *The Logic of Philosophy and the Theory of Categories*, published in 1911, 'irrationality' is synonymous with 'impenetrability', i.e., the quality of resisting a complete rational apprehension, the impossibility of a total and transparent rationalization of reality (Lask 1923a, 121). For Lask, what characterizes the relation between form and matter is the fact that form embraces matter and gives it theoretical intelligibility; form infuses meaning to matter so that the latter becomes a possible object of our understanding. So things can be apprehended by means of rational forms, but these do not exhaust the reality of things and thus cannot explain them in their entirety. The individual, empirical and thereby historical reality of things has a remnant of contingency and irrationality that defies any attempt at universalization. This basic substrate of reality is the necessary condition of all activity, be it theoretical and abstract or historical and practical. This is the reason why Lask rejects Hegelianism as an attempt to reduce all the real and particular to the rational and universal.

The core of Heidegger's *Habilitationsschrift* revolves around the debate over idealism and realism which is the main focus of the neo-Kantian discussions of the time. Officially, Heidegger worked under Rickert's supervision, and it is to Rickert that the *Habilitationsschrift* is dedicated. In Rickert's seminars, Heidegger came in touch with the work of Emil Lask, who was trying to bring together Rickert and Husserl by means of a new reading of Aristotle. Against the psychologistic interpretation of Kant, Lask argued that forms are not purely a priori structures. For him, we live within the embracing framework of forms: 'What is objectivity, being, reality, if not a particular objective conformity that has to face sensible, a-logical contents? Objectivity, being and reality are nothing but a compact protective wrapping that covers the a-logical with a logical crust' (Lask 1923a, 69).

For Lask, the Kantian doctrine of the a priori overlooks a fundamental phenomenical moment: the pre-theoretical understanding of what is given. The fact that a form is a 'moment of clarity' means that understanding does not depend on the subject. A form illuminates something that was already there. Each form is embedded in a structure that is pre-theoretically comprehensible and which originates in concrete historical life. Therefore, matter belongs to form, for form cannot be thought without matter. This primordial pre-theoretical structure was understood, both by Lask and Husserl, under the name 'categorial intuition' (HU XIX/2, 694≠720/Log. Inv. 2, 803–824). The pre-theoretical is not subjective. It is something 'pre-predicative' (*vorprädikatives Etwas*), it is an originarily given domain of experience and a condition for any act of thinking. Facticity is thereby a structure that cannot be apprehended in a theoretical manner. Primordial truth opens up, primordially, in the categorial intuition. We think always within the sphere of pre-theoretical comprehension, or, to put it another way, we always already live in a horizon of meaning.

Lask criticizes the static character of idealism on the account that it overlooks the intrinsic historicity of human knowledge and its categories. He argues, for instance, that in the face of the abstract universality of juridical norms, philosophical inquiry should not lose sight of the irreducible reality of that which is particular. Philosophical knowledge opens up a path towards life and its capacity to apprehend the world in a categorial manner. In this way, Lask's thinking is located one step above logic and so inquires into the kind of validity the logical categories of thought have. What is the category of the categories, the form of all forms? Human life, perhaps? There is no doubt that Georg Simmel's and Wilhelm Dilthey's philosophies of life, as well as Friedrich Nietzsche's vitalism and Søren Kierkegaard's existentialism permeate the intellectual environment of the time, but one cannot find any neo-romantic or poetizing elements in Lask's neo-Kantian outlook. In his view, in all Western ontologies, the categories – i.e. the fundamental concepts with which we are supposed to interpret the relation of human being to the world, other human beings and to itself – have served the purpose of thinking and articulating only the sphere of the sensible. In contrast, for Lask, the doctrine of the categories needs to extend itself to the sphere of the supra-sensible, that is to say, all that which distinguishes the human world from mere experience. This programme, the reconstruction of metaphysics, suits Heidegger's interests perfectly well. Just like Heidegger, Lask also makes reference to Scotus's famous dictum *'fides non est habitus speculativus, sed practica'*. This means that it is not possible to deduce the fundamental questions regarding human life from the existence of an objective being. Rather, these questions come out of lived activity itself, out of the intrinsic movement of life itself.

Aristotle's categories are not all the categories there are, for they pertain to only one domain of reality (GA 1, 211). Far from being applicable to any object of knowledge, traditional categories regard only the sphere of nature, as Duns Scotus had already noted (GA 1, 287–288). The classic doctrine of categories is blind to all other spheres. Categories cannot be deduced by means of abstraction, or draw from an analogy to an ultimate metaphysical entity. They can only be discovered by means of a phenomenological inquiry (GA 1, 213). A phenomenological approach allows us to make visible a third type of reality. Over and above the psycho-physical sensible reality and the metaphysical supra-sensible reality, there is the domain of validity of judgements: 'next to the "is" there is the "is valid": the meaning, the identical and constant element that remains irrevocable in all judgment' (GA 1, 179; quotation marks in the original). Heidegger joined the Laskian project of expanding the doctrine of the categories so that it comprised other domains of reality, such as history and art, without suppressing them or reducing them to other domains, which was what naturalism and psychologism attempted to do. The knowledge offered by the empirical sciences was incomplete and in need of further ontological grounding.

In this context, Heidegger entered into a fruitful philosophical dialogue with Lask. Kant having established the valid categories for the knowledge of natural reality, the task of philosophy was now to explore the categories of philosophical knowledge itself. Lask thought this was the crucial philosophical enterprise (Lask 1923a, 22ff.). If each of the various domains of knowledge – art, literature, history and so on – obey their own logic, then it is necessary to find a fundamental logic that unifies, and differentiates between, all these logics. Heidegger asserts on his own behalf Lask's contention that 'logic requires its own categories: 'There must be a logic of logics' (GA 1, 288). Philosophy becomes thus an primordial science, whose aim is to analyse the nature of categories and which situates itself in the pre-cognitive level at which pure forms present themselves as given.

Where do the spheres of real being and of ideal meaning encounter each other? What distinguishes Lask's view from traditional epistemology? The answer to this question is that for Lask, the ideality of validity can only be given in a context of signification. The prior existence of a heterogeneous and fluctuating reality, that is to say, the existence of a world of particulars, each with its own singular form, is what makes the application of categories possible. Lask's starting point is not the transcendental operations of a subjective understanding, but the objective and valid content that precedes all cognitive activity. For him, it is unthinkable to suppose that form can exist independently of matter (Aristotle) or that it is imposed on the latter by thought (Kant). On the contrary, if forms are plural (Lask), then the principle of individuation must reside in matter itself. This is the gist of Lask's principle of the material determination of form, according to which no object can be reduced to a mere logical concept. We get to know the matter of thought by means of the form in which thought presents itself. Form envelops matter, and matter is immediately experienced even if not immediately known. We live in categories as if in a context that we only perceive as illumination. Form determines objects as well as the way in which these find their place in the world. Lask maintains that form enjoys a certain conformity with particulars, and thus provides a certain ordering to things, a moment of clarity bestowed upon objects. For this reason, form is not a metaphysical principle but one of intelligibility. Lask's novelty, as Heidegger acknowledges, is the application of Husserl's principle of the internal correlation of form and matter. Both elements respond to pure relationality, that is, form has a tendency towards the actual reality of things. In this way, form and matter manifest what Lask calls the 'primordial relation' between validity and being (Lask 1923a, 173):[17] 'Forms are nothing other than the objective expression of the different ways in which consciousness intentionally directs itself towards objects. Form is a correlative concept; form is form of a matter' (GA 1, 319). Forms are then to be completed, fulfilled, by matter.

The principle of the material determination of form implies that categories have no meaning apart from their correlate, that is, the intuition of the represented object. If one leaves aside the relation to a subject, the logical clarity of the object becomes unintelligible. Here, reference to Husserl is crucial for understanding the conformity between judgement and object. The *noema*, i.e. the meaningful content of what is given, is nothing but the object itself insofar as it is apprehended in the *secunda intentio* of reflection. In contrast to *prima intentio*, in *secunda intentio* consciousness is not directed towards 'the real object in its immediate reality, but towards its own content' (GA 1, 279). In this way, validity is no longer an irreducible transcendental category; it is grounded in intentionality: 'intentionality is the category that defines the logical domain' (GA 1, 279), that is to say, it is 'the moment at which an order is determined and which characterizes the domain of logic'.

Kantian-oriented theories of knowledge have it that forms are the active elements that determine matter. In the view being discussed, in contrast, one has to go back from the order of knowledge to the order of being, that is to say, the order in which consciousness encounters objects. In contraposition to Hegel's panlogicism, individual forms do not hold logical relations to one another; individual forms lie before us as part of a heterogeneous continuum, an irreducible multiplicity. Ultimately, forms partake of a reality that unfolds as an inexhaustible field of possibilities. As we enter into contact with this brute facticity of individual things, we can but accept its a-logical order of existence and accept the limited nature of human reason. The young Heidegger illustrated the moment of the factical encounter between an existing thing and the faculty of knowledge by reference to the contraposition of *simplex apprehensio* and *judicium*: 'The truth of "*simplex apprehensio*," its having an object, does not have falsity as its contrary. Its contrary is not-knowing, not being aware of [...] In strict sense, to represent something can only be called "false" if the object has been already apprehended under some type of determination' (GA 1, 320; italics and quotation marks in the original).

Heidegger is here hinting at the pre-predicative, pre-propositional level of that which is directly given to consciousness, and is therefore prior to the distinction between false and true judgements. Echoing Husserl's *Sixth Investigation*, Heidegger asserts that 'we live in the truth', that we move in the heart of intentionality and so we are 'directed towards the object itself in the noematic realm' (GA 1, 310). This is the true universal principle of reality: that of the material determination of form. To put it another way, the immediate experience of reality involves a categorial experience, or to use the Husserlian expression, it involves a categorial intuition that rests in the pre-theoretical ground in which we live prior to any thinking about reality itself. We live in an a-thematic and pre-reflective dimension of meaning. We can only know objects because we already move within a certain understanding of reality, because we are already somewhat familiar with logical form: '[...] entities of any kind can only be given in a context of meaning that is valid' (GA 1, 279).

Heidegger borrows from Lask the idea of a pre-theoretical and pre-reflective absorption in a world that has always been already understood, even if only in a a-thematic manner: '[...] that which is always known, that about which judgments are also always enunciated, only in that is it possible to know and to judge. Only insofar as I live in validity, can I have knowledge of what exists' (GA 1, 280).[18]

To live in the domain of validity is tantamount to what in *Being and Time*'s language is called 'to have a preontological understanding of reality'. Most of Heidegger's inquiry during the first Freiburg lecture courses focused precisely on the priority of the pre-theoretical sphere. As he acknowledged in the post-war semester, 1919, 'the only person who was troubled by the problem [of the theoretical] was Emil Lask' (GA 56/57, 88/IP, 74).[19] However, Heidegger already asserts in the conclusion to this *Habilitationsschrift* that 'in the realm of formations of the living spirit, the theoretical attitude is only *one* among many others' (GA 1, 406; italics in the original). The question concerning the pre-theoretical not only regards a primordial mode of human existence but also has to do with the Laskian idea that logical forms are grounded in a horizon of meaning that has always been already opened, and in this way, forms allow us to apprehend the domain of the immediate experience of life in a way similar to that in which formal indicators allow us to articulate Dasein's modes of being. It was not long before the idea of a pre-theoretical, absorbed, flowing and meaningful life, together with the principle of the material determination of form, enabled the young Heidegger to pave the path towards the facticity of human life and thus break away from the philosophical priority of the subject of knowledge.

From the epistemic subject to human life

The publication of Heidegger's early work allows us to see in a different light the pathway that goes from his doctoral dissertation, *Theory of Judgement in Psychologism*, from 1913, to *Being and Time*, from 1927. This path constitutes an attempt to reconcile, on the one hand, the so-called vitalist, historicist and existentialist currents of the time, with the Husserlian ideal of philosophy as strict science, on the other. While he was training in the scholastic tradition, always with an attentive eye on the philosophical currents of his time, such as phenomenology and neo-Kantianism, Heidegger started to delineate a programme for the renovation of the metaphysical tradition. This programme followed the thread of the explicit elaboration of the question regarding the being of human life, which is precisely the subject matter that occupied Heidegger during his teaching in

Freiburg, starting in 1919. In the lecture courses of this period, the project of a phenomenology of factical life, understood as the ground from which to tackle the question regarding the meaning of being, began to coalesce. For this purpose, pure logic and the theory of knowledge, even though necessary in a preliminary stage, were sterile insofar as they take the theoretical attitude to be the philosophical attitude *par excellence* (GA 1, 186-87, 200, 403, 415). For Heidegger, this privilege of theory over the immediate reality of life was unwarranted. But at the same time, and contrary to the views of such relativist thinkers as Nietzsche, Dilthey and Kierkegaard, whose radical defence of human existence involved an outright rejection of all systematic thinking, Heidegger's interpretation of the phenomenon of factical and historical life was conceived of as granting the starting point for grounding logic and renovating metaphysics.

What is the nature of this philosophical grounding of logic for Heidegger? For him, this enterprise consists in the search for the conditions of possibility of logic. As shown, logical judgements presuppose a pre-logical and pre-comprehensive experience of objects, an experience that is intimately linked to our way of life and to the way we relate to objects and the circumstances of our life: 'It is not possible to see logic and its problems in all their dimensions without taking into account the trans-logical context in which they originate. *In the end, philosophy cannot do without that which is most proper to it, and thereby, without metaphysics*' (GA 1, 405; italics in the original).

In the remarkable programmatic epilogue that closes the published version of his *Habilitationsschrift* on Scotus, Heidegger grounds the objective validity of categories in the life of consciousness, the most characteristic features of which are temporality and historicity.[20] By no means does this betray a return to psychologism. The type of subjectivity at play here does not preclude the validity of categories. The aim is, on the contrary, to bring together the historicity of human life and the a-temporal validity of categories. However, this task does exclude a strictly transcendental solution in which categories are mere operations of thought. The traditional systems of categories are blind to the phenomenon of life. In Heidegger's view, one needs to insert the system of categories in the meaningful nexus of the immediate life of the subject and its intentional correlates, i.e. the objects. As the passage quoted above indicates, the logical problems of categories and judgement need be framed within the trans-logical context of the historical existence of the human spirit.

The real essence of the subject is historical. The categories cannot be deduced from a pure transcendental consciousness. Logic is grounded in a prior openness to the world, access to which is granted by the extra-logical and lived substrate of factical life. This is to say, logic is not given to an epistemic subject but to a being that is concerned with the world. Consequently, the meaning of logical judgements has to be disclosed by means of a hermeneutics of factical life (like the one the young Heidegger started to elaborate from 1919 onwards). A close reading of Scotus allowed Heidegger to come to a possible solution to the problem of the categories and meaning that draws on a theory of subjectivity and its immanent connections to meaning. Heidegger emphasizes that a purely formal approach to the problem of the categories is doomed to fail, insofar as it would not take into account the historical and cultural context in which those categories are operative. Taking Hegel as a point of reference, Heidegger talks of the 'living spirit' (*lebendiger Geist*), which encompasses the diverse theoretical, practical and aesthetic expressions of the human spirit: '*The living spirit as such is essentially a historical spirit in the widest sense of the term.* [...] The spirit can only be understood when it gathers the totality of its products, that is to say, *its history*' (GA 1, 407–408; italics in the original).

The living spirit is what ultimately gives meaning to reality and gives rise to the historical events that the human sciences[21] investigate. By the same token, insofar as the spirit is temporal, the historical elements acquire for the first time, in the young Heidegger's thinking, complete primacy over the universality that was traditionally ascribed to logic. Logic provides a way of apprehending the contents that stem from factical life itself, that is to say, logic ultimately goes back to material life. Now, understanding the spirit as that which is absolutely primordial involves showing how it grounds all other domains. Heidegger is perfectly aware of this, as he writes: 'A category is the most universal determination of the object. Object and objectivity only make sense, as such, for a subject' (GA 1, 403).[22] This declaration shows the fundamental correlation of object and subject: they do not come together only as two moments necessary for knowledge, but they actually determine each other. Heidegger takes up Rickert's formula to assert that the 'object of knowledge' relates to a 'knowledge of the object' (GA 1, 402). The task is to think of a spirit that refers to objects, in an essential manner, 'in the totality of its products'. But it is also possible to accept a concept of object that involves a spiritual determination. In sum, the living spirit is an authentic form of apprehension of reality. It embodies, so to speak, a logic of life that unfolds according to the articulation of the historical realizations of the living spirit – an idea that is similar to what Heidegger later says about the 'hermeneutics of facticity'.[23]

The point of departure and ultimate ground of logic is the living spirit, which is to say, human life: concrete historical existence with all the necessities and expectations of its time. The traditional hegemony of the epistemological subject is now replaced by the phenomenon of life. Undoubtedly, it is this attempt at reconciling the purity of thought with the immediacy of life – this capacity to place the most abstract problems of logic within the sphere of the individual – that, for Heidegger, was most seducing about Scotus philosophy (GA 1, 203).[24]

Over and beyond having been a fashionable academic trend in its time, the *grammatica speculativa* shows the subtle sensibility of mediaeval thinkers to the life of the subject. This is brilliantly encapsulated in the expression '*haecceitas*', which refers to the singularity of things, and which clearly shows that our reason is capable of making abstraction of itself and distinguishing between what things are by themselves and what our thought puts in them. The *haecceitas* denotes the factical and concrete individuality that escapes the control of universal concepts and at the same time enables us to pay heed to the immediate life of the subject and its vital manifestations. The individual becomes thus primary and irreducible, or, as Scotus puts it, the *individuum est ineffabile*. In its unicity, the individual is intimately linked to its concrete spatiality (*hic*) and its concrete temporality (*nunc*) (GA 1, 253).[25] For this reason, 'the form of individuality (*haecceitas*) is called to offer a primordial determination of actual reality' (GA 1, 253).[26] Actual reality is composed by a heterogeneous continuum, which cannot be grasped in all its richness by using universal concepts. In other words, individuality is not something irrational, a *factum brutum*, but rather it has meaning, form and perspective.

All intentions are grounded in the domain of primordial givenness that the pre-theoretical *haecceitas* constitutes. In phenomenological terms, what is given is the *intentum* of an primordial *intentio*. This primordial *intentio (Ur-intentio)* is not something the subject does, it is the surrounding world of ordinary life, a structure in which I normally live prior to any act of reflection. In this way, the primordial *intentio* is not an attitude I can change, but the way I factically exist in the world. The concrete *haecceitas* is the ultimate, though indefinable, determination of beings. It cannot be articulated in terms of a theoretical discipline, of *scientia*, for this approach can only offer a partial and limited view of the reality of things. In contrast, the *haecceitas* can only be grasped by an immediate intuition, what Scotus denominates *simplex apprehensio*. Abstraction is not an primordial way of knowing; on the contrary, it presupposes a prior understanding of reality. The *haecceitas* can be known only through experience:

> [...] the fact that there is a domain of reality that resists being demonstrated *a priori* by means of deduction. Real and actual things can only be shown. What is the meaning of this *showing*? That which is shown is there in front of us in its sameness, it can be immediately apprehended, it needs no reference to other reality.
> GA 1, 213; italics in the original

In one way or another, Heidegger recognized in the doctrine of the *haecceitas* Lask's domain of the pre-theoretical and Husserl's categorial intuition. Lask shows how abstraction covers up the primordial ontological structure. Husserl's categorial intuition also refers to a pre-predicative level of understanding, which, similar to Scotus's *simplex apprehensio*, anticipates Heidegger's later interpretation of *aletheia* as disclosedness. Lasks's and Scotus's ontology demand thematizing this pre-theoretical domain. But *haecceitas*, as it has been mentioned, cannot be defined by using scientific concepts. Its internal temporality precludes any attempt at universal definition. From the point of view of *Being and Time*, one of the main conclusions of the *Habilitationsschrift* is that time is the horizon of understanding of the *haecceitas*. The particular temporality of the latter reappears in *Being and Time* in terms of the concept of Dasein's particular whileness (*Jeweiligkeit*).

The philosophy of *haecceitas* targets the scholastic tendency to interpret history as a theatre of incomprehensible singularities (*singularitas repugnat intellectioni*). Scotus, on the contrary, defends the thesis that individuality is linked to time. The *haecceitas* is understood in a pre-categorial intuition of historical being. In the aforementioned work, *The Concept of Time in the Science of History* (1915), Heidegger designates the *haecceitas* as 'the comprehensible unicity' of our historical life (GA 1, 427). The nature of singularity is temporality:

> The individual is *something ultimate and irreducible*. It means the real object *prout includit existentiam et tempus*. Two apples from the same tree do not have the same position in relation to the sky, each of them is distinct in relation to its spatial determination. Everything that exists is really a 'so-here-now'. The form of individuality (*haecceitas*) is called to offer an primordial determination of reality.
> GA 1, 253; quotation marks in the original

Our historical life moves within the sphere of concrete singularities. Rejecting the knowledge of singularity puts into question the intelligibility of history. Merging the notion of *haecceitas* with that of categorial intuition enables Heidegger to transform Husserl's reflective phenomenology into a phenomenological analysis of historical life, that is to say, a hermeneutics of facticity.

In his dissertation on Duns Scotus, Heidegger drew a conclusion that was to become immensely important for his philosophy, namely, that the heterogeneity, richness and diversity of reality has no place in a science governed by the ideal of identity. Rather, that is the domain of a spoken language in all its historicity, 'the living language in the peculiar *movement* of signification and its fulfillment'[27] (GA 1, 336; italics in the original). Heidegger's conviction that the most proper *organon* of philosophy is not pure logic but spoken language in its historicity is a constant that remains unaltered throughout all the stages of his thinking. In this way, immersed in the neo-Kantian lexicon and doctrine, the young Heidegger finds himself facing problems that can no longer be addressed within that framework. These problems relate to the recognition of the historicity of the living spirit, that is, to use *Being and Time*'s wording, the recognition of the facticity of existence. This makes it impossible to keep considering the subject of knowledge as the pure subject that all transcendental philosophy presupposes. This accent on life leads Heidegger to interpret and ground logic in a sphere that extends beyond it. For the living spirit, the theoretical attitude does not exhaust it all. Heidegger states that 'a summary of the totality of what can be known' is not enough, the point is to 'penetrate into true reality and real truth' (GA 1, 406). The grounding function the subject of knowledge has enjoyed so far in the sciences progressively shifts toward historical and temporal human life. In this way, the transition from the epistemological subject to factical and concrete life comes to its completion. Reality cannot be interpreted as the literal translation of a logical language, much less as a reflection of psychological solipsism. Rather, reality displays all its richness in the socio-historical existence of human life, as it is exposed to the contradictions of immediate experiences and the constant flow of time.

In some manner, this way of thinking of life as an instrument for philosophy was already incubating in the young Heidegger's mind from the start, even if during the first years of his intellectual life he was not able to exploit it to the fullest on account of his theological and academic roots.

> The value of philosophical thought lies in something more than that of a scientific discipline to which one devotes one life because of personal preferences and for the willingness to contribute to culture. Simultaneously, philosophy stands in tension with living character and delineates its contents out of the depth of life's plenitude. Nietzsche, with his pietistic method of thought and plastic capacity of representation, has made manifest that philosophy is determined by the subject, which is the one that fuels philosophy.
>
> GA 1, 195–196

It was only after the Great War, during the early 1920s, that this philosophical capital could start to surface – slowly but fruitfully. This shift in perspective paved the way towards a phenomenology understood as the primordial science of life. This phenomenological approach was fully operative from the lecture courses of the post-war semester of 1919 onwards, and started to acquire the character of a hermeneutics of facticity in 1923. As mentioned at the beginning of this work, from that time onwards, the young Heidegger's philosophical programme was structured along two axes: on the one hand, a *methodological axis* that responded to the problem of how to gain access to the primary reality of factical life and give it an articulate expression by means of philosophical concepts, without slipping into the objectivization that characterizes the theoretical attitude; and on the other hand, a *thematic axis*, along which the main ontological structures of factical life were to be analysed and distinguished from each other. Approaching the problem related to the methodological axis resulted in establishing the methodological principles that govern phenomenological hermeneutics *vis-à-vis* the postulates of Husserl's reflective phenomenology, and in discussion with Dilthey's work. Tackling the demands of the second axis led Heidegger to a novel, ontology-oriented, reading of Paul, Eckhart, Luther, Schleiermacher, Augustine and, above all, Aristotle. All these authors make manifest in one way or another the different modes of being that belong to factical life. Throughout his various attempts at analysing the ontological texture of factical life, the young Heidegger eventually appropriated and transformed, in a productive manner, what these thinkers discovered about these modes of being. All these attempts, which received different labels throughout the years (primordial science of life – 1919, phenomenological ontology – 1922, hermeneutics of facticity – 1923 and exhaustive analytics of Dasein – 1925), anticipate *Being and Time*'s fundamental ontology (1927).

4

From the Being of Factical Life to the Meaning of Being as Such

A quick look at the table of contents of the volumes dedicated to Heidegger's Freiburg (1919-1923) and Marburg (1924-1928) lecture courses makes it clear that the phenomenon of life played a fundamental role in his early work. His phenomenological interpretations of mediaeval mysticism, St Paul's epistles, Augustine's account of his experience of factical life and Aristotle's practical philosophy show a clear interest in tracing the footprints of existence. These investigations also led the young Heidegger to a deep philosophical confrontation with Rickert, Natorp, Windelband, Dilthey, and above all, Aristotle and Husserl.

Heidegger's first academic writings partially move within the sphere of Rickert's neo-Kantian philosophy. However, in contrast to the traditional conception of a subject of knowledge, which renders this subject blind to its own life-world, Heidegger's dissertation, *Theory of Judgement in Psychologism*, from 1913, manifests an increasing interest in the horizon of meaning presupposed by all cognitive activity. For Heidegger, the theories of knowledge never paid attention to reality as it is immediately lived, to the world's primary meaningful openness. He insists repeatedly in his *Habilitationsschrift*, *The Theory of Categories and Meaning in Duns Scotus*, that the capacity human being has to move effectively within the practical sphere is due to universal categories. Insofar as human reality belongs to a historical world, it defies any attempt at logical systematization and conceptual compartmentalization. This change in perspective opens up the path towards a phenomenology, understood as primordial science of life. This phenomenology started to take form precisely during Heidegger's first years as a lecturer in Freiburg, particularly during his lecture courses, *The Idea of Philosophy and the Problem of Worldview*, from 1919, and *The Basic Problems of Phenomenology*, from 1919-1920.

The importance Heidegger gives to the sphere of life grew at the beginning of the twenties. In the lecture course from 1920-1921, *The Phenomenology of Religious Life*, he perfects his analysis of the modes of comportment of practical life and endeavours to determine its ontological structures. For Heidegger, the factical experience of life that early Christians had provides a historical paradigm for the phenomenology of life that he started to develop in his first Freiburg period. The phenomenological interest in the religious experience of early Christians is mainly philosophical, that is to say, it does not stem from Heidegger's religious convictions but from his interest in this early way in which the possibilities of the factical experience of life were actualized.

Cases in point are his interpretations of the phenomenon of *parousia* in St Paul's epistles, Augustine's *cura*, Luther's theology of the cross and his rediscovery of Schleiermacher's account of religious experience. From the point of view of *Being and Time*'s existential analytic, these lecture courses anticipated some of Dasein's fundamental structures and tendencies, such as the fall, the one, idle talk, voice of conscience, care and the kairological experience of time. In all the aforementioned interpretations, Heidegger expresses the idea that human life is subject to a continuous process of historical, and thereby temporal, realization. Human life has a dynamic nature, and the modes of comportment it involves respond, ultimately, to practical ways of relating to the world.

Heidegger's appropriation and subsequent radicalization of Aristotle's practical philosophy follow precisely these lines. The lecture course from the semester 1921–1922, *Phenomenological Interpretations of Aristotle*, the *Natorp-Bericht*, from 1922, the lecture course from 1924, *Basic Concepts of Aristotelian Philosophy*, and above all the lecture course from the winter semester 1924–1925, *Plato's Sophist*, offer an excellent overview of Heidegger's novel ontological reading of passages from the *Metaphysics*, *Physics* and especially *Nichomachean Ethics*. For Heidegger, inspired by Aristotle's concept of *praxis*, the direct experience of the world is the source of all knowledge. For this reason, the starting point of the ontology of human life is our dealing with things, persons and ourselves. A phenomenological reading of *Nichomachean Ethics* allows us to see that the roots of philosophy sink very deep into human activity.

This chapter presents Heidegger's take on the sources of Christianity and Aristotle's philosophy.

First, I will reconstruct the complex itinerary of Heidegger's phenomenology of religious life. After offering a brief account of its theological origin, I explain how factical life, as a topic, emerges in his readings of mediaeval mysticism, Schleiermacher and Dilthey. Then, I will analyse Heidegger's appropriation of St Paul's epistles, particularly those passages that highlight the factical and kairological nature of life.[1]

Second, I address Heidegger's appropriation and transformation of Aristotelian philosophy. I start by providing a general assessment of the meaning that Heidegger's (re)discovery of Aristotle had for his early philosophical programme. Next, I show how Heidegger's appropriation of Aristotle is structured according to the following three questions: the question regarding truth, which leads to the problem of disclosedness, the question regarding Dasein, which ultimately results in the ontology of factical life, and the question regarding time, which points at the primordial temporality of Dasein.

Third, I explain the way Heidegger integrates into his own philosophical programme Kant's reformulation of the ontological constitution of subjectivity in terms of temporality. After showing how the presence of Kant in Heidegger's reflections increases during the second half of the twenties, I spell out the master lines of Heidegger's dialogue with Kant; a dialogue inspired by his reading of Aristotle and framed by his increasing distance from Husserl. This engagement with Kant results in the idea of what Heidegger calls a 'phenomenological chronology'.

The phenomenology of religious life

During the first years of his academic training at the School of Theology of Freiburg University (1909–1911), Heidegger was exposed to an environment characterized by religious fervour and dominated by Thomistic debates. The biographies published in recent years give us plenty of information regarding Heidegger's early Catholic education (1903–1909), his numerous applications for scholarships to study theology (1909–1911) and philosophy (1911–1913) and, finally, his failure at securing a post as lecturer on Catholic philosophy (1916).[2] Some of the things that have come to light are Heidegger's numerous articles for the anti-modernist magazine, *Der Akademiker*, which manifest a conservative tone that, on the one hand, condemns the spiritual shallowness of his time, and, on the other, defends the tradition and discipline of the ecclesiastic hierarchy.[3]

As his doctoral dissertation, *Theory of Judgement in Psychologism*, from 1913, and his *Habilitationsschrift*, from 1915, corroborate, following the theological stage of his academic training, Heidegger's interests shifted towards Rickert's neo-Kantianism and Husserl's phenomenology.[4] These works evince scholastic, neo-Kantian and phenomenological features. However, in the epilogue to the published version of his *Habilitationsschrift*, Heidegger expresses for the first time doubts about the validity of logic. In this short text, he makes the case for the necessity of explaining logic on the basis of a trans-logical reality, which, echoing Hegel and Dilthey, he identifies with the living spirit.

After the World War I hiatus, Heidegger began to lecture at Freiburg and to delineate his early philosophical programme regarding a primordial science of life, which aimed at understanding the phenomenon of the factical experience of living reality. In these lecture courses, it starts to become apparent that Heidegger is shifting away from the neo-Kantian, phenomenological and theological principles that were still at work in his dissertation and the *Habilitationsschrift*. Heidegger breaks away from the neo-Kantian idea of a pure logic of knowledge, from Husserl's reflective phenomenology and from theological anthropology. This shift came to its final point with Heidegger's famous letter to Engelbert Krebs in 1919.

From that moment onwards, Heidegger focused on an exegetical reading of St Paul's epistles, Augustine's work, mediaeval mystics and Luther. His aim was to trace the factical experience of life and to analyse its various modes of realization. This task followed no apologetic or justificatory agenda. His phenomenology of religion is not the result of applying philosophical concepts to the religious domain. Rather, the idea is to remain faithful to the spirit of Christian religiosity. Having the phenomenological framework as a background, Heidegger identifies the different structures and tendencies that make up factical life and thereby human existence – the kairological experience of time, anxiety, the fall, inauthenticity and care, among others. All these inquiries into the phenomenology of life are framed by a productive appropriation of Dilthey's analyses of the genesis of historical conscience and primitive Christianity. In addition to this, the experience of history that stems from the self-understanding that the individual has of his own concrete situation opens the door for the metaphysical question regarding being, a question that arises out of the experience of time and which leads Heidegger to reconsider the generative operations of the transcendental self. These operations become the historically situated life-project of a Dasein that finds itself, factically, in the world.

Irrespective of whether he was discussing Duns Scotus, St Paul, Luther, Eckhart, Schleiermacher or Augustine, during these early years as a lecturer in Freiburg, Heidegger always ended up directing his efforts towards the phenomenon of the primordial experience of religious life. The young thinker found in Christian religiosity a historical paradigm for his phenomenology of life: first, in mediaeval mysticism, then in St Paul's epistles and finally in Augustine's work. The lecture courses from the winter semester, 1920–1921, *Introduction to the Phenomenology of Religion*, the summer semester, 1921, *Augustine and Neoplatonism* and the winter semester, 1921–1922, *Phenomenological Interpretations of Aristotle*, are all inspired, in different ways, by Christian sources. The imprint of these sources is still perceptible in *Being and Time*.

'Without this theological background I would have never have come upon the path of thinking'

In his well-known poem, '*On the Secret of the Bell Tower*' (1954), Heidegger describes how he lived his childhood in the Catholic environment of his hometown and how he came back several years later, filled with nostalgia, to see Meßkirch's old bell tower, the guardian of the secrets of being (GA 13, 115ff.). Bernhard Welte, a Catholic philosopher born in the same town, says that 'Heidegger was always very close to his homeland and native town, and identified himself with his little town of birth and the wide landscapes that surrounded it' (Welte 2003, 148).[5] The publication of his first poems and magazine articles from between 1909 and 1912 also bears witness to the influence that the Catholic environment of his town had on him. Heidegger's early poems, which are not particularly significant from a literary point of view, give an interesting glimpse at his relation with Christianity. He published four poems as a student: '*Sterbende Pracht*' (1910), '*Ölbergstunden*' (1911) and '*Wir wollen warten*' (1911) in the magazine *Allgemeine Rundschau*, and '*Auf stillen Pfaden*' (1911) in *Der Akademiker*. Both magazines were deeply anti-modern and Catholic. All four poems celebrate the merciful nature of life and warn the reader to stay away from agnosticism and atheism, on the one hand, and from the triumphalism of absolute truths, on the other. Heidegger commends himself to 'the angel of mercy' and hands himself over to the religious experience of the Mount of Olives, with the purpose of entering into a solitary dialogue with Christ. Divine grace was a recurrent theme for Heidegger up until 1919. In a letter addressed to Elisabeth Blochman of 1 May 1919, he criticizes the lack of humility of a world dominated by pain, frustration and irrationality (Heidegger and Blochman 1989, 14). Only the love of Christ can lead to salvation.

Heidegger himself acknowledges in several autobiographical testimonies, the better known of which probably is his dialogue with a Japanese person – from *A Dialogue on Language* – the importance of his theological roots for the subsequent development of his thinking:

> Without this theological background I would have never have come upon the path of thinking. But origin always comes to meet us from the future. [...] Later on, I met the term 'hermeneutic' again in Wilhelm Dilthey, in his theory of the History

of Ideas. Dilthey's familiarity with hermeneutics came from that same source, his theological studies and specially his work on Schleiermacher.

US, 96/OWL,10

Even Husserl recalls, in a letter to Rudolf Otto dated 5 March 1919, the weight theological tradition still had for 'Heidegger's religious personality' (in Schütte 1969, 139).[6] For this very reason Husserl encouraged his young assistant to work on a phenomenology of religion. But the young Heidegger was frustrated by the little value Husserl gave to his work. The purpose of Heidegger's lecture courses on mediaeval mysticism (1919-1920), the phenomenology of religion (1920-1921) and Augustine (1921) was not to offer an interpretation of the Christian conscience but to achieve a clear understanding of the most essential task of philosophy. No doubt, Heidegger's broad theological knowledge allowed him to understand that philosophy is born out of the experience of life, but by 1919 he was completely sure of his philosophical vocation (GA 56/57, 5/IP, 4-5).[7]

Rather than offering a collection of historical and biographical information I am interested in stressing the importance of Heidegger's theological origins. For this purpose it is useful to have in view the intellectual debate that characterized the theological context of his time.[8] The year 1907 marks the beginning of a lively debate regarding the relation between Catholicism and modernism in Germany.[9] The encyclical *Pascendi dominici gregis*, from 8 September 1907, openly opposes the use of scientific methods in theology, immanentist vitalism – which defended the idea that religion should be based in experiences – and evolutionism, which held that religious dogma is subject to historical progress. Against these modernist ideas, of which Kant is considered a founding father, neo-scholastic philosophy and theology saw themselves as the last keepers of the values of authority and tradition. Between 1910 and 1913, Heidegger aligned with the anti-modernist camp in several magazine articles for the Catholic *Heuberger Volksblatt* and apologetic talks in Meßkirch: he stands for a refutation of Darwinism, a critique of subjectivism and the aesthetics-obsessed urban model of life, a rejection of liberalism and socialism, and a defence of ecclesiastic authority and freedom of research.[10]

In his review of Friedrich Wilhelm Förster's book, *Authority and Freedom*, from 1910, Heidegger warns theology students against the dangers of unlimited freedom (GA 16, 5). Modern individualism, so Heidegger argues, is incapable of addressing the real problems of religious life. The lack of focus and the shallowness of modern life destroy the spiritual dimension of human existence, and so the possibility of transcendence is lost. But without transcendence there is neither God nor truth. Only Catholic tradition can guarantee transcendence. According to Förster and Heidegger, there can be but one truth. For this reason, it is superfluous to distinguish between the truth of science and the truth of faith. The higher and most fundamental truth belongs to theology. Philosophy is nothing but theology's servant and a reflection of the eternal. God's eternal order sets limits for thought. Hence, as Heidegger writes in his 1911 essay 'Toward a Philosophical Orientation for Academics', if one is to devote oneself to a truly scientific enterprise, one must have enough ethical strength and capacity for suffering (GA 16, 11).

In these early texts, the outlines of Heidegger's later philosophical path are already somewhat perceptible. If we set aside easy reductive interpretations – such as those that focus on the young Heidegger's militancy against modernism – and read Förster's book, several indications of Heidegger's subsequent philosophical evolution become apparent. Förster does not declare himself an enemy of the autonomy of the individual. Rather, his is a reflection on the true capacities of the individual. Förster conceives his book as a contribution to a critique of individual reason: '[...] a truly free thinking presupposes a heroic act of ethical emancipation' (Förster 1910, 28). The most crucial decisions of our existence respond to God's authentic authority rather than to social trends. As a consequence, the Church does not demand from individuals 'the sacrifice of the intellect, but the sacrifice of arrogance' (Förster 1910, 86). Förster also discusses the question regarding the domain and limits of particular sciences. For him, each science has its own field of study and methodology. For instance, while physics studies inert nature, biology studies living nature. This means that all sciences lack a foundation. The questions 'What is physics?' and 'What is biology?' are not of the kind those sciences address and therefore cannot be answered by them. Following Braig and Husserl, Heidegger defines philosophy, in his 1912 article, 'New Research on Logic', as a logic or doctrine of science: '[...] logic is the theory of theory, the doctrine of science' (GA 1, 23). As long as they remain aware of their limits, particular sciences will not clash with the dogma of faith. Problems arise when scientists incur in categorial mistakes, like taking the method of physics to be the method of science in general.

In writings from some years later, Heidegger argues that modern cosmological views such as historicism, psychologism and monism make that type of categorial mistake, and thus subscribes to Förster's demand: 'He who demands undivided attention to objective truth in the religious domain, has to demand the same type of attention to objective truth in nature and history' (Förster 1910, 184). These open the doors for history. As Heidegger would soon learn, modern logic, mathematics and natural sciences were the result of a long historical process. As he says in his review of Joseph Gredt's book (1912), philosophy '[...] is not a collection of axioms that one is to memorize or to bring back home in black against white; philosophy is a constant struggle for truth' (GA 16, 29).

Heidegger's religious tone, however, should not make us lose sight of the peculiar way in which he understood religiosity. He speaks out of his religious and theological roots but uses his own lexicon. It is true that the prevailing neo-scholastic Catholic theology of his time granted human reason access to the Christian dimension of life. But there were other traditions in which the unpredictable moment of grace, human being's fall, the divine abyss, the singularity of the historical and personal situation of the individual, and the finite nature of human reason, played a fundamental role. St Paul, Augustine, St Francis of Assisi, Eckhart, St Bonaventure, Luther, Pascal, Dostoyevsky, Nietzsche and Kierkegaard are central figures of these other traditions. And so, in addition to Heidegger's theological background, other religiosity-related readings were crucial for his intellectual development, as he himself acknowledges in the prologue to his *Frühe Schriften*: 'It is difficult to put into words what the exciting period between 1910 and 1914 meant for me. Briefly, it is worth mentioning the extended edition of Nietzsche's *Will to Power*, the translation of Kierkegaard's and

Dostoyevsky's work, the increasing interest in Hegel and Schelling, Rilke's and Trakl's poems and Dilthey's *Collected Works*' (GA 1, 56).[11]

This period is also important because these readings allowed Heidegger to adopt a distance from his theological and religious roots, a move that opened up new paths for his thought. In this early stage, Heidegger's relation to Christianity was not only characterized by neo-scholastic features, but also by other interests and motivations that were to become apparent before long (for instance, Protestant theology, Pauline tradition and the question regarding historicity). Heidegger speaks the language of his theological roots in his own dialect, a dialect that expresses his own historical facticity, including his experience of religious life and his conception of theology.

Between 1913 and 1914, Heidegger's attitude started to change. By 1919, this resulted in his breakup with Catholicism. The first reason for his discontent was the Roman Congregation's decision, from 29 June 1914, to tie Catholic philosophy to a strictly Thomistic framework. In 1915 Heidegger's change of mind deepened: 'At the beginning of my academic work, it was already clear to me that an authentically scientific investigation, one that had no reservations or hidden bounds, was not possible within the standpoint of Catholic faith' (GA 16, 43). As mentioned, these tensions with Catholicism continued to intensify until 1919, the year of Heidegger's definite breakup. In the well-known letter Heidegger wrote to Engelbert Krebs in January, he makes it clear that:

> [e]pistemological insights extending to a theory of historical knowledge have made the *system* of Catholicism problematic and unacceptable to me, but not Christianity and metaphysics – these, though, in a new sense. [...] I believe that I have the inner calling to philosophy and, through my research and teaching, to do what stands in my power for the sake of the eternal vocation of the inner man, and *to do it for this alone*, and so justify my existence and work ultimately before God.
> In Casper 1980, 541, italics in the original

These 'epistemological considerations,' which in the letter are left unexplained, coalesce in his first Freiburg lecture courses by way of a new conception of philosophy as primordial science of life. Heidegger's change of opinion regarding Catholicism was a reversal of his anti-modern oath from 1910 at Freiburg University, particularly in relation to what he then said about freedom of research and the possibility of a presuppositionless science.[12] This explains why, in 1922, Heidegger alludes to the anti-modern oath when explaining why he left his theological studies. The oath hindered impartial and independent research and thus threatened science's freedom.

In this way, by the time Heidegger began his academic career as a doctoral candidate under Heinrich Rickert's supervision, he was moving between scholasticism and neo-Kantianism. In the *Curriculum Vitae* he wrote for the defence of his *Habilitationsschrift* in 1915, he insists that it is necessary to make scholastic categories much more flexible and achieve a better grasp of their theoretical content by means of philosophical inquiry (GA 16, 39). Heidegger's first contact with modern philosophy, including Kant's, took place in the context of the modernism debate. According to the *Pascendi* encyclical and anti-modernists, 'Kantian philosophy', 'German idealism' and 'protestant philosophy' are interchangeable terms. Kant, the philosopher of modernism, was the direct antagonist of St Thomas, the philosopher of Catholicism. Even though the young Heidegger held scholastic views in his letters of application for scholarships – most probably more for strategic reasons than for theoretical ones – one should not forget that he abandoned his theology studies in the winter semester 1911–1912 in order to begin studying philosophy with Rickert, who, in Heidegger's words, taught him to identify philosophical problems. Between 1911 and 1912 Heidegger was still criticizing Kant and Hegel, but before long he had shaken off all religious scruples about these authors. In a letter dated 12 October 1913, Heidegger confesses to Rickert: 'To this date, in all the literature of "Catholic philosophy", there is no one book, no one essay, that offers an even approximately correct understanding of *Kant*' (Heidegger and Rickert 2002, 12, italics and quotation marks in the original).[13]

Additional stimulus came from Carl Braig, Heidegger's professor of dogmatics in the School of Theology of Freiburg University, who introduced him to a theology that was much more historical and life-directed than traditional theology. In *My Way to Phenomenology*, Heidegger recalls: '[...] on a few walks when I was allowed to accompany him [Carl Braig], I first heard of Schelling's and Hegel's significance for speculative theology as distinguished from the dogmatic system of Scholasticism. Thus the tension between ontology and speculative theology as the structure of metaphysics entered the field of my search' (ZSD, 82/MWP, 75). The source of Heidegger's interest in being as a topic was Braig's *On Being: An Outline of Ontology*.

However, what ultimately triggered Heidegger's breakup with the system of Catholicism was the problem of the relation of philosophy to history. The problem of historicity cannot be addressed within a framework in which the ultimate goal is to secure eternal, immutable truths. Such is the Thomist framework, within which Heidegger spent his years as a student of theology and composed his writings on the subject. Heidegger's interest in history was closely linked to the Protestant understanding of religion. In his 1917 comments on Schleiermacher's second discourse *On Religion*, Heidegger asserts: '*History*, in its most authentic sense, is the highest object of religion, religion begins and ends in it' (GA 60, 322/PRL, 244, italics in the original). Discovering historicity led him to a new understanding of religion and philosophy. This became patent in his first Freiburg courses and was a constant element of his thinking thereafter. But the main causes of the biographical storm of 1919 were Heidegger's failure at securing the chair of Catholic philosophy at Freiburg University, his conversion to Protestantism after his marriage to Elfride Petri and the interruption of his teaching activities due to his recruitment for military service when World War I began. As Gadamer points out, Heidegger embarked on a deep questioning of Catholic dogmas and of his religious convictions. This questioning not only obeyed confessional concerns but also implied a wide-ranging theological and philosophical transformation. From that moment onwards, a breach began to open up in Heidegger's mind between faith and reason, between theology and metaphysics; all for the sake of finding out the authentic roots of religious experience. This is why it became necessary for him to undertake a phenomenology of religion capable of setting aside dogmatic influences in order to reach the purity of religious experience. In this way, Heidegger's breakup with Catholicism coincided with a growing interest in primitive Christianity.

It is not surprising, then, that after finishing military service, Heidegger resumed his academic and philosophical activities with a keen focus on the phenomenon of religious conscience and the experience of factical life as it emerges in the first Christian communities. On the basis of his reading of works such as Schleiermacher's *On Religion: Speeches to Its Cultured Despisers* (1843), Dilthey's *Introduction to the Human Sciences* (1883) and Deißmann's *Paul, A Study in Social and Religious History* (1911), Heidegger began to realize that the concept of 'life' had been distorted by the categories of ancient philosophy and religious dogma. Authors such as St Paul, Augustine, Luther and Kierkegaard, in contrast, revitalized the phenomenon of the subject's interior life. In addition to the notion of factical life, Heidegger perceived in Christian thought another characteristic feature, namely, the evolution of historical conscience. In an attempt to establish a new model of inner Christian life, the figure of Jesus provided a new historical conception. The fact that God reveals himself as a reality that is given in the process of redemption made it possible to locate that reality apart from transcendence and in the very heart of history.

The lecture courses from the winter semester 1920–1921, *Introduction to the Phenomenology of Religion* and the summer semester, 1921, *Augustine and Neoplatonism*, are the pinnacle of Heidegger's path towards a phenomenology of Christian religious life. In a letter to Karl Löwith dated 19 August 1921, Heidegger states his position regarding Christianity: 'I work, in a concrete and factical manner, on the basis of my "I am," my origin, the milieu and nexus of my factical living. [...] To this facticity belongs that to which I summarily refer when I say that I am a "theo*logician*" [and that facticity is based on] historical conscience' (in Papenfuss and Pöggeler 1990, 29). Heidegger's italization of '*logician*' points toward the idea that phenomenology is the only method capable of getting to the root of the philosophical foundations of theology, that is, of grasping the true essence of the experience of religious life. Heidegger's reading of Dilthey, Schleiermacher, Bernard of Clairvaux, Eckhart, Luther, St Therese of Jesus and Kierkegaard made it plain to him that philosophy and theology are intimately linked. In another letter to Löwith, from 20 of August 1927, Heidegger insists on the breach that separates facticity and systematicity: 'Inquiry is the essential existential way in which my facticity articulates. The motivation and goal of philosophy is not to extend the domain of objective truths. [...] We have to stay away from any "system," "doctrine" and "stance" and immerse ourselves in existence' (in Papenfuss and Pöggeler 1990, 36–37).

This rejection of the Catholic dogma and the subsequent search for a personal form of religiosity that arises out of one's factical situation are framed by Heidegger's phenomenological project of a destruction of metaphysics and of opening up a new beginning for philosophy. Thus, in the winter lecture course 1921–1922, *Phenomenological Interpretations of Aristotle*, Heidegger asserts:

> The ideal of values (or of anything else bruited about as super-temporal and presumed to be eternally valid) will float away like a phantom. [...] Philosophy, as knowledge of principles, must thereby learn to renounce the swindle of an aesthetical befogging of itself and of its confederates. [...] Philosophizing is nothing other than the radical actualization of the historiology of the facticity of life.
>
> GA 61, 111/PIA, 83

In this way, the young *Privatdozent* that strove for a philosophy sensitive to the historical and dynamic nature of life, in opposition to the neo-Kantian obsession with values and logical discipline, immersed himself in the world of mediaeval mysticism and Scotus's scholastics and searched for the track of factical life.

The emergence of the problem of life

In the epilogue to his *Habiliationsschrift*, Heidegger emphatically asserts that the phenomenon of life cannot be captured by means of dogmatic and purely theoretical apparatuses. As an antidote to 'a theory divorced from life' he sets out to return to the 'living spirit', as it is fulfilled in its different manifestations (GA 1, 407ff.). The merit of thinkers such as Scotus, Eckhart, Schleiermacher and Dilthey resides precisely in the keen attention they paid to the immediate life of the subject and the nexus of meaning in which he moves.[14] This calls for a return to history: in contrast to the neo-Kantian view, history manifests itself, not only teleologically and in the theoretical domain, but also in the non-theoretical spheres of ethics, aesthetics and religion: 'Given the plethora of manners of realization of the living spirit, the theoretical attitude is only *one* among many others. For this reason, philosophy, as a world-view, makes a fatal mistake when it is content with merely describing reality' (GA 1, 406, italics in the original). In Scotus's case, Heidegger emphasizes that one of the invariable features of mediaeval scholastic thought was the lack of a strong notion of a subject independent of divine tutelage (GA 1, 198). For the mediaeval man, reality as such, as real and effective surrounding world, has meaning only in light of transcendent principles. The flow of life itself, in the multiplicity of its facets, the richness of its displays and the ramification of its conditions, remains unknown for the most part because of the prevalence of the idea of a transcendent ordering of 'reality' (GA 1, 197ff.). The dogmatic rigorousness of medieval scholasticism, together with its excessive conceptual and theoretical load, dissolves all trace of spontaneity and blocks all manifestation of life as such. None of this has a place in Scotus's philosophy. For Heidegger, Scotus 'stayed in close proximity to real life, like none of the scholastic thinkers that preceded him did' (GA 1, 203).

According to Heidegger's reading, Scotus's *haecceitas* provides a first primordial way of accessing the real happening of life (GA 1, 254ff.).[15] The role of philosophy is simply to stay alert and listen to the immediate life of subjectivity. The *haecceitas*, which embodies a form of concrete factical life, escapes the control of universal concepts, makes it possible to focus on the immediate life of the subject and of his vital manifestations. Heidegger applies this concept to all existent beings and extrapolates it to the domain of factuality (*Tatsächlichkeit*). The individual as individual is something irreducible: the *individuum est ineffabile*. In its unicity, this individual being is bounded to its spatiality (*hic*) and temporality (*nunc*): 'Everything that exists is such here-and-now. [For this reason] the form of individuality (*haecceitas*) is called to offer an primordial determination of actual reality' (GA 1, 253). Actual reality is composed by a heterogeneous continuum that cannot be grasped in all its richness by means of universal concepts. In other words, individuality is not something irrational, a *factum brutum*, but, rather, it has meaning, form and perspective.

The discovery of a *modus essendi activus* in Scotus's texts equipped Heidegger with the necessary means to study the fundamental correlation between the object and the subject in relation to Eckhart's mysticism. The intentional structure of religious experience manifests itself in the *unio mystica* 'I am Him, He is me'. This union requires a prior and gradual suspension of all multiplicity and particularity so that access to immediate religious experience can be granted (GA 60, 48). Heidegger alludes to Eckhart's concept of *Abgeschiedenheit* ('seclusion' or 'solicitude') and his idea that the soul belongs entirely to God, which, in metaphysical terms is tantamount to saying that human intellect stands in a relation of internal harmony with being. This idea, that thought is always inscribed in the sphere of being, would become a constant in Heidegger's philosophy. According to mediaeval mystics, whom Heidegger had read at the Front during the war and who were part of the bibliography of a lecture course he was planning to deliver in the winter semester 1918–1919 but was ultimately cancelled, mysticism was an effective way of getting to know God by means of the strength of Truth itself.[16] In the case of Bernard of Clairvaux and Eckhart, for instance, recognizing one's own nothingness is an indispensable condition for freeing oneself from all corporal chains and identifying one's life as whole with the love of God.[17]

According to Heidegger's outline of the aforementioned lecture course on the phenomenology of religion, he was planning to resume the attack, initiated in his *Habilitationsschrift*, against the idea that mystical experience is irrational. He also planned to countenance a rejection of the claim that the facticity of living experience is inaccessible and shapeless. In this way, the hermeneutic phenomenology of factical life and the phenomenology of religious experience were starting to converge. The latter has a validity of its own; it is a sphere of knowledge distinct from those of science and logic. Religious experience does not involve an irrational element; it is concerned with the historical dimension of the experience of life (Pöggeler 1983, 69). Religious experience is a form of authentic experience that keeps in view the personal and factical nature of one's life, the fact that it is always in-each-case-mine and historically and temporally rooted. The encounter with God becomes the more real, the more one assumes the finitude of human temporality and stops trying to surpass the limits of one's own factical life.

The phenomenon of life in primitive Christianity

The DeGreekanizing of Christian experience

The lecture courses from the winter semester 1920–1921, *Introduction to the Phenomenology of Religion* and the summer semester 1921, *Augustine and Neoplatonism*, are an inflexion point in Heidegger's path toward a phenomenology of Christian religious life. His interpretation of St Paul's epistles seeks to shown how the facticity of life was articulated in the first Christian communities.[18] This phenomenological approach to the epistles equipped Heidegger with a good part of the conceptual apparatus that constituted the backbone of his fundamental ontology. Phenomena such as conscience, the fall, anxiety, the world, care and death, are existential determinations that Heidegger would later give an ontological form in *Being and Time*.

The Heideggerian analysis of the Christian experience of life in Pauline literature focuses on a phenomenon that has been forgotten in Western philosophical tradition, namely, life in its here and now: the factical experience of life. In this regard, Heidegger ascertains:

> The Christian life-conscience of the early and high scholastic eras, the conscience in which was carried out the genuine reception of Aristotle and thus a quite definite interpretation of Aristotle, had already passed through a 'Greekanizing' *(Gräzisierung)*. The life-nexuses of the original Christianity had already matured within a surrounding world whose life was co-determined, in regard of its way of expressing itself, through the specifically Greek interpretation of existence and through Greek conceptuality.
>
> GA 61, 6/PIA, 6

For Heidegger, the 'Greekanizing' process accelerated during the patristic period and mediaeval Scholasticism in the context of the development of Christian theology and philosophy.

In effect, Heidegger thought that insofar as Christian theology was based on the Greek conceptual model, it buried the primordial experience of the first communities under a layer of objectification. In order to recover this hidden experience it is necessary to destroy or 'deGreekanize' traditional theology. Heidegger considers, however, that the primary task is not to deGreekanize Christian theology but Greek metaphysics, on which the former depends. In the aforementioned lecture courses on the phenomenology of religious life Heidegger tries to dismantle the Greek conceptual apparatus, which hampers the surfacing of the primordial experience of life. Thus, the historical content of the Incarnation, the Crucifixion and the Second Coming is construed in terms of the Greek notion of the divine as a present absolute being that is also the supreme good in a hierarchical-theological order of being. In this way, the relation between believer and God fits the notion of *theion* as first cause and knowledge of knowledge. The mistake of metaphysics resides in thinking being as constant being present. Such conception cannot suit the temporality of factical life (GA 60, 257–258/PRL, 192–193). The pure knowledge that the theoretical-contemplative relation to the divine is supposed to yield, a knowledge stripped of all emotion and religious sentiment, takes the form of a constant being in act, pure presence at hand. By taking up the Greek conceptual repertoire, Augustine and other patristic thinkers open the door to the adoption of neo-Platonism and Aristotelism, a process that consolidates in scholasticism.

Now, the main task of a phenomenology of religious conscience is precisely to follow the trail of the Christian primordial experience of life by means of a destruction of traditional theology. Dismantling the Greek conceptual heritage results in establishing a model of theological deconstruction and contains the seed of Heidegger's later project of a destruction of Greek, mediaeval and modern metaphysics as a means to take up again and reformulate the fundamental question of the historicity of being. For Heidegger, the beginning of Christianity constituted a first reaction to classical science and its metaphysical notion of objectivity, and a vindication of the phenomenon of life.

Heidegger had already addressed the problem of the phenomenon of life in the lecture courses that he imparted immediately after the end of World War I, *The Idea of Philosophy and the Problem of Worldview*, 1919, and *The Basic Problems of Phenomenology*, 1919–1920. Here the phenomenological research focuses on the interpretation of the movement of factical life, its structures, comportments and fundamental categories. All these methodological efforts, the goal of which was to shed light on ontology through a phenomenology of religion, are possible only by using the conceptual apparatus borrowed from Husserlian phenomenology, and are part of his broader search for an answer to the question regarding the being of factical life. In terms of the phenomenological method, religious experience fits the model of intentional correlation: the effectuation of life consists in a series of acts which refer, in different ways, to a world, and which involve a form of self-conscience insofar as all these acts involve awareness of their own referring. The different modes of experience and what is experienced cannot be separated from the factical experience of life. Insofar as factical experience of life is different from mere cognitive experience or the acquisition of knowledge, philosophy has to change: what is lived and effected in factical life is not equivalent to a pure object for a subject, it is a world in which one can live and which one shares with others (GA 60, 10–11/PRL, 8–9).[19]

This formal indication of the world and its relational structure of sense is included *in nuce* in the concept of life of primitive Christianity. This tradition also equipped Heidegger with the concept of the happening of history, i.e. a concept of history as something that cannot be objectified, and according to which concrete living is essentially a process, something that unfolds and is carried out. In Pöggeler's words, Pauline epistles allow us to appreciate 'how being directed towards the facticity of life consists in renouncing to visions and revelations characterized by an intrinsic content, and in the rejection of taking pride out of being the recipient of some type of particular grace instead of embracing one's own weakness' (Pöggeler 1983, 37). The experience of life is factical and historical at the same time, and for this reason Heidegger states in 1919 'the historical belongs to the essence of Christianity' (GA 56/57, 26/IP, 22).

The factical experience of life in the the Pauline epistles

In the second part of *Introduction to the Phenomenology of Religion* Heidegger offers a thorough commentary to St Paul's epistles to the Corinthians, Thessalonians and Galatians. His aim is to achieve a genuine comprehension of the phenomenology of the factical experience of life in primitive Christianity.[20] Now rather than appealing to a mystical experience – the mysterious and non-objectifiable manifestation of divine life – Heidegger embraces the apostolic *kerygma* or proclamation of a crucified and resurrected Christ, as it is described in the Scriptures.[21] In contrast to historical theories, Heidegger thinks that the peculiarity of Christian religiosity makes it incomparable to any other objective manifestation of religious phenomena. In order to illustrate this, he makes appeal to one of the central elements of Christian religious experience, namely, the Second Coming of Christ or *parousia* (1 Thess. 2–4). As Buren points out, Heidegger deconstructs the mediaeval scholastic triad: *summum ens*, contemplation and presence, and favours instead the triad of primitive Christianity: *Deus absconditus*, faith and kairological time, on which he bases the triad of his own ontological project: world, Dasein and historicity (Buren 1994b, 157).

The first order of business, for Heidegger, is the problem of the facticity of primitive Christian religiosity. The term 'facticity' appears for the first time at the end of the 1920 lecture course, and is fully developed in the context of the hermeneutic phenomenology of facticity in the lecture course of the summer semester 1923 (GA 59, 172–173, and GA 63, 5–6, 14–20, 67–105).[22] The historical and concrete self that figures timidly in the inaugural lecture *The Concept of Time in the Science of History* (1915) in terms of the 'living spirit' is taken up in the lecture course from 1919 under the label 'pre-theoretical life' and consolidates as 'Dasein' in the lecture course from 1923 on the hermeneutics of facticity. Also in the 1919 lecture course, Heidegger coins the disconcerting and fascinating expression 'to world', which apparently captivated his students (Gadamer 1983a, 30). Heidegger does not direct his attention toward the theoretical self as much as toward the lived experiences of a surrounding world, experiences that constitute a way of 'worlding' and in which that self is immersed. These experiences do not put anything forward, they simply happen (GA 56/57, 70ff./IP 59ff.).[23] In this way, we step out of the theoretical sphere and recognize it as a phenomenon that derives from a pre- or extra-theoretical sphere that Heidegger assimilates to life. This does not mean that life is irrational. Phenomenological intuition is now supplemented by a hermeneutic intuition that stems out of the immanent historicity of life itself. It is not surprising then that in the 1921–1922 lecture course, *Phenomenological Interpretations of Aristotle*, Heidegger addresses the problem of factical life from the standpoint of a problem regarding *kinesis*: 'It is therefore a matter of pressing on interpretively to a movement which constitutes a *genuine movedness of life, in* which and *through* which life *exists*, and from which, accordingly, life is determinable in its own sense of Being' (GA 61, 117/PIA, 87, italics in the original). Life – and later on, Dasein – is not considered by Heidegger in terms of a *what*, i.e. an objective content. He understands life in terms of a *how*: the manner in which it realizes temporally and historically.

According to the courses on religion that followed these early phenomenological investigations on the primordial domain of life, the phenomenon of factical life makes its first appearance in the context of Christian communities. And even though Heidegger does not make it explicit, the case he makes for the claim that with primitive Christianity historical conscience appears in the West for the first time, coincides, almost literally, with Dilthey's view in his *Introduction to the Human Sciences*. Heidegger's investigation focuses on the phenomenon of historicity and historical conscience. Just as neo-Kantians start out from the *factum* of knowledge, Heidegger takes the *factum* of primitive Christian religiosity as the starting point of his inquiry. Having this *factum* as the model of his phenomenology of life, Heidegger establishes the following two formal indicators of the religious phenomenon: on the one hand, primitive Christian religiosity takes place within the factical experience of life; on the other, the factical experience of life is historical, that is to say, it occurs and is realized in a temporal manner.

Heidegger reads the epistle to the Thessalonians along the lines of these two formal indicators and concludes that St Paul recognizes in the Thessalonians two modalities of being. On the one hand, they feel and understand their factical existence as Christians;

on the other, their religious experience of that knowledge depends on the *parousia*, which is kairological in nature. This way of realization of Christian facticity surpasses human strength, escapes human being's speculative capabilities and can only be reached by means of the phenomenon of grace.

In the lecture course of the semester 1920–1921, Heidegger pays especial attention to the epistles to the Corinthians and to the Thessalonians. St Paul reminds the Corinthians that there is but one message: the salvation by the Cross as union with Christ in the true knowledge of faith. This is the only true wisdom (1 Cor. 1, 20ff.).[24] Put otherwise, God is not apprehended as an abstract substance. He is rather experienced as a hidden God that manifests himself historically in the Crucifixion and the Incarnation – a God that is to return in the *parousia* of the Second Coming (1 Thess. 4, 13–18). The Second Coming is characterized by uncertainty and therefore believing in it is, unavoidably, a matter of individual faith, independent of any type of objective knowledge (2 Cor. 12, 5–10). This shift towards the individual human believer, that is, towards a life that is in each case mine, goes hand in hand with a number of existential characterizations, of which 'care', 'disposition', 'understanding', 'anxiety', 'death', 'fall' and 'conscience' are some of the most relevant and which will occupy a central role in *Being and Time*'s existential analytic.

Heidegger's phenomenological interpretation of the first epistle to the Thessalonians allows him to illustrate how attunement, understanding and language are actively involved in the phenomenon of care (GA 60, §§ 23–26). What St Paul is trying to convey with the famous passage: 'concerning times and seasons, brothers, you have no need for anything to be written to you. For you yourselves know very well that the day of the Lord will come like a thief at night' (1 Thess. 5, 1–2), is that this type of knowledge is not theoretical, but rather consists in a type of practical understanding that, from Heidegger's point of view, can be dubbed a comprehension of immediate life or understanding of the situation in which God historically comes to meet us: 'This knowledge is entirely different from any other knowledge and memory. It arises only out of the situational context of Christian life experience. [...] It is about an *absolute turning-around*, more precisely about a turning-*toward* God and a turning-*away* from idol-images' (GA 60, 94, 95/PRL, 65, 66, italics in the original).

Paul also praises the Thessalonians' disposition or attunement and particularly their 'work of faith and labor of love and endurance in hope for our Lord Jesus Christ' (1 Thess. 1, 3). This disposition is intimately linked to the arrival of a discursive message thanks to which the Thessalonians 'became imitators of us and the Lord, receiving the Word in great affliction, with joy from the Holy Spirit' (1 Thess. 1, 6). As Buren points out, 'this emphasis on language and interpretation was taken up into the tradition of theological hermeneutics, where *hermeneúein* means both "to say" and, more specifically, "to interpret" sacred writings in the light of not only past but also present circumstances' (Buren 1994b, 176). The Word takes place in a living world that is interpreted out of the concrete situation of each individual.

For Heidegger, care is the basic meaning of life in primitive Christianity and, in the New Testament, takes the following two forms: caring about the things of the Lord and caring about the things of the world (1 Cor. 7, 32–33).[25] In a way that echoes Kierkegaard's words about going from the one to the other, Paul distinguishes between two basic and irreconcilable ways of existing, corresponding to two types of people: on the one hand, we have those who live away from grace and therefore in darkness – inauthenticity, to use Heidegger's lexicon – on the other, we have those who are aware of their real situation and await the arrival of Christ living in the light – i.e. authentically. The Pauline epistle warns all those who live occupied and preoccupied with material day-by-day matters that they are running the risk of ending up entrapped in worries about reputation, fame, prestige and power. This clearly is the background of Heidegger's later claim that 'in Christianity and its interpretation of existence this particular matrix of being that obtains between existence's authentic being and fallen concern has undergone a specific conceptualization' (GA 21, 232/LQT, 194). In *Being and Time* this state of fallenness is taken up from the point of view of the existential determinations of the being of everyday life, that is, idle talk, curiosity and ambiguity.

Keeping oneself excessively busy with everyday and public matters results in bringing oneself to a state of anxiety and blindness to the Second Coming of Christ. The fall in the world creates the illusion of a safe, confident and meaningful life, but in reality the world of public norms throws us human beings into a state of blindness, confusion and inauthenticity that prevents us from grasping the moment of the Second Coming (GA 60, 102–103/PRL, 71–72). At the same time, the uncertainty regarding the moment of the *parousia* causes a deep feeling of anxiety, a form of existence that impregnates all the Christian experience. This anxiety accompanies the believer and causes her to feel restless, but in this she realizes her own fall into the everyday inauthentic 'they'. In the face of the phenomena of being lost in the constant flow of public opinions and anxiety, conscience appears as that which reactivates the believer's relation to God.[26] In primitive Christianity, anxiety is closely related to the phenomenon of death. For Paul, death is not something that occurs at the end of one's life, as much as something that accompanies us day by day: 'Every day I face death; I swear it by pride in you brothers that I have in Christ Jesus our Lord' (1 Cor. 15, 31).[27] The proclamation of Christ's death and resurrection, which is the core of the Christian message, and its acceptance by men, transform the human relation to death that hovers over mankind in general and each individual in particular into a spiritual force that is the principle of eternal life.

In this state of anxiety, weakness of faith and disenchantment, conscience becomes what reactivates the relation between believers and God, rescuing the individual from the fall and causing him to turn to God. According to the studies on moral conscience that were published at the time Heidegger was studying St Paul, the latter was the first person to incorporate the Greco-Roman concept of conscience into the Christian context.[28] In the New Testament, conscience has multiple facets: it is personal, it is related to memory, it carries the manifestation of what is hidden, it warns about the erratic character of human existence, it reminds the individual of her primordial guilt and keeps her attentive to the coming of Christ (1 Cor. 10, 29; 2 Tim. 1, 3–9; 2 Cor. 4, 2–6; Rom. 13, 5–8; Heb. 10, 22–31). With the consolidation of Patristics and scholasticism, the Greek term '*synteresis*' is replaced by the Latin *conscientia*, understood either in relation to Aristotelian habits regarding practical principles and ends, or in relation to the application of those principles and ends to particular situations.[29] In contrast, mystics use the concept of conscience in the sense of receptive tendency towards God. Nevertheless, both in the moral interpretation and in the mystic one, conscience has the power of illuminating and uncovering, of counteracting the tendency towards the fall and self-deception.

In Luther, conscience is the faculty by means of which the individual receives the divine word without any mediation from the Church. Along the same lines, Kierkegaard distinguishes between individual conscience and a conscience that is marked by public and institutional norms, such as the dogmas of the Church. It is conscience that liberates individuals from the distractions and anonymity of the public sphere and so leads them back to their most proper, authentic, personal and inalienable existence. In conclusion, conscience lays bare the guilt and finitude of each human being, and thus points to the inflexion point at which each individual can be singularized. At the beginning of the twenties, however, the concepts of conscience and guilt were not well developed in Heidegger's work. It was only at the composition of *Being and Time* that these concepts would be systematically elaborated.

For Heidegger, as for Kierkegaard, conscience has nothing to do with the public sphere of the 'they'. On the contrary, Heidegger thought of conscience as something that is personal and in-each-case-mine, and understood it as a call. In *Being and Time*, this call is not heard in the idle talk of the 'they'. Rather, it calls in a silent way. Conscience, as the call of care, urges Dasein to come out of its state of being lost in the 'they' and puts it in front of its possibilities. For this reason, as conscience discloses the self and rescues it from sinking in everyday life, it attests to one's possibility of being one's proper self and prepares one to project oneself in a resolute way towards essential guilt. This makes manifest Dasein's double lack: it is thrown into existence and it cannot actualize all its possibilities. Heidegger conjoins this double lack under the concept of 'thrown project' (*geworfener Entwurf*). The formal similarity to *Being and Time* is truly surprising. In this work, Heidegger takes the concrete individual, namely, Dasein, as his starting point. Dasein is anchored to the world together with others and is immersed in dealing with his everyday businesses. Dasein, whose 'there' is existentially structured in terms of attunement, understanding and discourse, is also bound by the everyday public interpretation of the world that the 'they' (*das Man*) offers; and so Dasein plummets into the inauthentic mode of being of the fall. On the basis of anxiety and the desire to take conscience of its fall into the 'they', Dasein is singularized and becomes responsibly free to resolutely and authentically project itself out of its primordial potentiality-for-being.

The kairological features of factical life

In the lecture course from the winter semester 1920–1921, *Introduction to the Phenomenology of Religion*, Heidegger offers an interesting analysis of the experience of time in the first Christian community. According to him, the intentional relation between the believer and God in the New Testament generates a truly kairological time. Heidegger interprets the kairological instant of the Second Coming of Christ on the basis of the third and fourth chapters of the first epistle to the Thessalonians. The phenomenon of the apostolic proclamation is inscribed in the context of the factical experience of life, which is the central element of a religion that is oriented towards the call of faith. Now, how is this experience actualized within the context of apostolic proclamation? In Heidegger's phenomenological interpretation, this process of actualization is understood out of the concrete historical situation (GA 60, 98/PRL, 67).[30] In this way, the recurrent image of Christ's calling – and the explicit repetition of this call – is part of the history of a process of actualization that factically affects each member of the community. Knowledge arises directly from the situational context of Christian experience. This shared knowledge is the basis for the divine message, which translates into serving and awaiting God out of absolute faith in the return of Christ: 'For they themselves openly declare about us what sort of reception we had among you, and how you turned to God from idols to serve the living and true God and to wait his Son from heaven, whom he raised from the dead, Jesus, who delivers us from the coming wrath' (1 Thess. 1, 9–10).

The message Paul ultimately conveys is this: do not pay heed to the present, rather look into your own self, your own life, which you know so well. As I have already noted, those who hold on to the security of the present moment and stay immersed in this world, that is to say, those who have forgotten themselves, cannot be saved, for they live in the darkness of inauthenticity. This means that those who live in the present, ignorant of their historical – and hence authentic – situation, will not recognize the moment of the Coming of Christ and thus will hamper their possibilities and cause their own ruin (GA 60, 103/PRL, 72). In contrast, those who stay in a state of expectation of, and openness to, the Lord's coming, live in authenticity, in the light of self-knowledge – that is the Day of the Lord. For Heidegger, the wordly determinations of the believer's life are completely irrelevant, for they do not determine the believer's existence. For this reason, Paul insists that 'everyone should remain in the state in which he was called' (1 Cor. 7, 20). Worldly relations slow down or even hinder actualization. It is therefore necessary to parenthesize the world with the purpose of reaching a full relation to God.

The aforementioned process of actualization involves a particular kairological moment of illumination which is attended by the believer's constant state of alert and disposition to wait. The meaning of the *when* in which the Christian believer lives acquires the nature of the factical experience of life, that is, a historical character (GA 60, 104, 106/PRL, 73, 75). The *when* of the *parousia* depends on the believer's own actions, which he performs armed with faith, love and hope:

> But you, brothers, are not in darkness, for that day to overtake you like a thief. For all of you are children of the light and children of the day. We are not of the night or darkness. Therefore, let us not sleep as the rest do, but let us stay alert and sober, [...] putting on the breastplate of faith and love and the helmet that is hope for salvation.
> 1 Thess. 5, 4–8

In contrast to late Judaism's eschatology, which gives primacy to a future event, the temporality of Christian facticity puts the accent on the moment of a decision that oscillates between past and future. This is why temporality stems from the context of actualization of our relation to God. This relation includes the dimension of the present, which is opened up in remembrance, but is also always already determined by the expectance of the imminent return of Christ, a return that will take place in the *kairos* – the fulfillment of time.

And yet, Paul never alludes to the actual moment of this Second Coming; rather, he suggests that it is unpredictable and that it will happen in the blink of an eye. He proclaims the instantaneous nature of the eschatological moment of salvation. Neither the time nor the circumstances of God's arrival are established. The unpredictable nature of salvific action involves something of a threat. Believers are to live always in a state of alert, constant insecurity and uncertainty, awaiting a moment that demands from them a decision in the present. This way of living in the present contrasts with living in the calculated prospect of an objectified future moment. Kairological features are not compatible with a calculation of time, they are part and parcel of the process of actualization of a life that resists objectification and quantification. Only on the basis of this imminent future arrival can one apprehend the primordial Christian experience of time and take upon oneself the facticity and historicity of life. Heidegger construes chronological time as a way of escaping anxiety and insecurity, and achieving the tranquility and peacefulness that a measurable, objective and present-at-hand reality is supposed to provide. But as Paul observes: 'when people are saying "Peace and security," then sudden disaster comes upon them, like labor pains upon a pregnant woman, and they will not escape' (1 Thess. 5, 3).

This allows us to consider Heidegger's second thesis: Christian experience generates primordial temporality. In this regard, the first questions one should ask are: What is the primordial condition of this experience? How is God present in factical experience? Both of these questions have one and the same answer: phenomenologically speaking, temporality is the modality in which God 'is given' or 'makes Himself present' in the factical experience of life. With the purpose of finding out the type of temporality that the Second Coming of Christ and the phenomenon of *parousia* involve, Heidegger undertakes a phenomenological analysis. One initial result is that late Judaic eschatology is not adequate to understand its Christian counterpart because the former makes use of an objective and lineal conception of time that has nothing to do with the actualization of Christian experience. On the basis of this, Heidegger interprets the sense of temporality that the Pauline epistle conveys. To his mind, in principle, the authentic Christian relation to *parousia* does not take the form of hope in a future event. As mentioned, the problem of the *when* is explained in the fifth chapter of the first epistle to the Thessalonians as follows: 'Concerning times and seasons, brothers, you have no need for anything to be written to you. For you yourselves know very well that the day of the Lord will come like a thief at night' (1 Thess. 5, 1-2). For this reason, the problem of the *when* of *parousia*, of *chronos* and *kairos*, which Heidegger renders as Zeit (time) and *Augenblick* (instant), cannot be solved by reference to objective time or to everyday time. On the contrary, as the expression 'you yourselves know' suggests, the problem of the *when* has to be dealt with in the context of the factical experience of life. This is why the problem of the temporality of Christian religious experience becomes a matter of how each person lives his own life (GA 60, 116–117/PRL, 83–84).

In this sense, authentic time is the result of the synthesis, in the present instant, of necessity and possibility, past and future. In contrast to Greek philosophy, which conceives the eternal as a past that is to be remembered, and to Judaism, which conceives it as a future that is to be anticipated, Christianity unifies both conceptions in the notion of *kairos*, which refers to the *parousia* that takes place in 'the fullness of time' (4 Gal. 4). The *kairos*, the instant of salvation, brings the believer to the razor's edge: the moment of decision. Kairological determinations do not regard a calculation or domination of time. Rather, as they refer to the future, they carry something of a threat, they belong to the history of the realization of a life that cannot be objectified. According to Heidegger, the experience of life is factical and historical insofar as in this experience the prevalent structure of life is actualization rather than content.[31] Leaving aside apocalyptic history and the idea of a datable final moment reinforces the radical orientation towards factical life. The *kairos* compels the believer to direct himself towards his own historicity and assume responsibility for his decisions, because each instant carries the possibility of the eschatological moment.

In contrast with this, in the quietist and static view of *vita beata*, the temporalizing relation that holds between the believer and God is de-historicized and mythologized to such a point so as to concern an immutable eternity. This ultimately results in the ossification of the present. Paul explains the primordial kairological experience that characterizes Christian temporality, and which excludes any metaphysics of presence, in the following passage from the epistle to the Romans:

> I consider that the sufferings of this present time are as nothing compared with the glory to be revealed for us. [...] We also groan within ourselves as we wait for adoption, the redemption our bodies. For in hope we were saved. Now hope that sees for itself is not hope. For who hopes for what one sees? But if we hope for what we do not see, we wait with endurance.
>
> Rom. 8, 18–25

Luther's critique to the scholastic *theologia gloriae* and favouring of a *theologia crucis* is also a movement away from Aristotle-based metaphysics of presence.[32] The human condition is not to have God but to search for Him once and again. The path towards Him, as human existence in general, is a constant circular *kinesis*, full of privations. Life is not static, it is in constant motion. Luther – and later on Heidegger – appropriates the dynamic relation between the individual and God. God does not become manifest in the static contemplation of a pure eternal presence. The Heideggerian destruction of the metaphysics of presence and the ontological repetition of the historicity of factical life in primitive Christianity put Heidegger in a position to reformulate the question regarding the meaning of being in the horizon of kairological temporality.

In the lecture courses he delivered in the ensuing years, Heidegger deepened this analysis of the primordial experience of time as a future arrival in which factical life unfolds and is actualized. All this came to fruition in the 1924 lecture 'The Concept of Time', the homonymous treatise from the same year, and the 1925 lecture course *History of the Concept of Time: Prolegomena*, where time is understood in terms of the transcendental horizon within which the question regarding the meaning of being can be formulated (GA 20, §§ 32–36). In particular, both in 'The Concept of Time' and in *Being and Time*, the state of resoluteness that anticipates death is the key to our understanding of temporality. Similar to the phenomenon of *parousia*, the phenomenon of the anticipation of death does not fit chronological dating parameters because it is essentially imminent and unpredictable. In order for Dasein to achieve its possibility of being-a-whole, it has to break with the everyday view that life is an uninterrupted flow that takes place in a homogeneous present time. Dasein actualizes and temporalizes its existence in a finite way and in accord with the primordial merge of past, present and future – even in if there is a particularly strong orientation towards the latter. Thus understood, temporality preserves the characteristic features of kairological time and has almost nothing in common with the idea of time as a lineal sequence of homogenous moments. Heidegger's interpretation of time and care in Augustine's *Confessions* follows the same lines.[33] In his doctrine of time, Augustine considers human beings in relation to their temporal dimension and as creatures that can either conquer or lose their existence. Only on the basis of the essence of time can one understand why the human being is capable of measuring and calculating time. Augustine equates the question regarding time with the question regarding what the human being is.[34] This is where Aristotle comes into the scene. Heidegger's interpretation of Aristotle, developed between 1922 and 1925, offers a detailed picture of the ontological structures and the fundamental modes of comportment of human being.

Heidegger and Aristotle's practical philosophy

Aristotle plays a major role in Heidegger's early thought. As we have seen, other important thinkers such as Dilthey, Kant, Luther and Augustine figure prominently in the young Heidegger's work. But there is no doubt his reinterpretation of Husserl's phenomenology together with his radicalization of Aristotle's practical philosophy are the bedrock of his complex early philosophical programme. His interpretation of Aristotle is a recurrent element in his courses from the early twenties. Heidegger himself frequently stressed the importance of Aristotle for the evolution of his philosophy.[35] This has been corroborated also in many of the numerous studies on the relation between Aristotle and the young Heidegger that have appeared over the years.[36] Finally, the documentary sources that have become recently available allow us to analyse in detail the minutiae of Heidegger's appropriation and radicalization of several themes and concepts inspired by Aristotle's philosophy.

After arriving at Freiburg as Husserl's assistant in January 1919, Heidegger focused on finding a phenomenological access to life. As explained in the previous section, Christian religiosity offered him an initial historical paradigm for his phenomenology of life. However, this attempt did not completely work out. Beside philosophical reasons, some personal reasons regarding Husserl might have played a role in this. It was Husserl who encouraged Heidegger to undertake that enterprise in the first place.[37] While in May 1919 Heidegger still considered the elaboration of a phenomenology of religion a central research topic, in the lecture course of 1920–1921, *Introduction to the Phenomenology of Religion*, he indicates that 'the complex of experience can be grasped only *out* of the origin of Christian life-context. [...] What is available only to us Christians is not sufficient for the task of arriving at Christian facticity' (GA 60, 121, 122/PRL, 86, 87, my italics). The possibility of a genuine phenomenology of life became available to Heidegger only with his rediscovery of Aristotle, as the *Phenomenological Interpretations in Connection With Aristotle. An Indication of the Hermeneutical*

Situation, better known as the *Natorp-Bericht*, makes evident. *Phronesis*, i.e. practical wisdom, substitutes primitive religiousness. *Phronesis* is evidently not just a virtue that helps us determine our comportments but certain openness to life, a fundamental mode of being that Heidegger refers to with the concept of care (*Sorge*). As is known, Heidegger's interest in this subject matter is ontological rather than ethical.

Now, what does Heidegger find in Aristotle? He considered Aristotle's work extremely congenial to his own, both thematically and methodologically. His interpretation of the phenomenon of factical life points at the proto-phenomenological dimension of Aristotle's work, which includes important comments on the dynamic and practical nature of life. Heidegger finds in the different types of truth Aristotle describes in *Nichomachean Ethics* an alternative to the traditional conception of contemplative truth, an alternative that gives primacy to those phenomena that involve a practical truth and give the historical situation of life a primordial role. In this way, as Volpi claims, Heidegger's appropriation of Aristotle devolves around three main questions: the first one regards truth, the second one Dasein and the third one time. These three questions are formulated within the unitary horizon of the question of being (Volpi 2003, 26–36). Having this in mind, the present section is structured as follows: *firstly*, I point out some important aspects of Heidegger's (re)discovery of Aristotle; then I address the question regarding truth; and *thirdly*, I consider Heidegger's radicalization of Aristotle's practical philosophy, which results in an ontology of factical life. Finally, I delineate the horizon of the question regarding time in the context of Heidegger's burgeoning dialogue with Kant.

The (re)discovery of Aristotle

Aristotle is present throughout Heidegger's thinking. His first contact with Aristotle was through Franz Brentano's *On the Manifold Meaning of Being according to Aristotle*, from 1862, which Heidegger read while in high school; then, Heidegger read Aristotelian philosophy during the years he spent studying theology in the Thomistic environment of Freiburg (1909–1911). His last direct academic engagement with Aristotle was in a seminar on Aristotle's concept of *physis* (GA 9, 239–301).[38] However, the crucial stage of Heidegger's philosophical relation to Aristotle takes place in the period that preceded the publication of *Being and Time* (1927), and particularly during the last years of his first appointment in Freiburg (1921–1922) and the beginning of his time in Marburg (1924–1926), when he elaborated his philosophical programme. In the first half of the twenties, Aristotle had a central role in the Heideggerian programme of an ontology of human life. This programme fed, especially, on the *Nichomachean Ethics*. The publication of the early lecture courses, which has been recently completed, constitutes a textual source that allows us to trace, semester by semester, the increasing importance Heidegger conferred on Aristotle. His (re)discovery of Aristotle's work, especially of his practical philosophy, is surprising because neo-Kantianism, hermeneutics, neo-scholasticism and phenomenology dominated the academic landscape of the time.

The lecture course of the winter semester, 1921–1922, and his interpretation of the first books of the *Metaphysics* and *Physics*, in the lecture course of the summer semester 1922 (GA 61 and GA 62, respectively) mark Heidegger's first approach to Aristotle during the twenties. From that moment onwards, his interest in Aristotle, particularly in the *Nichomachean Ethics*, became central to his work. Heidegger found in Aristotle's practical philosophy an inexhaustible source of inspiration for his own philosophical programme, which is first articulated in the *Natorp-Bericht*, from 1922 (NB, 237–274). In this work, which was initially planned as the sketch of a monograph on Aristotle that Heidegger never wrote, he elaborates an ontology of human life on the basis of a brilliant interpretation of the sixth book of the *Nichomachean Ethics*.[39] This interpretation is later complemented, first, with the analysis Heidegger developed in the summer 1924 lecture course, *Basic Concepts of Aristotelian Philosophy*, on the role of sentiments (*pathos*) and discourse (*logos*) as fundamental modes of being; and then, with his long introduction to the winter lecture course, 1924–1925, *The Sophist* (GA 18, 113–160 and GA 19, 21–187, respectively).

After *Being and Time*, Aristotle remained a central reference in Heidegger's thought, especially during the last years of the twenties and the beginning of the thirties. Proof of this are Heidegger's analysis of the notion of *logos* in the lecture course from the winter semester, 1929–1930, *The Fundamental Problems of Metaphysics* (GA 29/30, § 72), his interpretation of being as presence in the lecture course from the summer semester, 1930, *The Essence of Human Freedom* (cf. GA 31, § 9), and the 1931 lecture course on Book IX of Aristotle's *Metaphysics* (GA 33). However, in these works, Heidegger starts to read Aristotle from the standpoint of the history of the forgetfulness of being, whose two main features are subjectivity and onto-theology. Finally, the seminar 'On the Essence of the Concept of *physis*', composed in 1939 but published in 1958, evinces the importance that Aristotle still had for the later Heidegger. However, in this work the focus is not on the practical determinations of existence – as it was in the early work – but on Aristotle's reflections on natural entities and particularly on the idea that in contrast to artefacts, natural entities move by themselves (GA 9, 239–301). Anyone who is aware of the significance that the relation between technology and nature had for the later Heidegger's diagnosis of the contemporary epoch has to appreciate the importance he confers on Aristotle in this context.

Our interest here is the penetrating interpretative work Heidegger developed during the years that preceded the publication of *Being and Time*. At this stage, Heidegger focused on the fundamental question regarding the being of human life. How to describe human life without sacrificing its intrinsic movement, without objectifying it by means of conceptual representation? How to apprehend it in a conceptual way without distorting its authentic dynamic nature? Aristotle not only accounts for the theoretical comportment of human life but also for the poietic and practical ones. This practical dimension of life, including the care for things and persons that it involves, is fully integrated into *Being and Time*. As Volpi has shown repeatedly, the existential analytic and Aristotle's practical philosophy are homologous in many respects, to the point that one could argue, no doubt provocatively, that *Being and Time* is a modernized version of the *Nichomachean Ethics*.[40] However, one should not lose sight of the fact that Heidegger's appropriation 'ontologizes' the fundamental concepts of Aristotle's practical philosophy, that is, strips them of their practical nature and makes of them fundamental modes of being human being.[41] Thus, practical philosophy turns into an ontology of human life.

The phenomenon of truth: *aletheia* and unconcealment

As Heidegger turns to Aristotle, he progressively assimilates truth to being.[42] It is worth remembering, though, that Heidegger becomes interested in the concept of truth through a critical discussion of Husserl's *Logical Investigations*. On the basis of Husserl's theory, Heidegger comes to the conclusion that judgement is not the locus of the primordial manifestation of truth, as the tradition has it. Truth is first and foremost unconcealment. As Aristotle says, human beings live in the truth. Heidegger's philosophical investigation on factical life is not limited to offering a number of characterizations of vital experiences. His inquiry ultimately aims at the truth, that is, at confirming its claims regarding life. Without corroboration or evidence, there is no philosophy. In this regard, Heidegger remains faithful to the Husserlian motto 'to the things themselves'. The idea is to analyse phenomena the way they are directly given before any act of reflection. Phenomenology as primordial science rests on the non-reflective proving of truth. The concept of truth as unconcealment, which Heidegger started to develop in his early courses, particularly in the lecture course of the winter semester, 1925–1926, *Logic. The Question of Truth*, feeds on the Husserlian notion of 'evidence' to a large extent.[43]

In the aforementioned lecture course, Heidegger offers an initial but detailed elaboration of the concept of truth. His critical assessment of the *Logical Investigations'* theory of truth leads him to argue that judgement, as synthesis (*synthesis*) or separation (*diairesis*) is not the primordial place for the manifestation of truth. Judgement derives from a phenomenon that is ontologically more primordial. Heidegger also subscribes to the idea that evidence is awareness and living unreflective experience of truth. What is given to consciousness is the intentional object pure and simple rather than a relation of adequacy between what is meant and what is given: 'When I live in intuition of a thing as a proving intuition, the act of intuiting does not lose itself in the thing and its content. Rather, this content is intuited as bodily present and explicitly as fulfilling, as identifying-itself with the empty idea' (GA 21,107/LQT, 88).

It is important to keep in mind that Heidegger does not accept the existence of a psychic domain, and this puts him at a distance from the *Logical Investigations* and makes his approach closer to that of *Ideas I* (HU III/1, § 136). Heidegger emphasizes that the primordial givenness of the object involves a direct unreflective knowledge that the act has of itself. For this reason, in the act of getting access to evidence, that is, the particular way in which the object manifests itself, that act is transparent to itself.

Naturally, Heidegger rejects the idea that this understanding in which the act becomes transparent to itself is a form of self-consciousness, as the ultimate warrant of truth. This ideal of evidence is still in debt to the Cartesian conception. Against Cartesianism, Heidegger sets out to restore the authority of all forms of evidence rather than to subject them, in an artificial manner, to the ideal of mathematical certainty. In the living experience of the surrounding world, pre-reflective evidence is also present and phenomenology cannot ignore this. In this sense, the model of a rigorous science that Husserl proposed is superimposed onto the field of the direct and primordial givenness of things. And with this, 'the principle of principles' from *Ideas I*, is suppressed.[44] One must free oneself from that extra-phenomenological attitude and grasp what is given in a way that is immediate and free of any positing. Hermeneutic intuition, the true core of Heidegger's programme of a primordial science, bears witness to the givenness of the thing itself.

Following the thread of the problem of truth, Heidegger dives into the crack that Husserl opened. However, his radicalization and transformation of Husserl's philosophy does not begin with the concept of truth but with that of givenness (*Gegebenheit*), a concept that is close to the Heideggerian notions of disclosedness (*Erschlossenheit*) and unconcealment (*Unverborgenheit*).[45] On the basis of this, Heidegger links openness to truth, a move that constitutes a radical shift in the approach to the later concept.[46] Truth is now considered in terms of unconcealment, that is to say, as the condition of possibility of propositional truth. The tradition handed down two convictions: that the proposition is the place of truth and that truth is correspondence of thought and beings. Besides, the tradition has attributes that are both claims to Aristotle (GA 21, 128/LQT, 108, and SuZ, 214/BT, 206). Heidegger sets out to expose these three claims as prejudices resulting from the scholastic approach to logic. His discovery of the connection between intuitive truth and propositional truth imposes on him 'the need to return to Aristotle' (GA 21, 109/LQT, 90).[47] He undertakes a destruction of the traditional theory of truth that, on the basis of an overly ontological reading of *On Interpretation*, Book I, *On the Soul*, Book III, *Metaphysics*, Book IX, and *Nichomachean Ethics*, Book VI, leads him to bring logic back to its Aristotelian origin.

The lecture course of 1925–1926, *Logic. The Question of Truth*, offers a first systematic elaboration of passages from these works and provides a good part of *Being and Time*'s conceptual battery. The leading thread of that lecture course is the concept of *logos*, understood as human being's most fundamental way of being, by means of which it reveals to itself, to others, and ultimately reveals its own being. To put it another way, the task of logic is to examine the possibility of the openness, discovery and unconcealment of beings in general within the horizon of truth. This means that Dasein, the others, the world and beings, are initially concealed: 'In other words, much of the world and much of human existence is by and large not un-covered. So beings can be drawn out of their not-un-coveredness, their concealment [*Verborgenheit*]. They can be un-covered or un-concealed. This uncoveredness or unconcealment [*Unverborgenheit*] of beings is what we call truth' (GA 21, 7/LQT, 6).[48]

Heidegger directs his criticism to the metaphysical tradition, which reduces *logos* to its propositional and categorial dimension, effectively giving priority to predication and judgement. Thus Heidegger rejects the definition of human being as the animal that has *logos*, for that definition has become reductive. The same goes for all other concepts and definitions applied to human being: all of them reduce the essence of human being to one thing among others. The conception of human being as *animal rationale* does not account for the movedness of human life, it is entrapped in a contemplative and static model of knowledge. The leading thread of Heidegger's new philosophical programme for a primordial and radical understanding of human life demanded a reinterpretation of the genuinely Aristotelian comprehension of the unconcealing dimension of *logos* (Courtine 1996b, 22–23; Volpi 1996, 34–35).

Logos is a structure that is prior to language and belongs to the field of the pre-objective openness and immediate understanding of the world. According to Aristotle, 'the thinking of indivisibles is among things concerning which there can be no falsity; but objects to which truth or falsity may belong are combinations of concepts *already* formed, like unities of things' (De an. III 6, 430a, 27–28, my italics). This 'already' refers to an ontological structure that was going to be very important for the development of the young Heidegger's philosophical programme. He would refer to it as the 'hermeneutic *as*' in which the 'apophantic *as*' of proposition is grounded.[49] To utter a proposition is to express something, to say something about something. But this predicative operation is derivative on the being already in the world that characterizes human existence. The world opens up to pre-predicative experience as a world that is in some way already meaningful, that is, a world that has already been interpreted: 'It [the being] is already posited in meaning – it already makes sense' (GA 21, 144/LQT, 121). In *Being and Time*, the *factum* of our meaningful relation to the world is the universal structure 'as'. This is the kernel of the hermeneutic transformation of phenomenology. The claim that 'any simple pre-predicative seeing of what is at hand is in itself already understanding and interpretative' (SuZ, 149/BT, 149) leads Heidegger to substitute the model of hermeneutic understanding for that of phenomenological perception.[50]

Therefore, propositions do not stand in a primordial relation to beings. In fact, their relating to beings is made possible by a prior state of disclosedness, which thereby becomes the condition of possibility of propositions:

> To say that a statement is *true* means that it discovers the beings in themselves. It asserts, it shows, it lets beings 'be seen' (*apophansis*) in their discoveredness [*Entdecktheit*]. The *being true* of the statement must be understood as *discovering*. Thus, truth by no means has the structure of an agreement between knowing and the object in the sense of a correspondence of one being (subject) to another (object).
>
> SuZ, 218–219/BT, 210, italics in the original[51]

Heidegger's analysis of the conditions of possibility of false propositions is useful to illustrate this point. Suppose, Heidegger says, I am taking a walk in a dark forest and suddenly it seems to me something is moving in the firs and comes towards me. First, I think it might be a deer. But as I approach the firs, I realize it is just a bush shaken by the wind, and therefore, that my initial judgement was false (GA 21, 187/LQT, 158). It is important to notice that the example evinces the following conditions: first, it is necessary that something comes to our attention. If this does not happen, we would not even have a reason to form a judgement. This means we are always already moving in the prior openness of the world. Second, the simple fact that I perceive the deer as 'something' that comes to my attention presupposes that this 'something' is already somehow understood. And third, things only appear in a context: only in the surrounding world 'forest' can something appear as a 'deer'. This surrounding world, which is part of the meaningfully structured whole that Heidegger calls being-in-the-world, is framed by certain pre-understanding that limits one's possibilities of seeing. So much so, that it is highly improbable that we could run into the King of Persia amidst the firs of a German forest (GA 21, 188/LQT, 158–159).[52]

Hence, the possibility of agreement or disagreement between a proposition and an object depends on the background of a world that has been always already understood. Now, recognizing disclosedness as the condition of possibility of both true and false propositions does not make for a complete account of truth, since the question is still open as to what decides whether a proposition is true or false. In the end, it is not possible to find any feature in Heidegger's account that allows us to connect his conception of truth with other theories of truth such as conventionalism or coherentism. In this sense, Heidegger's account cannot be considered complete, as Tugendhat (1967) and Gethmann (1991) have argued. The fact that beings can only be understood on the basis of prior disclosedness blocks the possibility of accounting for the binary nature of truth. The truth of propositions, as Tugendhat points out, is to be understood as progressive unconcealing, a gradual approach to the thing itself. We are always on our path towards truth but propositions are never completely verified. This path is to be understood as the goal of a movement, a tendency that has not yet reached its end, and this gives truth the character of a constant dynamic approaching (Tugendhat 1967, 331–348, in particular 345–348).

According to Heidegger's explanation of the three conditions of false propositions, the pair unconcealed/concealed is not tantamount to the pair false/true. Heidegger does not provide a definition of falsity, he just spells out its conditions of possibility. Disclosedness offers a necessary though not sufficient condition for truth. Putting truth and disclosedness at the same level allows Heidegger to connect the problem of facticity to the problem of truth. Thus, the problem of truth loses its counterfactual aspect, but at the same time, Heidegger's move leaves open the path towards dealing with the problem of truth in terms of disclosedness and unconcealment: 'But we showed in our earlier analysis of the worldliness of the world and innerwordly beings that the discoveredness (*Entdecktheit*) of innerwordly beings is *grounded* in the disclosedness (*Erschlossenheit*) of the world. [...] *With* and *through* it is discoveredness; thus only with the disclosedness of Da-sein is the *most primordial* phenomenon of truth' (SuZ, 220, 221 /BT, 212, italics in the original).

Equating truth and meaning constitution makes it impossible to make room for the traditional properties of the concept of truth related to its validity, such as universality, necessity and unconditionality. As a result, truth can only be spoken of in terms of a historical and factual happening.[53] Thus, insofar as Dasein's disclosedness presupposes an interpretation of the world, all propositions depend on the factic understanding of the world that in each case Dasein has. The 'epistemologization' of the concept of truth becomes visible precisely at this point. For by asking about the nature of truth and its ontological foundations – 'What is true?' and 'How is truth possible?' – Heidegger transforms the traditional question of truth into the question of truth as uncovering (Lafont 1994, 160ff.).

But what is really at stake here is Heidegger's equation of truth to unconcealment. The question regarding the meaning of being and its relation to truth motivates Heidegger to establish the ontological structure of human life with regard to its power for unconcealing. And here, the paradigm that Heidegger follows is no doubt Aristotle, whose *Nichomachean Ethics* leaves behind the Platonic assimilation of knowledge to eidetic vision. In the framework of the typical phenomenological problem of the constitution of the subject, Heidegger turns to the Aristotelian idea that the soul lives in the truth, and makes Aristotle's concept of *praxis* his own. With this, Heidegger attempts to find a way out of Husserl's aporetic conception of a transcendental subjectivity, where the subject is referred to the world while at the same time constitutes it. Heidegger distances himself from the transcendental view of his teacher, who considers consciousness from a predominately epistemological point of view, and finds his footing in Aristotle.

In this sense, the importance of Husserl and Aristotle in Heidegger's work is much more significant than that of a mere historical and critical reference. Both authors delineate the horizon of the problems in which Heidegger was interested. The discovery of Aristotle as the thinker that formulates the primordial question of philosophy, that is, the question regarding the meaning of being, connects with the discovery of Husserl as the thinker that lays down the right method for inquiring about things themselves. For Heidegger, addressing Husserl and Aristotle was not simply a matter of studying and incorporating some of their ideas; it was part of the *mise en scène* in which one single problem played out: the question regarding being. The meaning of being showed itself in human being's life. Heidegger saw Aristotle through the eye of Husserl's phenomenology, but at the same time, his encounter with the former transformed the way he regarded the latter. On the one hand, Heidegger interprets Aristotle in a phenomenological key rather than in the metaphysical and theological way of Christian scholastics. On the other hand, he reads Husserl from an ontological point of view, and not in an idealist and transcendental way. What shows itself in the understanding openness of human being remains irreducible to the objective representation of a cognitive subject. But at the same time, the fact that human being's intentional openness is irreducible to cognitive, psychological and anthropological determinations is what lets things show themselves in their beings. During those early years, each time Heidegger read Aristotle, he was led to the genuinely phenomenological task of an ontology of life, or in other words, to an ontology of Dasein.

From *Nichomachean Ethics* to the ontology of human life

The fundamental modes of unveilment: theoria, poiesis and praxis in the articulation of fundamental ontology

Heidegger's analysis of the phenomenon of truth makes manifest that theory is only one of the different possibilities and modalities by which human being understands beings and its own being. Aristotle's practical philosophy offers a richer and more consistent approach than that of Husserl. Aristotle's approach starts out from the everyday relations we are ordinarily engaged in. His exposition of the virtues, as they figure in *Nichomachean Ethics*, offers a broad spectrum of human modes of comportment that Husserl did not take into consideration in his project of philosophy as rigorous science. The rejection of Husserl's theoretical attitude and the appropriation of Aristotle's ethical thinking are the two indispensable ingredients of Heidegger's analysis of human existence.

In the long introduction to the lecture course of the winter semester, 1924–1925, *Plato's Sophist*, Heidegger undertakes a detailed analysis of the sixth book of *Nichomachean*

Ethics (GA 19, 21–188/PS, 15–129).⁵⁴ The point of departure is the being of beings. What is the leading thread of the ontological inquiry? Truth, or *aletheia*, understood as unconcealment. What being gives us an adequate access to the openness of truth? Human life, that is, Dasein, who by being ontologically determined by truth, makes the unveilment of being possible (GA 19, 17/PS, 11). On the basis of this general reflection, Heidegger analyses the five modes by means of which, according to Aristotle, the human soul can possess the truth: 'art, scientific knowledge, practical wisdom, philosophic wisdom, intuitive reason' (Nic. Eth. VI 3, 1139b, 15–17). Heidegger is interested in finding out which of these modes provides the most primordial manifestation of the world and of being. With this purpose, he examines the following three modes of unveilment: *theoria*, *poiesis* and *praxis*, and their respective forms of knowledge: *episteme, techne* and *phronesis*. One consequence of Heidegger's productive appropriation of Aristotle's account is that it is possible to establish a certain correspondence between the latter and the ontological determinations of *Being and Time*. The most evident of these correlations are probably those between *poiesis* and readiness-to-hand, and *theoria* and *being-present-at-hand*.⁵⁵ Each of these modes of unveilment corresponds to a particular form of knowledge and comportment. Schematically, the correspondence can be put as shown in Table 4.1. By the same token, these modes of comportment can be distinguished from each other by the goals and modes of being each of them involves.

(a) *Praxis* and *theoria*. It is critical to distinguish between these two modes of unveilment right from the outset. *Praxis* denotes human acting insofar as it is directed to success under the guidance of practical wisdom (*phronesis*), which in each case dictates the adequate way of comportment given a concrete situation. For its part, *theoria* is the result of observation and description, and aims at apprehending the being of beings in an abstract manner. The philosophical tradition has privileged theoretic activity and thus marginalized the practical dimension of human life. Moreover, this dimension has been subordinated to the categories of the theoretical domain. Aristotle offers a good platform for overcoming this situation and securing the autonomy and particularity of *praxis*. In his discussion of Plato, Aristotle distinguished for the first time between the theoretical comportment (*theorein*) and the practical one (*praktein*). In conformity to this distinction, he clearly separated the verifiable knowledge of wisdom from the practical knowledge of *phronesis*.

(b) *Praxis* and *poiesis*. Ethical and political action (*praxis*) is different from the production of objects (*poiesis*). The latter is an activity directed towards the production of artefacts and tools that thus becomes instrumentally available to us. Given the similarity between practical action and poietic production it is necessary to distinguish

Table 4.1 Life and the main modes of being of truth

Modes of unveilment	Forms of knowledge	Forms of comportment
Theoria	*episteme*	being-present-at-hand
Poiesis	*techne*	readiness-to-hand
Praxis	*phronesis*	care

between their respective modes of being. *Praxis* embodies a practical-moral knowledge, *poiesis* a technological-instrumental one. The criterion for distinguishing them from one another is the fact that practical action is an end in itself. Success in practical action lies in the perfection and virtue that accompany the action itself. In contrast, the end of production lies outside the productive activity, it is the produced object as such. Heidegger makes Aristotle's concept of *praxis* his own and construes it as the fundamental ontological determination of human life. This poses the risk of turning the existential analytic into a form of solipsism in which Dasein, as primordial *praxis*, is left naked in the face of its destiny, as it were. In this regard, two notable students of Heidegger's, Herbert Marcuse and Hannah Arendt, restate this view in an inverted way: Marcuse locates life in the material conditions of existence, while Arendt elaborates on the interpersonal, public and plural nature of *praxis*.

(c) Phronesis. Aristotle distinguishes the practical knowledge or wisdom in which *phronesis* consists from the productive knowledge of *poiesis* and the theoretical knowledge of *sophia*. The distinction between practical and theoretical knowledge lies in the difference between *praxis* and *theoria* and their respective domains of inquiry. The practical knowledge that *phronesis* involves is below the theoretical knowledge of *sophia* because its object – the contingency of human action – is not as perfect as the object of the theoretical sciences, which belong to the domain of divine eternity. However, *phronesis* involves a remarkable element that theoretical knowledge lacks, namely, its imperative directedness towards action. *Phronesis* demands to make decisions and to act accordingly (Nic. Eth. VI 10, 1143a, 8).

For its part, the distinction between practical and poietic knowledge cannot be established on the same grounds as the distinction between practical and theoretical knowledge. The reason is that both *phronesis* and *poiesis* pertain to the contingent, that is to say, what can be otherwise. In Book VI of *Nichomachean Ethics*, Aristotle offers a somewhat subjective criterion for distinguishing between *phronesis* and *poiesis* based on the different attitudes each of them involves. First, in contrast to *techne, phronesis* does not pertain individual actions but takes into consideration success in life in general. Practical wisdom aims at happiness (*eudaimonia*) rather than mere utility, as productive knowledge does. Second, *phronesis* and *techne* are different modes of knowledge that refer to different modes of comportment, *praxis* and *poiesis*, respectively (Nic. Eth. VI 5, 1140b, 3ff.). As mentioned, the end of *poiesis* lies outside poietic activity, while the end of *praxis* is involved in the action itself. Third, even though Aristotle characterizes both *phronesis* and *techne* as modes of knowledge, there is a subtle difference between these characterizations. While in his definition of *techne* Aristotle stresses the technological knowledge of the truth of *logos*, in his definition of *phronesis* he insists on the truth of the attitude behind moral knowledge, which is attended by skillfulness and cleverness (Nic. Eth. VI 4, 1140a, 20ff., and Nic. Eth. VI 5, 1140b, 5, respectively). Fourth, *techne*, unlike *phronesis*, involves a rule establishing the standard of perfection. Through the continuous practice of medicine, a physician can improve his diagnostic abilities and surgical techniques. A carpenter can perfect his manual and instrumental skills to the point of excelling in his craft. Practical-moral wisdom, for its part, is not reducible to the application, to each person's life situations, of the model of action that the morally knowing man (*phronimos*) embodies, as if life could be modelled by imitating the techniques of a master sculptor. In other words, *techne* allows for a gradual and accumulative approximation to perfection, but *phronesis* can be enacted in one single way and does not involve the application of a universal model of action (Nic. Eth. VI 5, 1140b, 22–24). In *techne*, perfection can be achieved through practice and error. This is not the case with *phronesis*, for one cannot become a virtuous person in a world of vice. One does not come back home any wiser from a walk in the red-light district.

Dasein and Aristotelian praxis

Heidegger's *praxis*-based interpretation of the structures of Dasein evinces certain structural, conceptual and sometimes even terminological correspondences to Aristotle's proposal. Heidegger himself declares that practical reason is an ontology of human life. In the context of 'practical science' (*episteme praktike*), which Heidegger renders as 'ontology of human existence', Aristotle assigns to human life a specific type of movement (*kinesis*). 'Life', Aristotle says, 'is action (*praxis*), not production (*poiesis*)' (Pol. I 4, 1254a, 5–6).[56] *Praxis* is not sheer Zen, that is, preservation and contemplation of life, but *bios*, that is, a life that projects itself onto reaching the best existence possible. Not even in his praise of the ideal of the practically knowing man and his defence of theoretical and contemplative life can Aristotle shake off the ties of temporality and reality: 'But, being a man, one will also need external prosperity; for our nature is not self-sufficient for the purpose of contemplation, but our body also must be healthy and must have food and other attention' (Nic. Eth. X 8, 1178b, 34–36). His apparently trivial fact introduces an element on which knowledge also depends.

This submission to actual reality constitutes the anchor that makes knowledge embodied in nature. Knowledge of ideas in themselves, irrespective of their genesis – from which they cannot be disassociated – becomes knowledge of mere theoretical schemes. And these do not apply to the domain of knowledge that pertains to actions and the projection of thought onto the space of culture and society. The end of politics and ethics 'is not knowledge (*gnosis*), but action (*praxis*)' (Nic. Eth. I 3, 1095a, 6). *Praxis* occupies centre stage in ethical reflection. In essence, *praxis* is comportment and life in the political context of a community. And this comportment possesses *logos*, which offers guidance and paths for perfection.[57] The link between *praxis* and *logos* not only indicates a way out of a purely natural horizon but inscribes the theory of human action in the sphere of intersubjectivity: 'Surely it is strange, too, to make the supremely happy man a solitary; for no one would choose the whole world on condition of being alone, since man is a political creature and one whose nature is to live with others' (Nic. Eth. IX 9, 1169b, 16–18).

This *logos* does not stem from the contemplation of eternal truths. Our dealings with things and the world enriches the content of our acts and thought (Nic. Eth. I 3, 1095a, 1–7). The unbreakable link between human being and its works is present both in Aristotle's and in Heidegger's interpretations of *praxis*. This means that human being, insofar as it is *zoon politikon logon echon*, has to deliberate (*boulesis*) and decide (*proairesis*) what path to follow and what meaning to give to its life. As is well known, the man that has practical wisdom (*phronimos*) is the man that knows how to deliberate and decide in the right way, and thus is capable of achieving happiness (*eudaimonia*), the ultimate end of a fulfilled life. This way of being, however, is the result of temporality, which intertwines with the fabric of *praxis*. And so *praxis* becomes an enterprise, a project, a creation. In the face of the acts of gods and heroes, human *praxis* starts to become a symbol of human autonomy. But this *praxis* requires multiple alternatives; it requires possibilities and freedom. For this reason, happiness – and all that this term seems to encompass – as Heidegger's own existence, is forged in a process that requires the present to be conceived, the past to be enriched and the future to be actualized. By understanding human reality in terms of *praxis*, Heidegger is able to project life towards the will, *logos* and, naturally, the real conditions in which existence unfolds.

Nevertheless, Heidegger's appropriation of the concepts of *phronesis* and *praxis* was quite selective. It involved a process of 'ontologization' that made it possible to integrate those concepts in his philosophical programme. He appeals to these concepts in his criticism of the metaphysical ambition for a system where absolute truth is warranted. In contrast, he purports to direct the philosophical inquiry towards the practical situations in which human being performs its everyday tasks, including the productive and intellectual ones. Reading the *Nichomachean Ethics* taught Heidegger that *phronesis*, as much as an ontological understanding of human reality, is not irreducible to theoretical parameters. Rather, it is relative to Dasein's project of self-determination. Heidegger takes up this fundamental intuition and reformulates it in an ontological manner. Dasein is a peculiar entity, for which its being is always at stake. Dasein is a factical being that always has to decide about the existential possibilities within its reach. Particularly, Dasein has to choose the types and modalities of its own self-realization. As Aristotle says, human being is the being that has to decide (Nic. Eth. VI 5, 1140a, 26). An authentic existence becomes available to Dasein only when it explicitly takes upon itself the responsibility of choosing among its possibilities. Even complete passivity or evasion in relation to the actualization of these possibilities is predicated upon a not-wanting-to-make-a-decision. Evasion necessarily leads to falling in a state of inauthenticity. In contrast, Dasein achieves the highest level of authenticity when, by paying attention to the voice of conscience, it accepts the necessity of deciding, in a resolute way, out of the projection of its own possibilities.

On the basis of the ontological interpretation of Dasein's practical structure, Heidegger drew a number of conclusions that would become decisive for the design of *Being and Time*'s fundamental ontology. *First*, against the metaphysical privilege of the present, Heidegger argues for the implicit priority of the future in each decision human beings make. He thematizes and conceptualizes this unity, which sustains the whole self-referential structure of care, in accord with the idea that Dasein is not fully realized in the present actuality of a pure act. Structurally, Dasein has the capacity to exceed the limits of the present and open itself up to the temporal dimensions of the future, as the horizon for the projection of possibilities, and the past, as the ineluctable context of those projections. It is precisely because Dasein's comportment involves deciding about its being that Dasein is always constantly projecting itself towards the future. For Aristotle too, deliberation and decision are linked to the future (Nic. Eth. VI 9, 1142b, 5–6).

Second, for Dasein, in all decisions, its being is always an issue; that is, the being that is always at stake is specifically its own. In other words, the being towards which Dasein is in each case directed is always *mine*. Dasein decides about its own being and not about that of the others. Heidegger calls this peculiar way of being '*Jemeinigkeit*' (mineness). This ontological determination is surely based on the type of self-knowledge that *phronesis* supplies (Nic. Eth. VI 8, 1141b, 30–34).

Third, Heidegger draws a radical distinction between the ontological constitution of Dasein's practical comportment and those beings that do not have Dasein's mode of being. This leads him to assert the ontic and ontological priority of Dasein and therefore also to criticize radical metaphysical distinctions such as those between human being and nature, subject and object, and consciousness and world, which in his view are based on an inadequate understanding of the fundamentally unitary structure of life.

Fourth, the practical nature of Dasein's being implies a radical rejection of the existence of a reflexive self-consciousness, understood as the knowledge we can obtain of the self through introspection. Dasein's identity is not constituted irrespective of its affective dispositions and relations to the world of things and human beings. Heidegger explicitly avoids the objective categories of the prevailing metaphysical doctrines of consciousness. His radicalization of *praxis*, a concept which he unties from particular actions and reformulates in ontological terms, allows him to displace metaphysical claims in favour of the fundamental and primordial action of Dasein's care. At this point, the differences between Aristotle and Heidegger become visible. Whereas for the former practical understanding of life is a specific form of understanding that interacts with others such as physics, biology and psychology, for the latter, practical conditions pertain to Dasein's ontological constitution and therefore precede all action.

Care and practical wisdom

Heidegger's attraction towards Aristotle's ethics is due, above all, to the priority the latter gives to the practical understanding over the theoretical one. It is clear that practical wisdom is not the knowledge of science. In this sense, Aristotle's distinction between practical wisdom, *phronesis*, and theoretical knowledge, *episteme*, is straightforward. All the more so, if one recalls that for the Greeks, mathematics was the paradigm of science. Mathematics was a knowledge of the immutable that rested on demonstration and therefore anyone could master it. In contrast, in acting, human beings have to deal with ever-changing situations that require cleverness and always demand that we make decisions. It is evident that insofar as practical wisdom pertains to particular cases it is not a science. In this way, it opposes the intellect, which is capable of establishing universal definitions (Nic. Eth. VI 8, 1142a, 25–26). This is the problem of moral knowledge, which is the focus of Aristotle's inquiry. The question one has to face is what is the right thing to do in each case? It is worth recalling that ethics is part of politics and for that reason the defining human characteristic in ethical inquiry is what Aristotle expresses with the formula *zoon politikon*. According to Greek thinking, the ability to establish a political ordering allowed human beings to free themselves from the ties of natural needs, and directly opposed natural forms of association such as domestic unity and family.

The development of the city-state meant, for human beings, the acquisition of something of a second nature, that is, *bios politikos*. This second nature pertains to the domain of human affairs, which have to do with action *(praxis)* and rational speech *(logos)*. This is why Aristotle says both that human nature is *zoon politikon* and that it is *zoon logon echon*. Each citizen belongs to both spheres: the private one and the public one. In this way, a clear-cut distinction is established between that which is the citizen's property and that which belongs to the community. This is not just an Aristotelian theory, but an actual historical fact: the foundation of the *polis* was preceded by the destruction of kinship-based communities. An outstanding analysis of the consequences of this fact has been offered by Hannah Arendt, a student of Heidegger precisely during the years he developed his interpretation of Aristotle's practical philosophy, in her book, *The Human Condition* (Arendt 1958, 7–21).[58]

Ethical knowledge does not aim at establishing universal rules of behaviour. It takes the concrete situations of human actions into consideration. Given that it is a knowledge that guides an activity, the Greek notion of *techne*, the knowledge or skill of the artisan that knows how to fabricate a tool may come to mind in this regard. At first sight, the similitudes between the practically knowledgeable man *(phronimos)*, who knows how to make the right choices in each circumstance, and the artisan, who acts according to a plan, seem plain enough. However, the differences between both types of knowledge cannot be ignored. It is clear, for one, that we do not have our own self at our disposal as the artisan has his material at his. The problem is how to distinguish the knowledge that we have of our own selves as ethical persons from the knowledge we could have regarding how to fabricate something. A technique can be learnt and forgotten. But ethical knowledge can be neither learnt nor forgotten. It is not like the knowledge related to a particular profession, which can be chosen. It is not possible to reject ethical knowledge in order to choose a different type of knowledge. The practically knowledgeable person is immersed in a concrete situation that calls for action here and now and is required to exercise her ethical knowledge according to the demands of the circumstances (Gadamer 1993, 85–86).[59]

To some extent, the capacity to decide involved by care is similar to that of practical wisdom. What is the centre of the reflection for both practical wisdom and care? Dasein itself. What is the nature of practical wisdom? 'Now it is thought to be the mark of a man of practical wisdom to be able to deliberate well about what is good and expedient for himself, not in some particular respect, [...] but about what sorts of things conduce to the good life in general' (Nic. Eth. VI 5, 1140a, 25–27). *Phronesis* pertains to the being that thinks. And in contrast to produced things, the being that thinks is human being, Dasein itself. 'Practical wisdom', Aristotle says, 'also is identified specially with that form of it which is concerned with a man himself –with the individual' (Nic. Eth. VI 8, 1141b, 30). Whereas the *telos* of *techne* is limited to intra-worldly beings, the *telos* of *phronesis* lies in the different factical situations of Dasein's existence. In this sense, practical wisdom embodies a mode of truth that uncovers Dasein in its concrete historical facticity (GA 19, 51–52/PS, 36–37). To the extent that Dasein ordinarily finds itself trapped by pleasures and everydayness, Dasein risks losing itself in the 'they'. Dasein's being dissolves in this type of existence, because '[...] the man who has been ruined by pleasure or pain forthwith fails to see any such originating cause – to see that for the sake of this or because of this he ought to choose and do whatever he chooses and loses; for vice is destructive of the originating cause of action' (Nic. Eth. VI 5, 1140b, 17–20). To which Heidegger adds: 'in this way, therefore, *phronesis* is involved in a constant struggle against a tendency to cover over residing at the heart of Dasein' (GA 19, 52–53/PS, 36–37). At the same time, practical wisdom constitutes the only type of comportment that enables human beings to conquer their authenticity. Human existence is always entangled in a constant dynamic process of decision-making that has the structure of what Kierkegaard called *entweder-oder*: authenticity or inauthenticity. For this reason, just as *phronesis* is not a self-evident and already secured mode of knowledge, but a task, life is not a finished act either, but is incessantly underway. It is the moment of decision (*kairos*)[60] and the possibilities of choice (*proairesis*)[61] that determine in each case the level of self-determination of human existence.

Phronesis embodies our capacity to master our own will and project our life. It is, on the one hand, a dianoetic virtue that pertains to the contingency of the self, and, on the other, constitutes the possibility of self-actualization of factual life. According to the lecture course, 1924–1925, *Plato's Sophist*, the truth that occurs in *phronesis* aims at unveiling 'the right mode of being of Dasein as such and as a whole' (GA 19, 49/PS, 34). In other words, truth unveils Dasein's authentic potentiality to be itself (*Selbst-sein-können*). However, Dasein is characterized by its proneness to fall and get immersed in everyday dealings. For this reason, *phronesis* expresses 'a constant struggle against a tendency to cover over residing in the heart of Dasein' (GA 19, 52/PS, 37). In this way, Heidegger's interest starts to shift toward an interpretation of *phronesis* in terms of the ontological and transparent truth (*aletheia*) of human existence. This truth cannot be apprehended by Dasein itself, although it has, for Dasein, a binding nature. The validity of the truth of *episteme* transcends our existence and thereby has an extra-temporal meaning. In contrast, the truth of *phronesis* is historical, that is, is bounded to the individual history of each person and ceases when the individual ceases to exist.

The possibility of self-determination at which Heidegger's analysis points, and which is always framed by the practical question regarding the meaning we want to confer to human existence, always involves facing a double possibility: to lead either an inauthentic or an authentic existence. It is manifest here, once again, that the practical question demands taking issue with oneself. Evading one's freedom is tantamount to fleeing from oneself. The space of decision that the practical question opens up has the character of 'deciding by yourself' and so offers a possibility of self-determination that escapes external prescriptions. This fits the phenomenon of singularization that Dasein undergoes in the face of anxiety, and which 'reveals to it authenticity and inauthenticity as possibilities of its being' (SuZ, 191/BT, 184).

Now, what type of relation does Dasein have with itself? Basically a practical and voluntaristic relation. For Heidegger, what distinguishes Dasein is 'the fact that in its being this being is concerned *about* its very being' (SuZ, 12/BT, 11, italics in the original). For this reason, Heidegger conceives existence as a 'to be' (*Zu-sein*): 'The "essence" of this being lies in its to be' (SuZ, 42/BT, 41, quotation marks in the original). Where does the question regarding being lead? Obviously, this is not a theoretical question one could answer with a proposition. It is a practical question that demands Dasein to make a concrete decision regarding its existence, an existence that has to be assumed and actualized in one way or another. No one can take away his existence from someone else. Existence is non-transferrable and, given Dasein's mineness (*Jemeinigkeit*), is personal. Existence is given to us as what we are to be, and therefore as something we have to take care of. For this reason, existence as comportment is essentially practical:

> Da-sein is always my own, to be always in this or that way. It has somehow always already decided in which way Da-sein is always my own. The being which is concerned in its being about its being is related to its being as its truest possibility. Da-sein is always its possibility. It does not 'have' that possibility only as a mere attribute of something objectively present. And because Da-sein *is* always essentially its possibility, it *can* 'choose' itself in its being, it can win itself, it can lose itself, or it can never and only 'apparently' win itself.
> SuZ, 42 /BT, 42, italics and quotation marks in the original

We can better understand this form of comportment if we compare it to the classical picture of what a human being is. The idea that human being takes issue with its own existence is by no means new. It is already present in Aristotle, who to a large extent defined the philosophical tradition. He even extrapolated this idea to animals and plants, the rationale being that the end of every living creature is to preserve its own life (De an. II 4, 415b, 1–2). However, non-rational animals, which lack the capacity to give expression to their states of consciousness through speech, are blind to the needs of their being. For Aristotle, only human being, who is capable of speech and reason (*logos*), is aware of its own being and the means necessary for its preservation (Pol. I 2, 1253a, 10–12). Therefore, human being is not only determined by sensation, but also dwells in the domain of actions and voluntary decisions. The term *praxis* is reserved precisely for this domain. Being is not only life, but also activity.[62] Aristotle, as Heidegger, asserts a practical relation to oneself. So, the question arises, what distinguishes Aristotle's view from Heidegger's? The answer, as Tugendhat has carefully showed, is threefold (1993, 179–190).

First, Aristotle only develops the active aspect of human being's comportment towards itself: for human being, what is at stake is always its own being. Heidegger adds the passive aspect: human being has to be its own being. This 'having-to-be' becomes concrete in the facticity of the responsibility that is necessarily linked to Dasein's thrownness. Whereas the first, voluntary, aspect implies a practical *possibility*, the second one implies the inevitable moment of a practical *necessity*. Possibility and necessity limit Dasein's practical behaviour. All decisions are determined by these two aspects. The fact that we always find ourselves in a particular context of action is what constitutes facticity, but at the same time all action is performed in a space of possibilities. Lack of possibilities would indicate that everything has become completely necessary or trivial. Therefore, there is a space of decision in which I ask myself how to realize my being even though the fact that I am to realize it is an ontologically necessary determination.[63]

Second, Heidegger's conception of *praxis* is different from Aristotle's in its ontological import. For Heidegger, the meaning of being is radically distinct from mere presence and verification. So the question arises as to what alternative conception is possible. Heidegger's solution is to prove that presence is derivative on the primordial unconcealing power of being.

Lastly, the fact that Heidegger vindicates and gives priority to Dasein's practical dimension allows him to direct his ontological inquiry in a way that is distinctly different from the one favoured by the modern tradition. That Dasein takes care of itself and primordially comports itself in a practical way takes away the priority of the subject/object epistemological scheme, which thereby becomes non-fundamental. The deliberative nature of *phronesis* bespeaks autonomy, and this is something Heidegger tries to preserve with the concept of resoluteness (*Entschlossenheit*). At the same time, deliberation, understood as directed toward the future, is intimately linked to time. While *nous* inquiries about eternal principles, wisdom and practical wisdom contribute to the philosophical interpretation of 'the ways how factical life temporalizes and relates to itself' (NB, 246). With this connection between being and temporality we arrive at the core of Heidegger's thinking: life as care acquires its full meaning by means of an interpretation of time.

The constitutive movedness of human life and the question regarding time

As explained, the traces of Aristotle's practical philosophy are quite evident in the young Heidegger's thought and delineate the path that results in the ontology of human life. Heidegger's painstaking interpretations of the *Nichomachean Ethics* enabled him to bring to light the eminently practical comportments that constitute human life. Life is action (*praxis*) as much as it is movement (*kinesis*). As Heidegger recalls: 'The problem of facticity is a *kínesis*-problem' (GA 61, 117/PIA, 87). The question regarding movement, and therefore also the question regarding time, undoubtedly play a crucial role in Heidegger's hermeneutic appropriation of Aristotle's philosophy.[64] In this sense, Aristotle's *Physics* is the fundamental reference for Heidegger's programme of the destruction of the history of ontology. Since the early Freiburg lecture course, Heidegger was completely aware of the fact that the elaboration of a hermeneutics of factical life and the critical dismatlement of the ontological tradition were two faces of the same coin. Heidegger's appropriation of Aristotle's *Physics* followed the same two coordinates: on the one hand, the ontological characterization of the kinetic nature of factical life; on the other, the critical assessment of ontological presuppositions with a view to get to the primordial sources of the phenomenon of movement. And finally, this phenomenon, which is the keystone of Heidegger's analysis of facticity, is brought back to its temporal foundation, that is, Dasein's temporality.[65]

Heidegger found in Aristotle's critique of Plato and in his radical ontological conception of movement the starting point for a genuine philosophical anthropology. Aristotle's conception of movement is not only at the bottom of Heidegger's interpretation of the Greek philosopher but becomes the fundamental phenomenon in his own hermeneutics of factical life. Human life, as he repeatedly reminds us, is not a mere objective process (*Vorgang*), but is characterized by the capacity to grasp the world that surrounds it in an understanding way (*Ereignis*). No doubt, Heidegger could have used the terms '*Handlung*' or '*Tätigkeit*' in order to highlight Dasein's active dimension, but in his attempt to distance himself from the philosophical tradition he preferred the expression '*Bewegtheit*' (movedness). 'Movedness' designates a type of movement distinctive of Dasein, and thus contrasts with mere '*Bewegung*' (movement) that corresponds to physical entities (Adrián 2009, 59–61).

The Aristotelian analysis of movement shows that physical entities belong to a world, to be precise, to the sublunary world, which is characterized by generation and corruption. This characterization is structurally parallel to the Heideggerian description of the character of being-in-the-world. *Physics* discovers the different ontological modalities of living beings (plants as vegetative beings, animals as perceiving beings), including human being (as thinking being). *Kinesis* itself is taken to be a primordial ontological determination of all physic beings that show up in the world. Heidegger defends his radicalized appropriation of Aristotle's *Physics* claiming that behind Aristotle's physicalism lies a true possibility to thematize Dasein, for the first time, as a being in a world of movement. Aristotelian movement is not so much a worldly feature as the fundamental principle on which all beings and all relation to the world rests. Once Heidegger completed the destruction of the notion of movement, which extended movement beyond the physical sphere, he was in a position to turn the Aristotelian notion of *kinesis* into an analytic of Dasein. With this ontologization, one goes from the Aristotelian category of movement to the movement of being-in-the-world. The ontic concept of movement (*Bewegnung*) leaves room for the ontological concept of movedness (*Beweglichkeit*). Heidegger's appropriation of the Aristotelian theory aims at understanding life in its primordial movedness (*Urbewegtheit*), the central topic of the hermeneutics of factical life: 'It is therefore a matter of pressing on interpretively to a movement which constitutes a *genuine movedness of life, in* which and *through* which life *exists*, and from which, accordingly, life is determinable in its own sense of Being' (GA 61, 117/PIA, 87, italics in the original). Thus, the appropriation of the Aristotelian concept of movement requires a demanding deconstructing work that lays bare both the ousiological presuppositions implicit in any theory of movement and the subsequent transformations Aristotle's philosophy underwent in the hands of scholastic and mediaeval philosophers. The hidden tendency of Greek philosophy, and hence of Aristotle's philosophy as well, is to give priority to the model of *physis* and production (*poiesis*) in detriment of human action (*praxis*). The paradigm of production (*poiesis*) reduces all beings to what is given as present, stable and usable. Heidegger stresses: '*Being* thus means to be produced. That corresponds to the original sense of *ousía*. *Ousía* meant possession, wealth, household chattels, that which is at one's disposal in everyday existence, that which stands in availability. *Being* means to stand there as available' (GA 19, 270/PS, 186, italics in the original).

In the lecture course of the summer 1927, entitled *The Basic Problems of Phenomenology*, Heidegger sums up the point:

> Disposable possessions and goods, property, are beings; they are quite simple that which is, the Greek *ousía*. In Aristotle's time, when it already had a firm terminological meaning philosophically and theoretically, this expression *ousía* was still synonymous with property, possessions, means, wealth. The pre-philosophical proper meaning of *ousía* carried through to the end. Accordingly *a being* is synonymous with an *at-hand disposable*.
> GA 24, 153/BP, 108–109, italics in the original[66]

Heidegger's destruction brings to light how the prevalence of the substance, the *ousia*, rests on a Greek presupposition: the everyday ordering of the world in terms of the availability of tools (*pragmata*). In light of this 'naïve' and 'totally natural' interpretation, Greeks understood 'the meaning of being *from the world as surrounding world*' (GA 19, 270/PS, 186, italics in the original). The being of beings is thus determined by its availability and everyday usefulness. For this reason, ancient philosophy construes the reality of the real, the being of beings, as presence and subsistence (*ousia*).

For Heidegger, the Greek tendency to think being in terms of the modality of presence permeated the whole course of the history of philosophy up until his time: from the Platonic figure of the Demiurge to the Christian conception of beings as created by God. Precisely the fact that 'createdness, in the broadest sense of something having been produced, is an essential structural moment of the ancient concept of being' (SuZ, 24/BT, 23–24) justifies a destruction of metaphysics that lays bare the implicit ousiological presupposition of Greek ontology. But even though Heidegger deconstructs the ontological assumptions of the *Physics*, he also exploits Aristotle's scheme in order to articulate a new way of understanding the movedness of life.

Aristotle's investigation of nature provides a new set of categories for the understanding of physical present beings. These categories, Heidegger thinks, cannot be applied to the analysis of the ontological structures of human life without reducing it to a present thing among other present things. In this way, he acknowledges the ontological difference between beings, which simply *are there* and *in movement*, and human existence, for which the term 'Dasein' is reserved. Heidegger already used this term in the *Natorp-Bericht*, from 1922, but the difference between physical beings and Dasein is not yet drawn in that text. The constitutive ontological feature that characterizes Dasein is facticity (*Faktizität*), which therefore distinguishes Dasein from the presence-at-hand (*Vorhandenheit*) of intra-worldly beings. As Heidegger says in the 1925–1926 lecture course: 'By "facticity" [*Faktizität*] we understand a specific determination of the being of Dasein. The term does not have an indifferent meaning that would be the same as the factuality [*Tatsächlichkeit*] of something merely there' (GA 21, 233/LQT, 194).

Even though Dasein lives ontically in the world, its being is not reducible to that which is merely present. Dasein is essentially unfinished, it is always in process of actualization, and therefore its being cannot be reduced to the structures of produced beings (*ens creatum*). Dasein's unfinished nature points to disclosedness, and this, in contrast to the production of tools, does not obey the model of production according to a concrete end (*telos*). Dasein has an end, but unlike Aristotelian ends, it is not teleological. Rather, Heidegger thinks of Dasein's end as a distinctive structure of Dasein's existence, which he already called in 1924 'being-towards-the-end' (*Sein zum Ende*). The only criterion for Dasein's existence is its immanence, its always being open to possibilities.

It is at this point that Heidegger's hermeneutics of facticity, which he started to elaborate in 1923, decisively turns away from the Aristotelian conception of movement. The movement of human existence cannot be thought of in terms of location in the world. The reason is that the pre-understanding of the world in which human existence moves is grounded in Dasein's movedness, which in turn is constitutive of care (*Sorge*).

Movedness (*Bewegtheit*) cannot be thought, as in the *Physics*, in terms of movement (*Bewegung*) as the mode of being of an entity. It is no longer possible to reduce existence to a mere *being there*, to being *in* the world in the sense of presence. Dasein actualizes itself in the different modalities of care, that is to say, through its different ways of relating to the world. Therefore, the world cannot be thought of as the container of the totality of existing entities. It is the horizon to which movedness, understood as care, points, that is, the direction in which life develops. The world is not the element in which the existence of human being and other creatures move but the horizon of meaning that Dasein has always already understood.

In this sense, the *Nichomachean Ethics* and *On the Soul* offer a much better characterization of Dasein's modes of comportment. In these two texts, the concept of movement pertains to Dasein's possibilities of understanding, which in Heidegger's interpretation are based on Dasein's uncovering and unveiling nature. Insofar as human being lives in truth (*aletheia*) and is determined by intelligence (*nous*), it has the capacity for uncovering. The fact that Dasein lives in the truth allows us to draw a distinction between the sphere of physical beings, governed by the immanent principle of movement described in the *Physics*, and the sphere of human action, governed by the soul (*psyche*). What distinguishes human being from the rest of living beings is its possession of an intelligent soul. Intelligence contains a principle of movement. In this way, human life is not limited to the aforementioned technological thinking of production (*poiesis*), but it freely determines itself on the basis of action (*praxis*). The soul allows human beings to conceive their own factual situation within the framework of their existence in the world.

In applying Aristotle's notion of movement to Dasein, Heidegger transforms that notion into the ontological principle of movedness. That is to say, he ascribes the dynamic movement involved in uncovering beings to Dasein's immanent movedness. For this reason, movedness is not determined by pure presence but by temporality. Having exposed the ontological assumptions of Aristotle's notion of *kinesis*, Heidegger shows how movedness stems from Dasein's primordial temporality. The same deconstructing strategy Heidegger uses as regards movement, he applies to the analysis of Aristotle's notion of time. This topic, announced in the general outline of *Being and Time* was finally developed in the 1927 lecture course, *The Basic Problems of Phenomenology*.

In this sense, the analysis and interpretation of the Aristotelian concept of time that Heidegger develops in this lecture course are crucial for understanding *Being and Time*'s general project. Such understanding is not possible if one limits oneself to the existential analytic of Dasein. Over and above the detailed reflections on the fourth book of the *Physics* and the correction of several mistakes that for Heidegger predate the modern conception of time,[67] what is really interesting in his analysis is the transit from the everyday experience of time to the implicit sense of temporality from which it stems. Heidegger purports to show in this regard how Aristotle's analysis is based on Dasein's primordial temporality: 'What Aristotle presents as time *corresponds to the common prescientific understanding of time. By its own phenomenological content* common time points to an original time, *temporality*' (GA 24, 362/BP, 257, italics in the original).

As has been pointed out, Heidegger's interpretation of Aristotle has to be assessed against the background of his own philosophical project. According to *Being and Time*, this project aims at elaborating the question regarding the difference between being and beings, that is, working out the question regarding being and time in a way that makes it possible to think being and time in their difference with beings. Heidegger reserves the Latinized term *Temporalität* for this third meaning of time. In this way, he opens the path for considering time as the horizon for the manifestation of being, the path *Being and Time* is to follow. He developed a good part of these ideas in the second part of his 1925–1926 lecture course, where he undertook a 'phenomenological chronology', that is, an inquiry into the temporality of all phenomena. Throughout this task, Kant was Heidegger's main interlocutor.

Kant as a preamble to the problem of temporality: Heidegger's early engagement with Kant

'I am often at Königsberg'

Since the publication of *Kant and the Problem of Metaphysics* in 1929, the importance of Kant for Heidegger's thinking became obvious. Heidegger himself confirmed this in many letters to his friends of youth: Karl Jaspers, Elisabeth Blochmann and Hannah Arendt. In a letter to Jaspers of 10 December 1925, Heidegger expresses how much he is enjoying teaching his seminars, in which Kant is starting to become a prominent subject: 'The most beautiful of all is that I am beginning to really love Kant' (Heidegger and Jaspers 1990, 57). This certainly is a surprising confession for someone that not many years before was moving within the coordinates of theology and Freiburg's philosophical Catholicism.

Heidegger's first contact with modern philosophy in general and Kant's in particular took place in the context of the debate with modernism. According to the *Pascendi* encyclical as well as anti-modernists thinkers, 'Kantian philosophy', 'German idealism' and 'protestant theology' are interchangeable terms. On this view, Kant, the philosopher of Protestantism and St Thomas, the philosopher of Catholicism, are fierce antagonists. But Heinrich Rickert taught Heidegger how to recognize genuine philosophical problems. Even though by 1911–1912 Heidegger was still critical of Kant and Hegel, soon afterwards he had already shaken off his confessional scruples in regard to them. As mentioned, in a letter dated 12 October 1913, Heidegger said to Rickert: 'To this date, in all the literature of "Catholic philosophy," there is no one book, no one essay, that offers an even approximately correct understanding of *Kant*' (Heidegger and Rickert 2002, 12, italics and quotation marks in the original).

Now, when does Kant begin to become a decisive figure for Heidegger's thinking? What explains the love Heidegger declares for Kant in his letter to Jaspers? The correspondence between Heidegger and his lover and confidante during his initial years at Marburg, Hannah Arendt, offers a valuable testimony. Heidegger writes on 23 August 1925: 'I am often at Königsberg: not only because I read Kant in order to "recover" but because, in doing so, I realize more and more that what is called nowadays philosophy has become miserable, even in style and attitude' (Heidegger and Arendt 2002, 45). In 1927, Heidegger stresses Kant's influence once again. In a letter to Elisabeth Blochmann of 21 October, he declares: 'I have read again the Kant's *Critique of Pure Reason* in one sitting, and have obtained from it many lessons, strength and clarification' (Heidegger and Blochmann 1989, 21). And on 12 February 1928, he writes to Jaspers: 'Right now I am "recovering" day by day through Kant, who can be interpreted even more powerfully than Aristotle. I think Kant has to be rediscovered in a completely new way (Heidegger and Jaspers 1990, 53).

All these epistolary references confirm Heidegger's increasing interest in Kant during the second half of the twenties. His systematic engagement with Kant began by the end of 1925, intensified in Marburg (1924–1928) and was still alive some years after his return to Freiburg (1929). The result is widely known: one of the most rigorous and productive dialogues with Kant in the twentieth century. But it is no less true that Heidegger's interpretation is difficult to follow because of its occasional exegetical violence, as is frequently the case, in general, with his readings of the greatest figures in the history of philosophy (Heraclitus, Parmenides, Plato, Aristotle, Leibniz, Hegel, Schelling and Nietzsche, to name the most relevant).

The secondary literature offers two lines of inquiry in this regard. On the one hand, there are studies that further Heidegger's approach and extend it to problems he did not address.[68] On the other hand, there are investigations that stress the thematic diversity of Heidegger's engagement with Kant, particularly in relation to *Kant and the Problem of Metaphysics* (1929) and the 1935–1936 lecture course, *What is a Thing?* (edited in 1962, just a year after the publication of the conference 'Kant's Thesis about Being').

However, the posthumous publication of the Freiburg (1919–1923) and especially the Marburg (1924–1928) lecture courses has made manifest that Heidegger's 1929 book on Kant was preceded by a deep and thorough discussion of the latter's philosophy.[69] In this regard, it is worth recalling that Heidegger devotes a whole section of his 1927 lecture course, *The Basic Problems of Phenomenology*, to discussing the Kantian thesis that being is not a real predicate (GA 24, 35–107/BP, 27–76). Immediately afterwards (winter semester 1927–1928), Heidegger gave the lecture course published under the title *Phenomenological Interpretations of Kant's Critique of Pure Reason* (GA 25), which offers a much more detailed analysis than the one that *Kant and the Problem of Metaphysics* supplies. Upon returning to Freiburg, Heidegger dedicated most of his 1930 lecture course to the problem of causality and freedom in Kant's philosophy (GA 31, 139–297), and even though it is frequently overlooked, the second part of the 1925–1926 lecture course *Logic. The Question of Truth* offers Heidegger's first exhaustive interpretation of the *Critique of Pure Reason*. This work analyses the transcendental aesthetics and analytic and stresses Kant's importance in relation to the problem of temporality (GA 21, 269–408/LQT, 223–337).[70]

The Marburg lecture course allows us to fathom the whole depth of Heidegger's dialogue with Kant. By the same token this course confirms that, together with Husserl and Aristotle, Kant is Heidegger's third main interlocutor as regards the formulation of the problem of being and the existential analytic of Dasein. As a consequence, Heidegger's discovery of Kant plays a crucial role in the genesis of *Being and Time*.

During the Marburg years, Heidegger was aiming at understanding the unity of sensibility and understanding on the basis of Dasein's primordial temporality. It is at this precise point that Kant comes into scene.

After laying bare the ontological presuppositions behind Aristotle's concept of *kinesis*, Heidegger purported to show how movedness stems from Dasein's primordial temporality.[71] This explains the increasing interest in Kant that Heidegger manifested from the second half of the twenties onwards.

Kant and the task of a phenomenological chronology

Heidegger praises the carefulness Kant demonstrates in not subjecting phenomena to the court of understanding in a premature way. This attitude is manifest in Kant's approach to the problem of time: 'In this field of the problem of time, Kant keeps the horizons open. [...] When it reaches his limits, he leaves the problems there – which is more helpful for later research than forcefully arranging some half-baked ideas into an imposing system' (GA 21, 201/LQT, 170). In this sense, Kant's approach to the problem of time is characterized by a peculiar mixture of phenomenological and dogmatic elements. For this reason, Heidegger says that Kant, just as Aristotle, was a phenomenologist even if he did not see himself that way. Both philosophers defend a conception of thinking that is faithful to phenomena. But at the same time, this interlacement of phenomenology and dogmatism explains the cryptic quality of the transcendental aesthetics.

Contrary to neo-Kantianism, which endorses a logical interpretation of the *Critique of Pure Reason* on which the aesthetics is absorbed into the analytic, Heidegger puts the accent on the transcendental aesthetics (GA 21, 278/LQT, 231). In this way, he takes a distance from Cohen's interpretation, which dominated the readings of Kant at the time. Even though this interpreter recognizes that the transcendental apperception and the Copernican turn – the idea that the subject plays a 'constitutive' role in relation to the object – are the core of Kant's thought, he is seduced by a unilateral reading on which the whole *Critique* is interpreted on the basis of the transcendental analytic. In consequence, the aesthetics completely loses its independence and thereby the receptive character of sensitivity dissolves into the spontaneity of understanding. This interpretation is one more chapter in the traditional metaphysical view that, since Plato and Aristotle, distinguishes between perception (*aesthesis*) and the faculty of reasoning (*noesis*); in Kantian terms, between aesthetics and logic. But, as Heidegger says in his 1929 book on Kant, it is crucial to keep in mind that knowledge is not only the result of categorial logic but also of pure sensitivity as creative receptivity (KPM 20ff.). In Cohen's logic-dominated reading, the decisive element of givenness disappears. For Heidegger, Kant's main contribution was to recognize the passivity inherent to all processes of knowledge, that is, the creative aspect of intuition.

Heidegger recalls the following passage from the *Critique of Pure Reason*: 'All that seems necessary for an introduction or preliminary is that there are two stems of human cognition, which may perhaps arise from a common but to us unknown root, namely sensibility and understanding, through the first of which objects are given to us, but through the second which they are thought' (Kant B 29).

Kant himself recognizes in the first edition of the book the stark distinction between these two sources of knowledge and in trying to solve the problem of their relation gave priority to understanding over sensibility. The Marburg School adopted a radical interpretation of this Kantian solution – which Kant developed in the second edition of the *Critique* – and thus took the transcendental aesthetic to be a pre-critical remnant that consequently was to be absorbed by the transcendental logic.

Heidegger takes upon himself the task of solving the problem of the unity of sensibility and understanding. From the outset, he rejects the idea that the aesthetics is a contingent or inessential part of Kant's proposal. He attempts to show that giving an essential role to the creative receptivity of sensitivity expresses an internal necessity of Kant's project. The transcendental aesthetics privileges the pure intuition of time. According to Kant himself, 'time is the a priori formal condition of all appearances in general' (A 34/B 50) and not only of internal phenomena. He even concedes certain primacy to time over space: all our representations are temporal, independently of their content, insofar as they are part of the flow of consciousness. Time is the immediate condition of internal phenomena and the mediate condition of external phenomena, which are given in a spatial manner (GA 21, 335–336/LQT, 276–277). Hence, all phenomena are given *in* time. This is the context of Heidegger's discussion of Kant regarding time in the second part of the aforementioned 1925–1926 lecture course, *Logic. The Question of Truth*.

In that section of this lecture course occurs a violent change of topic. After a long preliminary consideration of Husserl's criticism of psychologism and an intense discussion of the problem of truth in Aristotle, Heidegger shifts the direction of his reflections and devotes most of the second part of the lecture course to Kant's conception of time in the context of what he calls a phenomenological chronology. The main task of this enterprise is 'to study the ur-temporal determinedness of phenomena – that is, their ur-temporality – and consequently to study [ur-]time itself' (GA 21, 200/LQT).[72] The first paragraphs of the second part of *Logic. The Question of Truth* address, in a preliminary manner, the problem of the temporality of care, the role Hegel gives to time in the *Encyclopedia*, and Aristotle's influence on Hegel's and Bergson's conceptions of time. After this, Heidegger provides a thorough analysis of Kant's conception of time in transcendental aesthetics and logic, with a special focus on the relation between the 'I think' and time (GA 21, §§ 18, 20–21, 23–24, 29). At first sight, the abrupt change of topic this lecture course undergoes might seem surprising, but if one pays heed to the deepest problem at issue, the shift becomes understandable. Heidegger wanted to lay bare the unquestioned presuppositions of Aristotle's conception of truth, particularly his underlying understanding of time. According to Heidegger, Kant is the only philosopher that intuits, if only in a timid way, the connection between being and time, and thus indicates the path to follow. He expresses this same idea again in *Being and Time*: 'Kant is the first and only one who traversed a stretch of the path toward investigating the dimension of temporality (*Temporalität*) – or allowed himself to be driven there by the compelling force of the phemonena themselves' (SuZ, 23/BT, 22). Heidegger begins by quoting a passage from Kant's *Reflexionen* that figures also in *Being and Time*: 'The business of the philosopher is not to give out rules but to dismember the secret judgments of common sense' (GA 21, 197/LQT, 167).[73] This means that the task of philosophy is to expose the comportments that ground the everyday comportment of Dasein. In this sense, Heidegger understands Kant's analytics not only as the breakdown of something into its constituent elements – the chemical paradigm – but as bringing that something back to its place of origin. The idea is therefore to go back to the genesis of phenomena and show the ontological conditions of possibility of their givenness. This explains Heidegger's Kantian-inspired talk of an existencial *analytic*, that is, an analysis that lays bare the ontological conditions of possibility of Dasein's different modes of comportment.

The analysis of proposition and truth in Aristotle, the topic of the first part of the lecture course, gives way to a thorough inquiry into time. But what exactly explains this change of topic? Propositions do not necessarily have the form of a judgement. Their most essential feature is that they discover something in an act of making it present (*gegenwärtigen*). Being is the presence of something that can be discovered (truth) or covered up (falsity):

Let us now take the dogmatic conclusion that we first arrived at and pose it once again in three theses:

1. Being means presence (*Anwesenheit*).
2. Truth means the now-present (*Gegenwart*).
3. Presence and presence-now, as characteristics of presenting (*Präsenz*), are modes of time (GA 21,199/LQT, 168).

And so the analysis of propositions, that is, *logos apophantikos*, is oriented toward time and thus highlights the temporal nature of logical phenomena. Aristotle does not ask about the meaning of this identity between being and truth. For this reason, in order to get at the root of the question of truth it is necessary to radicalize this question by directing it toward the genesis of truth out of temporality.

This is where the project of a phenomenological chronology comes into play. This enterprise seeks to analyse the temporal structure of phenomena, which ultimately involves an inquiry into time itself. The phenomenological chronology includes an analytic and genetic reading of the *Critique of Pure Reason*. The short-lived name 'phenomenological chronology' does not indicate the foundation of a new philosophical discipline but a redefinition of the task of philosophy. From a strictly etymological point of view, the phenomenological chronology conceives of thought (*logos*) in its own temporalization (*chronos*). This avoids falling into a simple subjectivization of time (Augustine) or an absolute subjectivization (Husserl), and at the same time allows one to think about the strange identity of Dasein and time, which is what Heidegger perceives in Kant's schematism.

Now, in what sense does this chronological phenomenology demand a debate with Kant? If the task of this chronology is to inquire into the temporality of all phenomena, then one should not consider time as the framework (*Rahmen*) of the showing themselves of phenomena and rather understand it as the structure (*Struktur*) of phenomena. In other words, time does not operate in terms of a general framework (*rahmenmäßig*) but in terms of structure (*strukturmäßig*). And insofar as it is a structure, a new conception of time is necessary, one in which it is not conceived in the natural sense of succession. The phenomenological chronology underscores that temporality is an essential feature of Dasein's comportment and not a feature of the world (GA 21, 205/LQT, 173). As Heidegger says in the 1924 conference, 'The Concept of Time' and the homonymous treatise of the same year, Dasein is time (BZ, 26 and GA 64, 57 and 61). This is not tantamount to a subjectivization of time, in which time is located *in* the soul or the subject. On the contrary, the point is to recognize the intrinsic temporal constitution of Dasein and to distinguish the ordinary understanding of time from primordial temporality.[74]

The brief history of the concept of time Heidegger sketched in the 1925–1926 lecture course gives Kant a place of privilege over Aristotle, Hegel and Bergson. The reason is well known: Heidegger saw in Kant's schematism an anticipation of phenomenological chronology, in which a new concept of time comes into play, a concept that cannot be understood only within the framework of the manifestation of nature and the objective world. Rather, according to this new conception, time is a constitutive element of all conscious phenomena. Kant finds in the depths of the human soul, in the schematism, a manifestation of the temporality of Dasein's comportments. This he calls, in a still traditional Cartesian fashion, 'transcendental apperception', the 'I think' that accompanies all the acts of understanding. He takes a further step and asks about the determinability of time, that is, about the condition of possibility of a connection between time in general and the 'I think' in general (GA 21, 309/LQT, 255). This problem of the unity of sensitivity and understanding, which is ultimately the problem of the unity of subjectivity, is exactly the problem post-Kantian philosophy tried to solve, but without questioning Kant's presuppositions. This is why post-Kantian philosophy, according to Heidegger's diagnosis, keeps moving within the Cartesian coordinates of the 'I think'. *Being and Time*, in contrast, attempts to explain this unity on the basis of the structure of care that ontologically determines Dasein in terms of primordial temporality.

5

Development and Methodological Presuppositions of the Hermeneutic Phenomenology

From 1919 onwards, life became one of the keystones of the young Heidegger's philosophical programme. This new perspective would not have been of much use, however, in the absence of a fully determined concept of 'life' and a good grasp of the correct way of getting access to life. The real phenomenologist has to ask himself: what attitude should I choose in order to make human life *show itself*? The answer determines the course of Heidegger's early programme: the critique to objectivization. Human existence slips through our fingers when we try to capture it by means of a purely theoretical attitude. For in objectivizing thought all the richness and nuances of the life-world disappear. And so Heidegger focuses all his energies on the unfathomable lived instant. The idea is not to recover some mysterious divine link, nor to descend to the subconscious world, or take refuge in vitalism. The essential task of philosophy is to make the relations of life with the immediate everyday world transparent and intelligible. The true object of philosophical inquiry – as Heidegger puts it in the *Natorp-Bericht* (1922) – is human existence insofar as it is interrogated as regards its being: 'Philosophy is concerned with the problem of the *being* of factical life' (NB, 242, italics in the original). From this moment onwards, the particular mode of being of human life becomes the leading thread of the question regarding the meaning of being. The question about Dasein's ontological status is the first step in the inquiry regarding being in general.

Broadly speaking, the lecture courses Heidegger gave during the post-war period aimed at elaborating a new concept of philosophy, one that did not subject the phenomenon of life to the scientific parameters of knowledge. The same question comes out again and again: how is it possible to capture the phenomenon of life in a genuine way, without deploying the objectifying tools of the philosophical tradition? The answer is straightforward: the primacy of the theoretical attitude must come to an end, and the dominant ideal of physical and mathematical sciences that pervades philosophy, from Descartes to Husserl, must be suppressed. The final result of the slow and systematic inquiry into the ontological structures of life appears in different ways in the analyses Heidegger undertook during the twenties: in 1919, he speaks of a primordial science of life; in 1922, of a phenomenological ontology of factical life; in 1923, of a hermeneutics of facticity; in 1925 and 1927, of an existential analytic of Dasein; and in 1928, of a metaphysics of Dasein. The core task around which the young Heidegger's philosophical efforts devolved was this: to show, in a phenomenological manner, Dasein's different modes of being, so as to apprehend the meaning of being within the horizon of historicity and temporality.

The preceding chapters have shown the importance of four influences in the development of the young Heidegger's thought, namely, Husserl's phenomenology, Christian tradition, Kant's philosophy and Aristotle's practical philosophy. In the preface to the 1923 lecture course, *Ontology. The Hermeneutics of Facticity*, Heidegger comments on his philosophical itinerary: 'Companions in my searching were the Young Luther and the paragon Aristotle, whom Luther hated. Impulses were given by Kierkegaard, and Husserl opened my eyes' (GA 63, 5/HF, 4). Heidegger's plurality as regards influences and lines of thought disappears at the end of the Freiburg period, with the first explicit formulation of his philosophical programme in terms of a hermeneutics of facticity. *Thematically* speaking, this enterprise results in an exhaustive analysis of the ontological structures of factical life or Dasein. *Methodologically* speaking, the enterprise involves the development of a hermeneutic phenomenology.

In this chapter, I spell out the methodological presuppositions of the hermeneutic phenomenology, which Heidegger started to develop in 1919 in terms of a primordial science of life. I start by clarifying the significance and scope of philosophy understood as primordial science of life. *Second*, I stress the methodological precautions that an analysis of factical life must have in the face of the prejudices handed down by the tradition. Once the hermeneutic situation is secured, I explain what is the right method for providing a correct categorial articulation of human life by means of formal indicators. *Third*, I break down the development of the hermeneutic phenomenology into stages and point out the deep differences this approach has from Husserl's reflective phenomenology. Then, I present Heidegger's criticism of Husserl, particularly as regards his misunderstandings concerning Cartesianism and transcendental idealism. Next, I assess the contributions of Husserl's genetic phenomenology. Finally, I show how the phenomenological ontology that starts to take shape in Heidegger's early work would have been unthinkable without an implicit recognition of the ontological difference.

The breakthrough of a new conception of philosophy as primordial science

The phenomenological imprint of the young Heidegger's thought is manifest. It is perceivable not only in the exercise of the method, in 'practicing the phenomenological seeing' (ZSD, 86/MWP, 78), but also in Heidegger's deep hermeneutic revision of phenomenology and his effort to elaborate a new conception of philosophy. This huge methodological endeavour, which begins with the Freiburg lecture courses, aims at achieving the right type of access to the primordial phenomenon of life. The constitutive meaningfulness and movedness of life cannot be captured within the framework of a philosophy of consciousness. The classic model of a pure subject of knowledge facing the reality of the external world does not satisfy the methodological demand to go to things themselves. The point of departure of a hermeneutically transfigured phenomenology is the immediate surrounding world in which all lived experience is given. The task is 'to grasp life in its full enactment sense' (GA 58, 97). In this sense, the young Heidegger redefined philosophy as primordial science of life (*Urwissenschaft des Lebens*). Before addressing the development of the hermeneutic phenomenology of factical life or Dasein, I will offer a preliminary characterization of philosophy as primordial science. First, I highlight the programmatic affinity between this philosophy as primordial science and Husserl's conception of philosophy as strict science. I also explain the radical difference between a primordial science and any worldview. Next, I clarify in more detail the meaning and the role of philosophy as primordial and pre-theoretical science of life.

Husserl's legacy of a new science and the problem of the worldview

Husserl began his post as professor in Freiburg University in 1916. Around that time, Heidegger was starting to distance himself from Rickert's neo-Kantianism and from Catholicism, and began to work as Husserl's assistant. During this time the collaboration between the master and the assistant was intense and close, to the point that Husserl himself told Heidegger 'you and I are phenomenology'. Given this close connection to phenomenology, the twenties are considered Heidegger's 'phenomenological decade' (Kisiel 1986, 24; Crowell 1995, 436–448).[1] And yet, the development of Heidegger's philosophy during these years is unthinkable without his dialogue with other authors, such as Aristotle, Augustine, St Paul, Luther, Dilthey and Kierkegaard. Heidegger's use of phenomenology during his years as lecturer in Freiburg is not as uncritical as it was in his doctoral dissertation and *Habilitationsschrift*.[2]

From 1919 onwards, Heidegger's philosophical worries are based on the necessity to reformulate the notion of intentionality. He applies this notion to the domain of the concrete historicity of factical life, rather than to the field of logic. He highlights the dynamic aspect of life, its intentional relation to the world. His efforts to develop a phenomenological interpretation of factical life are clearly far removed from the ideal of knowledge that dominates in exact sciences. However, there are no direct attacks against science and its methods in Heidegger's output from these years. His focus is on underscoring the pre- or a-theoretical origin of science and postulating that the life-world is the condition of possibility of all knowledge. Heidegger's work on Scotus's doctrine of the categories had already made some scattered references to locate pure logic within the framework of 'a philosophy orientated towards a worldview' (GA 1, 205/note 10). However, the first serious criticism of Husserl's phenomenology occurs during the post-war semester of 1919, and results in what is called in the literature the hermeneutic transformation of phenomenology.

In the lecture course from the same year, *The Idea of Philosophy and the Problem of Worldview*, Heidegger levels against Husserl the charge of reducing philosophy to purely theoretical reflection (GA 56/57, 12, and GA 59, 9–12). In order to understand Heidegger's view, it is worth recalling what Husserl understands as science. Philosophy, for Husserl, is not one more science among others. According to the *Logical Investigations*, philosophy is the highest science. Insofar as phenomenology is the foundation of all particular sciences, it is the most rigorous and elevated of all sciences. The problem Heidegger identifies is that the knowledge phenomenology provides is the result of evident intuition understood in a theoretical-reflective manner.[3]

In my opinion, despite Heidegger's rejection of the rationalist ideal of modern philosophy that Husserl endorses, there are three elements of his early work that come directly from Husserl's *Philosophy as Rigorous Science* (Rodríguez 1997, 18–21). The first one is the claim that philosophy is completely independent of theoretical sciences. Philosophy has not been able to achieve the level of a rigorous knowledge because its conception of knowledge has followed the model of particular sciences. The debate with naturalism made evident that extending the method of natural sciences to the domain of consciousness could produce results that were incompatible with reality (HU XXV, 11–12). The second element is the dispute with historicism and the consequent refusal to reduce philosophy to the role of a creator of worldviews. For Husserl, natural and human sciences made a mistake right from the outset: the former built their theories exclusively on empirical data, the latter only led to worldviews. In contrast, Husserl sets out to develop a science that is not limited to the opposing claims of empirical facts and worldviews. Rather, this science must concern something that is universally valid: the essence of things (HU XXV, 46, 51–52).[4] Husserl's criticism in *Philosophy as Rigorous Science* is directed to worldviews that purport to be a science, but not to the fact that worldviews might guide living experience and symbolic representations of individuals and communities. The philosophy of worldviews draws on the spiritual, historical and contingent life of humanity in order to elaborate an ideal of exemplary existence (HU XXV, 47–51). However, science deals with that which is apodictic and eternal: 'The "idea" of worldview varies from one epoch to the other [...] The "idea" of science, in contrast, is trans-temporal, this means that it is not limited by a relation to the spirit of the epoch' (HU XXV, 52). Phenomenology offers a new foundation for philosophy as a rigorous science that is capable of solving the mystery of knowledge – as asserted in the 1907 lecture course, *The Idea of Phenomenology* (HU II, 36).

At this point, Heidegger also takes distance from Jaspers' thesis in *Psychology of Worldviews*. Feeding on Husserl's debate with historicism, Heidegger rejects the idea that philosophy must produce a worldview (*Weltanschauung*). It is important to be very careful in relation to this, because the young Heidegger's affinity to Dilthey and the philosophies of life might suggest that it is the aim of the hermeneutics of facticity to provide a worldview of our time.[5] A *Weltanschauung* is a comprehensive perspective on the historical and natural reality of human life and is capable of guiding human action in the world. From critical realism and philosophies of life to neo-Kantianism, philosophy tried to build a rationally valid conception of the world, one that was based on scientific facts independent of political, religious and artistic values.

There is no such thing in Heidegger's philosophy. From his first lecture courses from 1919 and 1920 onwards, he engages the more important philosophical currents of his time: neo-Kantianism in its two branches (Cohen's and Natorp's Marburg School and Windelband's and Rickert's Baden School) and the philosophies of life. Against the transcendental and logic-based theory of value of the former, on the one hand, and the vital exaltation of the latter, on the other, Heidegger defends a phenomenological posture, which searches for a primordial science of life (GA 56/57, §§ 18–20; GA 58, §§ 15–19; GA 59, §§ 2–4). For him, the idea of philosophy as primordial science is not already given and at our disposal; on the contrary, it has to be enacted, that is, it is a historical development.

In this way, the 1919 lecture course initiates a philosophical journey that ends with *Being and Time*. The point of *The Idea of Philosophy and the Problem of Worldview* is not to address one specific question but to start working on a new project concerning the essence and object of philosophy. The first step of this project is to clearly distinguish philosophy from worldview, the second to conceive philosophy in terms of primordial science (GA 56/57, 11/IP, 9–10). On this new conception, philosophy must set life apart from the domain of the theoretical attitude and consider the way life comports itself in its immediate experiences with the surrounding world, with the persons with which it shares the world, and with itself *qua* concrete historical existence. The young Heidegger characterized the mode of being of life in a way that was completely different from those handed down by the tradition. Particularly, this new characterization differs starkly from that of Husserl's reflexive phenomenology, which considered life from a theoretical point of view on which the subject reduces to a pure objective stance. Philosophy as primordial science endeavours to capture life phenomenologically, in its immediate givenness, and irrespective of any theory. This explains Heidegger's definition of philosophy as the primordial and pre-theoretical science of life.

Philosophy as primordial and pre-theoretical science of life

What is the meaning of the terms 'science', 'primordial' and 'pre-theoretical' in a philosophy that defines itself as 'primordial science of life'? What should we understand by 'philosophy'? What is the subject matter of this new science? A proper answer to these question will allow us to understand the significance and depth of Heidegger's proposal.

The meaning of 'pre-theoretical'

What should we understand by 'theoretical' (*theoretisch*)? What do the expressions 'a-theoretical' (*atheoretisch*) and 'pre-theoretical' (*vortheoretisch*) mean? Is '*pre-philosophical*' equivalent to '*pre-scientific*'? When one speaks of philosophy as pre-theoretical the question might arise, given the Husserlian project of a rigorous science, as to whether 'pre-theoretical' denotes the pre-scientific character that the *Logical Investigations* ascribes to phenomenology. We need to clarify the meaning of Husserl's term 'pre-scientific' in order to get a good hold on the Heideggerian notion of 'pre-theoretical'. The term 'pre-scientific' (*vorwissenschaftlich*) refers to the essential feature of what Husserl calls the natural attitude. This attitude involves an uncritical acceptance of the existence of the world and worldly things. The shift from the natural attitude to the phenomenological attitude that the reduction produces can be understood as a shift from a pre-scientific attitude to a scientific one, or even from a pre-transcendental sphere to the transcendental one – the sphere in which the conditions of possibility of scientific knowledge are established. Husserl also applies the term 'pre-scientific' to phenomenology insofar as it is the fundamental science that precedes all the other particular sciences. In both uses, the term 'pre-scientific' is determined in a theoretical way. Hence, the 'pre-scientific life' of the natural attitude is in no way to be identified with Heidegger's talk of 'pre-theoretical life'.

Primordial pre-theoretical science analyses, in its immediacy, the different modes in which life actualizes itself; that is to say, analyses the primordial modes of life. In contrast, the particular sciences of life, such as biology, zoology and anthropology, as well as modern philosophy, turn life into an inert object of study from which all vital movement has been extracted, and isolate it from the historical process of its genesis. Contra the priority given to the theoretical way of analysing life, Heidegger asserts the necessity of going back to the more basic and pre-theoretical substrate of life. Putting the accent on theory distorts the way we have access to the world, for this leads to tearing apart, by objectification, the primordial sphere of our experience. In artificially extracting our immediate lived experiences from the life-world in which they emerge, theory falsifies them. In Heidegger, then, 'theoretical' does not refer to this or that theory but has a literal meaning: to contemplate, to observe (*betrachten*). Observation entails distance from that which is being observed. And so, through this reflective modification, lived experience loses its vital force.

Heidegger urges us to take a step back and actualize that theory and reflection start out of what is given immediately in the pre-theoretical and a-theoretical life-world (*Lebenswelt*). This is one of the central thematic and methodological keystones of Heidegger's early work. In this context, his later interpretations of Aristotelian *praxis* and practical wisdom are very clarifying. These interpretations allow Heidegger to incorporate in his reflection a number of human comportments that Husserlian phenomenology does not consider.[6] By incorporating practical knowledge, Heidegger puts into question the ideal of evidence connected to the traditional notion of subject and the mathematical order that Descartes', Kant's and Husserl's conceptions of consciousness impose on reality. Some years later, Heidegger articulated the different forms that the practical dimension of life can take, by appealing to the notion of care (*Sorge*).

The meaning and object of 'science'

Heidegger's phenomenological affiliation also raises the question as to how close is what he means by 'science' to Husserl's notion of science as pure knowledge. On the one hand, Heidegger's understanding of science is different from Husserl's insofar as for the former science as pure knowledge is in fact grounded in the primordial sphere of life. On the other hand, both ways of understanding the term 'science' are related insofar as Heidegger uses the term 'science' in reference to a form of knowledge of life itself. But for Heidegger, as mentioned, this knowledge is not theoretical in nature but a-theoretical and hermeneutical. The source of this knowledge is a hermeneutic intuition and not a reflexive intuition as it was for Husserl. Primordial science is not theoretical in the sense of being grounded and scientific. It is not theoretical because it is hermeneutic, that is, it opens up in a comprehensive way the a-theoretical sphere of the immediate experience of the surrounding world. Heidegger's ultimate goal was to break with the prevalence of the theoretical domain and show that 'the theoretical itself and as such refers back to something pre-theoretical' (GA 56/57, 59/IP, 50).

In this sense, one can say that primordial science is not scientific knowledge, that is, a set of propositions and rules, but a form of comportment. Kovacs (1990) goes as far as to say that it is a method for opening up and thereby unveiling life's modes of comportment. So the point is not to determine the properties of life as the object of scientific observation. In essence, life is not a 'what' (*Was*), like the observable objects of study of particular sciences. The philosophical method cannot impose a form of manifestation on life without distorting it. Therefore, philosophy has to adapt to the being of life itself, and this requires a new method, one that is capable of bringing the object out of its initial hiddenness. As we will see below, the task of hermeneutic phenomenology is to conquer and get a hold on the primordial domain of life. Hermeneutics characterizes a type of approach to phenomena, particularly, to life. How does life show itself primordially? Not as an object that has a thing-like nature, but as an object that possesses meaningfulness (GA 58, 197). Meaningfulness pertains to the primordial mode of being of life and the way life understands itself. For this reason, Heidegger defines hermeneutics in 1923 as facticity's self-interpretation.

The new meaning of 'philosophy'

The last question we set out to answer was: what is the essence of philosophy? What task does it have? In the first Freiburg lecture courses, Heidegger started to tackle this question. He was looking for an original answer of his own. From the outset, he rules out the various meanings that have been usually assigned to the term 'philosophy'. Philosophy is neither an abstract representation of entities, nor what provides the confirmation of the obvious truths of everyday life, much less a strictly utilitarian and calculative knowledge. It is not the task of philosophy either to reach the ultimate understanding of the world and human existence *vis-à-vis* other particular types of knowledge. And finally, it is also a mistake to think of philosophy as a critical science of values and culture built upon the acts and rules of consciousness. Heidegger sketches a new alternative: to show the radical incompatibility of philosophy and any kind of worldview (GA 56/57, 7–12/IP, 6–10). In this way, philosophy loses its traditional privilege as the top of the pyramid of human knowledge. On the basis of a discussion with neo-Kantianism and phenomenology, Heidegger conceives of philosophy as a ground knowledge, a 'primordial science' that urges us to rethink the very essence of life.

Now, what is the contribution of the idea of philosophy as primordial science to philosophy as such? To begin with, this idea shows that philosophical thinking is more rigorous and fundamental than scientific knowledge. It is more radical and essential than the inquiry into nature by means of theoretical artifice. Philosophy is not a speculative science. It is pre-theoretical: it lays bare lived experience as it is prior to any abstract modification. How is philosophy as primordial science completely different from natural and human sciences? In order to understand the answer to this question it is necessary to consider Heidegger's search for a method of analysis that allows him to get undistorted access to the origin of life. Philosophy as primordial science does not rely on the inductive method of particular sciences (GA 56/57, 22–28/IP, 18–23). It is of no use to try and clarify the nature of philosophy in terms of methodological considerations. The point is not merely to establish a specific method. A whole new idea of knowledge and truth is to be recognized. The mere confirmation or discovery of regularities does not make human sciences advance and therefore neither does so for philosophy. The adoption of such a methodological method hinders appreciation of how experience is embedded in a social and historical world. As a consequence, the goal of philosophy is not to explain phenomena as instances of a general rule. Philosophy's ultimate aim is to understand the phenomenon of life in its historicity, singularity and unicity. By way of example, historical science should not purport to find out how human beings, peoples and nations develop in general, but rather how *this* person, *this* people and *this* nation has come to be what they are. From this new perspective, primordial science is not a field of knowledge, but a phenomenon that enables us to know. It does not provide us with an objective content (*Was-Gehalt*) but it does give us as way of knowing objects (*Wie*). In this way, primordial science places us in a transcendental domain, in the fundamental and irreducible disclosedness that gives us access to all those beings that come to our encounters and allows us to understand them.

How is this primordial and a-theoretical disclosedness possible? Is it thanks to a 'theory of theory', as Husserl proposed? The answer is evidently no. For Heidegger, we have to learn to 'see' by parenthesizing all theoretical prejudice. This reduction (*epoche*) enables us to distinguish between the comportment of living experience and that of the knowledge of objects. At the same time, it uncovers the true essence of philosophy: philosophy is 'primordial science' (*Urwissenschaft*). Philosophy is not the result of a speculative approach that, on the basis of the model of phenomenological reduction proposed in *Ideas I*, attempts to deduce pure or transcendental consciousness. According to Heidegger, in order to free philosophy from the reflective ties imposed on it by Husserlian phenomenology, it is necessary to study concrete life in its immediate givenness. This entails developing a new concept of philosophy and phenomenology: philosophy as primordial science of life and phenomenology as hermeneutically oriented. Taking life as the new field of phenomenological investigation has a number of methodological consequences, all of which stem from the same question: how is it possible to apprehend the originally pre-theoretical sphere of life without the objectifying tools of philosophy? On the one hand, it becomes necessary to radicalize Husserl's 'principle of principles', on the other, the supposedly evaluative neutrality of neo-Kantianism has to be put into question.

The hermeneutics of facticity

Hermeneutics as factical life's self-interpretation: critical deconstruction and appropriation of the hermeneutic situation

For Heidegger, hermeneutics is not a method of interpretation of historical, literary and sacred texts. Hermeneutics gives us immediate access to human life. It penetrates life's nexus of meaning and articulates the understanding that life in each case has of itself. In other words, hermeneutics offers the possibility of interpreting human facticity, of understanding the facticity of our life, which from 1921 onwards Heidegger called 'Dasein':[7]

> Hermeneutics has the task of making the Dasein which is in each case our own accessible to this Dasein itself with regard to the character of its being, communicating Dasein to itself in this regard, hunting down the alienation from itself with which it is smitten. In hermeneutics what is developed for Dasein is a possibility of its becoming and being for itself in the manner of an *understanding* of itself.
>
> GA 63,15/HF, 11, italics in the original[8]

Heidegger stresses that by using the concept of facticity he purports to avoid use of the notions of self, person, ego, subject and rational animal, for each of these notions places facticity in a specific categorial domain from the start and thus distorts the primordial determination of human existence as care of the world in general. Similarly to the notion of primordial science Heidegger developed in 1919, hermeneutics offers the possibility of understanding the reality of life, that is, it is nothing other than facticity's self-interpretation.

This change in perspective allows Heidegger to break with the Husserlian ideal of philosophy as transparent, presuppositionless, neutral, that is, as rigorous science. Husserl's principle of evaluative neutrality rests on two presuppositions: the exclusion of all previous theory and the criteria for phenomenological evidence (HU XIX/1, 227–228, HU XXV, 340–341). Heidegger endorses this principle in such a way that he ends up turning it against Husserl himself. Husserl uses the model of the theoretical attitude without previous justification which, in Heidegger's terms, involves a prejudice: 'If the term is to say anything at all, *freedom from standpoints* is nothing other than an explicit *appropriation of our position of looking*' (GA 63, 83 /HF, 64, italics in the original).

The way Husserl accesses lived experiences is based on a subjective representation of objective processes, and therefore obeys the model of the theoretical attitude. Heidegger's analysis, for its part, yields a very different result. The original meaning of lived experiences is very different from the one provided by the theoretical knowledge of objectifying reflection. Theory is not the natural attitude of thought, but the result of a very specific stance. Having established this, Heidegger draws a distinction between the theoretical and the phenomenological attitudes.

In this way, he goes from Husserl's reflexive consciousness, which has intuitive access to its object, to what he calls the 'hermeneutic situation'. The hermeneutic situation is prior to our seeing, or better, is inexorably linked to it. All interpretations move within a threefold structure constituted by a prior having (*Vorhabe*), a prior seeing (*Vorsicht*) and a prior conception (*Vorgriff*). These three elements constitute every primordial projection of understanding.[9] No interpretation is a presuppositionless apprehension of what is given. Hermeneutics as such, insofar as it is factical, moves within the sphere of the pre-ontological understanding that life has of its own being. In this sense, hermeneutic phenomenology elaborates the conditions of possibility of all ontological investigations. The true hermeneutic task is to gain an adequate methodological access to life's primordial disclosedness. The phenomenological seeing must be directed to factical life as such. The philosophical act that provides access to life, and thus makes it possible to express primordial life experience, depends on a specific type of intuition, namely, hermeneutic intuition. Hence, the mission of philosophy is to make the meaning of the being of factical life explicit. By appropriating the hermeneutic situation, one secures the prior horizon in which life always already moves.

Now, among all possible horizons, which one is phenomenologically closest to human life so as to guide the hermeneutics of facticity? A crucial decision is at stake at this point, for 'it is all important that the initial approach to this "object" of hermeneutical explication does not already in advance, and this means once and for all, lose sight of it' (GA 63, 29/ HF, 24). Heidegger chooses the situation in which we *de facto* are: the actuality of everyday, the 'today' (*das Heute*). The interpretation starts out of the specific way in which we already see ourselves, that is, the ordinary and levelled-out understanding that the 'they' (*das Man*) imposes:

> This being-interpreted in the today is further characterized by the fact that it is in fact not explicitly experienced, not explicitly present. [...] Everyone thinks that ..., everyone has heard that ..., everyone expects that ..., everyone is in favor of ... The talk in circulation belongs to no one, no one takes responsibility for it, every-one has said it. 'One' even writes books on the basis of such hearsay. This 'everyone' is precisely *the* 'no-one' which circulates in factical Dasein and haunts it like a specter, a how of the fateful undoing of facticity to which the factical life of each pays tribute.
>
> GA 63, 30–31/HF, 26

This means that life always moves within a publicly established interpretation that limits in different manners the way we deal with things and our comportment in relation to the other persons that we encounter as we go about our everyday business. Phenomenological appropriation targets this open space of publicness (*Öffentlichkeit*). This space, however, acquires different forms, be they historical, political and economical, or philosophical, psychological and religious. Which of them is most appropriate? There is no clear answer to this question. In the 1923 lecture course, *Ontology. The Hermeneutics of Facticity*, Heidegger points at two interpretative directions: historical consciousness and the philosophy of the time. But there could be others, such as sociological polls, scientific development, or, as in Emil Durkheim, the suicide indicators. None of this warrants that we could gain privileged access to the hermeneutic situation.

In any case, appreciation of the fact that the public interpretation in which we move includes elements capable of distorting, covering up or hiding our authentic understanding of facticity, leads Heidegger to actualize that it is methodologically necessary to introduce in his reflection a critical moment of destructuring (*Abbau*) or destruction (*Destruktion*) of the prior orientation. In collective representations, the set of norms, values, world-pictures and social roles constitutive of the tradition in which factical life is thrown prior to any decision and action becomes a sediment, unconsciously or not (GA 63, 75/HF, 59). The problem is that traditions hand down to us a use of concepts that lacks a clear understanding and appropriation of their meaning. For this reason, the first task of the phenomenological investigation is to recognize the weight of the tradition and to identify, through self-reflection, the prejudices it involves. The critical destructuring of tradition, however, is not its annihilation. As Heidegger makes clear in *Being and Time*:

> The destruction has just as little the *negative* sense of disburdening ourselves of the ontological tradition. On the contrary, it should stake out the positive possibilities

of the tradition, and that always means to fix its *boundaries*. [...] Negatively, the destruction is not even related to the past: its criticism concerns 'today' and the dominant way we treat the history.

SuZ, 22–23 /BT, 22; italics in the original

This eminently methodological procedure aims at reaching an adequate appropriation of tradition and therefore of the past.

The horizon of the present is not independent of the past. From a formal point of view, the past only provides us with an indication, a meaningful hint, which the interpretation has to follow. Acceptance of our historical embeddedness should help us understand how, in our time, life actualizes in historical consciousness and philosophy.

Having laid out these methodological cautions, Heidegger can initiate his hermeneutics of facticity, that is to say, can undertake the task of making explicit the categorial modes of being of life. Heidegger asserts: 'The theme of this investigation is facticity, i.e., our own Dasein insofar as it is interrogated with respect to, on the basis of, and with a view to the character of its being' (GA 63, 29/HF, 24). Dasein's implicit understanding of being is the particular way of existing in which Dasein has to be. And it is the task of hermeneutics to articulate in a conceptual way the pre-philosophical self-understanding that Dasein has in relation to its own being.

Formal indication and the categorial articulation of factical life

The result of the young Heidegger's methodological worries can probably be considered one of the most important philosophical legacies for contemporary thought. Heidegger's first lecture courses evinced his interest in finding a solution to the difficult problem of how to gain access to the domain of the immediate givenness of the historical existence of human being. The main task of the hermeneutics of facticity is precisely to articulate in a categorial manner the understanding that life has of itself. The basic concepts hermeneutics deploys in order to make explicit the understanding that life has of itself and to know how life unfolds in the world are called, in Heidegger's early work, 'formal indicators'. These concepts correspond to *Being and Time*'s 'existentials'. The young Heidegger's terminological decision is an alternative to the epistemologically loaded term 'categories'. All his writings from the twenties make use of the expression 'formal indication' (*formale Anzeige*) in one way or another.[10] Formal indication is analysed in some detail in the lecture courses from 1920–1921, *Introduction to the Phenomenology of Religion*, and from 1921–1922, *Phenomenological Interpretations of Aristotle*.[11] Heidegger stresses the importance of formal indication for understanding his phenomenological-hermeneutic project in a 1924 letter to Löwith: 'Unfortunately, I had to leave important topics aside, above all, "formal indication," which is indispensable for a complete understanding and on which I have worked intensely' (in Storck and Kisiel 1992–1993, 214).[12]

Basically, the formal indication is a methodological device that assists Heidegger in gaining access to the primordial reality of factical life. In the 1921–1922 lecture course Heidegger asserts: 'Yet in order to make at all intelligible today the problematic of the ontological sense of this objectivity (factical life), it is necessary to bring the expression here into a formal indication of very sharp form. From this first access, it is possible to make one's way back step by step in the appropriation' (GA 61, 172/PIA, 130).

Antecedents of the formal indication can be traced back to Kierkegaard's model of indirect communication and Husserl's phenomenological analysis of occasional expressions.[13] What is important for our purposes is to clarify the meaning and role of formal indicators in the conceptual articulation of human life and determine the way in which Heidegger understands Husserl's 'categorial intuition' as presented in the Sixth Investigation.

The meaning and role of formal indicators

In the 1920–1921 lecture course, *Introduction to the Phenomenology of Religion*, Heidegger explains that the origin of the formal indication goes back to the distinction Husserl draws in the *Logical Investigations* (HU XIX/2, §§ 48, 50–52) and *Ideas I* (HU III/1, § 13) between generalization and formalization.[14] In the latter text, Husserl explains that generalization is applied within a particular field of experience and progressively moves from the particular to the general. By way of example, we go from the red colour to the sensible quality of red, from happiness to feeling and from feeling to lived experience. Generalization concerns a specific domain of things and aims at organizing content in terms of hierarchy of generalizations in the framework of a regional ontology (say geometry, biology, botany, and so on). Regional ontologies are the result of specific organizing generalizations. In contrast, formalization makes abstraction of all material content and regards only the logical and formal structures that are presupposed by knowledge. When we say 'the stone is an object' we use a formal category that does not belong to the nature of the thing. Formal categories like 'object', 'essence', 'plurality' and 'relation' apply directly to the content, the 'what'. The formal aspect does not belong to the thing or to its content, like, say, the surface belongs to the stone or the colour to the chair (HU III/1, 32–33). In contrast to the material categories of generalization, the categories of formalization do not imply a relation to the object.

In the aforementioned course, Heidegger explicitly distances himself from Husserl's ambition of developing a purely analytic ontology, a *mathesis universalis*. Thus, Heidegger asserts that 'the *formal indication* has *nothing* to do with this. It falls outside of the attitudinally theoretical' (GA 60, 59/PRL, 41, italics in the original). Heidegger's deployment of formal indicators in his interpretations of Augutine's texts and St Paul's epistles ('care', 'conscience', 'they', etc.) as well as of Aristotle's works (*phronesis, praxis, proairesis,* etc.) is characterized by a strenuous effort to relativize theory. Formal indication does belong to the theoretical interest of organizing and labelling beings. We have to keep in mind that hermeneutics starts out from a previous orientation corresponding to a determinate meaning of the being of factical life. Dasein does not occur as a mere set of properties standing out there. Dasein's existence is conditioned by the *factum* that it has to be and to take care of its own being. The decisive point of Heidegger's existential view is that the features that constitute Dasein's essence are to be actualized, brought to practice. The being that is pre-understood in the previous orientation is not an essence to which a 'what' (*Was*) belongs, a material or eidetic content, but a 'how' (*Wie*), a way of being. In Heidegger, self-reference acquires an active meaning rather than a cognitive one, it has more to do with self-creation than with self-knowledge. To put it another way, in existing, the type of being we are is at stake. Escaping the circle is not an option, for we are committed to ourselves from the start. Not to stake one's being is already a modality of existence. Heidegger articulates the inevitable self-reference of existence with the expression 'human being is a being for which its own being is at issue'.

The meaning of a formal indication is not an objective entity, whose *eidos* need be apprehended. Literally, a formal indication points at something, gives us a direction. It lacks content and only points in some direction: 'Accordingly, the content, the determination given of the object, must, as such, precisely *not become the theme*. Instead, the grasping comprehension has to follow the indicated direction of sense' (GA 61, 32/PIA, 25, italics in the original). In this way, in living, human being is actualizing its being. Life and actualization are not different. They are the same act, which is completed in the execution of one's own living. A formal indicator such as 'being-in-the-world' does not express a property of human being, or a real predicate, such as 'has the capacity to manipulate objects'. Rather, it indicates the way in which the ability is exercised. Heidegger underscores the execution-orientated character of formal indication. It is not guided by the content (the 'what', *das Was*), but indicates the mode of actualization (the 'how', *das Wie*), the sense of the execution (*Vollzugssinn*).[15] In the few pages Heidegger devotes to discussing this device in the 1929–1930 lecture course *The Fundamental Concepts of Metaphysics. World – Finitude – Solitude*, he asserts that, without transmitting any content, the formal indication points at a mode of actualization of human being's individual existence (GA 29/39, 429). By way of examples of formal indication, Heidegger names 'death', 'resolution', 'history' and 'existence'. But what are the implications of having a formal-indicative understanding of a concept such as 'existence'? The actualization of one's own existence is an indication that each of us has to understand by themselves. By no means is this an abstract postulate. On the contrary, it has an eminently concrete meaning that points at the factical situation in which we, in each case, find ourselves. The material indetermination of philosophical concepts is not so much a sign of insufficiency but one of true potential: 'The meaningful content of [formal indicators] is not that to which they refer; it offers an indication, a hint that exhorts he who understands it to carry out a transformation of his existence' (GA 29/30, 429–430). The primordial purpose of these concepts is to show to the individual the concrete situation in which he lives without imposing an evaluation. Formal indicators are ultimately dynamic. As Heidegger recalls: '[Formal indicators] initiate, methodically, a hermeneutic endeavor that provides philosophy with a starting point. Formal indicators must not be understood as normative links, what is indicated must not be reified' (GA 59, 85).

Hermeneutic concepts make us face the moment of decision while leaving the concrete decision open. Formal indicators are not predetermined schemes of action; rather, they delineate various possibilities for the being of life. The understanding of formal indicators does not involve a content, for their function is just to highlight the meaning of content (*Gehaltssinn*), of reference (*Bezugssinn*) and of execution (*Vollzugssinn*), which, as mentioned, can only be experienced in the very actualization of life, and not in the domain of theoretical thought.

Understanding a hermeneutic category does not give us information about the correspondent intuition because the category does not refer to an object. This evinces Heidegger's reservations regarding Husserl's concept of evidence, understood as the intuitive fulfilment of an empty form, by means of an adequate perception. Extracting the categories is a hermeneutic endeavour that is completely focused on the meaning of phenomena. There is no room here for a neutral, intentional and reflexive act. The belief in evidence, that is, in the idea that things are offered in a primordial way to the self's regard, is very dangerous insofar as it seems to rule out the mediation of an effort of appropriation (GA 63, 46/HF, 37). Heidegger's critique targets the belief that evidence is capable of grasping meaning simply as long as the thing is out there immediately in front of the subject. The presence of the thing does not exempt us from the task of understanding. Here a crucial question for hermeneutics arises regarding whether all self-understanding of life is equivalent to primordial understanding.

Formal indicators such as 'being-in-the-world', 'they', 'anxiety', etc., refer only to a specific mode of actualization of being. This poses the question as to how to apprehend formal indicators. The answer is: by means of a specific type of intuition, namely, hermeneutic intuition. This type of intuition concerns the pre-reflective evidence life has of itself, evidence that is equi-primordial with the unfolding of existence. For this reason, Heidegger holds:

> The categories are not inventions or a group of logical schemata as such, 'lattices'; on the contrary, they are *alive in life itself* in an original way: alive in order to 'form' life on themselves. They have their own modes of access, which are not foreign to life itself, as if they pounced down upon life from the outside, but instead are precisely the preeminent way in which *life comes to itself.*
>
> GA 61, 88/PIA, 66, italics in the original[16]

The categories of life express, in a conceptual manner, the understanding that life has of itself. The indicative and formal character of the categories shows that understanding meaning requires the actualization of the comportments to which the categories point: 'A *'concept'* is not a scheme, but a possibility of being' (GA 63, 16/HF, 49, italics in the original). The meaning of the word *'hermeneuein'* encompasses this double aspect of understanding and comportment: both are actualized in the same act. Hermeneutic categories express a way of being of facticity itself.

The background of the categorial intuition

Formal indicators, that is, the categories of factical life or hermeneutic concepts, express life's understanding of itself. But the fact that life can be made explicit through categories suggests that it involves something similar to what Husserl called in *Logical Investigations* 'categorial intuitions'. Heidegger's allusions to the 'Sixth Investigation' and particularly to the problem of being that arises in the discussion of categorial intuitions are frequent and occupy a prominent place in the 1925 lecture course *History of the Concept of Time* (cf. GA 20, § 6).[17] This makes it quite likely to find some traces of the categorial intuition in the categories of life.

Husserl talks of signifying acts and of their fulfilment. However, Husserl's concept of object is quite rich and wide-ranging. Basically, any thing one can predicate something of is an object. In the 'Sixth Investigation' Husserl distinguishes between two types of objects, real (perceptive) and ideal (categorial). One cannot only think of apples, cars or the Grand Canyon. It is also possible to think of ideal notions such as justice, freedom, pi, the principle of non-contradiction or states of affairs such as 'the sheet of paper that is on the desk is white'. When we think in a categorial manner we transcend the perceptual sphere. In the forty-eighth paragraph of the 'Sixth Investigation' Husserl illustrates this in the following way: at first, we are directed toward objects, say the sheet of paper, in a perceptual way. At this level, the object is given to us with all its general determinations, such as colour, shape, size, material and so on. Next, we focus on one property, say the sheet's white colour. And finally, and it is here that the categorial articulation takes place, we relate the previous two moments. We take the object *as* a whole and relate it to the part *as* a part of the whole. This is given expression in a judgement like 'the sheet of paper that is on the desk is white'. This predicative articulation is the result of a categorial act.

At this point the question arises: how are categorial intentions fulfilled? Let us keep using the example of the proposition 'the sheet of paper that is on the desk is white'. In this proposition, the meanings 'sheet', 'desk', 'paper' and 'white' can be fulfilled by perceptual intuitions. But what happens with the words 'the', 'of', 'on' and 'is'? Do they correspond to a perceptual intuition? Evidently not. It is not possible to see an *is* or an *on* (HU XIX/2, 658/Log. Inv. 2, 774). So one is to conclude that the proposition includes intuitions that cannot be covered by mere perception (HU XIX/2, 660/Log. Inv. 2, 775). Hence, the objective correlates of categorial forms are not real. The 'is' of the copula, together with all other words that express logical constants, such as 'and', 'therefore', 'because', 'where', and so on, do not correspond to an intuitive content in perception.

In other words, there is a whole domain of objects, including the ideal ones, that one cannot experience in a perceptual manner. None of these objects can be smelled, heard or seen. And yet, intuiting the white paper sheet is only possible on the basis of a superior act, one that although based on the perception of the white sheet and the desk, transcends what is immediately perceived and establishes the unity of the perceived parts. Broadening the concept of intuition is one of Husserl's main contributions: there are not only perceptual intuitions but also categorial intuitions (HU XIX/2, 670–676/ Log. Inv., 784–788). The intuition is an act by means of which the object is given to us in person, and, frequently, this is the result of a complex intellectual activity. In this way, Husserl broadens empiricism's concept of experience. We are not limited to experiencing concrete particular objects but can also experience abstract and universal objects. As Husserl explains in the *Encyclopedia Britannica* article, one of the tasks of phenomenology is to replace the narrow empiricist concept of experience with a broader one, and to clarify the different aspects of the latter (such as, apodictic evidence, intuition of essential structures and so on) (HU IX, 300).[18]

Still, the question is open as to the origin of the concept of being as well as of the other categories. One possibility, championed by Locke, is to say that the source of these concepts is internal perception, that is, reflection. The problem with this answer, so Husserl's objection goes, is that when we pay heed, in a pre-phenomenological way, to consciousness, all we find is psychic processes and not categorial forms. Being, and categories in general, are objective and their fulfilment takes place in specific acts. To each object belongs a specific form of givenness. It would be a mistake to treat an object as if it had the type of givenness of another object. The acts by which mathematical truths are given to us are different from those by which a table, a person or a dog are given to us. The way I understand '$a^2 - b^2 = (a + b)(a - b)$' is different from the way I perceive a table, say. The distinction between perceptual intuition and acts of categorial intuition plays a fundamental role in Husserl's phenomenology. It its worth remembering that something like this is already present in all Western theories of knowledge. The distinction can be traced back to the ancient distinction between the perceptual and the categorial, between perception (*aesthesis*) and understanding (*noesis*). In the traditional view, perception gives us basic access to the world and to things, whereas understanding enables us to apprehend perception. For this reason, in perceptual intuition 'an object is directly apprehended or is itself present, if it is set up in an act of perception *in a straightforward manner*. What this means is this: that the object is also an *immediately given object*' (HU XIX/2, 674/Log. Inv. 2, 787, italics in the original). In perception, the thing is immediately presented to me in person (*leibhaftig*) and from one single direction. This givenness in person is the specific and primordial way in which things themselves are given. Despite the different perspectives from which we can perceive a given thing and its numerous properties, that thing is presented in the act of perception as a simple unity (HU XIX/2, 677/Log. Inv. 2, 789). This means that even though I see the object from a certain point of view, I always see the same object as simply given to me. In contrast, Heidegger does not accept this view of the object as given 'in person', for this presupposes that things show themselves, primordially, as already present to a subject that contemplates them and perceives them instead of understanding them *in* the world.

Now, any act of perception can function as a basic act in which other acts are grounded. This may be the source of new objective contents, all of which refer back to the founding acts (HU XIX/2, 675/Log. Inv. 2, 787). It is precisely these acts, which give birth to a new objectivity, that Husserl calls 'categorial intuitions'. The categorial is not something that floats in the air, but something that needs be understood through the perceptual. The crucial point is that categorial intuitions are not founded acts, even though their objective character only shows itself through another simple act. This means that categorial formation does not entail a real transformation of the object. The object shown in perception is not affected by the new objectivity that stems from categorial intuition. This objectivity is grounded in the objectivity of mere sensible intuition, even though the former opens the latter in a new way. The object is no longer available in a perceptual way and in one stroke, but is opened in a different manner. The new objects that categorial forms give rise to are not objects in the primordial sense, they do not give shape to a material as the potter's mould does. Otherwise, what is primordially given in perception would be modified in its objectivity.

Thus, categorial forms leave primordial objects intact (HU XIX/2, 714–715/Log. Inv. 2, 819–820). 'Being', 'substantiality', 'plurality' and all the other categorial forms are not arbitrary determinations that are imposed on the object. They are what makes the givenness of the perceptual object possible. Through categorial intuition, phenomenic synthesis is possible. This is what in the tradition was characterized as the transit from *aesthesis* to *noesis*. Husserl follows this interpretative tradition when he claims that through categorial intuition we abandon the domain of sensibility and enter that of understanding. Then again, as I will show below, the phenomenic synthesis is only possible by means of reflection.

In categorial intuition, the object is presented in a new form of apprehension, which explicitly manifests the reality of the object. Heidegger follows Husserl in thinking that categorial intuition makes the presentation of the objectivity of objects, and therefore also an explicit understanding of reality, possible. The 1925 lecture course, *History of the Concept of Time*, is straightforward in this respect:

> By way of understanding what is present in categorial intuition, we can come to see that the objectivity of an entity is really not exhausted by this narrow definition of reality, that objectivity in its broadest sense is much richer than the reality of a thing, and what is more, that the reality of a thing is comprehensible in its structure only on the basis of the full objectivity of the simply experienced unity.
>
> GA 20, 89/HCT, 66

Heidegger's interpretation of the categorial intuition as a constitutive moment of the apprehension of beings as such evinces his efforts to avoid Husserl's transcendental standpoint. This is done by locating being out of the subjective domain and in the objective space of our understanding of the world. Heidegger does not regard categories as means to delimit the different regions of being but as projections that anticipate and guide our understanding of objects within their respective ontological regions. Put another way, categories are first and foremost anticipations that allow us to operate in a given context. Categories provide us with an illuminated space, a prior disclosure of being, and thus make possible an initial understanding of the phenomena that are given to us in a space of meaning that is always already discovered and available. In this sense, one could say that Heidegger thinks the Husserlian notion of categorial intuition in terms of what in 1921–1922 he called 'relucence' *(Reluzenz)* (GA 61, 117–121/PIA, 87–90), that is, the sphere that illuminates, in a pre-theoretical way, the understanding of life. This is what in *Being and Time* figures as Dasein's disclosedness (*Erschlossenheit*). From this point onwards, being can be a phenomenon, something that shows itself in a primordial space of meaning that is not modified by the subject/object scheme. For Heidegger, it is crucial that the categorial domain is not subjectively bounded, that it does not obey an internal reflection of consciousness:

> The category 'being', 'and', 'or', 'this', 'one', 'several', 'then' are nothing like consciousness, but are correlates of certain acts. [...] Categorial acts constitute a new objectivity. This is always to be understood intentionally and does not mean that they let the things spring up just anywhere. '*Constituting*' does not mean producing in the sense of making and fabricating; it means *letting the entity be seen in its objectivity*.
>
> GA 20, 79, 97/HCT, 59, 71, italics and quotation marks in the original

With this in view, the question regarding the meaning of being, that is, that which is understood by the word 'being', can be formulated. For Heidegger, Husserl was not able to find the meaning of being because he understood it as given to intuition rather than as the horizon of illumination and unveilment of beings. Nevertheless, in the 'Summary of a Seminar on the lecture "Time and Being"', Heidegger acknowledges that categorial intuition paves the path to the elaboration of the question regarding the meaning of being (VS, 116).[19] What really attracts the young Heidegger is the possibility of conceiving of being as a phenomenon pertaining to lived experience that can be made explicit in a categorial way.

The problem with Husserl is that his characterization of being is limited to the domain of theory. In his theory, the basic meaning of being is being-an-object, being-a-thing, reality and nature (GA 56/57, 87; GA 61, 91–92; GA 20, 83). My purpose is not to discuss whether with the categorial intuition Husserl asked himself the question of being, but just to show that whatever access he had to this question, it was always based on reflection. And so, the question of being is addressed always within the field of consciousness, and hence being can only appear as reflectively known. This way of approaching the problem is completely different from Heidegger's. It certainly does not fit the unreflective and pre-theoretical focus of hermeneutic phenomenology. For Heidegger, Husserl is content with posing the question in the traditional way, that is, by understanding being as perceivable thing. In this way, Husserl forgets to discuss explicitly the question of the meaning of being. This is an enterprise that Dilthey had already started when he took the Husserlian notion of intentional objectivity out of its logical context and located it in the vital sphere of the practical and cultural world. Following Dilthey's lead, Heidegger broadened the space of openness beyond the purely theoretical field of Husserl's transcendental *ego* and thus made room for historical, sociological and ordinary contexts.

In the young Heidegger's view, the reflexive stance of consciousness no longer has a place of privilege. Confirmation of the categories can only be achieved through the pre-reflective evidence that life has of itself. The origin of formal indicators is, therefore, the primordial understanding that life has of its own structures. This understanding does not obey the methodological rules of scientific rigorousness. Rather, it is the basic motion of human existence. In this sense, philosophy turns its back on eternal essences. In Heidegger's view, the purpose of philosophy is only to offer formal indications that point to things themselves. But being as factical, historical and temporal as they are, things demand a constant process of appropriation. In sum, Heidegger's thinking goes from Husserl against Husserl himself. All in the name of a radical new beginning and a return to things themselves. In order to safeguard the priority of being, a radical application of the Husserlian motto requires an internal critique of the phenomenology of pure consciousness. The incipient ontology of factical life perforates the logical structures of phenomenology and at the same time the idea of the self-givenness of being prevails over the idea of the reflective productivity of consciousness. In this way, Heidegger goes from the Husserlian logic of transcendental subjectivity to the fundamental ontology of Dasein's being-in-the-world.

Development and meaning of the hermeneutic phenomenology

Throughout this work I have pointed out several differences between Husserl's reflexive phenomenology and Heidegger's phenomenological hermeneutics. Now the time has come to sum up those differences. Both thinkers share the phenomenological motto, 'to the things themselves'. However, their approach and way of access to things differ. The basic difference between these two conceptions of phenomenology lies in their respective understanding of the phenomenological intuition: Husserl thinks of it in terms of 'reflexive seeing', while Heidegger, in turn, understands it in terms of 'hermeneutic intuition'. As Herrmann has repeatedly pointed out, Husserl's phenomenology is grounded in an eminently theoretical and reflective attitude, whereas Heidegger's is characterized by an a-theoretical and pre-reflective approach (Herrmann 1981, 1990, 15–12, 2000, 11–98). Put another way, Husserl moves within the coordinates of reflexive phenomenology; Heidegger elaborates a hermeneutic phenomenology.[20] In what follows I focus on the way the young Heidegger develops his hermeneutic phenomenology *vis-à-vis* Husserl's reflexive phenomenology, during the twenties. In general, this development has four stages: the first one takes place during the post-war semester, 1919, in the lecture course *The Idea of Philosophy and the Problem of Worldview*, in which Heidegger undertakes an initial critique of the theoretical postulates of Husserl's phenomenology while at the same time laying the ground for hermeneutic phenomenology, by giving primacy to the pre-theoretical. The second stage corresponds to the 1923–1924 lecture course, *Introduction to Phenomenological Research*, where Heidegger praises Husserl for his discovery of intentionality as the fundamental structure of consciousness in the *Logical Investigations*, but at the same time accuses him of straying from phenomenology in *Ideas I*, where he interprets subjectivity from the point of view of the Cartesian *ego cogito*. Heidegger's move away from Husserl comes to completion in the third stage, with his extensive immanent criticism of Husserl in the 1925 lecture course, *History of the Concept of Time*. Here, Heidegger takes a stance regarding the key elements of Husserl's phenomenology, namely, intentionality, consciousness, being and categorial intuition. The fourth and final stage, in which the hermeneutic phenomenology of Dasein is fully developed, is *Being and Time*.

The need for a hermeneutic phenomenology

As seen in Chapter 3, the young Heidegger's interest in phenomenology goes back to his first articles, doctoral dissertation and *Habilitationsschrift* (ZSD, 81–82/MWP, 74). It is also known that the reason he went to Freiburg to study under the supervision of the neo-Kantian Heinrich Rickert rather than to Gotinga to study with Edmund Husserl was strictly financial. It is not surprising, then, that during his time as a student and doctoral candidate Heidegger resorted both to neo-Kantianism and phenomenology in his search for a pure logic or a priori grammar, that is, a doctrine of categories capable of explaining 'the multiple modes of reality that constitute the whole sphere of being' (GA 1, 186).

In the conclusion to his *Habilitationsschrifft* on Scotus, in which Heidegger integrates ideas from Meister Eckhart's mysticism, German idealism and Carl Braig's neo-Hegelian theology, he uses phenomenology in the context of a speculative and religious metaphysics, whose object is the true reality of God's absolute spirit (GA 1, 409–411). During this period, his appropriation of phenomenology remains within the boundaries of what he called, many years later, in *Identity and Difference*, 'ontotheology', that is, an understanding of the event of being as divine ground.

Heidegger's first academic writings endorse the critique of psychologism held in *Logical Investigations*. Now, once a clear distinction between the psychic acts of thought and the validity of logical content is drawn, that is, once the autonomy of logic is secured against relativist takes, the question arises as to the foundation of logic. Heidegger's solution points to the existence of a trans-logical context, a proto-hermeneutic horizon from which human thinking can be understood. In this way, the idea that all subjects have a pre-understanding of the world enters the scene: only if one has certain prior understanding of the object of study, is it possible to carry out a scientific enterprise.

For all that, Heidegger's hermeneutic turn occurred only during the first Freiburg lecture courses, particularly during those of the post-war semester, 1919, *The Idea of Philosophy and the Problem of Worldview*. The slogan in this context is *let us go back to the primordial nature of life!* This vindication, perfectly suited to the intellectual environment of the time, translates into a radicalization of Husserl's principle of principles. This entails suspending traditional philosophical strategies, mistrusting dogmatically transmitted authority and giving preference to phenomenological description over theoretical constructs. From this moment onwards, Heidegger would hold that phenomenology is neither a discipline, nor a philosophical method among others, but the highest possibility of philosophy itself (GA 56/57, 110; GA 58, 139, 233; GA 61, 187; GA 63, 72; GA 19, 9; GA 20, 184; GA 21, 32; SuZ, 38; GA 24, 1, 3). His slogan could be something like 'against phenomenology in the name of phenomenology'. As we will see, the effort to rethink phenomenology ultimately aims at securing an immediate and direct mode of access to life. This comes to fruition, first, in the understanding of philosophy as primordial science of life (1919), then as hermeneutic phenomenology of Dasein (1922), next as hermeneutics of facticity (1923), and finally as existential analytic (1925 and 1927). The idea is to deploy all the potential of phenomenology, taking factical life as the starting point.

Before considering the thematic horizon of this transformation, it is important to keep in mind the following caveats. First, hermeneutic phenomenology is also an ontology. A hermeneutic transformation of phenomenology entails an ontological transformation. Heidegger redirects Husserl's phenomenology, which was limited to the investigation of the constitutive acts of transcendental consciousness, toward the question regarding being, and thus gives rise to a phenomenological ontology. For Heidegger, the 'thing' phenomenology should allow us to see, is being. Like phenomenology, hermeneutics also acquires an ontological dimension that, formally, it did not have before. In Heidegger's hands, hermeneutics is no longer the auxiliary discipline of human sciences that fixes the rules for the exegesis of classical, sacred and juridical texts. It becomes a philosophical attitude according to which human beings conceive themselves as interpretative animals that act in all domains of ordinary life. This is the reason why human being always has the capability to interpret being in one way or another.

Second, it is necessary to distinguish between carrying out the aforementioned transformation and offering an explicit assessment of that which is being transformed. It is one thing is to transform Husserl's phenomenology in a hermeneutic-ontological way, and a very different one to elaborate a detailed critique of the former. By all appearances, Heidegger undertook the first task during the Freiburg years, whereas he explicitly confronted Husserl in a thoughtful way only during the 1925 lecture course, *History of the Concept of Time*.

Third, Heidegger's approach to phenomenology is by no means neutral. Several elements that originated in his affinity to some aspects of the philosophies of life are at odds with phenomenology from the outset. His true interest is to rethink the question of being out of the horizon of factical life. He offers a wonderful portrait of this project of a phenomenological ontology in his review of Jaspers' *Psychology of Worldviews* (1919–1921):

> When phenomenology first erupted onto the scene with its specific aim of appropriating the phenomenon of theoretical experience and knowledge in a new and primordial manner (the Logical Investigations, i.e., a phenomenology of theoretical logos), the goal of its research was to win back an unspoiled seeing of both the sense of those objects that are experienced in such theoretical experience and, correlatively, the sense of 'how' these objects become experienced. But if we are to understand the philosophical sense of the tendencies of phenomenology in a radical manner, and appropriate them genuinely, [...] we need to see that experiencing in its fullest sense is to be found in its authentically factical context of enactment in the historically existing itself. And this self is one way or another the ultimate question of philosophy. [...] The concrete self should be taken up into the starting point of our approach to philosophical problems, and brought to 'givenness' at the genuinely fundamental level of phenomenological interpretation, namely, that level of interpretation that is related to the factical experience of life as such.
>
> AKJ, 34–35/CKJ, 30, italics and quotation marks in the original

For this reason, phenomenological science does not aim at providing an encyclopaedic catalogue of all the manifestations of life. Life is to be understood in its origin, that is, as it takes shape within the sphere of pre-theoretical experience. Where does this leave phenomenology? What are the conditions that allow phenomenology to carry out its vocation as primordial science of life as such and as it is for itself? A general answer to this question leads, methodologically, to a hermeneutic transformation of phenomenology, and results in the elaboration of a primordial science of life.

The first step in the development of a hermeneutic phenomenology

The initial formulation of the hermeneutic phenomenology provided by the 1919 lecture course, *The Idea of Philosophy and the Problem of Worldview*, responds to an interest in apprehending the primordial experience of pre-theoretical life *thematically*, and in fulfilling the *methodological* need of achieving an adequate access to the domain of the pre-theoretical. Theme and method are intimately intertwined. The phenomenological thematization of a new field of inquiry, pre-theoretical life, demands a new method of analysis. The domain of the pre-theoretical cannot be accessed by reflection and theory. The need to find a method capable of grasping the nexus of meaning in which life is primordially given results in the elaboration of the hermeneutic phenomenology of factical and a-theoretical life, as we find it in the first Freiburg lecture courses. This enterprise is formulated in different terms throughout the years: primordial science of life (1919), phenomenological ontology of Dasein (1922), hermeneutics of facticity (1923) and existential analytic (1927). However, all these approaches start out of the primordial experience of life and determine the methodology of Heidegger's inquiry. For this reason, one can say that the discovery of the pre-theoretical dimension of life in the first lecture course from 1919 is the keystone on which the hermeneutic transformation of phenomenology rests, and marks the beginning of a philosophical path that Heidegger followed during his time in Freiburg and Marburg up until he composed *Being and Time*.

The dissolution of the theoretical attitude and the discovery of the pre-theoretical dimension of life

The aforementioned lecture course from 1919 delineates a whole new philosophical programme in which Heidegger redefined the object of study, i.e. factical life, and the methodology, i.e. hermeneutics. The subject matter and the methodology are closely linked. The method is not the application of a general technique; it has to respond to the mode of being of the object of study. As Heidegger acknowledges in the 1919–1929 lecture course, *The Basic Problems of Phenomenology*, 'the philosophical method is rooted in life itself' (GA 58, 228). In this way, from the point of view of the subject matter, philosophy is conceived as primordial science of life and lived experiences. The methodological counterpart is the hermeneutic phenomenology, which, like life and lived experiences, is a-theoretical and pre-theoretical in nature.

The question Heidegger sets out to answer is how to gain primordial access to pre-theoretical life, which had been ignored by philosophy thus far. The task of the first Freiburg lecture courses is, therefore, to show the possibility and feasibility of a non-reflexive phenomenology capable of delimitating and articulating, in a systematic way, the primordial domain in which life shows itself. Because of the longstanding primacy of the theoretical attitude, life is hidden or distorted. It is thereby necessary to break with this primacy in order to gain access to the primordial soil from which life stems in its immediate givenness. This involves grasping life in its pre-theoretical and a-theoretical nature. So what exactly is the domain of a philosophically primordial science? In the 1919 lecture course, Heidegger starts to focus on the primordially practical relation we have with the life-world. The possibility of elaborating a new conception of philosophy arises from this relation between life and world. The origin of philosophy is the underground that has not yet been pierced by reflection and categorial determination. Philosophy as primordial science is 'a catastrophe for all previous philosophies' (GA 56/57, 12/IP, 10). But here, 'catastrophe' is understood in the Greek sense of *katastrophe*, that is, 'turn', 'shift', 'change'. Aristotelian metaphysics, Kantian transcendental philosophy, Hegel's absolute science and Husserl's transcendental phenomenology are the outcome of a long and difficult process of theoretical abstraction, the goal of which is a logically transparent philosophical system. The new concept of philosophy Heidegger elaborates corresponds to a change in the way of seeing things: rather than starting from the domain of theoretical reflection, one is to start from the pre-theoretical sphere of life.

The theoretical attitude is the most apparent in the field of science and of the theory of knowledge. As the history of philosophy attests, this attitude has a place of privilege as the ultimate source of truth. Right from the start, however, the theoretical attitude involves an evaluative judgement on which other domains of knowledge such as art, literature and history are underestimated. But it poses an even bigger threat: it eliminates all trace of our immediate, pre-theoretical and unreflective experience of the world, and thus hinders free direct access to life's primordial space of givenness. Hence, as Heidegger says, 'this primacy of the theoretical must be broken' (GA 56/57, 59/IP, 50). This does not mean that one is to hastily and blindly dive into the domain of *praxis*, with its sets of values and natural routines. The very distinction between theory and *praxis*, between the rational and the irrational, is a creature of the theoretical attitude itself.

As Heidegger says, full *pathos*, at this point of the philosophical reflection, we find ourselves 'at the methodological cross-road which will decide on the very life or death of philosophy' (GA 56/57, 63/IP, 53): either we keep going down the road of philosophical tradition and thereby keep to the reflective way of explaining the phenomenon of life, or we open up a new way of access to life that takes us along paths that philosophy has not yet travelled and allows us to reach a different world. Naturally, this is the world of life and lived experiences, the world of the a-theoretical and unreflective; in sum, the symbolically structured world in which life always already finds itself. In this sense, the world is not a receptacle that contains the totality of perceived things. It is filled with meaning from the start. As we are in the world, we do not first encounter objects but deal with tools and persons. We have direct access to this world through a certain degree of familiarity, on the basis of which the world is always intelligible to us to some extent. Hence, the world is open to us in a hermeneutic way and not in a reflective one: 'We have gone into the aridity of the desert, hoping, instead of always *knowing* things, to intuit understandingly and to *understand intuitively*' (GA 56/57, 65/IP, 55, italics in the original). Heidegger does not reject knowledge, only the unwarranted primacy that has been given to theoretical and objectifying knowledge. The knowledge of the world of life rests on an a-theoretical seeing rather than on a reflective inquiry. The pre-theoretical knowledge we acquired in our direct dealings with the world is a matter of understanding and not of explanation. This does not mean that reflective access to lived experiences is a mistake or yields false judgements. The point is just that that is a derivative form of access that depends on a prior, non-thematic and pre-reflective understanding of the immediate world of life and lived-experiences.

In sum, reflexive phenomenology has access to reality through theory, whereas hermeneutic phenomenology draws a clear-cut distinction between the theoretical and phenomenological attitudes. From this point of view, the 1919 lecture course is critical insofar as it anticipates Heidegger's programme of a hermeneutics of facticity and clearly establishes the main differences between Husserl's and Heidegger's conceptions of phenomenology.

The hermeneutic structure of the experience of the surrounding world

The second part of the 1919 lecture course, *The Idea of Philosophy and the Problem of Worldview*, shows how carrying out a primordial science of life is closely linked to a hermeneutic transformation of phenomenology. Heidegger asks himself: how do we experience life? How do we apprehend reality before any scientific or evaluative consideration, before any conception of what the world is? In the first place, Heidegger invokes the principle of all principles: 'Everything that presents itself ... *originarily in "intuition" is to be taken simply ... as it gives itself*' (GA 56/57, 109/IP, 92, italics and quotation marks in the original). Then, he adds that Husserl's application of this principle is limited to a description of the different ways in which things are given to a theoretically directed consciousness. However, as we experience our surrounding world, our comportment rarely follows theoretical protocols. The primordial attitude attached to lived experiences is not of this kind. To illustrate this, Heidegger uses the example of 'seeing a lectern'. He offers the following rich phenomenological description:

> Focus on this experience of 'seeing *your* place,' or you can in turn put yourselves in my own position: coming into the lecture-room, I see the lectern. We dispense with a verbal formulation of this. What do 'I' see? Brown surfaces, at right angles to one another? No, I see something else. A largish box with another smaller one set upon it? Not at all. I see the lectern at which I am to speak. You see the lectern from which you are to be addressed, and from where I have spoken to you previously. In pure experience there is no 'founding' interconnection, as if I first of all see interesting brown surfaces, which then reveal themselves to me as a box, then as a desk, then as an academic lecturing desk, a lectern, so that I attach lectern-hood to the box like a label. All that is simply bad and misguided interpretation, diversion from a pure seeing into the experience. I see the lectern in one fell swoop, so to speak, and not in isolation, but as adjusted a bit too high for me. I see – and immediately so – a book lying upon it as annoying to me (a book, not a collection of layered pages with black marks strewn upon them), I see the lectern in an orientation, an illumination, a background. [...] This object, which all of us here perceive, somehow has the specific meaning 'lectern.'
> GA 56/57, 70–71/IP, 59–60, quotation marks in the original

In the experience of seeing the lectern something is given *to me* from out of an immediate environment. This environmental milieu (lectern, book, blackboard, notebook, fountain pen, caretaker, student fraternity, tram-car, motor-car, etc.) does not consist just of things, objects, which are then conceived as meaning this and this; rather, the meaningful is primary and immediately given to me without any mental detours across thing-oriented apprehension. Living in an environment, it signifies to me everywhere and always, everything has the character of world. It is everywhere the case that '*it worlds*' (GA 56/57, 72–73 /IP, 61, italics in the original).

The disconcerting verb 'worlds', which Gadamer was very fond of, refers to the fact that one experiences the meaningfulness of the lectern, its function, location and the memory of the path one has to follow along the university corridors in order to get to the lectern, in front of the students, and so on.[21] The lectern's 'worldling' gathers a whole spatial and temporal world. In this way, if, for instance, in a different time, we evoke the experience of the lectern, we recall a whole life situation, just like Proust's protagonist did when he tasted the madeleine he had just dipped in his tea. Evoking the lectern lays out a whole universe of memories before us, and thus makes plain our own world of experiences, past and present.

The example of the lived experience of the surrounding world (*Umwelterlebnis*) connected to the lectern illustrates the primordial way in which things are given to us. These do not show themselves, primordially, in the inner space of consciousness, as the traditional subject/object scheme might lead us to think. On the contrary, things become accessible and intelligible thanks to the subject's prior belonging to a symbolically articulated world, that is to say, from out of the pre-understanding horizon that all human beings possess. My immediate experience of the surrounding world is not an experience of a sphere of objects present in front of me but one of a network of tools with which I take care and understand my self. We don't first see the colours and surfaces of an object, and then assign a meaning to that object. Rather, because of our familiarity with the world that we ordinarily inhabit, we always have an understanding of things from the beginning. The lectern shows itself, primordially, in a context of signification, a determinate hermeneutic situation, namely, the lecture that is taking place in the usual lecture room. Only at a second moment, we perceive objective qualities such as colour, shape, location, weight, and so on. Reflecting on the act 'seeing a lectern' does not take us to a context of perception. In the context of perception we are still thinking in terms of the subject/object scheme: there is a self that perceives an object and its properties. But Heidegger argues that understanding perception as private experience of an isolated subject runs the risk of falling into a form of methodological individualism, which would severely distort the human experience of the world. Heidegger offers a hermeneutic account of our experience on which it becomes possible to understand human being as inhabiting a symbolically structured world, in which each thing is already understood in some way. The meaning of the experience of the lectern is grasped in one fell swoop and not after breaking it down, reflectively, to the perception of several different features. The whole set of objective determinations 'is simply a bad and misguided interpretation, diversion from a pure seeing into the experience' (GA 56/57, 71/IP, 60).

By the same token, the meaning of the lectern is not isolated; it is not grasped in a closed and complete act of understanding. The meaning of the lectern is framed by a whole context of signification. One might object that the concrete meaning of the lectern is only intelligible to those that are familiar with a university lecture room. For this reason, a peasant from the Black Forest might not be able to completely grasp the meaning of the lectern. He might just *see* the place the lecturer occupies. And yet, the peasant wouldn't just perceive a material body; he would perceive the lectern as something within his own horizon of understanding. So even if the peasant sees the lectern as a box or some sort of barricade he wouldn't be seeing it as a bare object, but as something with the meaning 'box,' or 'barricade'. Moreover, Heidegger says, suppose a Senegalese person has never been to a classroom comes through the door. The Senegalese person would assign to what we call 'lectern' a meaning that is incorporated in his cultural context. For instance, he might *see* the lectern as 'something to do with magic, or something behind which one could find good protection against arrows and flying stones' (GA 56/57, 72/IP, 60). Just like the Black Forest peasant, the Senegalese individual wouldn't just gather a collection of sense data. No, he would understand the thing in this or that way. Most probably, his *seeing* would not be familiarized with the same horizon of understanding that the German student's seeing is. But still, in no way would the Senegalese persons seeing be reduced to a simple act of perception. His lived experiences, like those of the German student, have a hermeneutic structure.

The example of the lectern makes it clear that it is essential to all human life, irrespective of nationality, geographic location, cultural context and system of beliefs, to move within a horizon of meaning. Insofar as human life understands itself on the basis of a certain horizon, it does not simply relate to things in terms of mere perception but in terms of a primordial comprehension. For this reason, the surrounding world is not the totality of perceived things, not even the totality of things in general. The world gathers the totality of significations in terms of which we understand the things and persons that we encounter in our everyday dealings with the surrounding life-world. Perception and knowledge do not only mean perception *of* something and knowledge *of* something, but perception and knowledge *in* a world, *in* a horizon. This horizon of meaningfulness precedes all acts of perception and knowledge; these *already* presuppose and put into play the horizon, either implicitly or explicitly.[22]

It is clear, then, that the philosophical investigation of life and lived experiences is only possible in the context of significations of life itself. In the 1919–1920 lecture course, *The Basic Problems of Phenomenology*, Heidegger offers another example that illustrates this.

> As I drink tea, I hold the cup in my hand. During the conversation I keep the cup in front of me. It is not like I perceive the sense data of certain color and this thing as a cup located in a spatial and temporal frame. 'The cup I drink' is really fulfilled in meaningfulness. In fact, I am always a *captive of meanings*, and each meaning joins other newer ones [...] I live in facticity as in a particular context of significances that intertwine all the time.
>
>   GA 58, 104–105; italics in the original[23]

The analysis of the structures of life does not follow the deductive procedure of scientific methodology. This procedure gradually extinguishes the worldly context of experience in order to grasp a content, the 'what' (*Was*) of an object. However, factical life does not fit the parameters of epistemological theories. To paraphrase another example Heidegger gives, when I see someone I know and he waves to me, I interpret the gesture, first and immediately, as a greeting, rather than as the movement of a material being in an objective space, which I interpret as a greeting only at a later moment. What is more, if I have a doubt, I won't ask my companion 'Have you seen the waving I have seen?', but rather, 'Has that man greeted us or not?' (GA 58, 105). Once again, here we have a phenomenological description anchored in the hermeneutic structure of life itself and directed to show the mode, the 'how' (*Wie*), of life's phenomenological manifestation (GA 58, 83–84).

And so we come back to the problem of the givenness of that primordial space of manifestation, a problem phenomenology cannot elude if it wants to shed light on the way life comports itself in relation to the world, others and itself. The origin of life is not an axiom or a mystical entity because the 'most primordial givenness is never directly given; on the contrary, it is the object of an arduous conquest' (GA 58, 27). Life is not a self-contained and finished entity; it is actualized progressively in the course of its own existential unfolding. It is not the result of an external source of authority either, and does not respond to an ontological hierarchy involving a transcendent order. Neither does it obey some religion or worldview. The fundamental phenomenological feature of life is its self-sufficiency (*Selbstgenügsamkeit*): 'Life is directed and responds to itself in its own language, so that it is structurally impossible for it to go out of itself' (GA 58, 42). We can thus formulate the following equation: facticity equals life's in-itselfness, and this equals self-sufficiency. Since this equation precedes all analysis of life, it is important to clarify certain possible misunderstandings. One of the most common mistakes is to identify self-sufficiency with some sort of self-satisfaction or complacency. But '[…] life is also enough for itself in imperfections and insufficiency' (GA 58, 35). The experiences of frustration and dissatisfaction are modalities that, just like the experiences of pleasure and happiness, are incorporated in the frame of self-sufficiency. According to another misunderstanding, which is the opposite of the last one, life is assimilated to some sort of brute, blind and meaningless facticity, similar to the Sartrean existentialist view of the absurd. Heidegger's interpretation of life is completely opposite to the idea of the absurd. The following passage, in which Heidegger takes distance from irrationalist views, is very clear in this respect: 'Life is not a chaotic cluster of dark flows, a weighty principle of strength, an unlimited monstrosity that devours everything; *it is what it is only because it possesses a concrete meaning*' (GA 58, 148, italics in the original). If, occasionally, life seems unintelligible to us, this is not the result of a lack of sense, but the result of an excess of meanings. Self-sufficiency admits of different forms of manifestation and meaningfulness. Recall that Heidegger insists in the worldly character of life and asserts that 'all life lives in a world' (GA 58, 36). This means that life has a necessary connection to the world. It is affected and addressed by the world.

In sum, with the recognition of the reference to the world (*Weltbezogenheit*), the context of signification (*Bedeutsamkeit*) and self-sufficiency (*Selbstgenügsamkeit*), as constitutive elements of factical life, a shift in the young Heidegger's perspective comes to completion: he moves from the paradigm of perception of the philosophy of consciousness to hermeneutic understanding. No doubt, these two views correspond to two different ways of 'seeing' the lectern: from the point of Husserlian phenomenology's theoretical attitude, on the one hand, and from that of the a-theoretical attitude involved in Heidegger's hermeneutics, on the other. And, in turn, these two ways of 'seeing' correspond to two forms of phenomenological access: that of Husserl's reflective description and that of Heidegger's method of hermeneutic comprehension.

Phenomenology is, first and foremost, an attitude that gives privilege to 'things themselves'. This means that things are not simply given to us in the natural attitude. In fact, the phenomenological reduction seeks to suspend the validity of precisely that attitude, which obstructs our free access to phenomena. For this reason, to the moment of the intuition of things, a moment of critical stepping back is added, all with the purpose of achieving an understanding of the meaningfulness we experience in an immediate way. Thus far, Husserl and Heidegger coincide. The difference between their postures lies in the standpoint from which the phenomenological description issues. Husserl's inquiry operates within a reflective framework. Lived experience is the object of a theoretical seeing. Heidegger, for his part, rejects the idea that reflection is capable of satisfying the phenomenological requirement to remain faithful to the primordial givenness of things.

The theoretical attitude that guides Husserl's phenomenological inquiry sacrifices the way experiences are lived in their immediacy. Husserl himself was aware that the reflective objectification of lived experiences altered in some way the primordial meaning of things (HU III/1, 165–169). In spite of this, he did not find any other way of making conscious life explicit. In contrast, in Heidegger's hermeneutic attitude, lived experiences like that of the lectern are understood without appealing to reflection or the mediation of the perception of a material object. For hermeneutic phenomenology, 'the meaningful is primary' (GA 56/57, 73/IP 61). The roots of perceptual experience sink deep in life's context of signification. This does not mean that one can just ignore perceptual experience. Perceptual experience is included in understanding meaning. But it no longer has a primordial and grounding character. The latter belongs to the immediate and a-theoretical understanding of life. Things, persons and situations in the everyday life-world do not show themselves primarily as perceived objects, but as objects that have a concrete meaning.

Heidegger seeks to make that primordial domain of lived experiences transparent to us. In the so-called theoretical attitude, in the objectifying attitude of science, the primordial meaningfulness of the surrounding world dissolves. Everything reduces to the artificial picture of a world-less subject facing an object. But for Heidegger, what modern philosophy, and consequently also modern science, establishes as the primordial, presuppositionless site of ultimate certainty, does not really obey the principle of evaluative neutrality. The primordial situation is not like that. Heidegger makes the criticism, 'a deeply ingrained obsession with the theoretical greatly hinders a genuine survey of the prevalent domain of environmental experience' (GA 56/57, 88/IP, 74). The theoretical attitude, no matter how useful it is and how much it helps us to improve our capacity to understand and explain the world, strips life of its meaningfulness.

The example of the lectern serves to illustrate both the theoretical way of access to life endorsed by Husserl's reflexive phenomenology and the pre-theoretical access of Heidegger's hermeneutic phenomenology. Husserl's starting point is a consciousness that perceives things; next he establishes the objective content of lived experiences by means of a mechanism of reflexive representation that ultimately breaks with the life-world. For his part, Heidegger starts from a factical life that comprehends the beings that show themselves in its everyday dealings with the world, by means of an understanding repetition that affords us a real appropriation of the lived experiences we have. Strictly speaking, the lived experiences of the surrounding world, rather than being given to us, are something we encounter. Talking of givenness does not characterize in a completely adequate manner the way we live the surrounding world. *'How do I live and experience the environmental. How* is it "given" to me? No, for something environmental to be *given* is already a theoretical infringement. It is already forcibly removed from me, from my historical "I"; the "it worlds" is already no longer primary' (GA 56/57, 88–89/IP, 74–75; italics and quotation marks in the original). The surrounding world is not *given* to life – in Husserl's case, to consciousness – but we *encounter it* in its meaningfulness. The lived experiences of the surrounding world have the character of *encountering (Begegnung)*. Givenness, as a theoretical mode of encountering, is different from the a-theoretical way of showing itself that the meaningfulness of that which surrounds us has in our dealings with the world. This is one further respect in which hermeneutic phenomenology is radically different from reflexive phenomenology.

Lived experience as process versus lived experience as appropriation

Having explained how the hermeneutic-phenomenological analysis of the experience of the surrounding world works, we can now spell out the structure of lived experiences. These do not obey the rules of a mechanism of objectification. Neither are they grasped by means of a representation ultimately anchored in a subjective pole. In Husserl's philosophy of consciousness, lived experiences show themselves in what Heidegger calls a 'pro-cess' (*Vor-gang*: passing before us), particularly, a process of theoretical objectification. The hyphen underscores the objectifying character of the process, the effect of distance from the perceiving subject. But for Heidegger, re-presentations grounded in a subjective pure self are not what is at play here. The theoretical self dissolves in immediate experience and becomes a factical self that follows the experience's rhythm and follows the flow of meaning of life itself (cf. GA 56/57, 73/IP, 62). We extract lived experiences from that current of meaning, we deny their primordial nature, and the result is a phenomenon Heidegger calls 'de-vivification' (*Ent-lebung*).[24]

The theoretical process in which the object's qualities are picked out is secondary to a prior primordial and understanding appropriation of experiences. Put another way, the theoretical lived experience is a modification of the pre-theoretical one. The example of the lectern refers precisely to this level of appropriation of life. At this level, life is in a relation of vital sympathy (*Lebenssympathie*) with things prior to any reflection about them. This relation makes the surrounding world transparent to us (GA 56/57, 110/IP, 92). Lived experience is no longer understood as an objective process. Heidegger offers a new view (GA 56/57, 75/IP, 63). From the point of view of hermeneutic phenomenology, lived experiences occur as an event of appropriation (*Er-eignis*). Essentially, life is an event, that is to say, an a-theoretical occurring or happening, and not a theoretical process. Appropriation is the way of getting unreflective and pre-theoretical access to the sphere of lived experience.[25] Lived experience refers, primarily, to ap-propriating (*er-eignen*) as something that stems from life itself, for it is what is proper to life (*eigen*), it is life's property (*Eigentum*). The German prefix 'er-' denotes the primordial and primary level from which all lived experiences emerge.

Process and *appropriation* connote two different phenomenological attitudes. In the former, lived experience is an object of the reflective act of pure consciousness. In the latter, one plunges into the meaningful current of lived experience and thus complies with the methodological requirement of executing and bringing to completion lived experiences in their full vitality. Heidegger uses the phenomenon of sunrise, as described by Sophocles in *Antigone*, to illustrate the difference between process and appropriation, theoretical and factical self. Evidently, the sunrise is not described as the mere natural process of the sun's moving across the arc of the circumference of the Earth. What the description seeks is an appropriation of the emotion that fills us when we see the sunshine and the sun-rays' interplay (GA 56/57, 75/IP, 63). The phenomenon of sunrise is not exhausted by mere observation (*Hinsicht*). In theoretical-contemplative observation, lived experience 'is posited as a thing' and figures as 'consciousness of givenness' (GA 56/57, 98/IP, 82). One can posit lived experience as a thing when one takes it as perceptual experience and it is in these terms that one refers to it. In this picture, the world is populated by perceived objects 'given' to consciousness. Heidegger prefers to talk of an immersion (*Hingabe*), that is, an a-thematic and pre-reflective absorption in the immediate reality of the meaningful world of lived experience. *Hingabe* is an essentially practical way of having access to the phenomena we encounter in our everyday dealings with the world. This form of access is substantially different from the objectifying seeing of the *Hinsicht*.[26] It is one thing is to be immersed in various activities in the world (*Hingabe*) and quite a different one to contemplate them by means of the distant and detached seeing of reflection (*Hinsicht*). As Heidegger says in the 1919 lecture course:

> The reflection makes something which was previously unexamined, something merely unreflectively experienced, into something '*looked at*.' We look at it. In reflection it stands before us as an object of reflection, we are directed towards it and make it into an object as such, standing over against us. Thus, in reflection we are totally orientated. All theoretical comportment, we said, is de-vivifying. This now shows itself in the case of life-experiences, for in reflection they are no longer lived but looked at. We set the experiences *out* before us *out of* immediate experience; we intrude so to speak into the flowing stream of experiences and pull one or more of them out.
>
> GA 56/57, 100/IP, 84–85, italics and quotation marks in the original

The difference between actualization and contemplation, *praxis* and *theoria*, hermeneutics and reflection, present throughout the young Heidegger's work, might be better understood in terms of the opposition of *Hingabe* and *Hinsicht*. Life is primarily actualized through direct contact with the beings of the surrounding world, whereas theoretical knowledge is acquired at a second moment, through observing with the intention of understanding the being of objects, that is, of apprehending the *eidos* of things.

Thus, there are two ways to have access to the sphere of lived experiences. As Heidegger puts it, what is at stake here is 'the problem of the methodological apprehension of lived experiences as such: how is a science of experiences as such possible?' (GA 56/57, 98/IP, 82). The question is how (*Wie*) should we articulate experiences, how should philosophy proceed, from a methodological point of view? Two different solutions are available: according to Heidegger, Husserl chooses the way of reflection and theory, within the framework of his ideal of philosophy as rigorous science. For his part, Heidegger takes the path of understanding and hermeneutics as the methods of philosophy understood as primordial science of life.[27]

Reduction versus anxiety

So far, I have explained the difference between Heidegger's and Husserl's ways of analysing lived experiences. I have also highlighted the ways in which each of them gains access to the phenomenological sphere of lived experiences: the method of descriptive reflection, in Husserl's case, and the method of hermeneutic understanding in Heidegger's. Now I will explain how they reach the core of their subject matter, namely, pure subjectivity and factical life, respectively. Once again, their procedures are very different. Husserl develops the method of reduction. By effecting certain forms of detachment from the world, and executing several levels of reduction, one arrives at transcendental subjectivity. For Heidegger, in contrast, primordial access to the world of factical life occurs or arrives suddenly and through a fundamental affective state, namely, anxiety. The main difference between Husserl and Heidegger is that the reduction can be executed freely: at any moment one can go from the natural to the reflective attitude. For its part, anxiety is an event that escapes the control of reflective life. As I will show, anxiety is central to Heidegger's methodology because it allows us to reach a form of self-understanding similar to the one reduction offers, but in contrast to reduction, anxiety allows us to do this in passive way.

When we discussed the topic of the appropriation of the hermeneutic situation by means of the phenomenon of everydayness, I warned that public interpretation imposes conditions on the possible ways in which one can see life, and this imposition might make these ways of seeing non-primordial. This suspicion is confirmed by Heidegger's early lecture courses. In many of them, life appears to have a structural tendency toward covering-up (*Verdeckung*), ruinance (*Ruinanz*), plummeting (*Sturz*), masking (*Maskierung*) and the fall (*Verfallen*) (GA 61, 131; GA 63, § 6; GA 20, § 29; SuZ, § 38). We also saw that the phenomenological analysis of factical life involved three fundamental intentional elements: the sense of holding (*Gehaltssin*), the relational sense (*Bezugssinn*) and the sense of actualization (*Vollzugssinn*). The first one makes direct reference to life and the world in which our actions take place; the second one points to the way we relate to the surrounding world through care; and the third one indicates the way in which life temporalizes itself in the modality of the ruinance (GA 61, 85–90, 90–124, 125–155). In this type of inauthentic actualization of existence, life's intrinsic tendency towards concealment and the fall becomes apparent. Insofar as life cannot fully appropriate its own existence, it takes refuge behind the mask of the dominant collective representations. The idea that the implicit self-understanding we have in our dealings with the world includes the possibility of distorting the very being of life is present throughout the aforementioned lecture courses. Our immediate everyday experience, in which life and world have a relation of co-belonging, does not seem to provide us with a definite understanding, and on the contrary, threatens to conceal the real phenomena from us. It is clear this is what *Being and Time* frames in terms of inauthenticity, although here the vocabulary is much more dramatic and expressionist.

The structural tendency toward concealment affects how primordial the experience of factical life can be. It is here that hermeneutics, as a movement of un-concealment, un-veiling and un-masking, enters the scene. Life also has a capacity to interrogate itself as regards its own existence. This pre-reflective search for transparency constitutes a tendency that opposes the fall. On the basis of that tendency, life is capable of neutralizing and suspending the validity of public interpretations and thus of opening up the possibility of a primordial understanding 'in *struggle against its own factical ruinance*' (GA 61, 153/PIA, 114, italics in the original). This countermovement ultimately rests on the fundamental experience that gives us awareness of our own being. In the 1924 conference, 'The Concept of Time', Heidegger starts to talk about that experience in terms of our anticipation of the extreme possibility of death (BZ, 16–17). Soon enough, the phenomenon of anxiety is introduced in this regard, first, in the 1925 lecture course, *History of the Concept of Time*, and then in *Being and Time*. The 'what about' of anxiety is nothingness, that is, the pure and bare experience of being in the world (GA 20, 401–402). Anxiety's lack of determination is precisely what makes us face our thrownness (*Geworfenheit*) and take upon ourselves the possibilities that we in each case are. As Heidegger puts it in *Being and Time*: 'However, in anxiety there lies the possibility of a distinctive disclosure, since anxiety individualizes. This individualizing fetches Dasein back from its falling prey and reveals to it authenticity and inauthenticity as possibilities of its being' (SuZ, 190–191/BT, 184). Anxiety opens up the space for the immediate self-givenness of life, and thus makes possible a primordial access to it. In this way, insofar as anxiety disconnects us from the everyday understanding in which we are habitually immersed, it bears some resemblance to Husserl's phenomenological reduction.

But it is still worth asking, what exactly happens with the moment of reduction in Heidegger's hermeneutic phenomenology? Is phenomenology possible without a reduction? For many years now, two answers have been on offer in the literature. On the one hand, some claim that there is no trace of reduction in *Being and Time*. Typically, this claim is substantiated either by alluding to Heidegger's intention of distancing himself from Husserl, or by arguing that the analysis of being-in-the-world excludes a moment of suspension of a prior mode of understanding (Landgrebe 1963; Schacht 1972; Biemel 1977). On the other hand, some commentators hold that Heidegger's analysis of the world presupposes the whole problem of reduction.[28] The absence of a moment of reduction in Heidegger's inquiry is not the result of abandoning the phenomenological-transcendental standpoint but of a radicalization of it. The absence of the *epoche* is the result of Heidegger's wanting to keep intentionality free from Husserl's theoretical and objectifying scheme (Tugendhat 1967, 263ff.). In the background of this debate, the question has been asked whether Heidegger ever really participated in the phenomenological project (García Gaínza 1997, 190) or at some point moved away from it (Pöggeler 1983, 92). Husserl himself declared in a 1931 letter to Pfänder that '[...] Heidegger's phenomenology is completely different to mine' (Husserl 1994, vol. II, 182) and then added: 'I have come to the sad conclusion that, from a philosophical point of view, I have nothing to do with this deep Heideggerian sense, with this brilliant a-scientificity' (1994, vol. II, 184).

In contrast, Held and Herrman do not accept this view and have repeatedly argued that Heidegger always worked within the framework of phenomenology, even if at certain point he stopped using the term. I would go even further and say that Heidegger radicalized phenomenology, understood, literally, as the enterprise of 'going to the root of things themselves' in their immediate givenness, and thus prior to all rupture, suspension, cancellation or reduction (*epoche*) of the world of lived experiences. Heidegger's numerous investigations, from his first Freiburg period onwards, on the being of factical life and Dasein move within a phenomenological framework, even if not a transcendental one – as was the case with Husserl. The fact that Heidegger does not apply a phenomenological reduction does not mean he abandoned phenomenology. What is characteristic of phenomenology is not the *epoche*, but the way it arrives at things themselves. And in this sense, Heidegger's work is profoundly phenomenological.

The publication of the Freiburg and Marburg lecture courses, especially those from 1925, *History of the Concept of Time*, gives us a clear picture of Heidegger's radicalization of Husserl's phenomenology. This process goes hand in hand with an immanent critique of the concept of reduction, as presented in *Ideas I*. The core of the critique is a characterization of the reduction as a way of going back to the constitutive acts of the absolute sphere of pure consciousness. 'In the reduction we disregard precisely the reality of the consciousness given in the natural attitude of factual human being. [...] In its methodological sense as a disregarding, then, the reduction is in principle inappropriate for determining the being of consciousness positively' (GA 20, 150/HCT, 109). This way of being of consciousness impedes any apprehension of the primordial ontological determinations.

In this context, Courtine proposes the suggestive hypothesis that anxiety is a repetition of the Husserlian phenomenological-transcendental reduction (1990, 232–234).[29] Over and beyond the initial existentialist interpretations of the notion of anxiety, what is important to appreciate is the methodological role of anxiety in the analysis of human life. Anxiety helps explain the transit from inauthenticity to authenticity. The starting point of fundamental ontology is the *factum* of inauthenticity, which involves ignorance of inauthenticity.

In this sense, the suspension of everyday certainties that anxiety produces is structurally similar to the parenthesizing of the natural attitude the reduction effectuates. Now anxiety is not the product of a reflective attitude adopted with the purpose of suspending the validity of the everyday world and going back to pure consciousness. Rather, anxiety embodies a way of finding one self in the world, a fundamental affective state (*Grundstimmung*) that puts us in front of ourselves. Heidegger criticizes Husserl's egological reduction precisely because it results in a private world-less self. Here is where the difference between anxiety and reduction becomes the most apparent: while the former originates in an affective state that gets hold of us, the latter is an attitude we can adopt for methodological reasons at any time.[30]

With anxiety, the method of transcendental reflection is inverted. Husserl cancels out the validity of the natural world in order to reach the domain of pure consciousness. Heidegger, in contrast, rejects the artificiality of transcendental reduction and takes the immediate experience of our surrounding world as the point of departure of his phenomenological-hermeneutic analysis. Lived experiences are no longer analysed from the point of view of subjectivity but from the point of view of the way we find ourselves in the world. Insofar as they are always opened to the world, these lived experiences have tremendous value for the existential analytic. This enterprise has to be faithful to the most relevant and wide-ranging of Dasein's possibilities in order to be able to clarify Dasein's being. Now, we do not gain access to the most 'relevant,' 'wide-ranging' and 'primordial' mode of being through reflection, but through anxiety. In this affective state and in the call of conscience, the possibility of authenticity, which is initially hidden, is attested to. Anxiety and the call of consciousness are methodologically crucial for Heidegger's fundamental ontology because they yield the same results Husserl expected from the self-transparency of reflection, although they do so in a passive way.

What is it that phenomenological reduction makes manifest? In Husserl, phenomenological reduction reveals transcendental subjectivity as the ultimate constitutive ground of the world. In Heidegger, phenomenological reduction reveals the being of Dasein in its different modes of existence. One could thus talk of two ways in which life is made manifest: in one, subjectivity runs away from the world; in the other Dasein calls for the world (Bernet 1994). Each of these ways in which life is made manifest is twofold: in Husserl, the subject constitutes the world and observes it. In Heidegger, Dasein faces the modalities of inauthenticity and authenticity. Even though both Husserl and Heidegger assign to the phenomenological reduction the role of making this double aspect of life manifest, they are far from saying the same. The way transcendental subjectivity manifests itself is radically different from the way Dasein does.

In Heidegger's case, the occurrence of certain malfunctions in natural life – for instance, a tool breakdown or a train delay – introduces a break in ordinary life that reveals the correlation between Dasein and the everyday world. Through the phenomenon of anxiety, which one may consider a second phenomenological-hermeneutic reduction, as opposed to Husserl's phenomenological-transcendental reduction, Dasein is able to understand the futility of its immersion into the things of the surrounding world. Thanks to anxiety and, especially, the call of conscience, Dasein discovers that its own being is split between absorption into everyday matters and the reactivation of its most proper possibilities. In this second reduction, Dasein is in a world that it no longer recognizes as its own, and has to face itself as regards the double possibility of authenticity and inauthenticity.

Comparative table of Husserl's reflexive phenomenology and Heidegger's hermeneutic phenomenology

We can summarize the difference between Husserl's reflexive phenomenology and Heidegger's hermeneutic phenomenology in Table 5.1.

The second step in the development of a hermeneutic phenomenology: the critique of Husserl's Cartesian turn

Heidegger's intense discussion of Descartes, which starts with the 1923–1924 lecture course *Introduction to Phenomenological Research* and is taken up again later in the 1969 Le Thor Seminar and the 1973 Zähringen Seminar (VS, 64–138), is also an indirect discussion of Husserl (Marion 1989, 121ff.; Greisch 1991, 50). Husserl himself praises Descartes and establishes him as a model to follow when laying the foundation

Table 5.1 The difference between Husserl's reflexive phenomenology and Heidegger's hermeneutic phenomenology

Reflexive phenomenology	Hermeneutic phenomenology
TRANSCENDENTAL SUBJECTIVITY Transcendental subjectivity, abstracted from the immediate world, is what constitutes reality	FACTICAL LIFE Factical life, which is always immersed in a hermeneutic situation, is the point of departure of the analysis
GIVENNESS (*Gegebenheit*) The sphere of intentional objects is primarily given through the objectivizing seeing of consciousness, which artificially isolates immediate lived experiences from the world in which they emerge	ENCOUNTERING (*Begegnung*) Immediate lived experiences of the surrounding world are not given in, or to, consciousness, but come to our encounter in the horizon of sense that articulates the symbolic world in which we ordinarily live
PERCEPTION (*Wahrnehmung*) Primordial access to the immediate world is grounded in the perception of the colours, shapes, surfaces and resistance of the intentional objects given to consciousness. These qualities are described according to the model of natural sciences	SIGNIFICATION (*Bedeutung*) Perception retains its validity but is no longer considered primordial and grounding. These features belong to the immediate a-theoretical understanding of human life. Things, persons and situations of the ordinary world are not, primarily, perceptible objects, but objects that have a concrete meaning
WHAT (*Was*) The theoretical attitude of natural sciences and the reflective attitude of phenomenology seek to establish and to express, in a categorial and conceptual way, the objective determinations of the extant things given to consciousness. Reflective phenomenology undertakes an analysis of the structures of consciousness, which, by following the deductive procedure of science, suppresses the worldly and historical context of experience in order to fix its objective content, that is, the 'what' of lived experience (like the colour, shape, weight, etc.)	HOW (*Wie*) The a-theoretical and genuinely phenomenological attitude does not establish the objective properties of the beings that show up in the world, but the way we are located in that world. The analysis concerns the structures of human life and is inspired by the hermeneutic method of the *Geisteswissenschaften*, which seeks to lay bare the roots of the meaningfulness of a world that is always already understood and to show how it manifests itself in a phenomenological way (for instance, in terms of 'being-in-the-world', care, solicitude, the they, the fall, etc.)
PROCESS (*Vorgang*) The mechanism of reflective representation by means of which lived experiences pass in front of the subject. This results in a phenomenon of de-vivification	APPROPRIATION (*Ereignis*) A mechanism of comprehensive repetition of the lived experiences of the surrounding world. By means of appropriation one apprehends lived experiences in a pre-reflective way and in their primordial way of givenness to a historical self
DE-VIVIFICATION (*Ent-lebung*) The result of applying the theoretical and reflective attitude, which analyses conscious lived experiences in an objective way but does not account for the factical, historical and temporal nature of life itself	LIVED EXPERIENCE (*Er-lebnis*) The result of applying the a-theoretical and hermeneutic attitude, which interprets lived experiences in their immediate givenness and as they arise from the primary ground of the life-world

EXPLANATION
(*Erklärung*)
A method consisting in laying down perceived things in front of consciousness in order to describe them and analyse their qualities thoroughly. In the case of natural science, the idea is to establish the causes of a phenomenon, in the case of Husserl's phenomenology, to bring every phenomenon back to the constitutive subjectivity of the transcendental ego

SCIENCE
(*Wissenschaft*)
Husserl's conception of phenomenology imitates the model of natural sciences and thus parenthesizes the natural world in order to reach an ideal access to the pure lived experiences of the ego. The eidetic description of phenomenological science still employs categories

INTENTIONALITY
(*Intentionalität*)
The starting point of the phenomenological description is the self, that is, an intentionality that is directed towards an immanent element of psychological consciousness which is the ground of lived experiences

REDUCTION
(*Reduktion*)
Access to pure subjectivity is achieved through an explicit reflective act, that is, depends on a reflective attitude the ego can adopt freely. In contrast, anxiety throws us to the world as such against our own will

REFLECTION
(*Reflexion*)
Husserl's point of departure is the suspension of the natural attitude and the world immediately given to the self. In this way he establishes an objectifying interpretation of the primordial way in which things present themselves. In his view, it is only in reflection that consciousness of oneself becomes possible

OBSERVATION
(*Hinsicht*)
The detached and reflective way of seeing things in the world, which starts from the lived experience of the immediacy of life and transforms it into a purely observed object

UNDERSTANDING
(*Verstehen*)
A method consisting in penetrating the nexus of signification that constitutes the world as an irreducible symbolic space and a horizon of meaning that is always already open and available to Dasein. It does not consist in an endeavour of objectification and representation but in an immersion in the historical texture of life

PRIMORDIAL SCIENCE
(*Urwissenschaft*)
Heidegger's conception of phenomenology concerns the sphere of factical life and not the region of a particular science. The understanding life has of itself, which life acquires directly from its own practical relation with the world, is expressed in terms of formal indicators

CARE
(*Sorge*)
Heidegger rejects the idea that there is a psychic region that is the specific domain of intentionality and puts the accent on life's care for its lived experiences of the surrounding world

ANXIETY
(*Angst*)
Primordial access to the world occurs through the fundamental affective state of anxiety. Anxiety has a crucial methodological role because, in a passive way – i.e. without the subject's adopting a particular attitude – it allows us to reach a point of self-transparency similar to the one associated with Husserl's reduction

REPETITION
(*Wiederholung*)
Heidegger's starting point is the idea that factical life reveals itself in a pre-reflective way prior to any reflective explicit articulation. The repetition is a prolongation of that movement of self-understanding; that is to say, life itself is aware of its primary and spontaneous level of understanding and pre-reflective givenness

IMMERSION
(*Hingabe*)
The essentially practical way of grasping the meaning of lived experience through absorption in the meaningful current of life and in direct contact with the things of the surrounding world

(continued)

Table 5.1 (Continued)

Reflexive phenomenology	Hermeneutic phenomenology
ACT OF CONSCIOUSNESS (*Bewußtseinsakte*) Reflective phenomenology focuses on the analysis of the different types of act that take place in the inner space of consciousness (seeing, remembering, imagining, and so on)	MODE OF COMPORTMENT (*Verhaltensweise*) Hermeneutic phenomenology analyses the different eminently practical modes of comportment of life in its dealing with the world (solicitude, care, taking care, etc.).

of a science of consciousness. Science originates in an effort to overcome the relativity of everyday experiences and their limitations for explaining the causality that governs the natural and worldly order. Hence, the scientific method tries to solve the problem of how to go from concrete to given things, whose content is determined by my senses, to the generalizing abstraction that focuses on the properties of things. In this way, in the modern age, a process of mathematization of the universe that eliminates all subjective elements starts to take place.

Now, in phenomenology, following the model of natural sciences involves an objectification and naturalization of consciousness that clearly need be avoided. Husserl himself was aware that the scientific ideal does away with a whole dimension of reality, namely, the subjective domain. The phenomenological distinction makes manifest the differences between the immediate experience of things in natural sciences and the lived experiences in phenomenological psychology.[31] Each type of experience has a different spatiality: nature and things are always given to us within a spatial perspective, whereas the psychic, insofar as it is not located in a place and has no corporal reality, is not given to us as belonging to a spatial dimension. Additionally, each type of experience responds to a different temporality: natural objects are framed by an objective temporal sequence; in contrast, the subjective time of consciousness admits of considerable variations. In this sense, it is possible to distinguish between the representation and thing represented, the desire and thing desired, and so on. The desire of eating the apple, say, cannot be located spatio-temporally by consciousness as I can locate the apple itself. The phenomenological seeing is not as interested in objective things as it is in the way these things are given, reflectively, to consciousness.

The world of things is given to us as essentially linked to an actual consciousness. And consciousness, in turn, is presented to us as having an absolute things-independent being (HU III/1, 69–74). The new science of consciousness has to face a very difficult problem, namely, that once the phenomenological reduction is performed, pure reflection finds itself immersed in a constant flow of phenomena. In general, it is peculiar to consciousness to float in a sea of ever-shifting phenomenological manifestations, reminiscent of the Heraclitean flux. In the face of this difficulty, Husserl argues that the investigation of consciousness regards the sphere of ideal essences rather than experiences per se. The science of facts (*Tatsachenwissenschaften*) moves within the field of observation and experimentation, while the science of essences (*Wesenswissenschaften*) does not have to appeal to experience, it advances by means of inference (HU III/1, 27–29/Ideas I, 61–63). In this sense, phenomenology is guided by the ideal of precision of mathematics, a decision of which Heidegger is severely critical. Husserl sees in the mathematical way of thinking an open door to consciousness in its purity. And so, in *Ideas I*, he appeals to the mathematical ancient eidetic disciplines, especially geometry and arithmetic (HU III/1, 149/Ideas I, 188).

The a priori thinking of mathematics allows one to free oneself from the fugacity of facts and focus on the study of the ideal possibilities and the necessary and universal laws of the eidetic science. At this level, the factical reality of particular phenomena is altogether irrelevant, for '*pure essential truths do not make the slightest assertion concerning facts*' (HU III/1, 17/Ideas 1, 57, italics in the original). The idea is to inquire into the domain of consciousness and its correlates according to its possibilities and laws, and irrespective of its concrete existence. Phenomenology, as science of essences, analyses consciousness and its transcendental structures. The meaning of a lived experience does not form throughout that experience. It forms later, when the self directs itself towards consciousness and connects it to something external so that it appears in abstraction from its sheer actuality. The meaning of a lived experience is constituted when one grasps, in a conscious and reflective way, a connection between the lived experience and something else, which in its simplest form is another lived experience with which the former enters into a relation of identity, similarity, difference, etc. Meaning is achieved in the reflective act of consciousness. As such, this idea is one of Heidegger's main targets.

The theoretical nature of Husserl's phenomenology does not allow us to get to things themselves. Rather, things appear distorted through the prism of reflective subjectivity. In the aforementioned 1923–1924 lecture course, Heidegger accuses Husserl of Cartesianism on the basis that he defends, both in his well-known paper from 1911, 'Philosophy as Rigorous Science', and in *Ideas I*, the modern ideal of certainty and evidence (GA 17, 43).[32] Heidegger judges Husserl's procedure more severely than he did in the first Freiburg lecture courses and affirms that his criterion of evidence is determined by '*the predominance of an empty idea of certainty and [is] therefore fantastic*' (GA 17, 43, italics in the original). Husserl's appeal to the notion of evidence is motivated by '*the concern for* an *absolute knowledge*' (GA 17, 43, italics in the original), which is in accord with his idea of phenomenology as rigorous presuppositionless science. The ultimate goal is to '*conquer and establish an absolute scientificity*' (GA 17, 72, italics in the original), inspired by the ideal of mathematical knowledge advocated by Cartesianism. But in this way things do not show themselves from out of themselves, but from out of the imposition of a determinate type of knowledge, one with claims to absolute certainty, just like physical-mathematical knowledge. The prevalence of the ideas of certainty and absolute knowledge explains why consciousness becomes phenomenology's true field of study. Husserl's criticism in *Philosophy as Rigorous Science* is directed toward the naturalism and historicism he perceived in philosophy and, especially, towards the naturalization of consciousness and ideas.

Husserl's ultimate goal was to purify the sphere of consciousness from all naturalist, historicist and psychologist remnants, and in this way lay the foundations of philosophy as rigorous science. For Heidegger, however, Husserl's procedure '*absolutizes the idea of a scientific treatment of consciousness*' (GA 17, 71, italics in the original). This means that Husserl privileges the criterion of scientificity and absolute certainty over the pure givenness of things themselves. From the outset, things are submitted to the ideal of scientificity, which explains why the mathematical knowledge of nature embodies the prototype of knowledge *par excellence*, that is, 'justified knowledge', 'valid knowledge' and 'evident and universally binding knowledge' (GA 17, 83, 101).

Husserl's interest in achieving a rigorous and scientific knowledge of the way the structures of consciousness work can be traced back to the Cartesian notion of the *cogito sum* understood as *cogito certum*. Husserl appropriates the *cogito sum* and its attendant *certitudo* as the starting point of eidetic transcendental reduction. However, the excessive emphasis on the Cartesian obsession with certainty warps some of Husserl's phenomenological findings, intentionality in particular. Intentionality is disfigured the moment one understands it as a primarily theoretical comportment; this determines the way one sees and analyses intentional acts (GA 17, 271).

This way of considering lived experiences paralyses and objectivizes the vital flux of consciousness. The description of something is already the thing represented. Thus, the phenomenological description always concerns a represented thing that has already been previously understood. As a matter of fact, this is one of the main objections Natorp made to Husserl after the publication of *Ideas I*: any experience, inasmuch as it is expressed with concepts, is objectified and subjected to a process of homogenization that dissolves its particularity (Natorp 1917/1918).[33] Pure subjectivity manifests itself as what is left after a process of phenomenological reduction that detains the vital flow of lived experiences. The application of the mathematical model of knowledge, which starts with Plato and comes to fruition with Descartes, cannot grasp the fluctuating movement of life; what is more, concepts fix reality and cause a reflective modification of the stream of lived experiences. Treating lived experiences in a scientific way robs them from their 'lived' character. The epistemological approach isolates lived experiences and transforms them into something object-like. But as Natorp points out, 'the streaming stream is something different of what is grasped and retained in reflection' (Natorp 1917/1918, 231).[34] Inasmuch as consciousness is infinite and unlimited, it is not possible to gain a finite and absolute knowledge of it. It is even less plausible that a mere disconnection from the world, that is, a purely negative comportment, could be capable of showing pure consciousness. From Natorp's point of view, it is necessary to dissolve the clear-cut dualism of consciousness and object and to underscore the intimate relation they have to each other on the basis of the primordial potentiality of life. Heidegger takes on board a good part of Natorp's critical observations and values his insistence on the dynamic and kinetic character of lived experiences.[35]

The third step in the development of a hermeneutic phenomenology: immanent critique of phenomenology and the emergence of the question regarding being

A full actualization of the phenomenological programme of a primordial science of life and a hermeneutics of facticity ultimately involves facing the question regarding being, as regards both being in general and the being of the intentionality that is at play in all the acts of factical life. For Heidegger, this twofold question is a result of an internal demand of phenomenology. In order to comply with this demand, it is necessary to assess both Husserl's notion of pure consciousness as the thematic field of phenomenology and the method of reduction. Heidegger carries out this enterprise in full detail in his long introduction to the 1925 lecture course, *History of the Concept of Time* (GA 20, 34-182/HCT, 27-131). Here Heidegger sets out his position regarding some of the main themes of Husserl's transcendental phenomenology, such as consciousness, being, intentionality, phenomenological reduction and categorial intuition. From that moment onwards, the relation between Husserl and Heidegger follows two tendencies: continuity and deviation. The continuity is formal and to some extent methodological; the divergence regards the basic claims and the answers to concrete problems. As mentioned, Heidegger's thinking here brings Husserl against Husserl, as it were, in the name of a new beginning, understood as a return to things themselves. Strict application of Husserl's motto demands an internal critique of the phenomenology of consciousness in order to safeguarding being. The resulting ontology perforates the logical structures of phenomenology, and the self-givenness of being ends up prevailing over the reflective productivity of consciousness. The main targets of Heidegger's critique are, as seen, the notion of consciousness, the issue of reduction, the conception of intentionality and the status of categorial intuition. Since I have already addressed the problem of categorial intuition when discussing formal indicators,[36] I will focus now on Heidegger's stance concerning consciousness, reduction and intentionality.

The ontological features of consciousness

The scope of Heidegger's critique of Husserl's notion of consciousness is basically limited to *Ideas I*. Heidegger draws attention to the fact that Husserl attempts to delimitate and define the primordial domain of consciousness. With this, Husserl would be going beyond a purely methodological concern and into an ontological enterprise that sees in consciousness a particular way of being. The question is whether, in delimitating the thematic field of phenomenology, Husserl poses the question regarding the being of consciousness. Heidegger's discussion goes through the consideration of four determinations of being: immanent being, absolute being, absolutely given being and pure being.

First, on the basis of distinguishing between inner and outer perception, Husserl ascribes to consciousness the property of being immanent (HU III/1, 84-86/Ideas 1, 123-125). Heidegger points out that 'immanence is not a determination of the entity in itself with regard to its being, but a reflection of two entities within the region of lived experience or consciousness' (GA 20, 142/HCF 103). However, Husserl remains silent regarding the being of this relation.

Second, absolute being refers to the distinctive way in which lived experiences are given. In contrast to external perceptions, in which the object is presented from different perspectives, lived experiences present things in their concreteness. 'We perceive the Thing through the "perspective" manifestations of all its determinate qualities which in any given case are "real," and strictly "fall" within the perception. *An experience has no perspectives*' (HU III/1, 96-97/Ideas 1, 134, italics in the original). Again, Heidegger recalls that calling lived experiences 'absolute' means that they can be thematized as possible objects of reflection and irrespective of the thing itself they represent (GA 20, 143/HCT, 104).

Third, after cancelling out the validity of the natural world through the reduction, the only thing that is given to me in an absolute manner is consciousness:

> It is this which remains over as the 'phenomenological residuum' we were in quest of: remains over, we say, although we have 'suspended' the whole world with all things, living creatures, men, ourselves included. We have literally lost nothing, but have won the whole of Absolute Being, which, properly understood, conceals in itself all transcendences, 'constituting' them within itself.
> HU III/1, 118–119/Ideas 1, 154–155; quotation marks in the original

Every being is relative to consciousness. And so the idealist primacy of subjectivity over objectivity comes fully into place. But in this way entities as such are not grasped in their being. All that one can do is to establish a priority order that 'assigns to [consciousness] in this a formal role of being earlier than anything objective' (GA 20, 145/HCT, 106).

And fourth, on Husserl's account, consciousness is defined as a pure transcendental field with no links to concrete reality (HU III/1, 195–196/Ideas 1, 233–234). For Heidegger, Husserl appeals to the ideal of consciousness, the a priori structure of intentionality, and forgets about the intentional being itself: 'This character of being, consciousness as pure, shows especially clearly that what matters here is not the ontological characters of the intentional but the determination of the being of intentionality, not the determination of the being of the entity which has the structure intentionality, but the determination of the being of structure itself as intrinsically detached' (GA 20, 146/HCT, 106).

Now, none of these four determinations of consciousness is warranted by a phenomenological approach to the thing itself, namely, the being of consciousness. What is at play in Husserl's notion of consciousness is a scientific prejudice that requires pure consciousness as the object of inquiry. Those four determinations prevent us from seeing the true being of consciousness; they only show the being of consciousness 'as *apprehended, given, constituting and ideating*' (GA 20, 146/HCT, 106, italics in the original). As seen when discussing Heidegger's criticism of Husserl's Cartesian shift in *Ideas I*, this view does not involve a return to things themselves as much as a return to the traditional idea of absolute certainty, typical of modern philosophy. This criticism resurfaces in the 1925 lecture course, *History of the Concept of Time*:

> Husserl's primary question is simply not concerned with the characters of the being of consciousness. Rather, he is guided by the following concern: *How can consciousness become the possible object of an absolute science?* The primary concern which guides him is the *idea of an absolute science*. This idea, that consciousness is to be the region of an absolute science, is not simply invented; it is the idea which has occupied modern philosophy ever since Descartes. The elaboration of pure consciousness as the thematic field of phenomenology is *not derived phenomenologically by going back to the matters themselves* but by going back to a traditional idea of philosophy.
> GA 20, 147/HCT, 107, italics in the original

Heidegger makes explicit that the Husserlian determinations of the being of consciousness express external features of the way consciousness presents itself to itself in reflection, but not of the 'very being' of consciousness. To this theoretically laden idea on which being is grasped by means of reflective consciousness, Heidegger opposes the notion of beings in themselves, that is, the idea that the specific way in which things present themselves as 'themselves' is correlative to a specific comportment.

The limit of phenomenological reductions

Having discussed the critique of consciousness, the next question to be considered is whether phenomenology can address the question regarding being, particularly, whether the method of phenomenological reduction is useful at all for the ontological inquiry. Heidegger is straightforward in ascertaining that since this method suspends the validity of the natural attitude, it is completely incapable of apprehending the being of consciousness. The reason is that 'it involves precisely giving up the ground upon which alone the question of being of the intentional could be based' (GA 20, 150/HCT, 109).[37]

Another obstacle the reduction places in the way of the ontological inquiry is the fact that it keeps us in the space of the 'what' (*Was*), that is, the eidetic content, and leaves the 'how' (*Wie*), the mode of being of concrete objects, aside. In this sense, the reduction permits us to, say, distinguish the essence of colour from that of tone, without even asking oneself about the being of their respective objects. When one establishes the *essentia* of colour and of tone, one is not considering the *existentia* of the real object. Through the reduction, pure consciousness only shows 'the what, the structure of the acts, but as a result does not thematize their *way to be*, their being as such' (GA 20, 151/HCT, 109, italics in the original). Now, if we ask ourselves about the mode of being of intentionality, the intentional being has to be given to us in a primordial way. Where does this happen? Precisely in the natural attitude that the *epoche* parenthesizes. In the natural attitude, being – the reality of intentionality – is co-apprehended (GA 20, 153/HCT, 111). Without saying it explicitly, here Heidegger is clearly thinking of Dasein, who has a pre-reflective understanding of being.

The core of the disagreement between Husserl and Heidegger is the way they understand the natural attitude. Heidegger objects to two aspects of Husserl's description of the natural attitude: the fact that it has a naturalistic character, and its theoretical load. As regards the first point, the question is how does consciousness manifest itself in the natural attitude? Does it manifest itself as something 'naturalized'? For Heidegger, consciousness has been naturalized by theoretical reason, which thus transmits a traditional view of human being as rational animal, person, spirit, and so on. In this way, a preconception of consciousness sneaks in. But this 'is an experience which is totally *un*natural. For it includes a well-defined theoretical position, in which every entity is taken a priori as a lawfully regulated flow of occurrences in the spatio-temporal exteriority of the world' (GA 20, 155–156/HCT, 113). Husserl's posture stays in the terrain of objectifying reflection, in which beings only show themselves as beings for the contemplation of consciousness. The study of consciousness as the thematic field of phenomenology does not include the question regarding the being of intentionality.

These considerations take us well into Heidegger's second objection. The true natural attitude, in which we live prior to any reflection, is not something we can alternatively and voluntarily switch on and off; it is at play at all times (GA 20, 156/ HCT, 113). The point of departure of Heidegger's critique is not a reflective subject that faces a definitely objectified world, but the primordial understanding of factical life; and factical life is always in a process of actualizing itself in the world. This idea is already present in the 1919 project of phenomenology as primordial science of life. Heidegger envisages this project as a return to the primordial source of intentionality, starting with concrete human existence.

But 'what is the point of this questioning of being?' (GA 20, 157/HCT, 114). Utility is not a criterion for knowledge. Up to this point, posing the question regarding the being of intentionality might look like just a possibility, but we will see that for Heidegger it is absolutely necessary. Heidegger describes Husserl's phenomenology as a-phenomenological, for the reason that it overlooks the ontological dimension of intentionality. Husserl was fascinated by the laws of ideal thinking, that is, laws that were independent of the real laws of psychic processes. As a consequence, his opposition to naturalism led him to Dilthey's personalist posture, as attested in Husserl's paper, 'Philosophy as a Rigorous Science'. Dilthey himself made manifest in his latter writings his debt to Husserl in relation to the problem of the grounding of the *Geisteswissenschaften*. But he was also appalled by what Husserl says about history in the aforementioned paper. Heidegger goes even further in his appraisal of Dilthey, and says that even though Dilthey lacked the required resources, one can perceive in his work an inclination toward the question regarding being that is stronger than Husserl's.

Being-in-the-world as the ground of intentionality

In the 1921–1922 lecture courses, Heidegger says: 'What has always disturbed me: did intentionality come down from heaven? If it is something ultimate: in which ultimacy is it to be taken? [...] In regard to all categorial structures of facticity, intentionality is their basic formal structure' (GA 61, 131/PIA, 98).

Heidegger does not hesitate to consider intentionality as grounded in our being-in-the-world. The structural starting point of Heidegger's reflection is the horizon of the previously given world and the being of a temporally extended consciousness. With this ontological framing in place, the naïve idea of consciousness as something that constitutes itself is destroyed. In the new view, the world and temporality are the conditions of possibility of consciousness, which is therefore no longer what constitutes other things but something that is constituted, and this in a worldly and temporal way. This is the root of the conception of Dasein as thrown project (*geworfener Entwurf*). Dasein has the capability of opening the world in an understanding way, but always within a horizon that has already been understood. And so Heidegger's break with the classic notion of *subjectum*, understood as the motionless, self-enclosed ground of reality, is completed.

But how does Husserl solve the problem of the world? That is, the problem of how a non-worldly consciousness is able to transcend towards the world? Husserl locates transcendence toward the world in the immanence of consciousness. Now how can the knowledge of objects be warranted? How can the subject go out of herself and reach out to objects? (GA 20, 139/HCT, 101). The real problem lies in the worldliness of the subject. Going back to things themselves leads us to face the mystery of the worldliness of the subject. This mystery concerns the relation between the interiority of subjective life and the exteriority in terms of which human beings see themselves. The transcendental standpoint forgets that the perception of something is itself a perception in the world, because the subject sees herself as being in the world. The act of perception does not take place outside of the world; it is part of bodily subjectivity, which can only perceive things insofar as it projects horizons that can be verified through bodily movements. Perception is an activity that belongs to a concrete and bodily determined consciousness, not to an abstract one.

Husserl's crucial mistake, as Merleau-Ponty noted, rests in his conception of pure consciousness and of reduction as the way of getting access to this consciousness. The problem is not only that a complete reduction could only be accomplished by a pure spirit – because even our reflections take place in the very temporal flow that the reduction seeks to capture – but, above all, that there is simply no such pure consciousness. Consciousness is always committed to the world. Our contact with the world does not rest in a constituting consciousness; quite the opposite, our consciousness is embedded in our vital contact with the world. 'We have to ask ourselves if we really perceive the world. It is just the opposite: the world is what we perceive. [...] The world is not what I think, but what I live; I am opened to the world, I communicate with it and without doubts, even though it is not my possession, for it is inexhaustible' (Merleau-Ponty 1945, xi–xii). We are committed to the world. Our body bounds us to the world with a myriad of intentional links, even before the world appears to us as a representation in consciousness. Representative consciousness is nothing but one form of consciousness (Merleau-Ponty 1945, iii–iv).[38]

And yet, according to Husserl's analysis of intentionality, the ways in which things are given to consciousness are never completely isolated. Rather, they interlock in a nexus of references which constitutes the background of intentional lived experiences. In this sense, were one to be completely strict in applying the principle of evidence, one should recognize but one phenomenological theme, namely, the horizon of the world. The categorial domain could be explained on the basis of the horizon of the world, which, as a totality, has a purely formal character. In discussing Husserl, Heidegger reformulates the phenomenological maxim, 'to the things themselves', in a singular form, 'to the thing itself' (GA 20, 104ff./HCT, 76). As Eugene Fink argued, this modification is completely justified, for in the end phenomenology is concerned with only one thing: the world as prior and unsurpassable disclosedness (Fink 1993, 339). Husserl's mistake was to locate the world in the domain of the immanent constitution of transcendental subjectivity. In my view, even though Heidegger brings the theoretical view of intentionality back to its original meaning as being-in-the-world, he is not able either to solve the paradox of the world. The reason is that Heidegger substitutes the constitutive function of intentionality with being, rather than with the world, as one would expect. This is the result of a process in which problems are increasingly seen as ontological in nature. As we will see in the final section, this process rests in the presupposition of the ontological difference.

The question regarding the essence of the world is the central problem of the phenomenological reflection. What do we find when we inquire into the world? Do we find a subject that lives the world as a conscious flux of intentional lived experiences or a subject that finds in the world a horizon for her own projects and possibilities? On both hypotheses, the world is the a priori where things are experienced in a particular way. We actualize this on the basis of our understanding of the world and of the languages that transmit the meaning of the world to us. Both formulas evince two opposed ways of understanding phenomenology. 'Life-world' is the central category of a phenomenology of consciousness; 'being-in-the-world' plays a similar role in the ontological-existential phenomenology of Dasein. Both consciousness and existence are in fact closely connected to the world, but they differ in the way they are connected to it. Consciousness relates to the world in an intentional way by means of the relation of reference that holds between lived experiences and their material contents. In contrast, the relation between Dasein and the world consists in the encounter and familiar dealing with things and human beings, by means of the practical attitudes of solicitude and taking care.

So here we have two conceptions of intentionality. The Husserlian one, on which intentionality is isolated from the world and enclosed in its own noetic activity; and the Heideggerian one, on which intentionality is opened to the world in its noematic dimension.[39] These two ways of conceiving intentional consciousness, one from the point of view of the *intentio*, the other from that of the *intentum*, correspond to two different ways of understanding the reduction and the categorial intuition. Husserl continually insists in the difference between the apprehension of perceptual objects and the apprehension of categorial objects. For his part, Heidegger purports to show the internal connection between both types of apprehension. Rather than having an isolated existence, ideas allows us to 'see' the perceived object. Husserl's reduction extracts things from the natural world and refers them to a logical and pure subjectivity. But that epistemological prejudice hides exactly what Heidegger is trying to find, namely, things themselves as they are in the world. The concept of reduction has to be reformulated in ontological terms, so that the transcendental reference is being, as it is discovered and understood in itself and from out of itself. In this way, whereas Husserl's notion of subjectivity attempts to solve the problem of knowledge, and Heidegger's notion of Dasein concerns the problem of existence. The theoretical-speculative priority of pure consciousness is replaced with Dasein, understood as necessarily related in everyday life to what is at hand, which Dasein takes care of. Consciousness, according to Heidegger, has to be conceived as being in the world. Husserl's phenomenological reduction, which relates every phenomenon to a pure self, is substituted by an ontological reduction that construes every entity as being in the world. The core of Heidegger's criticism of Husserl is that the subject must be understood in terms of the ground of intentionality. In *Ideas I*, the goal of the phenomenological meditation is to expound the phenomenological reduction and establish the structures of pure consciousness. Consequently, intentionality gets trapped in a scheme of the epistemological geography of the domain of pure consciousness and its capabilities for constitution. The purpose of the second section of *Ideas I* is to secure an autonomous field of study for phenomenology. This explains why Husserl insists in separating pure consciousness from its natural embeddedness in the world.

For Husserl, in order to preserve the pure and independent essence of consciousness, its empirical connection to the body must be parenthesized. In his view, there is a form of access to the pure self that is different from, and superior to, the one us human beings have in our empirical existence. This more primordial form of access is reflection. For Husserl, reflection guarantees evidence, clarity and rigorousness, which are not within the reach of the natural attitude. Reflection is an intentional act, and the apodictic evidence it yields is grounded in the subject's interiority. Husserl extrapolates this model of reflection to all the other intentional acts, such as those of perception, memory, fantasy, imagination and so on. For Heidegger, this is nothing but a subjectivization of intentionality and a return to some kind of Cartesian metaphysics (GA 24, 91, 446/BP, 67, 313–314). Before posing the phenomenological question regarding the being of consciousness, Husserl has already construed it as a present and available object, that is, he has already located it in the subject/object scheme of knowledge. As the transcendental idealist he is, Husserl reduces the meaning of every being to a modification of a constitutive consciousness.

In arguing that neither the subject nor the object can be considered independently of the world and of history, Heidegger is rejecting the idea of pure transcendental subjectivity. All in the name of a return to things themselves. The historical world is given before the knowing subject and the object of knowledge. The subject and the object do not exist outside of the world. Both are given and understood in the world. The subject and the object, Dasein and beings, discover themselves in the concrete a priori of the world to which they belong. As Heidegger asserts in *Being and Time*: 'These determinations of being of Da-sein, however, must now be seen and understood *a priori* as grounded upon that constitution of being which we call *being-in-the-world*' (SuZ, 53/BT, 53, italics in the original). The phenomenological investigation of intentionality must show Dasein's transcendence, which is what makes being directed towards something possible (GA 24, 447/BP, 315).

Heidegger's reproach to Husserl is that in his hands the phenomenological reduction creates a breach that is directly opposite to the relational character of intentionality. The *distinctio pheamenologica* Husserl talks about in his 1910–1911 lecture course separates human being from consciousness, the immanent *intentio* from the transcendent *intentum*, the constituting being from the constituted being, and absolute consciousness from the world. The eidetic reduction effects this separation. For Husserl this reduction allows us to go from empirical phenomenology to an a priori phenomenology of pure consciousness. Heidegger thinks this a-temporal structure of the transcendental *ego* transforms phenomenology into some kind of 'noumenology' that forgoes the individual facticity of human beings. Heidegger aims at a much more natural and direct approach to intentionality. He emphasizes the fact that, at the very core of intentionality, *intentio* and *intentum* stand in a relation of co-belonging. And he finds no arguments that could justify, in a phenomenological manner, a separation between human factical existence and human pure consciousness. For in the end, in which of these two domains would one expect to find the being of intentionality? For this reason, Heidegger asks about the a priori of intentionality on the basis of the concrete individual effectuation of human intentional comportments.[40]

The phenomenological description of the process in which intentionality is actualized is the leading thread of the analysis of the being of intentional objects and of the subject of intentionality. The intentionality of being-in-the-world allows us to understand the being of things as serviceable and the being of ourselves as care. In our ontic comportment toward existent things and care, we reach an experience of transcendence, or to put it otherwise, the pre-understanding of the world that intentionality presupposes is revealed to us. This pre-understanding of the world is precisely what takes us to the being of intentionality as existential disclosedness and transcendence. Therefore, intentionality is grounded in a world that is yet to be discovered. For this reason, Heidegger talks about the ontological difference between intentionality and transcendence: 'Intentionality is the ratio cognoscendi of transcendence. Transcendence is the ratio essendi of intentionality in its diverse modes' (GA 24, 91/BP, 65). In this view, the unity of the subject is no longer supratemporal, but is disseminated across the temporal horizon of the world.

Briefly, Heidegger's critical discussion of Husserl's conception of intentionality can be summarized in three points. First, reducing every transcendent object to consciousness implies overlooking the ontological difference between *intentio* and *intentum*. Second, rather than being the result of the mental activity of an immanent subject, the being of intentionality is expressed in the disclosedness of, and transcendence toward, the world. Third, in opposition to Husserl's distance from the facticity of human existence, for Heidegger, the point of departure of the phenomenological inquiry into the being of intentionality must be the analysis of human intentional comportments in concrete and ordinary life. In this way, the transition from a pure self to factical Dasein, from reflection to care, comes to completion. And so the priority of *praxis* over *theoria* is established. From Heidegger's point of view, Husserl's phenomenological reduction is a procedure of separation that goes against intentionality's relational and transcendent nature.

The fourth step in the development of a hermeneutic phenomenology: the elaboration of the full concept of the hermeneutic phenomenology of Dasein

The foundation of hermeneutic phenomenology in the post-war semester of 1919 is grounded in a primordial thematic experience that demands a similarly primordial methodological treatment. From the thematic point of view, what is at stake here is the primordial experience of a-theoretical life; but this, in turn, calls for a primordial methodological experience that shows us that reflection does not grant us access to the domain of the a-theoretical. Husserl's reflective phenomenology, which Heidegger knew perfectly well on account of his work as Husserl's assistant and through his reading of Husserl's works, gives us access to, and allows us to describe, lived experiences, but only from a theoretical point of view; it does not give us the tools to understand the phenomenon of pre-theoretical life. Consequently, Heidegger transforms Husserl's phenomenology in a hermeneutic manner and so establishes a whole new conception of phenomenology. As Herrmann has shown (1994, 7–12; 2000, 119–121), all subsequent developments of hermeneutic phenomenology, as we find them in the Freiburg and Malburg lecture courses, are grounded in the discovery of the a-theoretical and pre-theoretical sphere of life and in the necessity of finding an adequate access to that sphere. The pathway of the hermeneutic phenomenology of factical and pre-theoretical life, which Heidegger started to travel in 1919, led him to the systematic hermeneutic phenomenology of Dasein presented in *Being and Time* (1927). It must be clear, in light of the three steps in the development of the hermeneutic phenomenology I have presented in the previous sections, that this enterprise is only possible against the background of Heidegger's discussion with Husserl's reflective phenomenology of consciousness. I have also pointed out the similarities and differences between both approaches.

What new elements does *Being and Time* bring to Heidegger's conception of hermeneutic phenomenology? Husserl and Heidegger share the same phenomenological starting point. Both adhere to the principle of going back to 'things themselves'. But there are stark differences between their respective methods of getting access to things themselves. Husserl favours the reflective method of reductions. For his part, in *Being and Time* and the 1927 lecture course, *The Basic Problems of Phenomenology*, Heidegger enriches the method of hermeneutic access to phenomena by incorporating hermeneutic reduction, construction and destruction.[41]

It is frequently forgotten that the term 'phenomenology' denotes, first and foremost, a mode of inquiry, a specific way of approaching phenomena. Phenomenology is not a philosophical discipline such as ethics, ontology and theory of knowledge. As a method, it does not refer to one specific and exclusive field of study. The thematic field of *Being and Time* is the being of beings and the meaning of being in general. And this field is approached in a phenomenological manner, that is, without drawing on a previous orientation. In this sense, Heidegger embraces many of the Husserlian formulations of the principle of the lack of presuppositions (HU XIX/1, 24/Log. Inv. 1, 263; HU III/1, 51/Ideas 1, 92). And just as Husserl invokes the methodological autonomy of phenomenology, Heidegger also vindicates the independence of his phenomenological seeing with respect to the phenomenological approaches of Husserl and Scheler.

Now, once one establishes that the subject matter of the inquiry is the being of beings, one has to show how to gain access to it. Which way will take us to the hidden being of beings? How can we wrest it from of its concealment? *Being and Time* is not fully clear in this respect. But it gives us the following hint: 'The way of encountering being and the structures of being in the mode of phenomenon must first be *wrested* from the objects of phenomenology. Thus the *point of departure* of the analysis, the *access* to the phenomenon, and *passage* through the prevalent coverings must secure their own method' (SuZ, 36/BT, 34, italics in the original). In the 1927 lecture course, *The Basic Problems of Phenomenology*, Heidegger spells out the three fundamental elements of the phenomenological method that allow us to carry out the triple task mentioned in the passage: phenomenological reduction, construction and destruction (GA 24, 26ff./BP, 19ff.). The phenomenological reduction secures the starting point of the inquiry, the phenomenological construction secures phenomenological access to the phenomenon of being, and the phenomenological destruction allows us to penetrate through the prevailing misconceptions that cover up the phenomena. Insofar as the phenomenological analysis looks away from intra-worldly beings and focuses on the a-thematic understanding we have of the ontological constitution of those beings, it is the first step toward an explicit thematization of the being of beings. The phenomenological construction unveils and opens up the proper mode of being of beings: on the one hand, the beings that do not have the mode of being of Dasein, are unveiled as concern (*Besorgen*) within the framework of a purposeful pattern; on the other, the being of Dasein is made manifest as existence and care (*Sorge*) within the meaningful horizon of the world. Finally, the phenomenological destruction allows us to penetrate, in a critical manner, the phenomena that cover up the being of beings, and thus enables us to distinguish between real phenomena and those phenomena that conceal the real ones; between phenomenon and appearance.

Husserl also talks of reduction as a method to get access to the pure domain of consciousness. We do not need to discuss the three levels of reduction again, suffice it to say that similar to Heidegger's three steps of the phenomenological method, the *epoche* and the reduction are also a method to gain access to the field of study of consciousness. Both Husserl and Heidegger talk about reduction but in very different senses. In Herrman's words, 'these senses of "reduction" are different to each other, as reflection and hermeneutics, as consciousness and Dasein' (2000, 150). Husserl's transcendental reduction is executed by a reflective attitude, while Heidegger's hermeneutic reduction proceeds in comprehensive terms. *Being and Time*'s methodological paragraph construes phenomenology as hermeneutics (SuZ, 37/BT, 35). The first task of hermeneutics is a phenomenology of Dasein, that is, an analysis of the fundamental ontological structures of Dasein and of the modes of being of the other entities. Now, insofar as the discovery of the meaning of being and of the fundamental structures of Dasein 'exhibits the horizon for every further ontological research into beings unlike Dasein' (SuZ, 37/BT, 35), one can say hermeneutics also establishes the conditions of possibility of all ontological investigation. In sum: 'Ontology and phenomenology are not two different disciplines which among others belong to philosophy. Both terms characterize philosophy itself, its object and procedure. Philosophy is universal phenomenological ontology, taking its departure from the hermeneutic of Da-sein' (SuZ, 38/BT, 36). As one can see, by incorporating three methodological devices, namely, reduction, construction and destruction, the hermeneutic phenomenology of Dasein, which was initiated as primordial science of life back in 1919, comes to completion.

Some caveats regarding Heidegger's interpretation of Husserl's phenomenology

Misunderstandings concerning Cartesianism and transcendental idealism

Husserl's query for a ground, such as consciousness, capable of providing us with a unique kind of evidence, has made him liable not only to the charge of Cartesianism – which Heidegger levels – but also of foundationalism. Husser's phenomenology has often been interpreted as an attempt to find a certain and indubitable ground that can become the starting point of any science.[42] No doubt, the title of one his better-known articles, 'Philosophy as Rigorous Science', is partly responsible for this interpretation. Husserl would say in response to this accusation that the phenomenological analysis of transcendental subjectivity has a very different status to that of a sociological inquiry into the consuming habits of the North American population, say. The idea is to inquire into the conditions of the possibility of experience, but this should not lead us to see in Husserl a defender of foundationalism, at least in the traditional sense of the term.

Husserl's view is different from classical foundationalism in at least two respects. On the one hand, he does not believe his own transcendental analysis to be conclusive. It can always be improved and extended. Philosophy, as a science that is based on ultimate justifications, can only be actualized in an infinite historical process (HU VIII, 186). On the other hand, Husserl explicitly distances himself from the ideally axiomatic and deductive method that is usually embraced by foundationalist rationalism. Phenomenology is not a deductive discipline, but a descriptive one, and for this reason Husserl insists that it is a kind of science different from mathematics (HU III/1, 171–174/Ideas 1, 209–211).

It is also important not to lose sight of Husserl's motivations. These are not primarily theoretical but practical, and express an ethical concern for a life of responsibility to oneself (HU VIII, 197). To live through the phenomenological attitude is not a neutral occupation, but reflects a personal decision. In other words, philosophy is closely linked to ethical life. In the first part of *Erste Philosophie*, Husserl refers to the Socratic-Platonic ideal of philosophy: 'Socrates's ethical transformation of life is characterized by understanding truly philosophical life as a life of pure reason [...] This means it is a life in which, through a constant gesture of self-reflection and radical responsibility, human being exercises a critique of his own goals, trajectory and significance' (HU VII, 9). This ethical motivation is particularly important in light of the fact that the task of finding an ultimate philosophical ground follows the ideal of an infinite search for truth, which demands from the philosopher, and therefore from the phenomenologist, a great amount of responsibility to oneself, to the others and to the community.

The most pressing and difficult objection to Husserl's philosophy, however, is the charge of transcendental idealism. For Husserl, every object has to be understood, necessarily, in relation to a constituting subjectivity. Hence, there is nothing independent of subjectivity. This seems to be a clear endorsement of idealism. Following the transcendental turn completed in *Ideas I*, and compellingly criticized by Heidegger, 'idealism' is understood as implying the primacy of transcendental subjectivity. This primacy is so central to Husserl that he often identifies phenomenology and transcendental idealism. But one should not understand the type of idealism Husserl defends either in opposition to realism, nor as a reduction of the reality of the world to mental contents. For Husserl, reality is not a brute, isolated fact, independent of all contexts of experience and conceptual apparatuses. Reality needs subjectivity in order to be articulated in a conceptual and comprehensive way. It is in this sense that reality depends on subjectivity. Objects only have a meaning to us thanks to our consciousness; particularly insofar as they are given to us according to different structures of presentation and with a determinate meaning. Talking about transcendent objects is talking about objects that are not part of my consciousness and cannot be reduced to my experience of them. Transcendent objects can always surprise us, that is, can show themselves in a different way than expected. But none of this implies that objects are independent of, and inaccessible to, consciousness, because it only makes sense to talk about transcendent objects insofar as they are transcendent *to us*. Evidently, this does not contradict or put into question the existence of the real world; it just amounts to a rejection of the objectivist interpretation of its ontological status. Husserl acknowledges as much in *The Crisis of European Sciences and Transcendental Phenomenology*: 'The fact that the world exists [...] is beyond doubt. But this is different from understanding this indubitable character and clarifying its legitimacy' (HU VI, 190–191). To paraphrase Putnam, the mind does not create the world, but is not limited to reflect it either (1978, 1).

Over and above the debate between idealism and realism, however, the true philosophical problem is how subjectivity constitutes the world. Many of the criticisms of Husserl insist that constitution is a creative process, and this entails an indefensible type of idealism. Husserl never clarified whether constitution was to be understood as creation or as reconstruction of reality. Be that as it may, claiming that the subject is the condition of possibility for the presentation of objects does not imply postulating a causal connection between the former and the latter. To use Dan Zahavi's suggesting image, constituting subjectivity must not be compared to some kind of Big Bang: it is not the beginning of a causal process determinative of objects.[43] What should we understand by 'constitution'? Briefly, it is the process that makes manifestation and meaning possible. As Heidegger observes, 'constituting' does not mean 'producing' in the sense of 'fabricating'; it means 'letting the entity be seen in its objectivity' (GA 20, 97/ HCT, 71). To dispel another common misunderstanding, this process is not deliberately initiated *ex nihilo* and controlled by the transcendental *ego*. For Husserl, at least in his later period, subjectivity is not the only necessary condition or possibility of constitution. Constitution involves several interrelated constituting elements, such as subjectivity, the life-world, the body and intersubjectivity. In other words, transcendental subjectivity can constitute the world only if it is embodied, is part of the social world and shares a historical-cultural world with others. As Husserl points out in *Ideas II*, I, we and the world belong to each other (HU IV, 288). Therefore, constituting subjectivity only accomplishes a full relation to itself in its relation to others, that is, in intersubjectivity. And this can only exist and develop as an interrelation between subjects that belong to the same world. Hence the world is to be understood as the sphere of a common and public experience. Seen this way, Husserl's analysis of the relation between the self, the world and others has striking similarities to the analyses of later phenomenologists such as Sartre and Merleau-Ponty, not to mention Heidegger himself.

It is particularly relevant for the present discussion that according to the analysis of passive synthesis that Husserl developed during the twenties, the process of constitution involves an element of facticity, of passive pre-givenness, free of any active contribution on the part of the ego (HU XI, 328, and HU XIII, 427). One should not interpret this as a new form of dualism. On the contrary, the idea is that subjectivity and the world cannot be understood independently of each other. Put another way, constitution is a process that takes place within the structure subjectivity-world, understood as the transcendental horizon in which objects can show themselves. For this reason, as we will see, in adopting genetic phenomenology, Husserl abandons the idea that there is a rigid correlation between what constitutes and what is constituted. What characterizes the constituting activity is a form of reciprocity in which the subject is constituted in the process of constitution. Consequently, saying that the transcendental subject remains unaltered throughout the process of constitution is also a misunderstanding that in light of the textual evidence one can gather from Husserl's work from the twenties on passive synthesis, intersubjectivity and the life-world, and needs to be eradicated.

The contributions of Husserl's genetic phenomenology

Naturally, explaining the fundamental ideas of Husserl's phenomenology and the stages it went through – static, genetic and generative phenomenology – goes well beyond the scope of this work. My goal in the present sections is just to dispel certain misunderstandings regarding Husserl's work and thus break with the widely held idea that Husserl was an idealist and defender of transcendental phenomenology.[44] This is important because many commentators still endorse Heidegger's classical interpretation of Husserl in an uncritical way.[45]

A particularly relevant indication of the influence of Heidegger's interpretation is the so-called transcendental turn of phenomenology. In contrast to positive science, phenomenology is not interested in the substantial nature of things, that is to say, their weight, colour or chemical composition, but in the way things are given to us. The phenomenological-transcendental question is, what are the conditions of possibility of the manifestation of things as such? Phenomenology tries to discover the essential necessary laws that govern the process by which consciousness constitutes a meaningful world.[46]

It is also common to hear that Husserl holds a transcendental view, whereas Heidegger and Merleau-Ponty reject the transcendental standpoint insofar as the constitutive structures they identify are located in being-in-the-world. But notwithstanding how widespread this interpretation is, it is a crude simplification. First, both Heidegger's Dasein and Merleau-Ponty's body – a concept that, by the way, is directly derived from Husserl – are transcendental in the sense that they make possible the openness of manifestation of the world as a meaningful totality. And second, even though a good part of Husserl's published work focuses on the constitutive structures of transcendental consciousness, the new material that has been recently published as part of *Husserliana* suggests that the mentioned focus is not completely representative of his later philosophical investigations.[47]

Husserl expanded his investigations significantly as his thought evolved. In this respect recall his analysis of the pre-egological structures of the body, his three volumes on the phenomenology of intersubjectivity and his works on historical and cultural life. His output from the twenties evinces that the transition from static to genetic phenomenology is an internal development of his work. Husserl starts to distinguish between the static and genetic methods of transcendental phenomenology in his lecture courses on transcendental logic, first given in the 1920–1921 semester, later expanded in the lecture courses from 1923 and 1925–1926 – they were partially published under the title *Analyses Concerning Passive Synthesis*. The distinction also appears in the 1922–1923 lecture course – an introduction to philosophy – and in his studies on active synthesis, which appeared as a supplement to the 1920–1921 lecture course on transcendental logic, *Active Synthesis. Lectures on Transcendental Logic*.[48] Genetic phenomenology distinguishes between active and passive synthesis. In the former, the subject plays an active role in the constitution of objects. The products of this constitution are tools, works of art, mathematical statements, scientific theories, and so on. All active syntheses, however, presuppose certain passivity that affects the subject. 'Passive' does not denote here inactivity. Rather, it refers to our being affected and influenced by habits, motor patterns, dispositions, motivations, emotions and memories. The phenomenological terrain is nowadays a particularly interesting field of study for psychological and neuroscientific research on emotions and cognitive processes.[49]

The task of transcendental logic is to show the transcendental-genetic origin of the highest products of thought, that is, categorial syntheses. This origin is pre-categorial experiences. While in *Experience and Judgment* Husserl distinguishes between pre-predicative and predicative acts, in the lecture courses on active synthesis he draws a distinction between passivity and activity. In Husserl's words: 'Passivity as such is the first thing, because all activity essentially presupposes a ground of passivity and a pre-constituted objectivity' (HU XXXI, 3).

The perceptive apprehension and identification of pre-constituted meaning in primordial passivity are forms of activity, but they belong to a pre-categorial level. It is precisely this activity within passivity that mediates between primordial passivity and full-blooded categorial activity. The self's tendency to active objectification is only possible on the basis of the primordial constitution of passive syntheses which originates in the constant flow of consciousness.

In sum, the genetic method broadens the elements of the structure of consciousness that *Ideas I* presented on the basis of the static analysis. In contrast to *Ideas I*'s analysis, in the new view the concrete self is understood, in an essentially relational way, as immersed in an intersubjective world, as situated in a historical community and as taking part of the horizon of meaning that the life-world is.[50] The genetic phenomenology Husserl started to develop in 1917 is not limited to the finished objective products of the constitution process, as static phenomenology was, but also takes into account the temporal situation of the subject. By making manifest the way the system of references emerges, Husserl expands considerably the field of phenomenological inquiry. In this conception, the experience of objects is based on layered habits; so when perceiving an object that has been perceived before, the self draws on features revealed in past acts of perception. Past experience predetermines, to some extent, the way future experience is expected to be, and this predetermination becomes more salient the more experiences of the same kind the self has. In this way, each confirmation strengthens the expectation, while each disappointment weakens it. Hence, each perception of an object is different from the previous ones. The self always has a horizon of acquired knowledge, a sphere of familiarity, as well as a system of typification, which is the result of a complex synthesis of association in which like attracts like, and which in this way becomes a permanent component of the object's meaning. This horizon is subject to constant modification insofar as it broadens and gets corrected with each new experience.

In this way, Husserl shows that the history of the transcendental subject is constituted by capacities that, as the genetic analysis reveals, are based on primordial foundational acts. Each of these acts is historical insofar as it is conditioned by previous acquisitions of knowledge and reflects past history, that is, the experience of a temporal horizon.

The self is not only the pole where intentional acts originate but also a substrate of habits, and this gives the self its own style, as it were, in the execution. This distinguishes the self from all other selves and this is why Husserl allows himself to talk of the self as a monad. As one can see, the self's relation to the world does not depend exclusively on conscious reflective acts but is also subject to bodily affections and to acquired habits and experiences. Put another way, the self is not only affected by perceptual data – primary passivity – but also by sedimented acts, understood as permanent acquisitions that at each moment connect to life by association – secondary passivity.

This explains the importance the topic of association acquires in the genetic analysis. The study of temporality does not supply an adequate view of the synthetic systems of the vital flux of consciousness. What is needed for this is a phenomenology of association that takes into account the constitutive role of the passive syntheses of similarity, uniformity, concretion, fusion, contrast, discretion and gradation, among other things. The crucial element of the phenomenological investigations carried out in *Analyses Concerning Passive Synthesis* is the phenomenon of affective allure (*Reiz*). Husserl gives the term '*Reiz*' a different meaning from the one it usually has, which has medical, physiological and mechanical connotations. *Reiz* denotes the motivational relation between the lived-body and the intentional object-like formations within a lived context. From this perspective, the affective allure is not an isolated or blind force but actually entails a motivational solicitation, i.e. that attention is drawn to something. This might receive an epistemic response – even though this response need not be self-involving (HU XI, §§ 26–35).[51] The process of association comprises a form of intentionality that belongs to the sphere of passivity and which is prior to the intentionality of an active self.

In any case, what is important to emphasize is that the inner evolution of Husserl's phenomenology is not only a matter of mere exegetical interest. A philosophical problem is at stake here. Transcendental phenomenology cannot limit itself to ego-logic philosophy of consciousness or of constituting subjectivity. 'Transcendental' denotes an attitude that is directed toward the root of phenomena; in other words, 'transcendental' embodies a type of philosophical explanation that purports to find the conditions of possibility of our experience of the meaningful world. These conditions lie much deeper than individual consciousness, they are anchored in our living bodies and the structures of our cultural and social world.

The ontological difference as an implicit premise

Having discussed the methodological scope of the hermeneutic transformation of phenomenology and spelled out the thematic analysis of the main ontological structures of human life, I finally want to draw attention to the implicit presupposition of the young Heidegger's thinking, namely, the ontological difference. With this element, the empirical/transcendental dichotomy of transcendental philosophy is replaced, in Heidegger's hermeneutic ontology, by the ontic/ontological dichotomy. At this point the question arises as to whether Heidegger is still moving within the coordinates of transcendental philosophy or is in fact de-transcendentalizing philosophy.[52] I do not intend to enter this debate. I think it is more interesting, first, to establish the similarities and differences between these philosophical approaches and then to show how Heidegger's appeal to the ontological difference allows him to perform a complex manoeuvre, namely, to deploy a transcendental strategy without a transcendental subject.

The similarities and differences between transcendental phenomenology and hermeneutic phenomenology

The context in which the Freiburg and Marburg lecture courses took place was characterized by the downfall of neo-Kantianism and an increasing enthusiasm for the philosophy of life. Dilthey, Nietzsche and Bergson substituted the productivity of life – no matter how opaque and diffuse – for the generative operations of the transcendental self. But they were not able to free themselves from the expressionist model of the philosophy of consciousness. For them, the idea that subjectivity exteriorizes itself in the objectifications of the human spirit but then these objectifications take the form of lived experiences was still valid. Heidegger fed on the reflections of these philosophers but nonetheless avoided the dominance that the concept of transcendental subjectivity had had since Kant. Both the primordial science of life and the hermeneutics of facticity rest on a radical critique of the transcendental subject of knowledge. The scientific method is by all accounts insufficient for understanding and articulating the context of meaning of human reality. Apprehending the meaningfulness of human life in its concrete facticity requires hermeneutic access, which is different from the type of access science offers. This critique, however, which implicitly rests on the ontological difference between being and beings, Dasein and other beings, still depends on the transcendental setting it is supposed to overcome. The attempt at dissolving the concept of subjectivity relies on a transcendental attitude that seeks to clarify, in a reflective way, the conditions of possibility of being-a-person as being-in-the-world. The philosophy of the subject can only be overcome by a philosophy just as systematic. This is what fundamental ontology provides.

Heidegger shares with neo-Kantianism and phenomenology the idea that philosophy has to provide the foundation of empirical sciences by means of an a priori inquiry into their basic concepts. Likewise, Heidegger agrees that it is necessary to extend Kant's transcendental project in order to deliver a genealogy of the different modes of being. In the intellectual context in which the young Heidegger was working, the main problem concerned the possibility of human sciences; that is, how to acquire scientific knowledge of human realities such as history, art and religion. This led many thinkers to search for a philosophical foundation not only of the *explanation* of natural phenomena but also of the *understanding* of cultural facts. To this effect, and taking Kant's *Critique of Pure Reason* as their starting point, Rickert, whom Heidegger knew perfectly well, and other neo-Kantians from the Baden and Windelband Schools, tried to extend transcendental philosophy toward a philosophy of values. In the Marburg School, Cassirer's project of a critique of culture had the same purpose. By the same token, the aim of Husserl's transcendental phenomenology was to provide a ground for all regional ontologies, not only for those of the natural sciences. Finally, within the historicist tradition, Dilthey's attempt at supplementing Kant's work with a critique of historical reason responded to the same motivations.

However all these attempts had to face the problem of how to reconcile the transcendental and the historical without sacrificing either. But, as the young Heidegger argues, the main problem of human sciences does not lie in their lack of a scientific grounding but in the idea that one can apply the scientific method in order to gain access to human reality as it is prior to any act of objectification. This explains Heidegger's obsession with destroying the 'primacy of the theoretical' and allows us to frame his efforts to develop a methodology adequate to the topic of the investigation, namely, human life.

It is not possible to address human life as the subject of inquiry without a methodology such as the one hermeneutic phenomenology provides and without clarifying first the meaning of being in general. This clarification has to establish the ontological conditions of possibility of sciences and their respective ontological regions. As early as 1922, in his *Natorp-Bericht*, Heidegger asserts: 'the basic problem of philosophy concerns the *being* of factical life. In this respect, philosophy is a *fundamental ontology* that deals with principles, so that this ontology of facticity provides the particular specialized regional ontologies of the world with a foundation for their problems a clarification of the sense of these problems' (NB, 254, italics in the original) This project comes to completion in 1927 with *Being and Time*. Here a new similarity with transcendental philosophy becomes apparent. Heidegger embraces an essential methodological element of all transcendental strategy: the priority of factical life or Dasein over all other beings.

The presentation of fundamental ontology in *Being and Time*'s introductory chapter – which basically sums up the results of the primordial science of life elaborated in 1919 and of the ontology of factical life, as presented in the *Natorp-Bericht* – is structured in three steps. First, Heidegger gives the transcendental approach an ontological meaning. Positive sciences concern ontical problems and formulate statements about nature and culture. However, he argues, science does not stem from cognitive elements that are available in subjectivity from the start. Rather, science is anchored in a concrete context, in the structure of being-in-the-world: 'sciences and disciplines are ways of being of Dasein' (SuZ, 13/BT, 12). One of the ingredients of a factically situated life is an understanding – no matter how blurry – of a world that is the horizon against which the meaning of beings has always been already interpreted. On the basis of this, beings can be objectified by the different sciences. We find this pre-ontological understanding of being when, through the transcendental attitude, we reach beyond the categorial constitution of beings. The outcome of the analysis of this prior understanding of the world is the description of the ontological structures Heidegger calls 'existentials'. Since these structures precede the categories of being as a whole, particularly the objectifying categories of science, the existential analytic of being-in-the-world deserves the name 'fundamental ontology'. This enterprise lays bare the transcendental-ontological foundations of regional ontologies.

The *second step* of Heidegger's presentation gives the phenomenological method the character of an ontological hermeneutics. Phenomena only show themselves indirectly. Entities hide their being in their ontic manifestations. Phenomenology seeks to bring to light that which remains veiled in beings. For this reason, it is necessary to uncover beings and thus make real phenomena present. In order to do this, Heidegger employs the hermeneutic method of interpretation rather than the Husserlian method of intuition. The way phenomena show themselves is not a process in which ideal essences make themselves present through intuition. What allows us to lift the veil that covers being is understanding the complex nexus of meaning in which the world consists.

In the third step, Heidegger connects Dasein's analytic to a motif borrowed from existentialism. Dasein understands itself out of the possibility of being or not being itself. Dasein finds itself facing the unavoidable decision between authenticity and inauthenticity. It is a being that, as Heidegger says several times, 'has to be' (BZ, 14; GA 20, 204–207/HCT,152–154; SuZ, 42/BT, 42). Human being has to choose itself and take control over its existence. Those who try to avoid this decision have already chosen a life in the mode of letting oneself go and in the state of the fall. Within the context of Heidegger's early interpretations of Aristotle, the tendency toward taking responsibility for one's own existence appears as a 'showing concern about one's own existence' (NB, 242; GA 61, 125–155/PIA, 92–115). The philosopher is not the only one that in asking the question regarding the meaning of being has to go back to the pre-understanding human beings have of the world and of themselves. The concern for oneself and the effort to secure the existential possibilities for one's most authentic potentiality for being are constitutive features of every Dasein. In this sense, human being as such is an ontological being that is compelled to ask about being. The existential analytic stems from the deepest impulse of human existence.

The hermeneutics of facticity puts an end to the methodological primacy of self-reflection, which was what forced Husserl to employ the transcendental reduction. And yet, the place self-consciousness occupied in Husserl's picture is now taken by the conceptual articulation of the pre-ontological understanding of being and the nexus of meaning in which everyday existence is always situated.

Human beings are embedded from their birth in an array of relations to the world and occupy a privileged position with respect to the rest of intra-wordly beings. This conceptual strategy is clearly an improvement over the philosophy of the subject: knowledge and action need not be considered as relations between a subject and an object any more. Now they can be understood as derivative on the subjacent modes of being in a world that has always been already intuitively understood. In conclusion, the project of providing a fundamental ontology by means of an existential analytic of Dasein is, in Lafont's words, 'the attempt to follow a transcendental strategy without a transcendental subject' (Lafont 2004, 268).[53] This is not possible, however, if one stays within the classical framework on which a distinction is made between the empirical and the transcendental. The hermeneutic transformation of philosophy demands a new conceptual framework. Here is where the ontological difference is called to play a role.

The ontological difference

From the first Freiburg and Marburg lecture courses up until *Being and Time*, Heidegger gives a special place to the *factum* of our meaningfully mediated relation to the world and to the universality of the structure of understanding. From a methodological point of view, this position results in a hermeneutic transformation of phenomenology, which comprises two fundamental modifications.

First, the model of hermeneutic understanding substitutes that of present perception: 'It is also a matter of fact that our simplest perception and constitutive states are already *expressed*, even more, are *interpreted* in a certain way' (GA 20, 75, italics in the original). This thesis had different formulations since the 1919 lecture course. In *Being and Time* it is rendered thus: 'any simple pre-predicative seeing of what is at hand is in itself already understanding and interpretative' (SuZ, 149/BT, 142). The central aspect of the hermeneutic transformation of phenomenology is the radical affirmation of the priority of understanding over perception. The example of the lived experience of the lectern perfectly illustrates the meaning and scope of this transformation. On the one hand, there is a shift from the mentalistic paradigm to the hermeneutic one: the world does not show itself in the inner sphere of consciousness; rather, the individual is already thrown into a symbolic world that makes the intelligibility of reality possible. On the other hand, the transformation shows that the primary structure of our relation to the world is meaningful in nature or, to put it another way, that the supposedly pure perception of beings is merely an abstraction derivative of our everyday experience of being in the world. The phenomenon that makes this claim plausible is the anticipation of meaning, that is, the fact that we always already move within an understanding of being which is the condition of possibility of our experience of the world.

Second, this transformation implies substituting the traditional concept of 'world' as the totality of entities with the hermeneutic concept of 'world', understood as a symbolically structured whole whose meaningfulness makes the intra-wordly experience of beings possible. Heidegger employed the same concept of world throughout the period we have been studying – in the 1919 lecture course *The Idea of Philosophy and the Problem of Worldview* (GA 56/57, § 14), in the 1919–1920 lecture course *The Basic Problems of Phenomenology* (GA 58, § 24), in the 1923 lecture course *Ontology*, in *The Hermeneutics of Facticity* (GA 63, § 24), in the 1925 lecture course *History of the Concept of Time* (GA 20, § 23; SuZ, § 18), and, of course, throughout *Being and Time*. With respect to our everyday dealings with things and physical objects in the world, Heidegger develops the idea of a referential context of signification (*Verweisungszusammenhang der Bedeutsamkeit*), and coins the term 'totality of signification'.[54] The results of Heidegger's analysis are particularly relevant for his critique of the philosophy of consciousness.

By asking 'who' is in the world, Heidegger extends his inquiry from the world of tools that Dasein as an individual employs to the domain of social relations between subjects:

> Is it then a priori self-evident that the access to Da-sein must be simple perceiving reflection of the I of acts? [...] The clarification of being-in-the-world showed that a mere subject without a world 'is' not initially and is also never given. And, thus, an isolated I without the others is in the end just as far from being given initially.
> SuZ, 115, 116/BT, 113, quotation marks in the original

From the perspective of interpersonal relations, the concept of world broadens considerably: from individual teleological action to symbolically mediated social interaction within the framework of an intersubjectively shared world.

In fact, the German world '*Welt*' retains the idea that human being and world belong to each other. The etymological origin of the word is the old High German word '*Weralt*', from the eighth century, which during the middle High German period transforms into '*Werlt*' and then into '*Welt*', acquiring the more familiar meaning of 'epoch, the totality of creation, the earth as the place man inhabits, in contrast to the inhospitality of the sea' (Pfeiffer 1993, 1555). Likewise, the Grimm brothers' etymological dictionary, which as mentioned Heidegger consulted frequently, says that Welt was initially conceived as 'the space where human communities live in the face of the life-threatening wilderness' (Grimm 1864–1960, vol. 28, 1458). In this sense, the Welt concerns the community dimension that Paul gives to the Greek term '*kosmos*' in his epistles. '*Welt*' is also used to translate the Latin terms '*saeculum*' ('genre', 'epoch', 'time', 'spirit of the time', 'age of humanity') and '*mundus*' ('world', 'world order', 'creation', 'universe') (Grimm 1864–1960, vol. 28, 1,459; Pfeiffer 1993, 1555). From the fifteenth century onwards the term is also applied to the domain of natural sciences both as regards the macrocosm of the universe and the microcosm of the individual. Clearly, this use coexists with the religious sense of divine creation. In this sense, '*weltlich*' (mundane) is linked to '*irdisch*' (earthy or terrestrial) and '*sinnlich*' (sensible) and opposed to '*himmlisch*' (heavenly) and '*geistig*' (spiritual). Mundanity is the characteristic form of human existence in this earthly world (*Diesseits*) and the opposite of future life in the hereafter (*Jenseits*). Throughout the eighteenth century the concept of Welt acquired the secularized meaning of Umwelt, that is, the surrounding world or environment, the totality of conditions for the life of a given individual or community.

The transformation of the term reflects the evolution of German spiritual life. The conception of the world as a community of individuals (*kosmos*) and a community of believers (*mundus* and *saeculum*) gives way, during the eighteenth and nineteenth centuries, and under the influence of natural sciences, to the more cultural notion of a Weltanschauung (worldview). This is reflected in Karl Jaspers' *Psychology of Worldviews*. In his 1920–1921 lecture course *Introduction to Phenomenology of Religion*, Heidegger vindicates St Paul's concept of *kosmos* as world shared by a historical community in which individuals carry out their everyday business and relate to each other.

For our purposes, it is worth emphasizing some aspects of the meaning the Grimm brothers ascribe to the term 'world'. In their account, the term refers to 'a closed autonomous space which represents a universe in miniature' and to 'the totality of perceptions and states of affairs that we can apprehend perceptually and intellectually'.[55] A good part of this conception is preserved in Heidegger's notion of world. The world is not the totality of entities, as if contained in a receptacle. The world is not primordially spatial but concerns the dimension of lived experience. The world is the domain, the sphere, the stage, the horizon or the context in which human life unfolds. And this is so with respect to three modalities: the relation to others (*Mitwelt*), the use of things in the surrounding world (*Umwelt*) and the world of the thoughts, feelings and lived experiences of each particular individual (*Selbstwelt*).[56] To each of these worlds corresponds a specific type of care (*Sorge*) and dealing (*Umgang*). And this determines the way human life comports itself with respect to the others, things and itself. Solicitude (*Fürsorge*) is a modality of care that indicates the relation of moral and practical interest and care that connects individuals to those with whom they share a world. Concern (*Besorgen*) expresses the modality of the relation, be it practical or theoretical, that life has with the beings that show up in the surrounding world. Finally, distress or uneasiness (*Bekümmerung*) points at the way in which life worries about itself.

These three worlds are equi-primordial and make up the structure of being-in-the-world. But the constitutive characteristic of the world is meaningfulness. At the primordial level, things do not show up in accordance with the scheme on which a subject contemplates objects. As mentioned on several occasions, things and persons become intelligible to us insofar as we, the 'subject', belong to a symbolic world from the outset. In other words, human life is part of a horizon of sense in which particular meanings relate to each other forming a holistically structured whole. The totality of these interwoven meanings that constitute being-in-the-world is called 'context of signification' (*Bedeutsamkeit*).

This shift in perspective has immediate consequences. While the philosophy of consciousness is based on the subject/object model on which an extra-worldly spectator stands in front of the totality of beings contained by the world, the hermeneutic transformation of phenomenology puts all the accent on human life, that is, a Dasein that is situated *in* a symbolically shared world. This amounts to a de-transcendentalization of inherited philosophical concepts. Appeal to a transcendental subject that constitutes the world is out of the question. For this reason, in this new perspective, facticity is the obligatory starting point: the subject does not constitute the world but participates in the constitution of meaning inherent to the world in which he has been thrown from the start.

The so-called *Kehre* in Heidegger's latter thought does not concern these two tenets – a holistically structured world and the de-transcendentalization of the subject – as much as a structural problem that is already apparent in the first lecture courses from the twenties and quite patent in *Being and Time*. As Tugendhat's (1967, 264) and Lafont's (1994, 25–45) incisive analyses of *Being and Time*'s methodological difficulties indicate, the root of the problem is the incompatibility between Heidegger's purpose of performing a hermeneutic transformation and the methodology he resorts to. In other words, the problem lies in is trying to base a fundamental ontology on an existential analytic of Dasein, or to ground the constitution of the world in Dasein's existential structure. Heidegger himself explains the *Kehre* as an attempt to overcome *Being and Time*'s dogmatic presupposition of the preeminence of Dasein.[57] What allows him to face this challenge is language.

As all extra-worldly elements are left out of the picture, Heidegger has to substitute the pair empirical/transcendental with the *ontological difference*. This technical term is not present in *Being and Time*, much less in the Freiburg and Marburg lecture courses. The first occurence of the term occurs in *The Basic Problems of Phenomenology*, from 1929, where it indicates the 'difference between being and beings' (GA 24, 22/BP, 17). Heidegger offers a more complete account of this concept in the lecture course from 1928 (GA 26, § 10). In my view, however, this concept is presupposed throughout the early lecture courses and the ensuing writings, including *Being and Time*.⁵⁸ Without it, one cannot fully grasp Heidegger's argument. Take for instance the analysis of the lived experience of the surrounding world in relation to the example of the lectern, from the 1919 lecture course, which we have already discussed in detail. In that example a fundamental ontological difference is announced between the prior disclosedness of a meaningful world, which makes our understanding of things possible, and the discovery of entities that stems from our dealings with them. In the early lectures and in *Being and Time*, Heidegger highlights how Dasein or factical life, as being-in-the-world, unveils the being of existent things. In this way, Heidegger puts the emphasis on the understanding of the world. Likewise, in our comportment we distinguish between the disclosedness of our existence in the world and the discovery of intra-wordly entities. In this sense, we can say that the ontological difference is implicitly present in Heidegger's analysis of the lived experience of the surrounding world. The ontological difference is a latent presence throughout Heidegger's work from the twenties.

Heidegger interprets the distinctive feature of human life – its priority over all other entities – differently from the way transcendental philosophy does. In contrast to Kant, Heidegger's analysis does not rest on the factum of reason but on the idea that human beings have a certain pre-understanding of being. This Heidegger characterizes as an '*average and vague understanding of being*' (SuZ, 5/BT, 4, italics in the original). It is precisely this understanding that allows Dasein to apprehend the difference between being and beings, and so reach an understanding of itself, the others and any thing that might show itself in the world. This interpretation of the ontological difference, however, involves much more than merely ascribing to Dasein an intuitive capacity to distinguish between being and beings. As Lafont indicates, it also implies, on the one hand, that beings are only accessible from out of a previous understanding of their being, which is tantamount to recognizing the transcendental priority of being over entities, and, on the other hand, acknowledging the de-transcendentalized nature of the understanding of being, which is a consequence of its contingent, historical, variable and plural character (2004, 268–269).

The claim that we can distinguish, intuitively, between the entities we talk about and the way we understand them is admittedly very plausible. The other implications are more problematic if one does not accept an additional presupposition, which one may call 'hermeneutic idealism'. The transcendental priority of being over other beings has to be referred back to Dasein's pre-understanding of being. This is the core of the hermeneutic transformation of phenomenology that starts in the 1919 lecture courses and which is encapsulated in the idea that 'the meaningful is primary and immediately given to me without any mental detours' (GA 56/57, 73/IP, 61).

The 1923 lecture course already hints at a connection between meaningfulness and being: '"significant" means: being, being-there, in the how of a definite signifying and pointing' (GA 63, 93/HF, 71). As the elaboration of the fundamental ontology advanced, the presupposition of a unitary meaning of being became less problematic, for the reason that the *difference* between the *ontological-formal* structures of Dasein in general and its concrete *ontic-historical* instances became increasingly patent. In the last Marburg lecture course, from 1928, *Metaphysical Principles of Logic*, Heidegger elaborates on this ontological difference and points out:

The internal necessity for ontology to go back to its origin can be clarified with the primordial phenomenon of human existence: that the entity 'person' understands being; in the understanding of being rests the actualization of the difference between being and beings; there is being only if Dasein understands being. In other words: the possibility that in the understanding of being beings is given is predicated upon the factical existence of Dasein.

GA 26, 199, quotation marks in the original

This passage evinces the foundational ambitions I discussed above. Sciences move in the ontic sphere, while philosophy moves in the domain of being itself. The categorial structure of objects is grounded in Dasein's pre-ontological understanding of being. In contrast to Husserl, however, transcendental subjectivity, as the ground of human life, disappears. In Heidegger's picture, Dasein's ontological role can only be understood in relation to the factical conditions of its intra-worldly existence. In this way, the transcendental question regarding the conditions of possibility of the constitution of the world is now referred to the prior structure of disclosedness:'[...] the discoveredness (*Entdecktheit*) of innerworldly beings is *grounded* in the disclosedness (*Erschlossenheit*) of the world' (SuZ, 220/BT, 212, italics in the original).

This new perspective has two very important implications for Heidegger's thinking. The first one is the idea that the relation between the subject and the object is always embedded in a structure of conformity, by reason of which intra-worldly entities always manifest themselves primordially as tools and not as objects of theoretical observation. The second implication is that this embeddedness in the open horizon of being-in-the-world that the objectifying consciousness and Dasein always presuppose has to be understood in a dynamic and temporal manner. In this way, Dasein not only depends on the constitution of meaning that takes place in disclosedness but in fact Dasein 'pre-is' in that space. The analysis of the structure of temporality as always-already-being-in-the-world necessarily leads to understanding the historicity of the finite Dasein. Heidegger's effort to de-transcendentalize philosophy boils down to these two implications. One could add to this diagnosis the commonly accepted idea, painstakingly elaborated by Gadamer,[59] that the structure of understanding, which conditions both ordinary life and science in a temporal and historical way, involves a linguistic pre-understanding that belongs to the public interpretation of the world of Dasein:

Dasein can never escape the everyday way of being interpreted into which Dasein has grown initially. All genuine understanding, interpreting and communication, rediscovery and appropriation come about in it and out of it and against it. It is not the case that a Dasein, untouched and unseduced by this way of interpreting, was ever confronted by the free land of a 'world,' merely to look at what it encounters.

SuZ, 169/BT, 163–164, italics in the original

Here the 'always-already' component of the prior and unsurpassable structure of the world is patent. With this, Heidegger's hermeneutic phenomenology distances itself from Husserl's optical and pre-linguistic model of phenomenological evidence. This brings us back to the Heideggerian project of a radicalization of phenomenology in which, as shown, Heidegger substitutes disclosedness for Husserlian intentionality. Intentionality is possible only against the background of being-in-the-world (GA 20, 153/HCT, 111; GA 26, 170). Gethman expressed several years ago Heidegger's perception of the limitations of the philosophy of consciousness:

> Heidegger's issue [with the philosophy of consciousness] can be put thus: How can self-givenness be productive? Whence can an object give itself? Doesn't it require an a priori space where it can show itself? [...] Consciousness cannot produce that on the basis of which it exists, that is, the reference to objects. This reference has to exist prior to consciousness and its possible operations in a space of objects previously opened, the meaning of being
> Gethmann 1974, 103

Heidegger puts the idea in the following way: 'In directing itself toward . . . and grasping something, Dasein does not first go outside of the inner sphere in which it is initially encapsulated, but, rather, in its primary kind of being, it is always already "outside" together with some being encountered in the world already discovered' (SuZ, 62/BT, 62, italics in the original). By incorporating the phenomenon of the world, fundamental ontology finds a satisfactory answer to the problem of the constitution of meaning. This answer presupposes the ontological difference.

In fact, this presupposition is always operative no matter whether the term is used or not. If the possibility of getting access to being belongs to Dasein, then it is there, in Dasein, that the ontological difference manifests itself. And the apprehension of being must stem from the mode of being of this entity, that is, existence, and not from a mere presence. In other words, the ontological difference occurs in Dasein in the sense that Dasein is the there of being, the place of the disclosedness of being. To be precise, Dasein is the place where the ontic and the ontological meet. We may call this crossroads the 'difference'. And it is always at Dasein's core. For this reason Dasein and being have to be thought of in their primordial co-belonging. It is clear that the sphere of being different is not different from the sphere of beings, for 'being' always means 'being of beings'. Otherwise, we would fall back into the metaphysical doctrine of the two worlds. In this way, the modern concept of subjectivity presupposed by traditional ontology dissolves and gives way to the ontological difference, a central methodological element that is going to be present throughout Heidegger's intellectual development and play a fundamental role in his project of renovating philosophy.

Conclusion

The question regarding the meaning of the being of factical life is present throughout the young Heidegger's thinking. Human life and its prior understanding of being are the leading thread of Heidegger's early thought. In this book I have analysed the genealogy and the thematic articulation of the question regarding the meaning of being, as well as the methodological requirements for addressing this question in a warranted way.

In the first Freiburg lecture courses, the problem of being appears in the context of a phenomenological inquiry into factical life. The purpose of this inquiry was not to think being along the lines of traditional metaphysics but to understand it as the being in each case mine. Now how can one go from the problem of the being of factical life to the problem of being in general? This issue, which was quite cloudy in the philosophies developed immediately after the war, was explicitly addressed by theological works. Ferdinand Ebner's *The Word and the Spiritual Realities* (1921) and Franz Rosenzweig's *The Star of Redemption* (1921) are cases in point.[1] As Fabris notes, this problem appears in Heidegger's review of Jaspers' *Psychology of the World-views*. Heidegger composed this review between 1919 and 1921, precisely when he was working on a phenomenological interpretation of factical life on the basis of proto-Christian texts, and on a reformulation of the problem of being as one of the fundamental topics of Greek and mediaeval philosophy.[2]

Put another way, one can consider Heidegger's procedure from two complementary points of view. On the one hand, his focus on the problem of factical life compelled him to develop new hermeneutic and methodological tools; on the other hand, that focus led him to undertake a destruction of traditional ontology that made his proposed analysis viable. Heidegger articulates this twofold project in his last Freiburg course, from 1923, entitled *Ontology* – qualified with the subtitle *Hermeneutics of Facticity*. He sums up the motivations for his inquiry thus: '*Facticity* is the designation we will use for the character of the being of "our" "own" *Dasein*. More precisely, this expression means: *in each case* "this" Dasein in its being-there *for a while at the particular time* [...] insofar as it is, in the character of its being, *"there" in the manner of be-ing*' (GA 63, 7/5, italics in the original). This project continues to develop during the Marburg period through a rich engagement with Greek philosophers (Heraclitus, Parmenides, Plato and Aristotle),[3] scholastic thinkers (St Thomas Aquinas and Francisco Suárez)[4] and modern and contemporary philosophers (Descartes, Husserl, Kant and Leibniz).[5] This work anticipates many of *Being and Time*'s analyses. During these years, the gap between positive sciences, which study beings, and philosophy as the science of being, becomes more radical. It is in this gap that the ontological meaning of the difference manifests itself.

The philosophical journey that will eventually lead to *Being and Time* started with the lecture courses from the post-war semester, 1919. In *The Idea of Philosophy and the Problem of Worldview* the goal is not to address a specific question but to develop a whole new project regarding the essence and object of philosophy. The first step is to distinguish with all clarity between philosophy and worldview; the second is to construe philosophy in terms of primordial science. The aim is to keep life away from the domain of the theoretical attitude and see how it comports itself in relation to the immediate lived experience of the surrounding world, of the persons with whom it shares a world, and of itself as concrete historical existence. The young Heidegger's characterization of the mode of being of life is completely different from the one inherited from the tradition, particularly from the characterization in terms of a reflexive attitude that regards lived experience from a theoretical standpoint that reduces the subject to a pure objective stance. Heidegger rejected this type of procedure. Philosophy as primordial science aims at apprehending, in a phenomenological way, the nature of life in its immediate givenness and over and above all theory.

The first Freiburg lecture courses start to address this issue and to search for an original way of thinking about it. Right at the outset, Heidegger distances himself from the usual definitions of the term 'philosophy'. Philosophy is neither an abstract representation of being, nor an endorsement of the self-evident truths of everyday life, much less a purely utilitarian and calculative knowledge. Likewise, the task of philosophy is not to accomplish an ultimate understanding of the world and of human existence *vis-à-vis* the results of other sources of knowledge. Nor is it a critical science of values and cultures based on the acts and norms of consciousness. Heidegger proposes a different view, one in which philosophy is radically incompatible with any kind of worldview. In this way, philosophy is no longer placed at the top of the pyramid of human knowledge. In the face of his discussions with neo-Kantianism and phenomenology, Heidegger sees philosophy as a primordial type of knowledge, a 'primordial science' that urges us to rethink the very essence of life.

Now, what is the contribution of this idea of philosophy as primordial science to philosophy as such? To begin with, it shows that philosophical thought is much more rigorous and primary than scientific knowledge; it is more radical and essential than the exploration of nature by means of theoretical artifices. Philosophy is not a speculative science but a pre-theoretical one. It lays bare the experiences of life prior to any abstract modification. How is philosophy radically different from natural and human sciences? In order to understand the answer to this question we have to have in view the method that makes undistorted access to the origin of life possible. Philosophy as primordial science does not follow the inductive method of generalization that characterizes particular sciences. In this sense, it is useless to try and clarify the nature of philosophy on the basis of purely methodological considerations. The point is not just to establish a method but also to recognize a very different idea of knowledge and truth. By merely confirming the discovery of certain regularities no progress is made in philosophy and human sciences. For this reason, the goal of philosophy is not to explain concrete phenomena as the instantiation of general rules. Its ultimate aim is to understand the phenomenon of human life in its historicity, singularity and unicity.

This project of a 'primordial science of life' comes together in the 1923 lecture course, *Ontology*. The term 'ontology' here is not a mere accident, nor does it designate a sub-discipline as in scholastic philosophy. It describes a task that is perfectly encapsulated by the subtitle of the lecture course in question, namely, *Hermeneutics of Facticity*. In contrast to the logical purity of the neo-Kantian subject of knowledge, facticity evokes a picture of life as hazy and foggy. By its very nature, life is dynamic and presents itself through different modes of manifestation. This does not mean that life is a chaotic mess or an inaccessible opaque phenomenon. Quite the contrary, all life involves an element of comprehension and the possibility of access. The task of hermeneutics is to shed light on this haziness. And for this, what is necessary is an interpretative effort capable of making transparent and intelligible the nexus of signification in which life is always already embedded.

One might think that the term 'ontology', in this initial stage in Freiburg, alludes to some sort of promised land that in fact the young Heidegger never reached. In my view, however, the problem of the meaning of being determines Heidegger's project from the start. The experience of history that stems from the individual's understanding of her own concrete situation opens the gates for an interpretation of the metaphysical question regarding being that is framed by the horizon of the experience of time. Such experience also leads Heidegger to reconsider the generative operations of the transcendental self. In this sense, phenomenological hermeneutics elaborates the conditions of possibility of any ontological inquiry. The truly hermeneutic task is to find a methodologically adequate mode of access to the primordial openness of life. The ontology of factical life that starts to develop in the first Freiburg years pierces through the logical structures of Husserl's phenomenology and, little by little, the self-givenness of being ends up prevailing over the reflexive productivity of consciousness. In this way, the transition from the Husserlian logic of transcendental subjectivity to the fundamental ontology of Dasein's being-in-the-world is completed.

Heidegger started to undertake the question regarding the meaning of being explicitly during the Marburg period (1924–1928), which was exceptionally productive and significant. Two things crucial to *Being and Time* happened during this period: Heidegger definitely departed from Husserl's phenomenology and ontology entered the scene hand in hand with an intense reading of Greek philosophy and Aristotle in particular. The presence of Aristotle, the definite breakup with Husserl's project and the burgeoning importance of Kant for the problem of Dasein's temporality reflect Heidegger's phenomenological passion for the problem of the being of factical life.

Whereas in Freiburg Heidegger's interest in the question of being was still vague, in Marburg much of his efforts were directed towards the ontological problem, particularly the relation between ontology and temporality. In this context, Aristotle is Heidegger's first interlocutor, but not long afterwards Kant takes his place. The titles and tables of contents of the Marburg lectures attest to this.

From Aristotle, Heidegger obtained a clear awareness of the universality of being, a conception of language and a notion of truth as unconcealment. The basic function of *logos* is to make things visible, to show that of which one speaks. In accordance with this conception of *logos*, truth is to be understood as unveiling or unconcealment (*Unverborgenheit*), not only in the sense that it brings something to light but also in the sense of uncovering that which has been hidden and forgotten. Heidegger's analysis of Aristotle's works led him to one of his most important discoveries: the unbreakable relation between being and truth. Inquiring into things (being) is at the same time inquiring into their uncovering (truth). In other words, the being of something can only be determined if that something shows itself as it is. By the same token, Heidegger claims that the notion that governs the Greek understanding of the relation between being and truth is presence. Accordingly, the uncovering comportment consists in presenting or bringing to presence.

Now 'what does *being* mean so that *truth* can be understood as *character of being*?' (GA 21, 191). Heidegger's answer is that being primarily means presence (*Anwesenheit*). On the basis of this conviction, he radicalizes the question regarding truth and relates it to temporality. In this way, this question converges with the need for a preparatory analysis of Dasein. Truth as unconcealment entails a tacit understanding of the being of beings in terms of presence. And this means that being is understood in terms of temporality, for presence (*Anwesenheit*), as a mode being determined by being in the present (*Gegenwart*), is necessarily linked to time. Put otherwise, the interpretation of being as presence presupposes a connection between being and time in which the dimension of the present has priority. In this way, being is revealed as temporal but only in terms of the dimension of the present. Greek thinking, however, was not fully aware of this relation between being and time. Neither was the ensuing philosophy. Only Kant envisages this relation, if only vaguely.

In the end, the deepest issue here is the temporal character of being. As mentioned, the departure point of the young Heidegger's thought is an analysis of life in its facticity. The aim is to articulate philosophically the meaning that has always already been understood as live. *Being and Time* establishes a terminology and elaborates a method, hermeneutic phenomenology, designed not only to analyse the ontological structures of human life, i.e. Dasein, but also to open up the space for the understanding of being within the horizon of temporality. From his first lecture courses onwards, Heidegger insists on the dynamic nature of all phenomena, particularly human life. This explains his constant efforts to develop a method of analysis and a conceptual apparatus capable of apprehending the diverse forms in which reality manifests itself. Thinking and giving expression to the intrinsic movedness of life without fixing it through categories and formal structures is one of the main tasks phenomenology has to take upon itself.

Being cannot be thought of as a real object, as a thing with certain properties. Even though our dependence on language forces us to nominalize it and treat it as a logical-grammatical subject of sentences, being is not something that acts. Addressing the question of being demands from us that we do not subject 'being' to representative thinking. Rather, we are to understand being as the horizon of intelligibility and meaning in terms of which reality is always already comprehended. This is why the latent presence of the ontological difference in Heidegger's early work is so important.

Notes

Chapter 1

1. GA 42/Heidegger, 1985, 98.
2. This question was present in Heidegger's work from his precocious reading of Brentano's book on the multiple meanings of 'entity' in Aristotle, in 1907, up until his last official letter, composed two weeks before his death and addressed to the participants of the Tenth Heidegger Colloquium that took place in Chicago (see GA 16, 747–748). For similar autobiographical comments, see *My Way to Phenomenology* (ZSD, 81-92/MWP, 74–82) and the *Preface* to the first edition of the first volume of the *Gesamtausgabe* (collected edition) (cf. GA 1, 55–57). In what follows I will refer to the *Gesamtausgabe* with the abbreviation GA, followed by the corresponding volume number. There is a full list of abbreviations at the beginning of the present work.
3. Heidegger, M., *Sein und Zeit*, Max Niemeyer, Tubinga, 1986. Henceforth I use for this work the abbreviation SuZ for the German edition and BT for the English one. When quoting Heidegger's *Being and Time* (BT) and *The Basic Problems of Phenomenology* (BP), and Husserl's *Logical Investigations* (Log. Inv.) and *Ideas I* (Ideas I) I preferably follow the English editions mentioned in the references section.
4. A word about my decision not to translate the German technical term '*Dasein*'. The usual meaning of the term, both in philosophical and ordinary contexts, is existence. In the seventeenth century the infinitive phrase '*da sein*' ('to be there', 'to be present', 'to exist', 'to be available') is nominalized as '*das Dasein*' and takes on the meaning of presence. In the eighteenth century the term 'Dasein' begins to replace, in philosophical contexts, the Latinized expression '*Existenz*', while in poetic circles the expression is used with the meaning of *Leben* ('life'). Heidegger distances himself from the canonical philosophical use, coined by Christian Wolff, on which *Dasein* is equated to *Existenz* ('existence') in the sense of *Wirklichkeit* ('reality' or 'actuality') and *Vorhandensein* ('subsistence' or 'presence'). Heidegger uses the term '*Dasein*' exclusively in reference to the ontological constitution of human life, characterized by its openness (*Da*) to being (*Sein*) and by its capacity to ask about its meaning. The term begins to acquire this technical character in the *Natorp-Bericht* (1922) where it is used to denote the being that asks about its own being. This shift in meaning is fully consolidated in the 1923 lectures, *Ontology. The Hermeneutics of Facticity*, where Heidegger gives the term '*Dasein*' the character of a formal indication that points at the way of being characteristic of human existence. For these reasons, when Heidegger uses the expression '*Dasein*' in his interpretations of other philosophers (such as Dilthey, Hegel, Kant, Natorp, etc.) I usually translate it for 'existence', but when Heidegger uses the expression in his own technical sense, I use the German 'Dasein' (without italics). It is worth noting that sometimes Heidegger hyphenates this term (*Da-sein*). This practice underlines Dasein's constitutive primordial openness and should not be confused with a merely local 'there'. Some years after

Being and Time Heidegger started to refer to this openness in terms of *Seinslichtung* ('clearing of being'). Beyond marking the physical separation that keeps two margins together, the hyphen highlights the idea of a continuous passage, a permanent 'between'. This 'between', 'open space' or 'passage' is what Heidegger really attempts to think. For more on this, see Leyte (2005, 46–47) and Adrián (2009, 63–67).

5   In the 'Introduction' Heidegger wrote in 1949 for 'What is Metaphysics?', he justifies the use of the term 'Dasein' as follows: 'To characterize with a *single* term both the relation of Being to the essence of man and the essential relation of man to the openness ("there" ["Da"]) of Being [*Sein*] as such, the name of "Dasein" [there-being] was chosen for the essential realm in which man stands as man. [...] "Dasein" names that which is first of all to be experienced, and subsequently thought accordingly, as a place – namely, as the locality of the truth of Being' (GA 9, 372–373/WM, 283).

6   Among others, see the editions of Buren and Kisiel (1994), Courtine (1996) and in particular Kisiel (1993). For a full list of the introductions and monographs on Heidegger's early work, see section 5.6.1 of the bibliographic appendix of the Spanish version of the present work, available at www.herdereditorial.com.

7   See the explanation Heidegger offers in *A Dialogue on Language* (p. 92, English edition) and his 1922 letter to Karl Jaspers, where he highlights the importance of devoting himself to the understanding of the meaning of the being of life rather than attending to the academic demands to publish (Heidegger and Jaspers 1990, 27–28).

8   Figal (1992, 49) is a case in point. For a reply to Figal's interpretation and a case in favour of an homogeneous reading of Heidegger's thinking, see Xolocotzi's compelling work (2004, 26–32).

9   See for instance, the autobiographical testimonies from *My Way to Phenomenology* (in ZSD, 81–90/MWP, 74–81), the scattered references of *On the Way to Language* (in US, 83–155) and the letter to Richardson (in Heidegger 1964/65, 397–402). For a list of Heidegger's readings see Kisiel (1993, 525–526); for students' recollections see Arendt (1978, 293–303), Biemel (1984), Gadamer (1986/87, 3–43), Neske (1977). The most valuable correspondence was with Engelbert Krebs, Karl Löwith, Hannah Arendt, Edmund Husserl, Heinrich Rickert, Elfride Petri and, especially, Karl Jaspers. For a full list of references see section 5.3 of the appendix available here: www.herdereditorial.com.

10 The *Gesamtausgabe* edition, however, has not been free of criticism. Particularly, on account of the decision of the editors to be completely faithful to the instructions Heidegger established in his will, it follows no chronological order, does not comply with philological criteria and lacks a critical apparatus. In relation to the impact of the *Gesamtausgabe* and the criticisms and rejoinders regarding its editorial criteria see the justification co-editor Herrmann offers (1986, 153–173), Emad's explanations (1993, 161–171), Jamme's contextualization (1996, 221–236), Kisiel's acid critique (1995, 3–15), Sheehan's reservations (1980) and Wetz's comments (1987, 13–25).

11 Among the numerous studies concerning Heidegger's early work (appendix, 5.6), the following are worth mentioning: Adrián (2000a), Berciano (2001), Buren (1994a), Courtine (1996a), Denker, Gander and Zaborowski (2004), Kisiel (1993), Buren and Kisiel (1994), Quesne (2003), Rodríguez (1997), Overgaard *et al.* (2003) and Xolocotzi (2004).

12 Before 1985, when the publication of Heidegger's first lecture courses in Freiburg began, access to his early work was indirect, mostly through Otto Pöggeler's *Martin Heidegger's Path of Thinking* (published in 1963 and composed with Heidegger's support and collaboration).

13 Heidegger is explicit in this respect in a letter from 20 September 1966, addressed to Professor Schrynemakers with the occasion a symposium on his philosophy held in Duquesne University: 'Today is barely necessary to insists that my thinking has nothing to do with existentialism or philosophy of existence' (Sallis 1970).
14 For a critical discussion of these two types of interpretation see Kalariparambil (1999, 69–74).
15 In this regard see for instance Rodríguez (1997), Gander (2001) and Lara (2008).

Chapter 2

1 For a general picture of the historical, social and political context of these years see Fergusson (1984), Gay (1984), Hughes (1972) and Watson (2002). For the philosophical context see Bambach (1995, 21–56), Gadamer (2000, 189–217) and Barash (1988, 17–89).
2 For more details on the intellectual environment during this period of Heidegger's career see Ott (1992, 117–132), Nolte (1992) and Safranski (1997, 101–137).
3 In this respect, see the correspondence between Heidegger and Jaspers from 1920 to 1924 (in Heidegger and Jaspers 1990). On the solidarity between both thinkers see Jaspers (1977, 93–96).
4 This point is documented in a well-known letter from 9 January 1919 to his friend, the priest Engelbert Krebs (in Casper 1980, 541), and qualified in his letters to Karl Löwith from 19 August 1921 and 20 August 1927, in which Heidegger defines himself as a 'Christian theologian', i.e., as someone interested in penetrating the primordial meaning of religious life, while remaining at distance from dogmatic positions, in order to dive into the current of human existence (in Papenfuss and Pöggeler 1990, 29, 36–37). Heidegger's lecture courses from 1920–1921, *The Phenomenology of Religious Life*, bear witness to this new attitude. Here, he offers a number of suggestive interpretations of Eckhart's, St Therese of Jesus and Bernard of Clairvaux mysticism, and of Saint Paul's epistles, Augustine's *Confessions*, Luther's *Disputations* and Schleiermacher's *Speeches on Religion*.
5 These works have been referred to in the second section of the first chapter.
6 These investigations, which began around 1919–1920 in the context of a discussion with hermeneutics, vitalism, neo-Kantianism and scholasticism, coalesce in the *Natorp-Bericht* (1922) and the lecture course *Ontology. The Hermeneutics of Facticity* (1923).

Chapter 3

1 All these works are collected in the first volume of the *Gesamtausgabe* (GA 1). It is worth remembering that Heidegger studied mathematics and natural sciences at the University of Freiburg during the 1911–1912 and 1912–1913 semesters. On Heidegger's interest in these disciplines, see the prefaces to the first edition of his *Frühe Schriften* and to his doctoral dissertation, *The Theory of Judgment in Psychologism* (in GA 1, 55, 61). More on this subject in Neumann (2004, 214–225).
2 See, among others, the lecture courses of the winter semester 1925–1926, *Logic: The Question of Truth* (GA 21), and of the summer semester, 1928, *The Metaphysical Foundations of Logic* (GA 26). Regarding secondary literature, during the seventies, a

first group of works on the link between Heidegger and neo-Kantianism and logic was published: Borgmann (1978), Caputo (1973), Fay (1974), Hobe (1971). These works were followed, in the eighties, by works by Kisiel (1983), Mohanty (1988) and Wolzogen (1989). Thanks to the publication of a good a part of Heidegger's early work during the nineties, interest in this stage of his career was renewed: Adrián (1999a), Borges (1995), Courtine (1996b), Crowell (1992, 1994, 1996), García Gaínza (1997), Heinz (2001), Kisiel (1996a), Lyne (2000), Orth (1992) and Rampley (1994). For a comprehensive assessment of the aforementioned works and a detailed exposition of the link between Heidegger's thought and neo-Kantianism, see Steinmann (2004).

3 For more details on Heidegger's fecund relation with science, the *Zollikoner Seminare* (1959–1969) are particularly relevant. See also Xolocotzi (2009, 73–91).

4 Here, the relation between the question of being and the question regarding language, a relation that will dictate Heidegger's future philosophical path, starts to become apparent.

5 Husserl, E., *Logische Untersuchungen*. First volume: *Prolegomena zur reinen Logik*, Husserliana XVIII. The Hague: Martinus Nijhoff, 1975; henceforth, HU XVIII, followed by the English translation abbreviated as *Log. Inv.* 1.

6 Courtine also offers an interesting presentation of Heidegger's critical destruction of logic as it appears in the 1915–1926 lecture course, *Logic. The Question of Truth*, and the 1929 conference 'What is Metaphysics?' The core of Heidegger's argument involves denouncing that logic has become increasingly scholarly, and as a result, judgement has been regarded as the locus of truth. In this way, the primordial capacity of *logos* for disclosure has been overlooked. The young Heidegger repeatedly levels, against the metaphysical tradition, the charge of reducing *logos* to the propositional and predicative dimension, thereby giving priority to *lógos apophantikós*. For Heidegger, *logos* constitutes an exceptional modality of uncovering, it makes possible openness and privileged access to beings, that is to say, it realizes the essentially uncovering character of Dasein.

7 In this context, it is important not to forget Frege's criticism of psychologism. In the aforementioned paper, 'New Research on Logic', Heidegger highlights Frege's notable place in philosophy of mathematics (GA 1, 20). As for the role Husserl's *Logical Investigations* played in the revitalization of logic, Heidegger makes several references in the Freiburg and Marburg lecture courses.

8 Frege painstakingly analyses the problems deriving from this psychologistic doctrine in his well-known work, 'Über Sinn und Bedeutung' ('On Sense and Reference'). By the same token, in his review of Husserl's *Philosophy of Arithmetic*, Frege stresses the difference between the representation of a thing and the thing itself that is being represented.

9 Psychologism overlooks the deep difference between the real being of 'judicative decision' and the ideal validity of judged content. Its main mistake is therefore 'ignoring the difference in the fundamental diversity of the being of beings' (GA 1, 50). This is a remark Heidegger made in his review of Charles Sentroul's *Kant und Aristoteles* (1914).

10 Heidegger is talking about expressions of the form '*es regnet*' (it rains), where the '*es*,' in contrast with its English counterpart (it) is not a noun (translator's note).

11 Heidegger uses the expression '*es blitzt*', which means 'it flashes' as when used in reference to a lightning. In English this expression would not work as an impersonal verb because the 'it' has a clear reference, i.e. the lightning.

12 This point is crucial to understanding Heidegger's hermeneutic shift. I come back to this in the next section.
13 See for instance Heidegger's expression of gratitude towards Lask in the preface to his *Habilitationsschrift*, finished a few months after Lask's death on the battlefield. See also Heidegger's letter to Rickert from 31 October 1916 (Heidegger and Rickert 2002, 23). In the lecture course of 1919, Heidegger asserts: 'Lask is one of the most important philosophical personalities of our time' (GA 56/57, 180). Even Heidegger's supervisor, Heinrich Rickert, highlighted, in his report on Heidegger's *Habilitationsschrift*, the connection between this work and 'Lask's metagrammatical theory of the subject-predicate, to whom the author [Heidegger] should thank, much more than he thinks, for his philosophical orientation as well as for his terminology' (quoted in Sheehan 1988, 118).
14 This problem has, by all lights, Aristotelian undertones. It eventually became one of the central worries of the young Heidegger's thinking, especially as he approached the problem of the unity of being and the multiple meaning of beings. Heidegger's early reading of Franz Brentano's *On the Manifold Meaning of Being According To Aristotle* plays an important role in his view on the problem. I give more thorough account of this issue in Chapter 4, as I discuss Heidegger's appropriation and radicalization of Aristotle's philosophy.
15 For an account of Heidegger's Laskian heritage see Adrián (1999c), Crowell (1992), Fehér (1992), Imdahl (1997), Kisiel (1996a) Steinmann (2004) and Strube (1993).
16 See the 1912 essay 'The Problem of Reality in Modern Philosophy' (GA 1, 1–15). In a short text published in the journal *Der Akademiker* in 1911, entitled 'Toward a Philosophical Orientation for Academics', Heidegger claims that the main task of philosophy is not only to find out the ultimate determinations of being but to take these as a starting point for offering an understanding of life as a whole (GA 16, 13).
17 The distinction between the categorial domains of that which 'is' and that which 'is valid' contains the seed of what Heidegger will later call the ontological difference of being and beings. Validity applies only on the basis of prior lived experience. The later Heidegger will say that beings only become visible against the illuminated horizon of being.
18 On the points of coincidence between Lask and Heidegger see Crowell (1994) and Kisiel (2001).
19 The importance Lask gives to the problem of the pre-theoretical has been acknowledged in the secondary literature. In particular, see Kisiel (1993, 27ff.).
20 The title of this epilogue, composed in 1916, is 'The Problem of Categories' (in GA 1, 399–411).
21 The author is referring here to what is called in German '*Geisteswissenschaften*', literally, 'sciences of the spirit' (translator's note).
22 On the genesis of Heidegger's notion of 'the living spirit' and its importance for the subsequent evolution of his thought, see Steinmann (2004, 77–105) and Steinmann (2004, 281–285).
23 The conceptual articulation of historical life is precisely one of the main tasks of the hermeneutics of factical life. Where Scotus talks about the *distinctio formalis*, Heidegger talks about formal indication. Both notions stem from the idea that the form shows that which cannot be said, namely, the concrete ontological relation between *intellectus* and *ens*, Dasein and world. The essence of the *distinctio formalis* rests on the assumption that the forms of ordinary language point at deep and hidden ontological structures. In a similar way, formal indicators allow us to make

the fundamental ontological structures of life phenomenologically visible. See Chapter 5 for a discussion of the methodological function of formal indicators in Heidegger's hermeneutics.

24   For more on this, see Adrián (1999a).
25   This peculiar temporal nature of the individual, irreducible to the concept of time used by physics, is the subject matter of Heidegger's interesting lecture from 1915, *The Concept of Time in the Science of History* (in GA 1, 413-434), given as part of his training as a lecturer.
26   As Heidegger himself indicates to Löwith in a letter dated 20 August 1927, the *haecceitas* is very close to what is discussed in *Being and Time* as the temporal and factical particularity of Dasein (in Papenfuss and Pöggeler 1990, 37).
27   At some moments in the young Heidegger's work, it is difficult not to hear the voice of the subversive self of the main character of Dostoyevsky's novel, *Notes from the Underground*. This voice demanded an independent and autonomous self. Heidegger would probably not agree with the nihilist tone, but surely would subscribe to the underground self's rejection of the Euclidian world of positivist rationalism, which purported to solve the complexity of human problems by means of the precise procedures of logic and arithmetic. Rather than submitting oneself to these procedures, the idea is to show the facticity and singularity of each individual.

Chapter 4

1   For reasons of space, I will not address Heidegger's interpretation of Luther's theology of the cross and his reading of Augustine's reflections on care and time. I have discussed this in Adrián (2010, 209-222).
2   Important references in this regard are Ott (1992, 45-119), Safranski (2000, 15-88), Casper (1980, 534-541), Sheehan (1981, 1988), Denker (2004) and Schaber (2004). With a critical tone, and with a view to addressing Heidegger's later rectorate period and relationship with National Socialism, Víctor Farías and Ernst Nolte also discuss this stage of his life (Farías 1989, 49-92; Nolte 1993, 514ff.). For a comprehensive assessment of various interpretative lines regarding this stage of Heidegger's work, see Holger Zaborowski's well documented paper (2004). I have discussed this topic elsewhere (Adrián, 1999a, 1999b). For more on the religious and theological dimension of Heidegger's thought, see Lehmann (1964, 1969), O'Meara (1986), Ott (1995), Schaeffler (1978, 3-34), Thöma (2003, 1-4) and Jung (2003, 5-8).
3   These short articles where discovered and first discussed by Víctor Farías (1989, 75-88). There is an English translation (Protevi 1991). In recent years, intense work on archives has also made many of the young Heidegger's publications available, particularly a good part of his poems, papers and reviews for journals like *Allgemeine Rundschau, Wochenschrift für Politik und Kultur* and *Der Akademiker* and *Heuberger Volksblatt*. Texts such as 'Allerseelenstimmungen' (1909), 'Das Kriegs-Triduum in Meßkirch' (1915) and some others from the same years have been partially edited and published as part of the *Collected Edition* (GA 16) and in Büchin and Denker (2005). All of Heidegger's minor writings from 1909-1915 are listed in the exhaustive appendix to the first volume of the journal *Heidegger-Jarbuch* (see Bremmers 2004).
4   Heidegger himself acknowledges the decisive influence of these two thinkers at the beginning of his philosophical life (see for instance the prologue to *Frühe Schriften*

and his autobiographical writing *My Way to Phenomenology*). In fact, Heidegger dedicated his *Habilitationsschrift* to Rickert and *Being and Time* to Husserl.

5   On the relationship of Heidegger and Welte and the meaning of the homeland for them, see Zaborowski (2003).
6   For his part, Gadamer even considers the *Natorp-Bericht*, composed in 1922, after Heidegger's breakup with Catholicism, a theological writing of youth (Gadamer 1989, 229).
7   Heidegger's brother, Fritz, wrote to him in a letter for his eightieth birthday that 'your path was to lead, after many years of law studies, to teaching at the philosophy classroom. Those four terms of theological studies were an inevitable intermediate stage' (Fritz Heidegger 1969, 60).
8   On the ecclesiastic and theological background against which Heidegger's posture develops, see Schaber (2004).
9   See for instance Conzemius (2003) and Arnold (2003).
10 See for instance Heidegger, 'Dem Grenzbot-Philosophen die zweite Antwort', *Heuberger Volksblatt* 43 (1911); 'Modernismus', *Heuberger Volksblatt* 41 (1911); 'Rede über naturwissen-schaftliche Themen und Erdbebenkunde', *Heuberger Volksblatt* 33 (1912); 'Die tierische Abstammung des Menschen und das Urteil der Wissenshaft', *Heuberger Volksblatt* 47 (1912); 'Spiritismus und Wissenschaft', *Heuberger Volksblatt* 101 (1913). On the Meßkirch talks, see Denker (2000, 2001).
11 In this context it is also worth mentioning Heidegger's early reading of Hölderlin (Heidegger and Bodmershof 2000, 132–133).
12 See Heidegger's article 'Dem Grenzbot-Philosophen zur Antwort', published in the local newspaper *Heuberger Volksblatt* 42 (7 April 1911, 1–2).
13 Between 1913 and 1914 Heidegger wrote reviews of three books on Kant (GA 1, 45, 49–53 and 54). To judge from the quoted passage, these books gave him a new view of Kantian philosophy, which was barely considered in scholastic literature (see Heidegger's résumé in GA 16, 38).
14 For a wider interpretation of these thinkers in relation to Heidegger's work on a phenomenology of religious life, see Adriàn (2010, 159–186).
15 On the role of the notion of *haecceitas* in the young Heidegger's thought, see Caputo (1974) and McGrath (2002).
16 Besides reading Eckhart between 1917 and 1919, Heidegger also read other mystics such as Bernard of Clairvaux, Hugh of St Victor, Tauler, Teresa of Avila and Thomas à Kempis. Heidegger's reading of these figures was concerned with the problem of *how* life is carried out. This he would later call the sense of realization of human existence (*Vollzugssinn des Lebens*). Heidegger's notes and some other material he prepared for the aforementioned lecture course were partially published in a volume on Heidegger's lecture courses on religion from the semesters 1920–1921 and 1920 (GA 60, 303-338/PRL, 231–254).
17 In describing this process of merging, Bernard of Clairvaux uses the beautiful image of a drop of water falling into wine, dissolving and acquiring its flavour and colour. An additional analogy is provided by iron, which, when sufficiently heated, becomes similar to fire and loses its form. Similarly, for saints all human affects dissolve and become God's will. In this return to the foundation, the particularity of the subject's concrete existence is somehow suspended and the subject rises up to the universal. This interpretation of the primary sense of spirituality guides the young Heidegger in his study of the vital core of intentionality.

18 Pöggeler (1983, 37) was the first commentator in calling attention to this fact. He did so in an early monograph on Heidegger, composed before much of the textual evidence we have nowadays was yet available. For an updated paper, see Pöggeler (1999, 249–252). The influence of dialectic theology, particularly Karl Barth's and Rudolf Bultmann's, in Heidegger's appropriation of St Paul's language is quite apparent (Barash 1988, 168ff.). Heidegger distances himself from the principles of liberal theology around the time he is reading Barth's comments to the *Epistle to the Romans* (1919) and is starting to become friends with Bultmann. The a priori of the actualization of life, historicity and the finitude of human existence is what ultimately makes the interpretation of the occurrence of faith possible.

19 I discuss the methodological evolution of the hermeneutic phenomenology of factical life further in Chapter 5.

20 Pöggeler (1983, 36–37), Sheehan (1979, 1980) and Kisiel (1993, 148–219) insist on the importance of the Pauline epistles in the subsequent development of some of the most important concepts deployed in *Being and Time*. On account of the incorporation of these concepts in Heidegger's fundamental ontology, some critics consider *Being and Time* a secularized Christian work. However, Heidegger's thinking always involves a tendency towards the 'this-worldly' (*Diesseitigkeit*) rather than towards the 'other-worldly' (or the transcendent) (*Jenseitigkeit*) that characterizes theology (Löwith 1969, 68ff.). This tendency is manifest in Dasein's questioning regarding the meaning of being, but is also manifest in other thinkers that were greatly influential for Heidegger: Husserl's intentional acts of conscience, Dilthey's meaning-bestowing conception of life and Nietzsche's radical questioning of meaning as such (human life has meaning insofar as it has will to power, but just as life is possible beyond good and evil, it is possible beyond meaning itself). For this reason, theological exegesis factically presupposes a prior understanding consisting in a projecting that gives us access to a world of meaningful nexuses. The immanent nature of the destiny of being contrasts with the theological notion of transcendence.

21 See for instance 2 Cor. 2:2.

22 The term '*Faktizität*' emerges in the context of neo-Kantian philosophy with the purpose of distinguishing the logicity (*Logizität*) of the supra-temporal, absolute and universal nature of knowledge in the domain of logic, from the facticity of that which is temporal, individual and contingent. Heidegger took part in the neo-Kantian debate regarding these matters while he was writing his *Habilitationsschrift* (1915), but he borrowed the term at the end of 1920 in order to denote the primary reality of the factical experience of life. The facticity of human life is not the *factum* of knowledge, nor the *factum brutum* of something that is 'out there', lacking all determination and resilient to any attempt at conceptualization. On the contrary, Heidegger's programme of a hermeneutics of facticity, which he sets to carry out in the lecture course from 1923, seeks to elaborate concepts capable of apprehending the phenomenon of life and the factical modes of existence. In his 1924 treatise, *The Concept of Time*, Heidegger uses a variation of the term, '*Facticität*', with the purpose of underscoring the specificity of his concept. As for the etymology of the term, it is worth noting that it comes from the German '*Faktum*' ('fact'), a transliteration of the Latin '*factum*'. '*Faktum*' is to be distinguished from '*Tatsache*', which was used for the first time in 1756 by the theologician Joachim Spalding to translate the English 'matter of fact', which in turn is the translation of the Latin expression *res facti* (see Krug 1832–1838, vol. III, 5). For more on this, see the entry '*Faktizität*' in Adrià n (2009, 88–90).

23 I come back to this in more detail in Chapter 5.
24 Faith is the acceptance of the word that actualizes itself in each person that accepts it – it is the event of salvation. Later on, post-Pauline theology insists on the structure of ministries, which effectively turns the Church into a salvific institution. Thus, faith is not understood as the acceptance of the kerygmatic message, but rather as the reception of a timeless and fixed doctrine. In his 1927 talk *Phenomenology and Theology*, Heidegger takes a deeply critical stance towards the institutionalization of faith and claims that faith is not a type of knowledge that is based on a theoretically loaded verification of internal experiences (GA 9, 53).
25 In the lecture course from the semester 1921–1922, Heidegger openly claims that life, in its literal sense, must be interpreted, according to its relational sense, as caring (GA 61, 90/PIA, 67).
26 This also explains Heidegger's interest in the Augustinian notion of care in his interpretation of the tenth book of *Confessions* (GA 60, 205–209/PRL, 151–155). Augustine already saw the risk of getting distracted in the world of public convention and being led exclusively by the interpretative criteria of everyday life and the rules of the public sphere. This guidance offers nothing but a pseudo-knowledge of reality and of one's self.
27 This notion of death is clearly present in *Being and Time*. He points out that 'the anthropology developed in Christian theology – from Paul to Calvin's *meditatio futurae vitae* – has already viewed death together with its interpretation of "life"' (SuZ, 249, n. 6 /BT, 239, n. 6).
28 See especially A. Ritschl's *On Moral Conscience* (1875), M. Kähler's *Moral Conscience in Antiquity and the New Testament* (1878) and H. Stoker's *The Moral Conscience* (1925), cited in *Being and Time* (SuZ, 272, n. 7/BT, 262, n. 7).
29 As I will show in the next section on Heidegger's appropriation of Aristotle's practical philosophy, this understanding of the situation is closely linked to *phronesis* or practical wisdom, a type of knowledge also present in the New Testament: 'Therefore, my beloved, avoid idolatry. I am speaking as to sensible people; judge for yourselves what I am saying' (1 Cor. 10: 14–15).
30 For more on the kairological features of factical life, see Haar (1996, 67–90), Greisch (1994, 30–34), Falkenhayn (2003) and Ruff 1997.
31 As mentioned, according to the second epistle to the Corinthians, what characterizes the facticity of life is the rejection of visions and revelations and the acceptance of one's own weakness (2 Cor. 12: 5–10). Paul firmly states that the strength of the believer lies in not being filled with pride, and it is with this purpose that God has subjected him to the sting of the flesh.
32 I give a more thorough account of this topic in Adrià n (2010, 209–218). On the influence of Luther's thought for the young Heidegger, see Pöggeler (2004), Buren (1994b, 159–174), Courtine (1992), Loewenich (1954), McGrath (2004, 273–280), Riedel (2003, 15–24) and Sommer (2005, 36–45).
33 For a more thorough discussion of Augustine's notion of *cura* and the question of time, see Adrià n (2010, 218–223). For Heidegger's analysis of time in Augustine, see *The Concept of Time* (conference of 1924, 5–8), *The Concept of Time* (the treatise from 1924, published in 2004 in GA 64, 17–19). Heidegger revisits the Augustinian conception of time in the talk he delivered on 26 October 1920, in the Beuron Monastery, *Agustinus: Quid est tempus? Confessiones lib. XI* (GA 80, forthcoming). For a detailed discussion of the relation between Heidegger and Augustine as regards the problem of time, see Cortí (2006).

34 See Flasch's interesting analysis (1993, 57ff.).
35 See for instance his autobiographical comments in the letter to Richardson (Heidegger 1964/65, in *My Way to Phenomenology*) (ZSD, 81–90/MWP, 74–82) and in the preface to the first edition of his early writings (GA 1, 55–57). No doubt, from his earliest lecture courses, to his latest seminars, Aristotle is one of the authors to which Heidegger devoted more time. As attested by the well-known *Natorp-Bericht*, from 1922, Heidegger even considered – though never completed – a book on Aristotle.
36 Among the abundant literature on this subject, it is worth mentioning Adrián (2001b, 2010), Bernasconi (1989), Brogan (1994, 213–230, 2005), Buren (1992), McNeill (1999), Sadler (1996), Yfantis (2009) and, above all, Volpi (1989, 1992, 1994). See also the monographic volume of the *Heidegger-Jahrburch*, which includes pieces by Figal, Courtine and Volpi, among other specialists, along with two unpublished seminars on Aristotle (Denker et al. 2007).
37 As Pöggeler mentions, in 1920 Heidegger expressed to Karl Löwith, his then student and later colleague, his frustration at the fact that Husserl considered him a theologian and paid little attention to his philosophical work (Pöggeler 1999, 249–252).
38 See also Heidegger's speech at the Heidelberger Akademie der Wissenschaften (Heidegger 1959, 20–21).
39 Heidegger was planning to publish the mentioned monograph in Husserl's journal, *Jahrbuch für Philosophie und phänomenologische Forschung*. The project was never finished. Moreover, the *Natorp-Bericht* itself was lost until 1989, when it was discovered as part of Josef König's legacy. It was later published with an introduction by Hans-Georg Gadamer.
40 See Volpi (1988, 1992, 1994, 2009). For criticism of this line of thought and a defence of the claim that Aristotle's and Heidegger's proposals need to be kept apart, see Rese (2007). Similarly, it is worth mentioning the dispute between Walter Brogan, on the one hand, and Jacques Taminiaux and Stanley Rosen, on the other. While Brogan reads Aristotle along the lines of Heidegger's interpretation and therefore sees him as a precursor of the latter (Brogan 1990, 137–146, 2005, 138–157), Taminiaux and Rosen criticize Heidegger's interpretation of the concept of *phronesis* arguing that he takes it out of context (Taminiaux 1991, 111–143) and Rosen (2004, 248–265). Finally, for a good comprehensive view of the relation between Heidegger and Aristotle, see Weigelt (2002, 12–19).
41 Some of the philosophers that advocate a return to Aristotle, such as Hans-Georg Gadamer, Hannah Arendt, Joachim Ritter and Hans Jonas, do not follow this line of interpretation. All of them attended Heidegger's early lecture courses and benefited from the experience. However, none of them follows the ontological programme of their teacher. On the contrary, they remain faithful to some of the basic epistemic intuitions of practical philosophy, particularly the idea human *praxis* has prevalence over the modern technological world. In this regard, Volpi shows how some of Heidegger's disciples develop these intuitions on the basis of their contact with Heidegger. Thus Hannah Arendt restores the concept of *praxis*, Hans-Georg Gadamer the concept of *phronesis* and Joachim Ritter that of *ethos* (Volpi 2007).
42 In this regard, Heidegger's early reading of Brentano's book, *On the Manifold Meaning of Being According to Aristotle*, is surely decisive. As late as 1973, in the seminar on Husserl's *Logical Investigations* that Heidegger taught in his Zähringen house, he claimed 'My Aristotle is Brentano's Aristotle!' (GA 15, 385). On the importance of Brentano for the evolution of the question of being, see Adrián (2010, 233–341).

Volpi's pioneer works on this subject are an obligatory reference (1976, 1978, 2001, 2004). See also Courtine (2007).
43 I will not address Husserl's conception of evidence here. For this, see Adrián (2010, 242–253). See also the brilliant exposition of this problem Tugendhat offers in his *Habilitationsschrift* (1967). On Heidegger's early concept of truth, see Courtine (1996b), Gethmann (1991), Ruggenini (1996) and Tugendhat (1969).
44 Heidegger formulates this objection as early as 1919 (GA 56/57, 109–110) and then elaborates it in the lecture course from the 1923–1924 semester (GA 17, 270ff.). I spell out in detail Heidegger's criticism of the Cartesian turn of Husserl's phenomenology in Chapter 5.
45 On the differences between Heidegger's and Husserl's postures, see Tugendhat (1967, 259–280).
46 Heidegger does this in the lecture course of the winter semester 1925–1926, *Logic. The Question of Truth* (cf. GA 21, §§ 11–14), and in *Being and Time* (SuZ, § 44). For more on this, see Ruggenini (1996) and Tugendhat (1969).
47 Heidegger's reconstruction of Aristotle theory of truth enables him to separate this phenomenon from a propositional scheme and thus free the question regarding being from the categorial approach (Vigo 1994).
48 I modify the translation in order to keep the consistency with our translation choices (translator's note).
49 The results of this analysis can be found in GA 21, § 12 and SuZ, § 33.
50 See Chapter 5 for a detailed account of the hermeneutic transformation of phenomenology.
51 This apparently arbitrary definition of 'being true as discovering' in fact echoes something ancient philosophy intuited and understood in a pre-phenomenological manner, namely, that *aletheia* refers to things themselves, that which shows itself. For its part, *logos* says something about how beings behave and for this reason it is disclosing in nature. In this sense, Heidegger's definition of truth as the state of discoveredness does not evince an attempt to shake off tradition but, on the contrary, to appropriate it in its most primordial sense.
52 For more on this, see Chapter 5, p. 143ff
53 The relativist consequences of this concept of truth *qua* unconcealment are plain in 'The Origin of the Work of Art'. This text preserves almost without alteration *Being and Time*'s account of truth. Meaning constitution and world openness are addressed there in terms of 'the foundation of truth' and 'the happening of truth', respectively. On the basis of this, Heidegger extends the question of truth beyond the limits of the problem of the proposition and knowledge and to all cultural domains: art, religion, history and philosophy. With this extension, Heidegger subordinates ontic-scientific knowledge to the deeper ontological understanding that characterizes these cultural domains.
54 For an exposition of the structure and content of these lecture course, see Adrián (2000b), McNeill (1999, 17–54) and, above all, Ingrid Schüßler (1996), the editor of that material.
55 I owe much of what follows to Volpi's sharp and original interpretation.
56 In *Eudemian Ethics,* Aristotle explicitly states that *praxis* is *kinesis tou bios* (*EE* II 3, 1220b, 27)
57 On the specific nature of *logos* and *doxa* as fundamental determinations of human being, see the interesting lecture course of the summer 1924, *Basic Concepts of Aristotelian Philosophy*, where Heidegger offers a detailed interpretation of Aristotle's

Rhetoric. In his own words, this work 'must be understood as the first systematic hermeneutic of the everydayness of being-with-one-another' (SuZ, 138/BT, 135). I have addressed this topic, as well as that of the relation between *logos*, *doxa* and *pathos* understood as fundamental determinations of human being in Adrián (2010, 296–308, and more thoroughly in 2013, 1–17).

58 An expanded German edition was later published under the name *Vita activa oder vom tätigen Leben* (1960). In a letter dated 28 October 1960, Arendt confides to Heidegger: 'the book was born suddenly during the first days in Freiburg, and owes you so much in all regards'. In fact, Arendt privately dedicated the German version of the book to Heidegger.

59 Like Arendt, Gadamer also attended Heidegger's classes during the early twenties. The chapters of Gadamer's *Truth and Method* dedicated to practical wisdom are clearly indebted to the young Heidegger's interpretation of the sixth book of *Nichomachean Ethics* (Gadamer 1986, 317–329), as developed in the 1925–1926 lecture course. It is also worth noting that Gadamer's draft of the chapter entitled 'Praktische Philosophie' was composed in 1930, though it was published in 1985 (Gadamer, 1985, 230–249). Gadamer highlights the role of practical philosophy in his late writings 'Hermeneutik als praktische Philosophie' (1972) and 'Vom Ideal der praktischen Philosophie' (1980) (see Gadamer 1976, 78–109, 1983b, 67–78, respectively).

60 In the end, all Heidegger does is to equate the moment of decision with the kairological time he found in Pauline eschatology.

61 *Proairesis* is not to be understood as a choice among the different existing possibilities available at a given time. Rather, it refers to a prior orientation, that is, it anticipates the moment of action: 'The origin of action – its efficient, not its final cause – is choice, and that choice is desire and reasoning with a view to an end' (Nic. Eth. VI 2, 1139a, 30–33).

62 This forces human being to go beyond mere self-preservation and reflect about the type of life it wants to have. For this reason, *Nichomachean Ethics* is not just about the preservation of life, but about the good life.

63 This conception of human existence as involving the two complementary aspects of possibility and necessity was probably suggested to Heidegger by his reading of Kierkegaard and Karl Jaspers' detailed exposition of the Danish philosopher in *Psychology of World Views*. A person is first and foremost a synthesis of necessity and possibility. In Heideggerian terms: Dasein is thrown project (*geworfener Entwurf*).

64 For more on this, see Brogan (2007), Jollivet (2007) and Weigelt (2004).

65 For a broader analysis of this point, see Adrián (2010, 310–337).

66 Heidegger also considers *ousia* as *hypokeimenon*, a concept he renders as *presence-at-hand* (*Vorhandenheit*) (GA 19, 24, GA 21, 244ff. and NB, 272–273).

67 In particular, Heidegger discusses Augustine's, Plotinus's, Simplicius's, Kant's and Hegel's conceptions of time. Heidegger also argues that Aristotle's conception was determinant for the development of the history of philosophy (GA 24, 328/BP, 231). It is surprising that Heidegger does not mention Husserl's investigations on the topic given that in 1927 Heidegger himself, together with Husserl's assistant, Edith Stein, edited Husserl's *The Phenomenology of Internal Time-Consciousness*.

68 Mörchen's classic study on the interpretation of transcendental imagination as temporality on the basis of an analysis of the *Critique of Judgment* (Mörchen 1930) and Vollrath's analysis of the metaphysical presuppositions of Kant's thought (1969, 93–160) are cases in point. See also Rosales (2000).

69 Among the numerous studies on Heidegger's reading of Kant, some of the most important are Blattner (1994), Dastur (1996), Han-Pile (2005), Rogozinski (2002) and Schalow (1992, 2002).
70 As Dastur points out, what Heidegger says in this lecture course anticipate many of the ideas of his book on Kant and include an interpretation of the schematism of the pure concepts of understanding that is lacking in the 1927–1928 lecture course (Dastur 1996, 114).
71 This topic, announced in *Being and Time*'s outline, is finally developed in *The Basic Problems of Phenomenology*, from 1927.
72 Heidegger employs here the Latinized term '*Temporalität*' in order to distinguish the temporal structure *(temporale Struktur)* of all phenomena – life and Dasein included – from temporality *(Zeitlichkeit)* in the natural and prephilosophical sense, which denotes the mere happening of things in time (GA 21, 199). In this lecture course he has not yet drawn the distinction between Dasein's temporality *(Zeitlichkeit)* and the temporality of being *(Temporalität)*, which is fully operative in *Being and Time*.
73 See also SuZ, 4/BT, 3.
74 This explains Heidegger's use of the expression '*Temporalien*' in the lecture course of 1925–1926. The *Temporalien* are the temporal *(temporal)* features of Dasein's existence and are to be distinguished from the temporal *(zeitlich)* determinations of all other phenomena. At the end of this course, Heidegger renames these structures with the term he uses in *Being and Time*, '*Existenzialen*'.

Chapter 5

1 Husserl had Heidegger in high esteem at first. During their first years of collaboration, Husserl is pleasantly surprised with Heidegger's intellectual capacities. A letter to Natorp of 11 February 1920, attests to this: '[Heidegger] has started to work in phenomenology with the highest strength' (Husserl 1994, vol. IV, 140). And as late as 1922, in another letter to Natorp, he recognizes Heidegger's philosophical potency: 'his phenomenological way of seeing, of working, and the very field of his interests, are not determined after me, all these are the result of his own originality' (Husserl 1994, vol. IV, p. 150). As it is well known, however, the idyllic phase of their relationship did not last too long. Their breakup became particularly severe in 1927, when Husserl wrote the article, 'Phenomenology' for the *Encyclopedia Britannica*. That same year, Husserl wrote to Roman Ingarden, 'the new article has been very difficult for me, particularly because I had to examine my path once again and confirmed that Heidegger, so I must believe now, did not understand that path, including the meaning of the method of the phenomenological reduction' (Husserl 1994, vol. III, 232).
2 The problem of the extent of the continuity and divergence between Heidegger's work and Husserl's phenomenology is very important in the critical literature. In general, two main positions can be identified. The first one stresses the way Heidegger distances himself from Husserl's work. Readings of this kind vary significantly. While authors like García Gaínza claim that Heidegger was never a phenomenologist (1997, 190), others think Heidegger progressively took distance from phenomenology (Rodríguez 1993, 88–92). Yet some others date the definitive breakup as late as 1929, when Heidegger wrote 'What is Metaphysics?' (Pöggeler 1983, 79; Jamme 1986/87, 89). The second line of interpretation insists in the continuity between Husserl's and

Heidegger's work. For some commentators, Heidegger's hermeneutics is necessarily grounded in certain aspects of Husserl's phenomenology (Crowell 1999, 208, 212) and Merker (1988, 268). Others stress that transcendental phenomenology is necessary for hermeneutic phenomenology. See for instance Merleau-Ponty's classic reading (1945, IX); also Caputo (1992, 100) and Marion (1989, 104, 108).

3   I will come back to the essentially reflective nature of this intuition and the Cartesianism charge on p. 119ff.

4   For a more detailed assessment of Husserl's criticism of naturalism and historicism, see Heidegger's lecture course, 1923–1924 (GA 17, §§ 8, 13 and 14).

5   This view is not infrequent. For some, Heidegger's hermeneutic phenomenology is the result of combining Husserl's phenomenology and Dilthey's hermeneutics (Gadamer 1987a, 198). Pöggeler goes as far as to speak of a combination of Husserl and Bergson (1992, 24). The assumption of these readings is that the alleged originality of the hermeneutic phenomenology reduces to broaden the paths opened by Husserl and Dilthey. See Grondin (1996, 272), Caputo (1986, 112, 120) and Makkreel (1990, 175ff.). Xolocotzi offers an interesting assessment of the methodological and therefore also thematic continuity between the young Heidegger's work and that of the aforementioned predecessors.

6   See Chapter 4 for a detailed analysis of Heidegger's appropriation of Aristotle's practical philosophy and its significance for the development of an analytic of human life (p. 70–96).

7   I explain why I do not translate this term in note 3 of the Introduction.

8   For detailed reconstructions of the development of the hermeneutics of facticity during Heidegger's first Freiburg years, see Fabris (1997), Imdahl (1997) and Rodríguez (1997). See also Adrián (2006), Kisiel (1996b), Lazzari (2002), Segura (1999) and Xolocotzi (2002).

9   For more on the structure pre-understanding and the hermeneutic circle see the *Natorp-Bericht* (NB, 237–238). By the same token, some very important passages from *Truth and Method*. Gadamer's philosophical hermeneutics develops in a very productive way many of the ideas Heidegger presented in the early lecture courses (1986, 270ff.).

10 Formal indication is widely discussed in the literature. See for instance Adrián (2004), Buren (1994a, 324–341), Dahlstrom (1994), Dijk (1991), Imdahl (1997), Lara (2008, 161–204), Oudemans (1990), Rodríguez (1997, 155–187), Streeter (1997), Xolocotzi (2004, 107–124). Pöggeler (1983, 354) and Kim (1988, 137) claim that Heidegger's appeal to formal indication corresponds to the intermediate period of his work that goes from the hermeneutics of facticity to *Being and Time*. In my view this is wrong. One might think that formal indication is no longer important in *Being and Time*, but in a 1927 letter to Löwith, Heidegger writes: 'Formal indication, critique of the doctrine of a priori, formalization, etc., all this is present to me even if I don't talk about it' (in Papenfuss and Pöggeler 1990, 37). In addition to this, formal indication figures in latter works, such as the 1929–1930 lecture course. Coriando (1998) shows how to understand formal indication in Heidegger's latter onto-historical thinking. Kisiel (1996b) also proposes a very problematic interpretation on the basis of Heidegger's post-war semester picture of his philosophical programme. Kisiel's proposal is powerfully questioned by Kalariparambil (1999, 93–98).

11 See GA 60, 11–13; GA 61, 16–41. There are some scattered allusions to the topic in Heidegger's review of Jaspers' book (GA 9, 8–11), the *Natorp-Bericht*, from 1922 (NB,

237–239, 247–249), and the 1929–1930 lecture course, *The Fundamental Problems of Metaphysics* (GA 29/30, § 70).

12 The study mentioned was never published but it is the textual foundation of the crucial 1924 treatise, *The Concept of Time*, unpublished until recently (GA 64, 1–103).

13 I have discussed this in Adrián (2010, 399–409). Gadamer construes the notion of formal indication on the basis of Kierkegaard's notion of 'actualizing' (*Aufmerksam machen*) (Gadamer 1983b, 148). For his part, Imdahl alludes to Simmel's 'formal moment' (1997, 45ff.). Xocolotzi focuses on the debt with Husserl (2004, 117–122). As I will explain in the next section, in my view Heidegger's motivations for the use of the notion of formal indication come from Kierkeggard but the notion takes shape as he engages in an intense consideration of Husserl's reflexive phenomenology.

14 It is worth remembering that Husserl's analysis is part of his attempt at providing a logical explanation of the mathematical methods of formalization and generalization.

15 For more on the executing nature of life, see my account of Heidegger's analysis of Aristotle's concept of *kinesis* in Chapter 4.

16 I come back to the difference between Husserl's reflexive intuition and Heidegger's hermeneutic intuition in the next section.

17 See also *My Way to Phenomenology* (ZSD, 86/MWP, 78), and the Zähringen seminar (VS, 116ff.). Among the numerous literature on the relation between Heidegger and Husserl and particularly on the problem of the categorial intuition, it is worth mentioning Dastur (1991), Held (1989), Herrmann (2000), Richter (1999), Rodríguez (1997, 173–197), Taminiaux (1978) and Watanabe (1993).

18 For an excellent discussion of the widely held accusation of essentialism Husserl has been subject to with regard to his idea of intuition of essences (*Wesensschau*), see Dan Zahavi's monograph (2003, 37–42).

19 However, as Held ascertains, the key to Husserl's view rests on his actualization that the categorial has the character of trans-subjective pre-givenness. This points to a trans-subjective space of openness (1989, 112). Put in the later Heidegger's terms, the categorial makes the presentation of beings possible and grounds the dimension of presencing in which beings become intelligible (VS, 116ff.). For this reason, the categorial has a double dimension: as *ratio essendi*, it discovers beings; as *ratio cognoscendi*, enables us to know them.

20 For more on the hermeneutic transformation of phenomenology, see, besides Herrmann's aforementioned works, Adrián (2005), Biemel (1978), Fabris (1997), Figal (2009), Gadamer (1986, 258–275), Gander (2001), Grondin (1991, 119–137), Jamme (1986/87), Kalariparambil (1999, 67–148), Lafont (2004), Merker (1988), Pöggeler (1994, 227–247), Richter (1999), Riedel (1989), Rodríguez (1997) and Thurner (1996).

21 One might think that Heidegger coined the expression 'to world' (*welten*). But this is not so. The verb figures in the Grimm brothers' dictionary as a derivation from the noun 'world' (*Welt*). In middle High German, 'to world' means 'to lead a relaxed, cheerful and hassle-free life', and even also 'to lead a jaunty life' (Grimm 1864–1960, vol. 28, 1562).

22 This '*already*' refers to an ontological structure that is central to the development of the young Heidegger's philosophical programme: it is the 'hermeneutic how' of primordial understanding, on which the 'apophantic how of the proposition' is grounded. To formulate a proposition, to express a judgement, is to reveal something, to say something about something. But this predicative act is derivative on being already in the world. The world opens up to the pre-predicative experience as a somewhat *meant* world, a world that is located within certain interpretation. As a

consequence, the proposition does not hold a primordial relation to beings; rather, the proposition is only possible on the basis of a prior disclosedness, which is the condition of possibility of any utterance. The universality of the 'how-structure' and *Being and Time*'s thesis that 'a pre-predicative seeing of what is at hand is in itself already understanding and interpretative' (SuZ, 149/BT, 140) are only possible against the background of the hermeneutic transformation of phenomenology that started with the first Freiburg lecture courses. I discussed Heidegger's concept of truth as unhidenness in Chapter 4, pp. 63ff.

23 It is worth noticing Heidegger's use of ingenious terminological devices in order to avoid the neo-Kantian vocabulary. In this case, he opposes the formal logic notion of 'state of affairs' (*Sachverhalt*) to the hermeneutic one of 'context of significance' (*Bedeutsamkeitsverhalt*) (cf. GA 58, 112).

24 This is another term Heidegger borrows from the brothers Grimm dictionary. Together with this text, the lexicographic sources Heidegger resorts to the most are Kluge's *Etymologisches Wörterbuch der deutschen Sprache*, and Kittel's *Etymologisches Wörterbuch zum Neuen Testament*. The verb '*entleben*' was used in the seventeenth century in the sense of killing or 'stealing a life' (*vita privare*) (Grimm 1864–1960, vol. 3, 568).

25 We should understand '*Ereignis*' here in opposition to '*Vorgang*'. Heidegger uses the former in order to highlight what is lived and experienced in life. In this sense, it has nothing to do with the key concept of the so-called *Kehre*, discussed, mostly, in *Contributions to Philosophy* (1936–1938). The later Heidegger's concept of *Ereignis* is characterized by a double movement of givenness and refusal, unconcealment and concealment. For a detailed analysis of the role, meaning, genealogy and peculiarities of the young Heidegger's philosophical vocabulary, see Adrián (2009, 15–20).

26 '*Hinsehen*' literally means 'to take a look at', 'to inspect.' Heidegger, however, uses this expression in the sense of observing or contemplating something in more of a theoretical and abstract way. This is a way of 'seeing' the world that is opposite to the intuitive and practical way in which we deal with things when we are immersed in the world. Heidegger recovers Lask's philosophical term, '*Hingabe*' to express this type of non-thematic absorption of life in the world. Lask uses the word '*Hingabe*' to denote our immediate experience of the forms of life, such as values, in which we are immersed. The Heideggerian use of the term certainly reflects Lask's influence and his principle of the material determination of form (see Chapter 3, pp. 30ff). According to this principle, our knowledge of objects does not rest in the reflective and theoretical activity of a transcendental subject as much as in the existence of a horizon of sense that has always been already understood in a pre-reflective way.

27 As Herrmann has shown in a very detailed way, here the deep differences between Husserl's method of descriptive reflection and Heidegger's procedure of hermeneutic understanding surface once again (Herrmann 2000, 67–98). For a critical assessment of the classical distinction between reflective and hermeneutic phenomenology, in light of some critical remarks regarding Heidegger's unilateral interpretation of Husserl, see Zahavi (2003).

28 The first one to see this implication was Merleau-Ponty in his famous preface to *Phenomenology of Perception* (1945, ix).

29 Courtine explains the similarities and differences between Husserl's reduction and Heidegger's appeal to anxiety. For other readings along the lines of Courtine's, see Marion (1989, 79–104) and Merker (1988, 153–193).

30 Merker offers an interesting description of the transit from inauthenticity to the primordial openness of authenticity. Leaving aside the methodological role of anxiety, Merker shows how, on Heidegger's account, the results traditionally associated with reflection are replaced by an event that happens to us suddenly and which, in analogy with the Pauline and Lutheran theological traditions, he construes as givenness and conversion (Merker 1991, 231–234).

31 The phenomenological distinction, which Husserl introduces in the 1910–1911 lecture course, *The Basic Problems of Phenomenology*, allows us to sever the connection between lived experience and the existence of things (HU XIII, 13). In *Ideas I*, this distinction points to the difference between being as lived experience and being as thing. While the former is immanent, absolute and necessary, the latter is transcendent, relative and contingent (HU III/1, 87–88, 118–119).

32 For more on this, see Gander (2004, 303–306).

33 For the relation between Heidegger and Natorp, see Lara (2008, 108–112) and Lazzari (2002, 112ff.).

34 Along these lines, Natorp claims that it is not possible to address lived experiences in their immediacy because they are always mediated by concepts. For this reason, Natorp favours a reconstructive method that seeks to neutralize the influence of reflection with the purpose of reaching the immediacy of the stream of experience. This can only be achieved in an asymptotic way, because it is not possible to reach the subjective immediacy of what is experienced.

35 Some echo of Natorp's objections to Husserl is apparent in the lecture courses from 1919 (GA 56/57, 99–108) and 1920 (GA 59, 92–147). In the latter lecture course Dilthey's influence is also patent, particularly as regards the historical character of the immediate reality of life and its capacity for self-understanding. I have addressed this point in Adrián (2005, 163–166).

36 See pp. 96ff of this chapter.

37 As we will see in the next section, the true being of intentionality is being-in-the-world.

38 Husserl's latter genetic phenomenology acknowledges this. He accepts that any reflection has to start by going back to a description of the life-world (*Lebenswelt*). In light of the textual evidence that the inquiries into the so-called genetic phenomenology has provided, it has become necessary to revisit the classical interpretations of Husserl as an idealist and as a defender of solipsism, which to a large extent have been widely accepted on the basis of Heidegger's criticism. I will come back to this in the section beginning on p. 134ff.

39 In this way, it becomes apparent that Heidegger never lost his interest in intentionality, as some authors suggest, but actually construed this notion in a radically primordial way. A case in point is Agamben, who talks about Heidegger's abandoning intentionality (1988, 65–66). In my view, Herrmann's posture (2002) is more adequate. For him, intentionality is the leading thread of Heidegger's phenomenology. Buchholz holds a similar view (1995, 54ff., 80ff.).

40 This idea is already present in Heidegger's review of Jaspers' book (1919–1921), where he asserts that 'the full sense of any phenomenon includes the following intentional characteristics: the intentional relation [established by the *intentio*], the intentional content [placed on the *intentum*], and the intentional enactment, so as to avoid any special emphasis on a theoretical sense of the intentional relation' (AKJ, 22/CKJ, 19).

41 In his extensive commentary to *Being and Time*'s introduction, Herrmann offers a detailed analysis of the methodological paragraph (§ 7) in which Heidegger breaks down the concept of phenomenology (Herrmann 1987, 277–390).
42 See for instance Habermas (1985, 129) and Rorty (1980, 4, 166–168).
43 In what follows I draw heavily on Zahavi's compelling argument (2003, 72–77).
44 At some point Husserl realized that transcendental phenomenology was similar in some respects to Fichte's idealism (see Gadamer 1987b, 161–162). In this last text Gadamer emphasizes the importance of the concept of world for avoiding the risk of falling into Cartesianism. As Gadamer points out in *Truth and Method* (1986), in order to definitely settle the question regarding Husserl's stance toward idealism and subjectivity, one would need to have access to a great part of his unpublished work. Fortunately, a good part of that material is currently available, and this should allow us to reassess Husserl's work as a whole.
45 In this respect, the critique presented in the lecture courses, *The Idea of Philosophy and the Problem of Worldview* (sec. 3.2), *Introduction to Phenomenological Research* (sec. 3.3) and *History of the Concept of Time* (sec. 3.4), which I discussed above, are particularly relevant. Now, one should not forget that irrespective of whether one embraces Heidegger's criticism of Husserl, this issue has been widely discussed for some time now with a view 'to set things straight', to use an expression that is frequent in the phenomenological arenas. Among others scholars one should mention Ludwig Landgrebe, Klaus Held, Rudolf Bernet and Walter Biemel in Germany; Javier San Martín, Miguel García Baró and Roberto Walton in the Spanish-speaking world; and Donn Welton, Dan Zahavi, Steve Crowell and Jitendra Nath Mohanty in the English-speaking world. There are many works that discuss the similarities and differences between the work of both thinkers, the possibility of interpreting these works as complementary and the legitimacy of Heidegger's appropriation, among many other subjects. My own view is that Heidegger's work started to diverge from Husserl's because of an internal critique and necessity rather than because of a rejection of Husserl's programme. I also think it is possible to establish a relation between their respective works that leaves each of them intact.
46 In this sense, one should not mistake phenomenology for psychological introspection, as so often happens. That is to say, phenomenology does not aim at establishing what a given person thinks of feels. Phenomenology explores transcendental subjectivity in its constitutive relation to the world. In contrast to private introspection, this exploration has to be intersubjectively valid, and therefore corrigible.
47 In this regard, see for example, Depraz (1995), Steinbock (1995), Welton (2000) and Zahavi (2003).
48 For more on this see the 1921 supplementary text 'Static and Genetic Phenomenological Method' (in HU XI, 336–345).
49 In this respect, numerous investigations on cognitive sciences have started to pay special attention to the contributions of phenomenology. Thompson's recent book (2007; particularly 16–36 and Appendix A, which corrects some of his critical views from previous works, such as Varela *et al.* (1991) is particularly relevant in this respect. For this reason the term 'neurophenomenology' has become increasingly frequent. See, for instance, Thompson *et al.* (2005) and Varela (1996). However, over and above the contributions phenomenology can make to cognitive sciences, it is also truth that phenomenology has to be complemented with psychology, neuroscience and biology.

50 Representative examples of this new take on Husserl's work, which breaks with the old Heidegger-inspired portrait of him as an idealist thinker, are Zahavi (2003) and the papers collected in *The New Husserl. A Critical Reader.*
51 For a brief and clear exposition of the central ideas of *Analyses Concerning Passive Synthesis*, see Steinbock's translation (2001, xv–xvii).
52 Schulz (1953–1954, 79) provides an early defence of the thesis that Heidegger's work remains within the confines of transcendental philosophy. The de-transcendentalizing thesis has been defended by Apel (1973, 22–52, 94–105 and 1989, 143–150).
53 In Lafont's cited book, one can find an interesting account of the conceptual framework of the ontological difference (2004, 268–274) that represents a development with respect to her previous book on the linguistic turn of Heidegger's hermeneutics (Lafont 1994, 30ff.).
54 In this sense, the pragmatic interpretation of the world as a totality of tools available for Dasein's use is completely wrong. Heidegger introduces a new concept of world that contrasts with the two traditional conceptions: the empirical one, on which the world is a totality of entities that includes human beings, and the transcendental one, which regards the totality of entities as constituted by an extra-wordly element, namely, transcendental subjectivity.
55 Grimm (1864–1960, vol. 28, 1459).
56 See, for instance, the first Freiburg lecture course, from 1919–1920 (GA 58, 33). In *Being and Time* this clear-cut distinction between what one may call the objective, intersubjective and subjective worlds disappears. In fact, this triple modality of being-in-the-world is not present in the 1923 lecture course. Likewise, Heidegger's early concern with what he calls the phenomenon of *distress* (*Bekümmerung*) is gradually displaced by a concern with *care* (*Sorge*). It is also worth noting that the technical term 'solicitude' (*Fürsorge*) is first introduced in the 1925–1926 lecture course.
57 Some of Heidegger's reflections on his own work point in this direction. See for instance his letter to Blochman of 20 December 1935, in which Heidegger expresses some self-criticism and the necessity of abandoning the philosophy of *Being and Time* (Heidegger and Blochmann 1989, 87). See also his letter to Arendt from 6 May 1950, where he talks about the threat of subjectivism implicit in the analytic of Dasein and the necessity of attempting a new formulation of the problem based on his work from 1937–1938, the years he was composing the *Contributions to Philosophy* (Heidegger and Arendt, 1998, 104). See also his 1937–1938 retrospective reflections (GA 66, 411–428), his thorough assessment of the 1940 lecture on the metaphysics of German idealism (GA 49, 26–74) and his well-known *Letter on Humanism* (GA 9, 301–360).
58 In this regard, Gadamer's testimony is very revealing. He recalls how, for him as a student, the expression 'ontological difference', which Heidegger used in Freiburg (1923) and Marburg (1924) was like a magical word. When he and his friend Gerhard Krüger asked Heidegger how was it possible to reach the ontological difference, Heidegger answered: 'But no! It is not us who make that distinction' (Gadamer 1995, 59). This happened in 1924! Just as interestingly, Gadamer points out that Heidegger saw in Parmenides's philosophy a clear predecessor of the ontological difference.
59 See the third part of *Truth and Method*. As is well known, Gadamer's world is profoundly inspired by Heidegger's hermeneutic transformation of phenomenology.

Conclusion

1. Casper (1980).
2. Fabris (2010, 21–22).
3. See for instance the 1926 lecture course *The Fundamental Concepts of Ancient Philosophy* (GA 22). For a detailed interpretation of Plato and especially Aristotle, see the lecture courses *The Fundamental Concepts of Aristotelian Philosophy* (GA 18), from 1924, and *Plato. The Sophist* (GA 19), from 1924–1925.
4. See the 1926–1927 lecture course *History of Philosophy, from Thomas Aquinas to Kant* (GA 23).
5. See Heidegger's criticism of Descartes in the 1923–1924 lecture course *Introduction to Phenomenological Research* (GA 17), his immanent critique of Husserl in the introduction to the 1925 lecture course *Prolegomena to a History of the Concept of Time* (GA 20), his engagement with Kant, which starts with the 1927–1928 lecture course, *Phenomenological Interpretations of Kant's* Critique of Pure Reason (GA 25), and later results in the book, *Kant and the Problem of Metaphysics* (GA 3), from 1929, and, finally, his work on Leibniz's thought in the 1928 lecture course *The Metaphysical Foundations of Logic* (GA 26).

Bibliography

Primary bibliography

Works by Heidegger (in chronological order – all references to Heidegger's work follow the *Gesamtausgabe* edition)

Heidegger, M., 'Allerseelenstimmungen' (publicado in *Heuberger Volksblatt* in 1909), in Denker, A., Gander, H.-H. and Zaborowski, H. (eds), *Heidegger-Jahrbuch* 1: *Heidegger und die Anfänge seines Denkens*, Karl Alber, Freiburg and Munich, 2004, 18–21.

——, 'Rezension zu F. W. Förster, *Autorität und Freiheit*' (*Der Akademiker, in* 1910), in *Reden und andere Zeugnisse eines Lebensweges* (GA 16, edited by H. Heidegger), Vittorio Klostermann, Frankfurt au Mein, 2000, 5–11.

——, 'Dem Grenzbot-Philosophen zur Antwort' (*Heuberger Volksblatt* 42, el 7 de abril de 1911), in Büchin, E. and Denker, A., *Martin Heidegger und seine Heimat*, Klett-Cotta, Stuttgart, 2005, 62–69.

——, 'Dem Grenzbot-Philosophen die zweite Antwort' (*Heuberger Volksblatt* 43, 10 April, 1911), in Büchin, E. and Denker, A., *Martin Heidegger und seine Heimat*, Klett-Cotta, Stuttgart, 2005, 71–74.

——, 'Modernismus', *Heuberger Volksblatt* 41 (1911), 1–3.

——, 'Zur philosophischen Orientierung für Akademiker' (*Der Akademiker*, in 1911), in *Reden und andere Zeugnisse eines Lebensweges* (GA 16, edited by H. Heidegger), Vittorio Klostermann, Frankfurt au Mein, 2000, 11–12.

——, 'Rede über naturwissenschaftliche Themen und Erdbebenkunde', *Heuberger Volksblatt* 14, no. 33 (1912).

——, 'Die tierische Abstammung des Menschen und das Urteil der Wissenshaft', *Heuberger Volksblatt* 14, no 47 (22 April 1912).

——, 'Rezension zu J. Gredts *Elementa philosophiae aristotelico-thomisticae*' (*Der Akademiker*, in 1912), in *Reden und andere Zeugnisse eines Lebensweges* (GA 16, edited by H. Heidegger), Vittorio Klostermann, Frankfurt au Mein, 2000, 27–30.

——, 'Das Realitätsproblem in der modernen Philosophie' (*Philosophisches Jahrbuch der Görres-Gesellschaft*, in 1912), in *Frühe Schriften* (GA 1, edited by F.W. v. Herrmann), Vittorio Klostermann, Frankfurt au Mein, 1978, 1–16.

——, 'Neuere Forschungen über Logik' (*Literarische Rundschau für das katholische Deutschland*, in 1912), in *Frühe Schriften* (GA 1, edited by F.W. v. Herrmann), Vittorio Klostermann, Frankfurt au Mein, 1978, 17–44.

——, 'Nikolai Bubnoff, *Zeitlichkeit und Zeitlosigkeit*' (*Literarische Rundschau für das katholische Deutschland*, in 1913), in *Frühe Schriften* (GA 1, edited by F.W. v. Herrmann), Vittorio Klostermann, Frankfurt au Mein, 1978, 46–47.

——, 'Spiritismus und Wissenschaft', *Heuberger Volksblatt* 15, no. 31 (14 April 1913).

——, 'Charles Sentroul, *Kant und Aristoteles*' (*Literarische Rundschau für das katholische Deutschland*, in 1914), in *Frühe Schriften* (GA 1, edited by F.W. v. Herrmann), Vittorio Klostermann, Frankfurt au Mein, 1978, 49–53.

——, *Die Lehre vom Urteil im Psychologismus. Ein kritisch-positiver Beitrag zur Logik* (published by J. A. Barth, Leipzig, 1914), in *Frühe Schriften* (GA 1, edited by F.W. v. Herrmann), Vittorio Klostermann, Frankfurt au Mein, 1978, 59–188.

——, 'Das Kriegs-Triduum in Meßkirch' (published in *Heuberger Volksblatt, in* 1915), in Denker, A., Gander, H.-H. and Zaborowski, H. (eds), *Heidegger-Jahrbuch* 1: *Heidegger und die Anfänge seines Denkens*, Karl Alber, Freiburg and Munich, 2004, 22–25.

——, 'Lebenslauf' (1915), in *Reden und andere Zeugnisse eines Lebensweges* (GA 16, edited by H. Heidegger), Vittorio Klostermann, Frankfurt au Mein, 2000, 38–39.

——, *Die Kategorien- und Bedeutungslehre des Duns Scotus* (1915), in *Frühe Schriften* (GA 1, edited by F.W. v. Herrmann), Vittorio Klostermann, Frankfurt au Mein, 1978, 189–411.

——, *Der Zeitbegriff in der Geschichtswissenschaft* (1915), in *Frühe Schriften* (GA 1, edited by F.W. v. Herrmann), Vittorio Klostermann, Frankfurt au Mein, 1978, 415–433.

——, 'Das Kategorienproblem,' in *Frühe Schriften* (GA 1, edited by F.W. v. Herrmann), Vittorio Klostermann, Frankfurt de Meno, 1978, 399–411.

——, 'Zu Schleiermachers zweiter Rede *Über das Wesen der Religion*' in *Phänomenologie des religiösen Lebens* (GA 60, edited by C. Strube), Vittorio Klostermann, Frankfurt au Mein, 1995, 319–322.

——, *Die philosophischen Grundlagen der mittelalterlichen Mystik*, in *Phänomenologie des religiösen Lebens* (GA 60, edited by C. Strube), Vittorio Klostermann, Frankfurt au Mein, 1995, 303–338.

——, *Die Idee der Philosophie und das Weltanschauungsproblem* (1919), in *Zur Bestimmung der Philosophie* (GA 56/57, edited by B. Heimbüchel), Vittorio Klostermann, Frankfurt au Mein, 1987, 3–117.

——, *Phänomenologie und transzendentale Wertphilosophie* (1919), in *Zur Bestimmung der Philosophie* (GA 56/57, edited by B. Heimbüchel), Vittorio Klostermann, Frankfurt au Mein, 1987, 121–201.

——, *Über das Wesen der Universität und des akademischen Studiums* (1919), in *Zur Bestimmung der Philosophie* (GA 56/57, edited by B. Heimbüchel), Vittorio Klostermann, Frankfurt au Mein, 1987, 205–214.

——, *Grundprobleme der Phänomenologie* (1919–1920) (GA 58, edited by H.-H. Gander), Vittorio Klostermann, Frankfurt au Mein, 1992.

——, *Phänomenologie der Anschauung und des Ausdruckes* (1920) (GA 59, editada por C. Strube), Vittorio Klostermann, Frankfurt au Mein, 1993.

——, (1976). 'Anmerkungen zu Karl Jaspers' *Psychologie der Weltanschauungen*' (1919–1921). In *Wegmarken* (1–44). Frankfurt am Main: Vittorio Klostermann (GA 9, edited by F.W. v. Herrmann). Trans. W. McNeill. 'Comments on Karl Jaspers' *Psychology of Worldviews* (1919/1921), in *Pathmarks* (1–38). New York, NY: Cambridge University Press, 1998.

——, *Einleitung in die Phänomenologie der Religion* (1920–1921), in *Phänomenologie des religiösen Lebens* (GA 60, edited by C. Strube), Vittorio Klostermann, Frankfurt au Mein, 1995, 3–159.

——, *Augustinus und der Neuplatonismus* (1921), in *Phänomenologie des religiösen Lebens* (GA 60, edited by C. Strube), Vittorio Klostermann, Frankfurt au Mein, 1995, 160–302.

——, *Phänomenologische Interpretationen zu Aristoteles. Einführung in die phänomenologische Forschung* (1921–1922) (GA 61, edited by W. Bröcker and K. Bröcker-Oltmanns), Vittorio Klostermann, Frankfurt au Mein, 1985.

——, 'Vita' (1922), in *Reden und andere Zeugnisse eines Lebensweges* (GA 16, edited by H. Heidegger), Vittorio Klostermann, Frankfurt au Mein, 2000, 41–45.

——, *Phänomenologische Interpretation ausgewählter Abhandlungen des Aristoteles zu Ontologie und Logik* (1922) (GA 62, edited by G. Neumann), Vittorio Klostermann, Frankfurt au Mein, 2005.

——, 'Phänomenologische Interpretationen zu Aristoteles. Anzeige der hermeneutischen Situation' (*Natorp Report*) (1922), *Dilthey-Jahrbuch* 6 (1989), 237–274 (in GA 62, por G. Neumann).

——, *Ontologie. Hermeneutik der Faktizität* (1923) (GA 63, edited by K. Bröcker-Oltmanns), Vittorio Klostermann, Frankfurt au Mein, 1988.

——, *Einführung in die phänomenologische Forschung* (1923–1924) (GA 17, edited by F.W. v. Herrmann), Vittorio Klostermann, Frankfurt au Mein, 1994.

——, *Grundbegriffe der aristotelischen Philosophie* (1924) (GA 18, edited by M. Michalski), Vittorio Klostermann, Frankfurt au Mein, 2002.

——, (1989). *Der Begriff der Zeit* (Conference, 1924). Tübingen: Max Niemeyer (reprinted in GA 64, pp. 105–125, by F.W. v. Herrmann). Trans. W. McNeill. *The Concept of Time*. Oxford: Blackwell Publishers, 1992.

——, (2004). *Der Begriff der Zeit* (Treatise, 1924). Vittorio Klostermann, Frankfurt am Main (GA 64, edited by F.W. v. Herrmann).

——, *Plato: Sophistes* (1924–1925) (GA 19, edited by I. Schüßler), Vittorio Klostermann, Frankfurt au Mein, 1992.

——, *Prolegomena zur Geschichte des Zeitbegriffes* (1925) (GA 20, edited by P. Jaeger), Vittorio Klostermann, Frankfurt au Mein, 1988.

——, 'Wilhelm Diltheys Forschungsarbeit und der gegenwärtige Kampf um eine historische Weltanschauung' (1925), in *Dilthey-Jahrbuch* 8 (1992/1993) (edited by F. Rodi), 143–180 (GA 80).

——, *Logik. Die Frage nach der Wahrheit* (1925–1926) (GA 21, edited by W. Biemel), Vittorio Klostermann, Frankfurt au Mein, 1976.

——, *Grundbegriffe der antiken Philosophie* (1926) (GA 22, edited by F.-K. Blust), Vittorio Klostermann, Frankfurt au Mein, 1993.

——, *Die Grundprobleme der Phänomenologie* (1927) (GA 24, edited by F.W. v. Herrmann), Vittorio Klostermann, Frankfurt au Mein, 1989.

——, *Geschichte der Philosophie von Thomas von Aquin bis Kant* (1926–1927) (GA 23, edited by H. Vetter), Vittorio Klostermann, Frankfurt au Mein, 2006.

——, *Phänomenologische Interpretationen von Kants* Kritik der reinen Vernunft (1927–1928) (GA 25, edited by Ingtraud Görland), Vittorio Klostermann, Frankfurt au Mein, 1995.

——, *Sein und Zeit* (1927), Max Niemeyer, Tubinga, 1986 (GA 2, por F.W. v. Herrmann). Trans. J. Stambaugh. *Being and Time*. Albany, NY: State University of New York, 2010.

—— (1978). 'Phänomenologie und Theologie' (1927). In *Wegmarken* (45–78). Frankfurt am Main: Vittorio Klostermann (GA 9, edited by F.W. v. Herrmann). Trans. W. McNeill. 'Phenomenology and Theology, in *Pathmarks* (39–62). New York, NY: Cambridge University Press, 1998.

——, *Metaphysische Anfangsgründe der Logik im Ausgang von Leibniz* (1928) (GA 26, edited by K. Held), Vittorio Klostermann, Frankfurt au Mein, 1990.

——, *Einleitung in die Philosophie* (1928–1929) (GA 27, edited by O. Saame and I. Saame-Speidel), Vittorio Klostermann, Frankfurt au Mein, 2001.

——, *Der deutsche Idealismus* (1929) (GA 28, edited by C. Strube), Vittorio Klostermann, Frankfurt au Mein, 1997.

——, *Die Grundbegriffe der Metaphysik. Welt – Endlichkeit – Einsamkeit* (1929–1930) (GA 29/30, edited by F.W. v. Herrmann), Vittorio Klostermann, Frankfurt au Mein, 1983.

——, *Kant und das Problem der Metaphysik* (1929), Vittorio Klostermann, Frankfurt au Mein, 1991 (GA 3, por F.W. v. Herrmann).

——, (1978). 'Was ist Metahpysik?' (1929). In *Wegmarken* (103–122). Frankfurt am Main: Vittorio Klostermann (GA 9, edited by F.W. v. Herrmann). Trans. W. McNeill. 'What Is Metaphysics?', in *Pathmarks* (82–96). New York, NY: Cambridge University Press, 1998.

——, *Vom Wesen der menschlichen Freiheit* (1930) (GA 31, edited by H. Tietjen), Vittorio Klostermann, Frankfurt au Mein, 1994.

——, *Aristoteles*, Metaphysik Θ, *1–3. Von Wesen und Wirklichkeit der Kraft* (1931) (GA 33, edited by H. Hüni), Vittorio Klostermann, Frankfurt au Mein, 1990.

——, *Die Frage nach dem Ding* (1935–1936), Max Niemeyer, Tubinga, 1987 (GA 41, edited by P. Jaeger).

——, *Schelling. Vom Wesen der menschlichen Freiheit (1809)* (1936) (GA 42, edited by I. Schüßler), Vittorio Klostermann, Frankfurt au Mein, 1988.

——, (1997). 'Ein Rückblick auf den Weg' (1937/38). In *Besinnung* (407–428). Frankfurt am Main: Vittorio Klostermann (GA 66, edited by F.W. v. Herrmann).

——, (1978). 'Vom Wesen und Begriff der *physis*. Aristoteles' *Physik* B, 1' (1939). In *Wegmarken* (239–301). Frankfurt am Main: Vittorio Klostermann (GA 9, edited by F.W. v. Herrmann). Trans. W. McNeill. 'On the Essence and Concept of *physis* in Aristotle's *Physics* B, 1', in *Pathmarks* (183–230). New York, NY: Cambridge University Press, 1998.

——, *Die Metaphysik des deutschen Idealismus* (1941) (GA 49, edited by G. Seubold), Vittorio Klostermann, Frankfurt au Mein, 2006.

——, (1978). 'Brief über den 'Humanismus'' (1946). In *Wegmarken* (301–360). Frankfurt am Main: Vittorio Klostermann (GA 9, edited by F.W. v. Herrmann). Trans. W. McNeill. 'Letter on 'Humanism'', in *Pathmarks* (239–276). New York, NY: Cambridge University Press, 1998.

——, *Die Grundfrage nach dem Sein selbst* (1946), in *Heidegger Studien* 2 (1986), 1–3.

——, (1978). 'Einleitung zu, as ist Metaphysik?' (1949). In *Wegmarken* (365–383). Frankfurt am Main: Vittorio Klostermann (GA 9, edited by F.W. v. Herrmann). Trans. W. McNeill. 'Introduction to 'What is Metaphysics?', in *Pathmarks* (277–290). New York, NY: Cambridge University Press, 1998.

——, (2006). *Zollikoner Seminare* (1959–1969). Frankfurt am Main: Vittorio Klostermann (GA 89, edited by Claudius Strube).

——, (1984). *Was heißt Denken?* (WS 1951–1952, and SS 1952). Tübingen: Max Niemeyer (GA 8, edited by P.L. Coriando).

——, 'Vom Geheimnis des Glockenturms' (Poem, 1954), in *Aus der Erfahrung des Denkens 1910–1976* (GA 13, edited by H. Heidegger), Vittorio Klostermann, Frankfurt au Mein, 1983, 113–116.

——, *Identität und Differenz*, Neske, Pfullingen, 1957 (GA 11, edited by F.W. v. Herrmann).

——, 'Antrittsrede Martin Heideggers bei der Aufnahme in die Heidelberger Akademie der Wissenschaften' (1959), *Jahreshefte der Heidelberger Akademie der Wissenschaften 1957/58*, Heidelberg, 1959, 20–21 (GA 1, edited by F.W. v. Herrmann, 55–57).

——, *Unterwegs zur Sprache* (1959), Neske, Pfullingen, 1990 (GA 12, edited by F.W. v. Herrmann).

——, (1978). 'Kants These über das Sein' (1961). In In *Wegmarken* (439–474). Frankfurt am Main: Vittorio Klostermann (GA 9, edited by F.W. v. Herrmann). Trans. W. McNeill. 'Kant's Thesis about Being', in *Pathmarks* (337–364). New York, NY: Cambridge University Press, 1998.

——, (1976). 'Mein Weg in die Phänomenologie' (1963). In *Zur Sache des Denkens* (81–90). Tübingen: Max Niemeyer (reprinted in GA 14, by F.W. v. Herrmann). Trans. J.

Stambaugh. 'My Way to Phenomenology', in *On Time and Being* (74–81). New York, NY: Harper & Row, 1972.

——, (1976). 'Das Ende der Philosophie und die Aufgabe des Denkens' (1964). In *Zur Sache des Denkens* (61–80). Tübingen: Max Niemeyer. Trans. J. Stambaugh. 'The End of Philosophy and the Task of Thinking', in *On Time and Being* (55–72). New York, NY: Harper & Row, 1972.

——, *Vier Seminare* (Thor Seminars from 1966, 1968, 1969 and Zähringen seminar from 1973), Vittorio Klostermann, Frankfurt au Mein, 1977.

——, 'Grußwort an die Teilnehmer des zehnten Colloquiums vom 14.-16. Mai 1976 in Chicago', in *Reden und andere Zeugnisse eines Lebensweges* (GA 16, edited by H. Heidegger), Vittorio Klostermann, Frankfurt au Mein, 2000, 747–748.

——, *Aus der Erfahrung des Denkens* (GA 13, edited by H. Heidegger), Vittorio Klostermann, Frankfurt au Mein, 1983.

——, *Seminare* (GA 15, edited by C. Ochwadt), Vittorio Klostermann, Frankfurt au Mein, 1986, 334–339 and 372–400.

Heidegger's correspondence

Heidegger, M., 'Brief an Engelbert Krebs' (9 January 1919), in Casper, B., 'Martin Heidegger und die theologische Fakultät Freiburg', *Freiburger Diözesan-Archiv* 100 (1980), 541.

——, 'Brief an Elisabeth Husserl' (24 April 1919), *Aut Aut* 223–224 (1988), 6–14.

——, 'Brief an Karl Löwith' (13 September 1920), in Löwith, K., *Mein Leben in Deutschland vor und nach 1933*, Stuttgart: Metzler, 1986, 30.

——, 'Brief an Karl Löwith' (19 August 1921), in Papenfuss, D. and Pöggeler, O. (eds), *Zur philosophischen Aktualität Heideggers*, vol. 2, Vittorio Klostermann, Frankfurt au Mein, 1990, 27–32.

——, 'Brief an Karl Löwith' (6 November 1924), in Storck, J. W. and Kisiel, Th. (eds), 'Martin Heidegger und die Anfänge der *Deutschen Vierteljahresschrift für Literaturwissenschaft und Geistesgeschichte*. Eine Dokumentation', *Dilthey-Jahrbuch* 8 (1992–1993), 214.

——, 'Brief an Karl Löwith' (20 August 1927), in Papenfuss, D. and Pöggeler, O. (eds), *Zur philosophischen Aktualität Heideggers*, vol. 2, Vittorio Klostermann, Frankfurt au Mein, 1990, 36–37.

——, 'Brief an Husserl' (22 October 1927), in Husserl, E., *Phänomenologische Psychologie* (Appendixes, *Husserliana* IX, Martinus Nijhoff), La Haya, 1968, 600–603.

——, 'Brief an Richardson' (1963), in Richardson, W., *Through Phenomenology to Thought*, Martinus Nijhoff, La Haya, 1974, xi–xxi.

——, 'Brief an Schrynemakers' (20 September 1966), in Sallis, J. (ed.), *Heidegger and the Path of Thinking*, Pittsburg, Duquesne University Press, 1970.

——, *'Mein liebes Seelchen!' Briefe Martin Heideggers an seine Frau Elfride 1915–1970*, Deutsche Verlags-Anstalt, Munich, 2005.

——, and Arendt, H., *Briefe 1925 bis 1975 und andere Zeugnisse*, Vittorio Klostermann, Frankfurt au Mein, 2002.

——, and Blochmann, E., *Briefwechsel 1918–1969*, Deutsches Literaturarchiv, Marbach, 1989 (edited by J. Storck).

——, and Bodmershof, I., *Briefwechsel 1959–1976*, Klett-Cotta, Stuttgart, 2000 (edited by B. Pieger).

——, and Jaspers, K., *Briefwechsel 1920–1963*, Piper and Vittorio Klostermann, Munich and Frankfurt au Mein, 1990 (edited by W. Biemel).

—, and Rickert, H., *Briefe 1912 bis 1933 und andere Dokumente*, Vittorio Klostermann, Frankfurt au Mein, 2002 (edited by A. Denker).
—, and Welte, B., *Briefe und Begegnungen*, Klett-Clotta, Stuttgart, 2003 (edited by B. Casper).
Heidegger, F., 'Ein Geburtstagsbrief des Bruders', in *Martin Heidegger zum 80. Geburtstag von seiner Heimatstadt Meßkirch*, Meßkrich, 1969, 58-63.

Works by Husserl

Husserl, E., *Texte zur Phänomenologie des inneren Zeitbewußtseins (1893-1917)*, Felix Meiner, Hamburgo, 1985.
—, *Logische Untersuchungen I, Prolegomena zur reinen Logik* (1900), *Husserliana* XVIII (edited by E. Holenstein), Martinus Nijhoff, La Haya, 1975.
—, *Logische Untersuchungen II, Untersuchungen zur Phänomenologie und Theorie der Erkenntnis* (1900), *Husserliana* XIX/1 and XIX/2 (edited by U. Panzer), Martinus Nijhoff, La Haya, 1984.
—, *Zur Phänomenologie des inneren Zeitbewußtseins* (1893-1917), *Husserliana* X (edited by R. Boehm), Martinus Nijhoff, La Haya, 1966.
—, *Die Idee der Phänomenologie* (1906), *Husserliana* II (edited by W. Biemel), Martinus Nijhoff, La Haya, 1973.
—, *Grundprobleme der Phänomenologie* (1910/1911), in *Zur Phänomenologie der Intersubjektivität*, *Husserliana* XIII (edited by I. Kern), Martinus Nijhoff, La Haya, 1973.
—, 'Philosophie als strenge Wissenschaft' (1911) (*Logos* I), in *Aufsätze und Vorträge* (1911-1921), *Husserliana* XXV (edited by Th. Nenon and H. R. Sepp), Martinus Nijhoff, La Haya, 1987, 3-67.
—, *Ideen zu einer reinen Phänomenologie und phänomenologischen Philosophie*. Libro primero (1913), *Husserliana* III/1 (edited by K. Schuhmann), Martinus Nijhoff, La Haya, 1976.
—, *Ideen zu einer reinen Phänomenologie und phänomenologischen Philosophie*. Libro segundo: *Phänomenologische Untersuchungen zur Konstitution* (1913), *Husserliana* IV (edited by M. Biemel), Martinus Nijhoff, La Haya, 1952.
—, *Die Bernauer Manuskripte über das Zeitbewußtsein* (1917-1918), *Husserliana* XXXIII (edited by R. Bernet and D. Lohmar), Kluwer Academic Publisher, Dordrech, 2001.
—, *Analysen zur passiven Synthesis. Aus Vorlesungs- und Forschungsmanuskripten* (1918-1926), *Husserliana* XI (edited by M. Fleischer), Martinus Nijhoff, La Haya, 1966.
—, 'Brief an Rudolf Otto' (5 March 1919), in Schütte, H.-W., *Religion und Christentum in der Theologie Rudolf Ottos*, Walter de Gruyter, Berlin, 1969.
—, 'Statische und genetische phänomenologische Methode' (1921), in *Analysen zur passiven Synthesis*, *Husserliana* XI (edited by M. Fleischer), Martinus Nijhoff, La Haya, 1966, 336-345.
—, *Aktive Synthesen. Aus der Vorlesung 'Transzendentale Logik'* (1920/21), *Husserliana* XXXI (edited by R. Breeur), Kluwer Academic Publisher, Dordrecht, 2000.
—, *Zur Phänomenologie der Intersubjektivität. Texte aus dem Nachlaß*. Parte primera: 1905-1929, *Husserliana* XIII (edited by I. Kern), Martinus Nij-hoff, La Haya, 1973.
—, *Erste Philosophie I, Kritische Ideengeschichte (1923/1924)*, *Husserliana* VII (edited by R. Boehm), Martinus Nijhoff, La Haya, 1965.
—, *Erste Philosophie II, Theorie der phänomenologischen Reduktion (1923/1924)*, *Husserliana* VIII (edited by R. Boehm), Martinus Nijhoff, La Haya, 1959.

——, *Phänomenologische Psychologie* (1925), *Husserliana* IX (edited by W. Biemel), Martinus Nijhoff, La Haya, 1962.
——, *Formale und transzendentale Logik* (1929), *Husserliana* XVII (edited by P. Janssen), Martinus Nijhoff, La Haya, 1974.
——, *Die Krisis der europäischen Wissenschaften und die transzendentale Phänomenologie*, *Husserliana* VI (edited by W. Biemel), Martinus Nijhoff, La Haya, 1954.
——, *Briefwechsel*, Kluwer Academic Publisher, Dordrecht, 1994.
——, 'Randbemerkungen zu Heideggers *Sein und Zeit* und *Kant und das Problem der Metaphysik*', *Husserl Studies* XI (1994), 3–63.

Other primary sources

Augustine, *The Confessions*, Hyde Park, NY: New City Press (Trans. Maria Boulding, O.S.A.).
Aristotle, *Metaphysics*, Oxford University Press, London, 1924 (edited by David Ross).
——, *Physics*, Oxford University Press, London, 1936 (edited by David Ross).
——, *Politics*, Oxford University Press, London, 1998 (edited by Ernest Baker and R.F. Stalley).
——, *On the Soul*, Oxford University Press, London, 2009 (edited by David Ross, revised by Lesley Brown).
——, *The Nichomachean Ethics*, Oxford University Press, London, 2009 (edited by David Ross, revised by Lesly Brown).
——, *On Rhetoric*, Oxford University Press, London, 2010 (translated by George Kennedy).
Brentano, F., *Von der mannigfachen Bedeutung des Seienden nach Aristoteles*, Georg Olms Verlagsbuchhandlung, Hildesheim, 1960.
Dilthey, W., 'Die Entstehung der Hermeneutik', in *Gesammelte Schriften* V, B. G. Teubner, Stuttgart, 1957, 317–338.
——, *Leben Schleiermachers*, in *Gesammelte Schriften* XIII/1, Walter de Gruyter, Berlin, 1970.
——, 'Christentum, Erkenntnistheorie und Metaphysik', in *Einleitung in die Geisteswissenschaften*, B. G. Teubner, Stuttgart, 1973, 250–267.
——, *Der Aufbau der Welt in den Geisteswissenschaften*, in *Gesammelte Schriften* VII, B. G. Teubner, Stuttgart, 1973.
Förster, F. W., *Autorität und Freiheit. Betrachtungen zum Kulturproblem der Kirche*, Kempten and Munich, 1910.
Jaspers, K., *Psychologie der Weltanschauungen*, Springer, Berlin, 1919.
——, *Philosophische Autobiographie*, Piper, Munich, 1977.
——, Kant, I., *Kritik der reinen Vernunft*, Hamburg, Felix Meiner, 1990. Trans. P. Guyer and A. W. Wood.
——, *Critique of Pure Reason*, Cambridge University Press, New York 1998.
Kierkegaard, S., *Abschließende unwissenschaftliche Nachschrift*, in *Gesammelte Werke* (vol. 7), Eugen Diederichs, Cologne and Düsseldorf, 1962.
——, *Philosophische Brocken*, in *Gesammelte Werke* (vol. 10), Eugen Diederichs, Cologne and Düsseldorf, 1952.
——, *Einübung im Christentum*, in *Gesammelte Werke* (vol. 26), Eugen Diederichs, Cologne and Düsseldorf, 1995.
——, *Die Krankheit zum Tode*, in *Gesammelte Werke* (vols. 24/25), Eugen Diederichs, Cologne and Düsseldorf, 1957.

Lask, E., *Die Logik der Philosophie und die Kategorienlehre*, in *Gesammelte Schriften* II, J. C. B. Mohr, Tubinga, 1923a.
——, *Die Lehre vom Urteil*, in *Gesammelte Schriften* II, J. C. B. Mohr, Tubinga, 1923b.
Luther, M., 'The Heidelberg Disputation,' in Forde, Gerard O., *On Being and Theologician of the Cross. Reflections on Luther's Heidelberg Disputation, 1518*. Cambridge: Williams B. Eerdmans Publishing Company.
Natorp, P., 'Husserls Ideen einer reinen Phänomenologie', *Logos* 7 (1917/1918), 215-240.
——, *Philosophische Systematik* (1958), Hamburg: Felix Meiner.
Paul, Letters, in *The New American Bible* (Saint Joseph edition), Catholic Book Publishing, New York, 1992.
Rickert, H., *Die Grenzen der naturwissenschaftlichen Begriffsbildung. Eine logische Einleitung in die historischen Wissenschaften*, J. C. B. Mohr, Tubinga, 1929.
Schleiermacher, F., *Hermeneutik und Kritik*, Suhrkamp, Frankfurt au Mein, 1977.

Secondary bibliography

Adrián, J., 'Fenomenología de la vida religiosa en el joven Heidegger, I: De la tesis de habilitación a los cursos de 1919', *Pensamiento* 55/212 (1999a), 217-243.
——, 'Fenomenología de la vida religiosa in el joven Heidegger, II: in torno a los cursos de religión (1920-1921)', *Pensamiento* 55/213 (1999b), 385-412.
——, 'Del sujeto epistemológico al horizonte translógico de la vida humana. Un estudio crítico del problema de la fundamentación de la lógica en los primeros escritos de Heidegger (1912-1916)', *Dianoia* XLV, no. 45 (1999c), 65-113.
——, *El joven Heidegger. Un estudio interpretativo de su obra temprana al hilo de la pregunta por el ser*, Ediciones UAB, Barcelona, 2000a.
——, 'Heidegger and la filosofía práctica de Aristóteles: de la *Ética a Nicómaco* a la ontología de la vida humana', *Taula* 33/34 (2000b), 91-106.
——, 'Der junge Heidegger und der Horizont der Seinsfrage', *Heidegger Studien* 17 (2001a), 11-21.
——, 'El joven Heidegger. Asimilación and radicalización de la filosofía práctica de Aristóteles', *Logos. Anales del Seminario de Metafísica* 34 (2001b), 179-221.
——, 'Prólogo', in M. Heidegger, *Interpretaciones fenomenológicas sobre Aristóteles. Indicación de la situación hermenéutica*, Trotta, Madrid, 2002, 9-22.
——, 'Heidegger and la indicación formal: hacia una articulación categorial de la vida humana', *Dianoia* XLIX/52 (2004), 25-46.
——, 'Hermeneutische versus reflexive Phänomenologie. Eine kritische Revision Heideggers früher Stellung zu Husserl ausgehend vom Kriegsnotsemester 1919', *Analecta Husserliana* LXXXVIII (2005), 157-173.
——, 'Die Funktion einer formal-anzeigenden Hermeneutik. Zu einer hermeneutisch-phänomenologischen Artikulation des faktischen Lebens ausgehend von Heideggers Frühwerk', *Philosophisches Jahrbuch* 113/1 (2006), 99-117.
——, *El programa filosófico del joven Heidegger*, Herder, Barcelona, 2008.
——, *El lenguaje de Heidegger. Diccionario filosófico (1912-1927)*, Herder, Barcelona, 2009.
——, *Heidegger e a filosofia prática de Aristóteles*, Nuova Harmonia, São Leopoldo (Brazil), 2010.
——, 'Heidegger on discourse and idle talk', *Philosophy Today*, 3/2 (2013).
Agamben, G., 'La passion de la facticité', in *Heidegger: questions ouvertes*, Cahiers du Collège International de Philosophie 6 (1988), 63-84.

Apel, K.-O., *Die Transformation der Philosophie*, I. *Sprachanalytik, Semiotik, Hermeneutik*, Suhrkamp, Frankfurt au Mein, 1973.

——, 'Sinnkonstitution und Geltungsrechtfertigung. Heidegger und das Problem der Transzendental-philosophie', in Forum für Philosophie Bad Homburg (ed.), *Martin Heidegger: Innen- und Außensichten*, Suhrkamp, Frankfurt au Mein, 1989, 131–175.

Arendt, H., *The Human Condition*, University of Chicago Press, Chicago, 1958.

——, 'Martin Heidegger zum 80. Geburtstag', *Merkur* X (1969), 893–902.

——, 'Martin at Eighty', in Murray, M. (ed.), *Heidegger and Modern Philosophy*, Yale University Press, London and New Haven, 1978, 293–303.

Arnold, C., 'Neuere Forschungen zur Modernismuskrise in der katholischen Kirche', *Theologische Revue* 90 (2003), 91–104.

Aubenque, P.: *El problema del ser in Aristóteles*, Taurus, Madrid, 1981.

——, *La prudencia in Aristóteles*, Crítica, Barcelona, 1999.

Bambach, Ch., 'Phenomenological Research as *Destruktion*. The Early Heidegger's Reading of Dilthey', *Philosophy Today* 37/2 (1993), 115–132.

——, *Heidegger, Dilthey and the Crisis of Historicism*, Cornell University Press, Ithaca and London, 1995.

Barash, J., *Martin Heidegger and the Problem of Historical Meaning*, Martinus Nijhoff, La Haya, 1988.

——, *Heidegger et son siècle. Temps de l'Être, temps de l'histoire*, PUF, Paris, 1995.

——, 'Heidegger's Ontological 'Destruction' of Western Intellectual Traditions', in Buren, J. and Kisiel, Th. (eds), *Reading Heidegger from the Start. Essays in his Earliest Thought*, State University of New York Press, Albany, 1994, 111–122.

Berciano, M., *La revolución filosófica de Martin Heidegger*, Biblioteca Nueva, Madrid, 2001.

Bernasconi, R., 'Heidegger's Destruction of *Phronesis*', *The Southern Journal of Philosophy* XXVIII (1989), 127–147.

Bernet, R., 'Transcendance et intentionnalité: Heidegger et Husserl sur les prolégomènes d'une ontologie phénoménologique', in Volpi, F. (ed.), *Heidegger et l'idée de la phénoménologie*, Kluwer Academic Publisher, Dordrecht, 1988, 195–216.

——, 'Husserl and Heidegger on Intentionality and Being', *Journal of the British Society for Phenomenology* 21/2 (1990), 136–152.

——, 'Phenomenological Reduction and the Double Life of the Subject', in Buren, J. and Kisiel, Th. (eds), *Reading Heidegger from the Start. Essays in his Earliest Thought*, State University of New York Press, Albany, 1994, 245–267.

—— et al., *Edmund Husserl. Darstellung seines Denkens*, Felix Meiner, Hamburgo, 1996.

Biemel, W., 'Husserl's *Encyclopaedia Britannica* Article and Heidegger's Remarks Thereon', in Elliston, F. and McCormick, P. (eds), *Husserl. Expositions and Appraisals*, University of Notre Dame Press, Indiana, 1977, 287–303.

——, 'Heideggers Stellung zur Phänomenologie in der Marburger Zeit', *Phänomenologische Forschungen* 6/7 (1978), 142–233.

——, *Martin Heidegger in Selbstzeugnissen und Bilddokumenten*, Rowohlt, Hamburgo, 1984.

Bien, G., Kleger, Hy Kobusch, Th., 'Praxis, praktisch', in Ritter, J. and Gründer, K. (eds), *Historisches Wörterbuch der Philosophie* (vol. 7), Basilea, 1989, 1277–1307.

Blattner, W., 'Is Heidegger a Kantian Idealist?', *Inquiry* 37 (1994), 185–201.

Borges, I., 'De lo lógico a lo translógico. La cuestión del sentido in el joven Heidegger (1913-1916)', in Arana, J. (ed.), *Saber and conciencia. Home-naje a Otto Saame*, Comares, Granada, 1995, 71–94.

Borgman, A., 'Heidegger and Symbolic Logic', in Murray, M. (ed.), *Heidegger and Modern Philosophy*, Yale University Press, New Haven, 1978, 3–22.

Bremmers, Ch., 'Schriftenverzeichnis (1909–2004)', in Denker, A., Gander, H.-H. and Zaborowski, H. (eds), *Heidegger-Jahrbuch* 1. *Heidegger und die Anfänge seines Denkens*, Karl Alber, Freiburg and Munich, 2004, 419–598.

Brogan, W., 'Heidegger and Aristotle. Dasein and the Question of Practical Life', in Dallerry, A. and Scott, Ch. (eds.), *Crisis in Continental Philosophy*, State University of New York Press, Albany, 1990, 137–146.

——, 'The Place of Aristotle in the Development of Heidegger's Phenomenology', in Buren, J. and Kisiel, Th. (eds.), *Reading Heidegger from the Start: Essays in his Earliest Thought*, State University of New York Press, Albany, 1994, 213–230.

——, *Heidegger and Aristotle. The Twofoldness of Being*, State University of New York Press, Albany, 2005, 138–157.

——, 'Die Frage nach der Zeit in Heideggers Aristoteles-Interpretation. Auf dem Weg zu *Sein und Zeit*', in Denker, A., Figal, G., Volpi, F. and Zaborowski, H. (eds), *Heidegger-Jahrbuch* 3: *Heidegger und Aristoteles*, Karl Alber, Freiburg and Munich, 2007, 96–108.

Buchholz, R., *Was heißt Intentionalität? Eine Studie zum Frühwerk Martin Heideggers*, Die Blaue Eule, Essen, 1995.

Büchin, E. and Denker, A. (eds.), *Martin Heidegger und seine Heimat*, Klett-Cotta, Stuttgart, 2005.

Buren, J., 'The Young Heidegger and Phenomenology', *Man and World* 23 (1990), 239–272.

——, 'The Young Heidegger, Aristotle and Ethics', in Dallery, A. and Scott, Ch. (eds), *Ethics and Danger. Essays on Heidegger and the Continental Thought*, State University Press, New York, 1992, 169–185.

——, *The Young Heidegger. Rumor of the Hidden King*, Indiana University Press, Bloomington and Indianápolis, 1994a.

——, 'Martin Heidegger. Martin Luther', in Buren, J. and Kisiel, Th. (eds.), *Reading Heidegger from the Start. Essays in His Earliest Thought*, State University of New York Press, Albany, 1994, 159–174.

——, and Kisiel, Th. (eds.), *Reading Heidegger from the Start. Essays in his Earliest Thought*, State University of New York Press, Albany, 1994b.

——, (ed.), *Supplements. From the Earliest Essays to* Being and Time *and Beyond*, State University of New York Press, Albany, 2002.

Camilleri, S., *Phénoménologie de la religion et herméneutique théologique dans la pensée du jeune Heidegger*, Viena and New York, 2008.

Caputo, J., 'Language, Logic and Time', *Research in Phenomenology* 3 (1973), 147–155.

——, 'Phenomenology, Mysticism, and the 'Grammatica Speculativa': A Study of Heidegger's *Habilitationsschrift*', *Journal of the British Society for Phenomenology* 5/2 (1974), 101–117.

——, 'Husserl, Heidegger and the Question of 'Hermeneutic Phenomenology'', in Kockelmans, J. (ed.), *A Companion to Heidegger's* Being and Time, University Press of America, Washington, 1986, 104–126.

——, 'The Question of Being and Transcendental Phenomenology: Reflections on Heidegger's Relationship to Husserl', in Macann, Ch. (ed.), *Martin Heidegger. Critical Assessments* II, Routledge, London and New York, 1992, 326–344.

——, 'Heidegger and Theology', in Guignon, Ch. (ed.): *The Cambridge Companion to Heidegger*, Cambridge University Press, Cambridge, 1993, 270–88.

——, '*Sorge* and *Kardia*: The Hermeneutics of Factical Life and the Categories of the Heart', in Buren, J. and Kisiel, Th. (eds), *Reading Heidegger from the Start. Essays in his Earliest Thought*, State University of New York Press, Albany, 1994, 327–344.

——, 'Martin Heidegger und die theologische Fakultät Freiburg', *Freiburger Diözesan-Archiv* 100 (1980), 534–541.

Casper, B., 'Martin Heidegger und die theologische Fakultät Freiburg', *Freiburger Diözesan-Archiv* 100 (1980), 534–541.

Chantrine, P., 'πρᾶξις', in *Dictionnaire étymologique de la langue grecque* (vols. 3/4), Paris, 1984, 932–940.

Cobb-Stevens, R., *Husserl and Analytical Philosophy*, Kluwer Academic Publisher, Dordrecht, 1990.

Colomer, E., *El pensamiento alemán de Kant a Heidegger* III, Herder, Barcelona, 1990.

Conzemius, V., 'Antimodernismus und katholische Theologie', *Stimmen der Zeit* 128 (2003), 736–750.

Coriando, P.-L., 'Die "formale Anzeige" und das *Ereignis*. Vorbereitende Überlegungen zum Eigencharakter seinsgeschichtlicher Begrifflichkeit mit einem Ausblick auf den Unterschied von Denken und Dichten', *Heidegger Studien* 14 (1998), 27–43.

Cortí, A., *Zeitproblematik bei Martin Heidegger und Augustinus*, Königshausen & Neumann, Würzburg, 2006.

Courtine, J.-F., 'Réduction phénoménologique-transcendentale et différence ontico-ontologique', in *Heidegger et la phénoménologie*, Jean Vrin, Paris, 1990, 207–247.

——, 'Heidegger entre Aristote et Luther', in Cassin, B. (ed.), *Nos Grecs et leurs modernes: les stratégies contemporaines d'appropriation de l'Antiquité*, Seuil, Paris, 1992, 337–362.

—— (ed.), *Heidegger 1919–1929. De l'herméneutique de la facticité à la métaphysique du* Dasein, Jean Vrin, Paris, 1996.

——, 'Les "Recherches logiques", de Martin Heidegger. De la théorie du jugement à la vérité de l'être', in Courtine, J.-F. (ed.), *Heidegger 1919–1929. De l'herméneutique de la facticité à la métaphysique du* Dasein, Jean Vrin, Paris, 1996, 7–31.

——, *Les catégories de l'être. Études de philosophie ancienne et médiévale*, PUF, Paris, 2003.

——, 'Zwischen Wiederholung und Destruktion – die Frage nach der *analogia entis*', in Denker, A., Figal, G., Volpi, F. and Zaborowski, H. (eds), *Heidegger-Jahrbuch 3: Heidegger und Aristoteles*, Karl Alber, Freiburg and Munich, 2007, 109–129.

Crétella, H., 'La théologie de Heidegger', *Heidegger Studien* 6 (1990), 11–26.

Crowell, St., 'Lask, Heidegger and the Homelessness of Logic', *Journal of the British Society for Phenomenology* 23/3 (1992), 222–239.

——, 'Making Logic Philosophical Again (1912–1916)', in Buren, J. and Kisiel, Th. (eds), *Reading Heidegger from The Start. Essays in his Earliest Thought*, State University of New York Press, Albany, 1994, 55–72.

——, 'Heidegger's phenomenological decade', *Man and World* 28 (1995), 435–448.

——, 'Emil Lask. Aletheiology as Ontology', *Kant-Studien* 87 (1996), 64–88.

——, 'Ontology and Transcendental Phenomenology Between Husserl and Heidegger', in Hopkins, B. (ed.), *Husserl in Contemporary Context: Prospects and Projects for Phenomenology*, Kluwer Academic Publisher, Dordrecht, 1997, 13–36.

——, 'Question, Reflection and Philosophical Method in Heidegger's Early Freiburg Lectures', in Hopkins, B. (ed.), *Phenomenology: Japanese and American Perspectives*, Kluwer Academic Publisher, Dordrecht, 1999, 201–230.

Dahlstrom, D., 'Heidegger's Method: Philosophical Concepts as Formal Indications', *Review of Metaphysics* 47 (1994), 775–797.

Dastur, F., 'Heidegger und die *Logischen Untersuchungen*', *Heidegger Studien* 7 (1991), 38–51.

——, 'Le projet d'une 'chronologie phénoménologique' et la première interprétation de Kant', in Courtine, J.-F. (ed.), *Heidegger 1919–1929. De l'herméneutique de la facticité à la métaphysique du Dasein*, Jean Vrin, Paris, 1996, 113–129.

Denker, A., 'Herr Studiosus Martin Heidegger und seine Heimat Meßkirch. Bausteine für seine Biographie, 1', *Meßkircher Heimathefte* 7 (2000), 5–16.

——, 'Herr Studiosus Martin Heidegger und seine Heimat Meßkirch. Bausteine für seine Biographie, 2', *Meßkircher Heimathefte* 8 (2001), 25–38.

——, 'Heideggers Lebens- und Denkweg 1909–1919', in Denker, A., Gander, H.-H. and Zaborowski, H. (eds.), *Heidegger-Jahrbuch 1: Heidegger und die Anfänge seines Denkens*, Karl Alber, Freiburg and Munich, 2004, 97–122.

——, Gander, H.-H. and Zaborowski, H. (eds.), *Heidegger-Jahrbuch 1: Heidegger und die Anfänge seines Denkens*, Karl Alber, Freiburg and Munich, 2004.

——, Figal, G., Volpi, F. and Zaborowski, H. (eds.), *Heidegger-Jahrbuch 3: Heidegger und Aristoteles*, Karl Alber, Freiburg and Munich, 2007.

——, and Zaborowski, H. (eds.), *Heidegger-Jahrbuch 4: Heidegger und der Nationalsozialismus*, I: *Dokumente*, Karl Alber, Freiburg and Munich, 2009a.

——, and Zaborowski, H. (eds.), *Heidegger-Jahrbuch 5: Heidegger und der Nationalsozialismus*, II: *Interpretationen*, Karl Alber, Freiburg and Munich, 2009b.

Depraz, N., *Transcendence et incarnation: le statut de l'intersubjectivité comme altérité à soi chez Husserl*, Jean Vrin, Paris, 1995.

Derrida, J., 'Ousía et grammê', in *Marges de la Philosophie*, Minuit, Paris, 1972, 31–78.

——, *La voix et le phénomène. Introduction au problème du signe dans la phénoménologie de Husserl*, PUF, Paris, 1979. (Trad. cast. de Patricio Peñalver, *La voz and el fenómeno. Introducción al problema del signo in la fenomenología de Husserl*, Pre-textos, Valencia, 1995.)

——, *Edmund Husserl's 'Origin of Geometry'. An Introduction*, University of Nebraska Press, Lincoln, 1989.

Dreyfus, H., 'Introduction', in Dreyfus, H. and Harrison, H. (eds.), *Husserl, Intentionality and Cognitive Science*, MIT Press, Cambridge, 1982, 1–27.

——, 'Husserl's Epiphenomenology', in Otto, H. R. and Tuedio, J. A. (eds), *Perspectives on Mind*, Reidel, Dordrecht, 1988, 90–95.

——, *What Computers Still Can't Do*, MIT Press, Cambridge, 1992.

Dijk, R. J. A., 'Grundbegriffe der Metaphysik. Zur formal-anzeigenden Struktur der philosophischen Begriffe bei Heidegger', *Heidegger Studien* 7 (1991), 89–100.

Drummond, J., *Husserlian Intentionality and Non-Foundational Realism*, Kluwer Academic Publisher, Dordrecht, 1990.

Elm, R., 'Heideggers früher Zugang zu den Griechen und seine Voraussetzungen', in Steinmann, M. (ed.), *Heideggers und die Griechen*, Suhrkamp, Frankfurt au Mein, 2006, 261–292.

——, 'Aristoteles – ein Hermeneutiker der Faktizität? Aristoteles' Differenzierung von φρόνησις und σοφία und ihre Transformation bei Heidegger', in Denker, A., Figal, G., Volpi, F. and Zaborowski, H. (eds), *Heidegger-Jahrbuch 3: Heidegger und Aristoteles*, Karl Alber, Freiburg and Munich, 2007, 255–288.

Emad, P., 'Zu Fragen der Interpretation und Entzifferung der Grundlagen der Gesamtausgabe Heideggers', *Heidegger Studien* 9 (1993), 161–171.

Esposito, C., 'Il periodo de Marburgo (1923–28) ed *Essere e tempo*: dalla fenomenologia all'ontologia fondamentale', in Volpi, F. (ed.), *Heidegger*, Laterza, Roma, 1997, 107–157.

Fabris, A., "L'ermeneutica della fatticità' nei corsi friburghesi dal 1919 al 1923", in Volpi, F. (ed.), *Heidegger*, Laterza, Roma, 1997, 57–106.

Falkenhayn, K., *Augenblick und Kairos: Zeitlichkeit im Frühwerk Martin Heideggers*, Duncker & Humblot, Berlin, 2003.

Farías, V., *Heidegger und der Nationalsozialismus*, Suhrkamp, Frankfurt au Mein, 1989 (Trad. cast. de Víctor Farías, *Heidegger and el nazismo*, Muchnik, Barcelona, 1989).

Fay, Th., 'Heidegger on Logic: A Genetic Study of His Thought on Logic', *Journal of the History of Philosophy* 12 (1974), 77–94.

Fehér, I., 'Lask, Lukács, Heidegger: The Problem of the Irrationality and the Theory of Categories', in Macann, Ch. (ed.), *Martin Heidegger. Critical Assessments* II, Routledge, New York, 1992, 373–405.

——, 'Phenomenology, Hermeneutics, *Lebensphilosophie*: Heidegger's Confrontation with Husserl, Dilthey and Jaspers', in Buren, J. and Kisiel, Th. (eds), *Reading Heidegger from the Start. Essays in his Earliest Thought*, State University of New York Press, Albany, 1994, 73–90.

Fergusson, A., *When Money Dies: The Nightmare of the Weimar Collapse*, William Kimber, London, 1975 (Trad. cast. de J. C. Gómez Borrero, *Cuando muere el dinero. El derrumbamiento de la República de Weimar*, Alianza, Madrid, 1984).

Figal, G., *Heidegger zur Einführung*, Junius, Hamburgo, 1992.

——, 'Heidegger als Aristoteliker', in Denker, A., Figal, G., Volpi, F. and Zaborowski, H. (eds), *Heidegger-Jahrbuch* 3: *Heidegger und Aristoteles*, Karl Alber, Freiburg and Munich, 2007, 53–76.

—— (ed.), *Heidegger und Husserl. Neue Perspektiven*, Vittorio Klostermann, Frankfurt au Mein, 2009.

Fink, E., 'Die phänomenologische Philosophie Husserls in der gegenwärtigen Kritik', *Kantstudien* 38 (1933), 319–383.

Flasch, K., *Was ist die Zeit? Augustinus von Hippo. Das XI. Buch der Confessiones. Historisch-philosophische Studie*, Vittorio Klostermann, Frankfurt del Meno, 1993.

Frege, G., 'Rezension: Husserl, *Philosophie der Arithmetik*', *Zeitschrift für Philosophie und philosophische Kritik* 103 (1894), 313–332.

——, 'Über Sinn und Bedeutung', *Zeitschrift für Philosophie und philosophische Kritik* 100 (1892), 25–50 (Trad. cast. de Luis Valdés Villanueva, 'Sobre sentido and referencia', in Valdés Villanueva, L. (ed.), *La búsqueda del significado*, Ariel, Barcelona, 1991, 24–45).

Fuchs, Y., 'Philosophy of Methodology in Heidegger's *Die Idee der Philosophie und das Weltanschauungsproblem* (1919)', *Journal of the British Society for Phenomenology* 25/3 (1994), 229–240.

Gadamer, H.-G., 'Die phänomenologische Bewegung', in *Kleine Schriften* III, J. C. B. Mohr, Tubinga, 1972, 150–189.

——, *Vernunft im Zeitalter der Wissenschaft*, Suhrkamp, Frankfurt au Mein, 1976.

——, *Philosophische Lehrjahre. Eine Rückschau*, Vittorio Klostermann, Frankfurt au Mein, 1977.

——, 'Die Marburger Theologie', in *Heideggers Wege*, J. C. B. Mohr, Tubinga, 1983a, 29–40.

——, 'Die religiöse Dimension', in *Heideggers Wege*, J. C. B. Mohr, Tubinga, 1983b, 140–151.

——, *Lob der Theorie*, Suhrkamp, Frankfurt au Mein, 1983.

——, 'Praktisches Wissen', in *Gesammelte Werke* (vol. 5), J. C. B. Mohr, Tubinga, 1985, 230–249.

——, 'Erinnerungen an Heideggers Anfänge', *Dilthey-Jahrbuch* 4 (1986/87), 3–43.

——, 'Die Geschichte der Philosophie', in *Gesammelte Werke* III: *Hegel – Husserl – Heidegger*, J. C. B. Mohr, Tubinga, 1987a, 191–205.

——, 'Zur Aktualität der Husserlschen Phänomenologie', in *Gesammelte Werke* X, J. C. B. Mohr, Tubinga, 1987b, 161–162.

——, 'Der eine Weg Martin Heideggers', in *Gesammelte Werke* III: *Hegel – Husserl – Heidegger*, J. C. B. Mohr, Tubinga, 1987c, 417–430.

——, 'Heideggers 'theologische,, Jugendschrift', *Dilthey-Jahrbuch* 6 (1989), 228–234.

——, *Wahrheit und Methode*, in *Gesammelte Werke* I, J. C. B. Mohr, Tubinga, 1986 (Trad. cast. de Ana Agud and Rafael de Agapito, *Verdad and método*, Sígueme, Salamanca, 1988).

——, *El problema de la conciencia histórica*, Tecnos, Madrid, 1993.

——, 'Hermeneutik und ontologische Differenz', in *Gesammelte Werke* X, J. C. B. Mohr, Tubinga, 1995, 58–70.

——, 'Sobre la filosofía alemana in el siglo xx', *ER. Revista de Filosofía* 26 (2000), 189–217.

Gander, H.-H., *Selbstverständnis und Lebenswelt. Grundzüge einer phänomenologischen Hermeneutik im Ausgang von Husserl und Heidegger*, Vittorio Klostermann, Frankfurt au Mein, 2001.

——, 'Phänomenologie im Übergang. Zu Heideggers Auseinandersetzung mit Husserl', in Denker, A., Gander, H.-H. and Zaborowski, H. (eds), *Heidegger-Jahrbuch* 1: *Heidegger und die Anfänge seines Denkens*, Karl Alber, Freiburg and Munich, 2004, 294–306.

——, 'La fenomenología hermenéutica del vivir fáctico in Heidegger', in Duque, F. (ed.), *Heidegger. Sendas que vienen*, UAM, Madrid, 2008, 141–171.

García Gaínza, J., *Heidegger and la cuestión del valor. Estudio de los escritos de juventud*, Newbook, Pamplona, 1997.

Gay, P., *La cultura de Weimar. La inclusión de lo excluido*, Argos, Barcelona, 1984.

Gethmann, C.-F., *Verstehen und Auslegung. Das Methodenproblem in der Philosophie Martin Heideggers*, Bouvier, Bonn, 1974.

——, 'Philosophie als Vollzug und als Begriff. Heideggers Identitätsphilosophie des Lebens in der Vorlesung vom Wintersemester 1921/22 und ihr Verhältnis zu *Sein und Zeit*', *Dilthey-Jahrbuch* 4 (1986/87), 27–52.

——, 'Heideggers Wahrheitsauffasung in seinen Marburger Vorlesungen. Zur Geschichte von *Sein und Zeit*', in Forum für Philosophie Bad Homburg (ed.), *Martin Heidegger: Innen- und Außensichten*, Suhrkamp, Frankfurt au Mein, 1991, 101–130.

——, 'Heidegger und die Phänomenologie', in *Dasein und Erkennen. Heidegger im phänomenologischen Kontext*, Walter de Gruyter, Berlin, 1993, 3–48.

Greisch, J., 'L'herméneutique dans la phénoménologie comme telle', *Revue de Métaphysique et de Morale* 96 (1991), 38–56.

——, *Ontologie et temporalité. Esquisse d'une interprétation intégrale de* Sein und Zeit, PUF, Paris, 1994.

——, 'La 'tapisserie de la vie'. Le phénomène de la vie et ses interprétations dans les *Grundprobleme der Phänomenologie* de Martin Heidegger', in Courtine, J.-F. (ed.), *Heidegger 1919–1929. De l'herméneutique de la facticité à la métaphysique du* Dasein, Jean Vrin, Paris, 1996, 131–152.

——, 'The Eschatology of Being and the God of Time in Heidegger', *International Journal of Philosophical Studies* 4/1 (1996), 17–42.

Grimm, J. and W., *Deutsches Wörterbuch*, Hirzel, Leipzig, 1864–1960.

Grondin, J., 'Die Hermeneutik der Faktizität als ontologische Destruktion und Ideologiekritik', in Papenfuss, D. and Pöggeler, O. (eds.), *Zur philosophischen Aktualität Heideggers* (vol. II), Vittorio Klostermann, Frankfurt au Mein, 1990, 163-178.

—, *Einführung in die philosophische Hermeneutik*, Wissenschaftliche Buchgesellschaft, Darmstadt, 1991.

—, 'Die hermeneutische Intuition zwischen Husserl und Heidegger', in Grethlin, Th. and Leither, H. (eds), *Inmitten der Zeit. Festschrift für Manfred Riedel*, Würzburg, 1996, 268-284.

Guignon, Ch., 'History and Commitment in the Early Heidegger', in Dreyfus, H. and Harrison, H. (eds), *Heidegger. A Critical Reader*, Blackwell, Oxford, 1992, 130-142.

Haar, M., 'Le moment *(kairós)*, l'instant *(Augenblick)* et le temps-du-monde *(Weltzeit)*', in Courtine, J.-F. (ed.), *Heidegger 1919-1929. De l'herméneutique de la facticité à la métaphysique du Dasein*, Paris, Jean Vrin, 1996, 67-90.

Habermas, J., *Der philosophische Diskurs der Moderne*, Suhrkamp, Frankfurt au Mein, 1985 (Trad. cast. de Manuel Jiménez Redondo, *El discurso filosófico de la modernidad*, Taurus, Madrid, 1989).

Han-Pile, B., 'Early Heidegger's Appropiation of Kant', in Dreyfus, H. and Wrathall, M. (eds.), *A Companion to Heidegger*, Blackwell, Oxford, 2005, 80-101.

Heidegger, G., 'Prefacio' (de la nieta de Martin and Elfride Heidegger, Gertrud Heidegger), in Heidegger, M., *Alma mía! Cartas de Martin Heidegger a su mujer Elfride 1915-1970*, Manantial, Buenos Aires, 2008, 29-34.

Heinz, M., 'Philosophy and Worldview: Heidegger's Concept of Philosophy and the Baden School of Neokantianism', in Rockmore, T. (ed.), *Heidegger, German Idealism and Neo-Kantianism*, Humanity Books, London, 2001, 209-237.

Held, K., 'Einleitung', in Husserl, E., *Die phänomenologische Methode: Ausgewählte Texte I*, Reclam, Stuttgart, 1985, 5-1.

—, 'Heidegger und das Prinzip der Phänomenologie', in Gethmann-Siefert, A. and Pöggeler, O. (eds.), *Heidegger und die praktische Philosophie*, Suhrkamp, Frankfurt au Mein, 1989, 111-139.

—, 'Heideggers Weg zu "den Sachen selbst"', in Coriando, P.-L. (ed.), *Vom Rätsel des Begriffes. Festschrift für Friedrich-Wilhelm von Herrmann zum 65. Geburtstag*, Duncker & Humblot, Berlin, 1999, 31-46.

Herrmann, F.W., *Der Begriff der Phänomenologie bei Husserl und Heidegger*, Vittorio Klostermann, Frankurt del Meno, 1981.

—, 'Edition und Interpretation. Die Edition der Vorlesungen Heideggers in seiner Gesamtausgabe letzter Hand', *Heidegger Studien* 2 (1986), 153-173.

—, *Hermeneutische Phänomenologie des Daseins. Eine Erläuterung von* Sein und Zeit (vol. 1), Vittorio Klostermann, Frankfurt au Mein, 1987.

—, *Wege und Methode. Zur hermeneutischen Phänomenologie des seinsgeschicht-lichen Denkens*, Vittorio Klostermann, Frankfurt au Mein, 1990.

—, *Heideggers* Grundprobleme der Phänomenologie: *Zur zweiten Hälfte von* Sein und Zeit, Vittorio Klostermann, Frankfurt au Mein, 1991.

—, *Augustinus und die phänomenologische Frage nach der Zeit*, Vittorio Klostermann, Frankfurt au Mein, 1992.

—, 'Augustinus und die phänomenologische Frage nach der Zeit', *Philosophisches Jahrbuch* 100 (1993), 96-113.

—, *Wege ins Ereignis. Zu Heideggers* Beiträge zur Philosophie, Vittorio Klostermann, Frankfurt au Mein, 1994.

—, *Hermeneutik und Reflexion. Der Begriff der Phänomenologie bei Heidegger und Husserl*, Vittorio Klostermann, Frankfurt au Mein, 2000.

—, 'Die Intentionalität in der hermeneutischen Phänomenologie', in *Die erscheinende Welt. Festschrift für Klaus Held*, Duncker & Humblot, Berlin, 2002.

Hobe, K., 'Zwischen Rickert und Heidegger. Versuch über eine Perspektive des Denkens von Emil Lask', *Philosophisches Jahrbuch der Görres-Gesellschaft* 78 (1971), 360-372.

Hogemann, F., 'Heideggers Konzeption der Phänomenologie in den Vorlesungen aus dem Wintersemester 1919/20 und dem Sommersemester 1920', *Dilthey-Jahrbuch* 4 (1986/87), 54-71.

Hoppe, H., *Wandlungen in der Kant-Auffassung Heideggers*, in *Durchblicke* (Martin Heidegger zum 80. Geburtstag), Vittorio Klostermann, Frank-furt del Meno, 1970, 284-317.

Hughes, H. S., *Conciencia and sociedad. La reorientación del pensamiento social europeo*, Aguilar, Madrid, 1972.

Imdahl, G., *Das Leben verstehen. Heideggers formal anzeigende Hermeneutik in den frühen Freiburger Vorlesungen (1919 bis 1923)*, Königshausen & Neumann, Würzburg, 1997.

Jamme, Ch., 'Heideggers frühe Begründung der Hermeneutik', *Dilthey-Jahrbuch* 4 (1986/87), 72-90.

—, '*Être et Temps* de Heidegger dans le contexte de l'histoire de sa genèse', in Courtine, J.-F. (ed.), *Heidegger 1919-1929. De l'herméneutique de la facticité à la métaphysique du Dasein*, Jean Vrin, Paris, 1996, 221-236.

Jaspers, K., *Philosophische Autobiographie*, Piper, Munich and Zúrich, 1977.

—, *Notizen zu Heidegger*, Piper, Munich and Zúrich, 1978.

Jiménez, G., 'La noción hermenéutica de indicación formal in el Heidegger temprano', *Escritos de filosofía* 39/40 (2001), 187-196.

Jollivet, S., 'Das Phänomen der Bewegtheit im Licht der Dekonstruktion der aristotelischen Physik', in Denker, A., Figal, G., Volpi, F. and Zaborowski, H. (eds), *Heidegger-Jahrbuch 3: Heidegger und Aristoteles*, Karl Alber, Freiburg and Munich, 2007, 130-155.

Jung, M., 'Die ersten akademischen Schritte (1912-1916). Zwischen Neuscholastik, Neukantianismus und Phänomenologie', in Thomä, D. (ed.), *Heidegger-Handbuch: Leben - Werk - Wirkung*, Metzler, Stuttgart and Weimar, 2003, 5-8.

Kalariparambil, T., *Das befindliche Verstehen und die Seinsfrage*, Duncker & Humblot, Berlin, 1999.

—, 'Towards Sketching the 'Genesis' of *Being and Time*', *Heidegger Studien* 16 (2000), 189-220.

Kim, I.-S., *Phänomenologie des faktischen Lebens: Heideggers formal anzeigende Hermeneutik (1919-1923)*, Lang, Frankfurt au Mein, 1988.

Kim, J.-Ch., *Leben und Dasein. Die Bedeutung Wilhelm Diltheys für den Denkweg Martin Heideggers*, Königshausen & Neumann, Würzburg, 2001.

Kisiel, Th., 'Heidegger (1907-1927): The Transformation of the Categorial', in Sallis, J., Seebohm, Th. and Silverman, H. (eds), *Continental Philosophy in America*, Duquesne University Press, Pittsburgh, 1983, 165-185.

—, 'Heideger's Early Lectures Courses', in Kockelmans, J. (ed.), *A Companion to Heidegger's* Being and Time, University of America, Washington, 1986, 22-39.

—, 'Das Entstehen des Begriffsfeldes 'Faktizität' im Frühwerk Heideggers', *Dilthey-Jahrbuch* 4 (1986/87), 91-120.

—, 'War der frühe Heidegger tatsächlich ein 'christlicher Theologe'?', in Gethmann-Siefert, A. (ed.), *Philosophie und Poesie. Otto Pöggeler zum 60. Geburtstag*, Frommann, Stuttgart, 1988, 59-75.

―, 'Das Kriegsnotsemester 1919: Heideggers Durchbruch zur hermeneutischen Phänomenologie', *Philosophisches Jahrbuch* 99 (1992), 105–122.

―, 'A Philosophical Postscript: On the Genesis of *Sein und Zeit*', *Dilthey-Jahrbuch* 8 (1992/93), 226–232.

―, *The Genesis of Heidegger's Being and Time*, University of California Press, Berkeley and Los Ángeles, 1993.

―, 'Heidegger (1920–21) 'On Becoming a Christian: A Conceptual Picture Show', in Buren, J. and Kisiel, Th. (eds), *Reading Heidegger from the Start. Essays in His Earliest Thought*, State University of New York Press, Albany, 1994, 175–194.

―, 'Heidegger's *Gesamtausgabe*: An International Scandal of Scholarsphip', *Philosophy Today* 39 (1995), 3–15.

―, 'Why Students of Heidegger Will Have to Read Emil Lask', *Man and World* 28 (1996a), 197–240.

―, 'L'indication formelle de la facticité: sa genèse et son transformation', in Courtine, J.-F., *Heidegger 1919–1929. De l'herméneutique à la métaphysique du Dasein*, Jean Vrin, Paris, 1996b, 205–210.

―, 'Heidegger – Lask – Fichte', in Rockmore, T. (ed.), *Heidegger, German Idealism and Neo-Kantianism*, Humanity Books, London, 2001, 242–255.

―― and Sheehan, Th. (eds.), *Becoming Heidegger. On the Trail of His Early Occasional Writings (1919–1927)*, Northwestern University Press, Evanston (Illinois), 2007.

Kittel, G., *Etymologisches Wörterbuch zum Neuen Testament*, Kohlhammer, Stuttgart (continuado por Gerhard Friedrich), 1933–1977.

Kluge, F., *Etymologisches Wörterbuch der deutschen Sprache*, Walter de Gruyter, Berlin, 1883 (revised and re-edited in 1910 por Alfred Götze and in 1957 por Walter Mitzka).

Kovacs, G., 'Philosophy as Primordial Science *(Urwissenschaft)* in the Early Heidegger', *Journal of the British Society for Phenomenology* 21/2 (1990), 121–135.

―, 'Philosophy as Primordial Science in Heidegger's Courses of 1919', in Buren, J. and Kisiel, Th. (eds), *Reading Heidegger from the Start. Essays in his Earliest Thought*, State University of New York Press, Albany, 1994, 91–110.

Krell, D. F., 'The 'Factical Life' of *Dasein:* From the Early Freiburg Courses to *Being and Time*', in Buren, J. and Kisiel, Th. (eds), *Reading Heidegger from the Start. Essays in his Earliest Thought*, State University of New York Press, Albany, 1994, 361–380.

Krug, W. T., *Allgemeines Handwörterbuch der philosophischen Wissenschaften*, Leipzig, 1832–1838.

Lafont, C., *Sprache und Welterschließung. Zur linguistischen Wende der Hermeneutik Heideggers*, Suhrkamp, Frankfurt au Mein, 1994.

―, 'Hermeneutics', in Dreyfus, H. and Wrathall, M. (eds.), *A Companion to Heidegger*, Blackwell, Oxford, 2004, 265–284.

Landgrebe, L., 'Husserls Phänomenologie und die Motive zu ihrer Umbildung', in *Der Weg der Phänomenologie*, Gerd Mohn, Gütersloh, 1963 (Trad. cast. de Mario A. Presas, 'La fenomenología de Husserl and los motivos de su transformación', in Landgrebe, L., *El camino de la fenomenología*, Sudamericana, Buenos Aires, 1963, 13–60).

Lara, F., *Phänomenologie der Möglichkeit. Grundzüge der Philosophie Heideggers 1919–1923*, Karl Alber, Freiburg and Munich, 2008.

―, 'Fenomenología and dialéctica. La crítica de Heidegger a la dialéctica', in Rocha, A. (ed.), *Martin Heidegger. La experiencia del camino*, Uninorte, Barranquilla, 2009, 95–122.

Lazzari, R., *Ontologia de la fatticità. Prospettive sul giovane Heidegger*, Franco Angeli, Milán, 2002.

Le Doux, J., *Synaptic Self. How Our Brains Become Who We Are*, Penguin Books, London.
Lehmann, K., 'Metaphysik, Transzendentalphilosophie und Phänomenologie in den ersten Schriften Martin Heideggers (1912-1916)', *Philosophisches Jahrbuch* 71 (1964), 333-367.
——, 'Christliche Geschichtserfahrung und ontologische Frage beim jungen Heidegger', in Pöggeler, O. (ed.), *Heidegger. Perspektiven zur Deutung seines Werkes*, Kiepenheuer & Witsch, Cologne and Berlin, 1969, 140-168.
Leyte, A., *Heidegger*, Alianza, Madrid, 2005.
Loewenich, K., *Luhters 'theologia crucis'*, Kaiser, Munich, 1954.
Löwith, K., 'Phänomenologische Ontologie und protestantische Theologie', in Pöggeler, O. (ed.), *Heidegger. Perspektiven zur Deutung seines Werkes*, Kiepenheuer & Witsch, Cologne and Berlin, 1969, 54-77.
——, *Mein Leben in Deutschland vor und nach 1933*, Metzler, Stuttgart, 1986.
—— et al., *Martin Heidegger im Gespräch*, Neske, Pfullingen, 1988.
Lyne, I., 'Rickert and Heidegger: On the Value of Everyday Objects', *Kant-Studien* 91 (2000), 204-225.
Makkreel, R., 'Heideggers ursprüngliche Auslegung der Faktizität des Lebens: Diahermeneutik als Aufbau und Abbau der geschichtlichen Welt', in Papenfuss, D. and Pöggeler, O. (eds), *Zur philosophischen Aktualität Heideggers*, Vittorio Klostermann, Frankfurt au Mein, 1990, 179-188.
——, 'Dilthey, Heidegger und der Vollzugssinn der Geschichte', in Denker, A., Gander, H.-H. and Zaborowski, H. (eds.), *Heidegger-Jahrbuch 1: Heidegger und die Anfänge seines Denkens*, Karl Alber, Freiburg and Munich, 2004, 307-321.
Marbach, E., *Mental Representation and Consciousness: Towards a Phenomenological Theory of Representation and Reference*, Kluwer Academic Publisher, Dordrecht, 1993.
Marion, J.-L., *Réduction et donation. Recherches sur Husserl, Heidegger et la phénoménologie*, PUF, Paris, 1989.
——, 'Heidegger and Descartes', in Macann, Ch. (ed.), *Critical Heidegger*, Routledge, London, 1996, 67-96.
Marzoa, F., *Heidegger and su tiempo*, Akal, Madrid, 2000.
McGrath, S. J., 'Die scotische Phänomenologie des jungen Heidegger', in Denker, A., Gander, H.-H. and Zaborowski, H. (eds.), *Heidegger-Jahrbuch 1: Heidegger und die Anfänge seines Denkens*, Karl Alber, Freiburg and Munich, 2004, 243-258.
——, 'Das verborgene Anliegen von *Sein und Zeit*. Heideggers frühe Luther-Lektüre', in Enders, M. and Zaborowski, H. (eds), *Phänomenologie der Religion. Zugänge und Grundfragen*, Karl Alber, Freiburg and Munich, 2004, 273-280.
McNeill, W., *The Glance of the Eye. Heidegger, Aristotle and the Ends of Theory*, State University of New York Press, Albany, 1999.
Merker, B., *Selbsttäuschung und Selbsterkenntnis. Zu Heideggers Transformation der Phänomenologie Husserls*, Suhrkamp, Frankfurt au Mein, 1988.
——, 'Konversion statt Reflexion. Eine Grundfigur der Philosophie Martin Heideggers', in Forum für Philosophie Bad Homburg (ed.), *Martin Heidegger: Innen- und Außensichten*, Suhrkamp, Frankfurt au Mein, 1991, 215-243.
Merleau-Ponty, M., *Phénoménologie de la perception* (prólogo), Gallimard, Paris, 1945, i-xvi.
Metclaff, R., 'Aristoteles und *Sein und Zeit*', in Denker, A., Figal, G., Volpi, F. and Zaborowski, H. (eds), *Heidegger-Jahrbuch 3: Heidegger und Aristoteles*, Karl Alber, Freiburg and Munich, 2007, 156-170.

Mohanty, J. N., 'Heidegger on Logic', *Journal of the History of Philosophy* 26 (1988), 107-135.
Montero, F., *Retorno a la fenomenología*, Anthropos, Barcelona, 1987.
Mörchen, H., *Die Einbildungskraft bei Kant*, Max Niemeyer, Tubinga, 1930.
Neske, G., *Erinnerungen an Martin Heidegger*, Neske, Pfullingen, 1977.
Neumann, G., 'Heideggers Studium der Mathematik und Naturwissen-schaften', in Denker, A., Gander, H.-H. and Zaborowski, H. (eds), *Heidegger-Jahrbuch* 1: *Heidegger und die Anfänge seines Denkens*, Karl Alber, Freiburg and Munich, 2004, 214-225.
Nolte, E., *Heidegger. Política e historia in su vida and pensamiento*, Tecnos, Madrid, 1992.
——, 'Martin Heidegger, die Weimarer Republik und die Konservative Revolution', in Großheim, M. and Waschkies, H.-J. (eds), *Rehabilitierung des Subjektiven*, Bouvier, Bonn, 1993, 505-520.
O'Meara, Th., 'Heidegger and His Origins. Theological Perspectives', *Freiburger Diözesan-Archiv* 106 (1986), 141-160.
Orth, E. W., 'Martin Heidegger und der Neukantianismus', *Man and World* 25/3-4 (1992), 421-441.
Ott, H., 'Der Habilitand Martin Heidegger und das von Schaezler'sche Stipendium', *Freiburger Diözesan-Archiv* 106 (1986), 141-160.
——, *Martin Heidegger. Unterwegs zu seiner Biographie*, Campus, Frankfurt au Mein, 1992 (Trad. cast. de Elena Cortez, *Martin Heidegger. in camino de su biografía*, Alianza, Madrid, 1992).
——, 'Heidegger's Catholic Origins', *American Catholic Philosophical Quarterly* 69/2 (1995), 137-156.
Oudemans, C. W., 'Heideggers 'logische Untersuchungen'', *Heidegger Studien* 6 (1990), 85-106.
——, Overgaard, S. and Schwarz, Th. (eds), *Den unge Heidegger*, Akademisk Forlag, Copenhague, 2003.
Papenfuss, D. and Pöggeler, O. (eds.), *Zur philosophischen Aktualität Heideggers* (3 vols.), Vittorio Klostermann, Frankfurt au Mein, 1990-1991.
Peñalver, P., *Del espíritu al tiempo. Lecturas de* El ser and el tiempo, Anthropos, Barcelona, 1988.
Petitot, J., J., Pachoud, B., Roy, J.-M. and Varela, F. J. (eds.), *Naturalizing Phenomenology: Issues in Contemporary Phenomenology and Cognitive Science*, Stanford University Press, Stanford, 1999.
Petzet, H. W., *Auf einen Stern zugehen. Begegnungen und Gespräche mit Martin Heidegger*, Societäts-Verlag, Frankfurt au Mein, 1983.
Pfeiffer, W., *Etymologisches Wörterbuch des Deutschen*, Akademie Verlag, Berlin, 1993.
Pietersma, H., 'Husserl and Heidegger', *Philosophy and Phenomenological Research* 40 (1979/80), 194-211.
Platón, *Fedro*, in *Diálogos* III, Gredos, Madrid, 1992.
Pöggeler, O. (ed.), *Heidegger. Perspektiven zur Deutung seines Werkes*, Kiepenheuer & Witsch, Cologne and Berlin, 1969.
——, *Heidegger und die hermeneutische Philosophie*, Karl Alber, Freiburg and Munich, 1983.
——, *Der Denkweg Martin Heideggers*, Neske, Pfullingen, 1983 (Trad. cast. de Félix Duqque, *El camino del pensar de Martin Heidegger*, Alianza, Madrid, 1986).
——, 'Heideggers Begegnung mit Dilthey', *Dilthey-Jahrbuch* 4 (1986/87), 121-160.
——, *Neue Wege mit Heidegger*, Karl Alber, Freiburg and Munich, 1992.
——, *Schritte zu einer hermeneutischen Philosophie*, Karl Alber, Freiburg and Munich, 1994.

——, *Heidegger in seiner Zeit*, Wilhelm Fink, Munich, 1999.
——, 'Heideggers Luther-Lektüre im Freiburger Theologenkonvikt', in Denker, A., Gander, H.-H. and Zaborowski, H. (eds) *Heidegger-Jahrbuch* 1: *Heidegger und die Anfänge seines Denkens*, Karl Alber, Freiburg and Munich, 2004, 185–196.
Poggi, S., *La lógica, la mística, il nulla. Una interpretazione del giovane Heidegger*, Edizioni della Normale, Pisa, 2006.
Protevi, J., 'Contributions to *Der Akademiker* (1910–1913)', *Graduate Faculty Philosophy Journal* 14–15 (1991), 486–519.
Putnam, H., *Meaning and the Moral Sciences*, Routledge & Kegan Paul, Oxford, 1978.
Quesne, P., *Les recherches philosophiques du jeune Heidegger*, Kluwer Academic Publishers, Dordrecht, 2003.
Rampley, M., 'Meaning and Language in Early Heidegger: From Duns Scotus to *Being and Time*', *Journal of the British Society for Phenomenology* 25/3 (1994), 209–228.
Rentsch, Th., *Martin Heidegger. Das Sein und der Tod. Eine kritische Einführung*, Piper, Munich and Zúrich, 1989.
Rese, F., *Praxis und Logos bei Aristoteles. Handlung, Vernunft und Rede in Nikomachischer Ethik, Rhetorik und Politik*, J. C. B. Mohr, Tubinga, 2003.
——, 'Handlungsbestimmung vs. Seinsverständnis. Zur Verschiedenheit von Aristoteles' *Nikomachischer Ethik* und Heideggers *Sein und Zeit*', in Denker, A., Figal, G., Volpi, F. and Zaborowski, H. (eds) *Heidegger-Jahrbuch* 3: *Heidegger und Aristoteles*, Karl Alber, Freiburg and Munich, 2007, 170–198.
Richardson, W., *Through Phenomenology to Thought*, Martinus Nijhoff, La Haya, 1974.
Richter, E., 'Heideggers Kritik am Konzept einer Phänomenologie des Bewußtseins', in Coriando, P.-L. (ed.), *Vom Rätsel des Begriffes. Festschrift für Friedrich-Wilhelm von Herrmann zum 65. Geburtstag*, Duncker & Humblot, Berlin, 1999, 7–29.
Ricœur, P., *La metáfora viva*, Cristiandad, Madrid, 1980.
Riedel, M., 'Urstiftung der phänomenologischen Hermeneutik. Heideggers frühe Auseinandersetzung mit Husserl', in Jamme, Ch. and Pöggeler, O. (eds), *Phänomenologie im Widerstreit*, Suhrkamp, Frankfurt au Mein, 1989, 215–233.
——, 'Reformation und deutscher Idealismus. Martin Heidegger zwischen Luther und Melanchton', in Seubert, H. (ed.), *Heideggers Zwiegespräch mit dem deutschen Idealismus*, Böhlau, Colonia, 2003, 15–24.
Rodi, F., 'Die Bedeutung Diltheys für die Konzeption von *Sein und Zeit*. Zum Umfeld von Heideggers Kasseler Vorträgen (1925)', *Dilthey-Jahrbuch* 4 (1986/87), 161–177.
Rodríguez, R., *Hermenéutica and subjetividad. Ensayos sobre Heidegger*, Trotta, Madrid, 1993.
——, *La transformación hermenéutica de la fenomenología. Una interpretación de la obra temprana de Heidegger*, Tecnos, Madrid, 1997.
——, and Duque, F. (eds), *Heidegger. Sendas que vienen*, UAM, Madrid, 2008, 175–204.
Rogozinski, J., 'Hier ist kein Warum! Heidegger and Kant's Practical Philosophy', in Pelligrew, D. and Raffoul, F. (eds), *Heidegger and Practical Philosophy*, State University of New York Press, Albany, 2002, 43–63.
Rorty, R., *Philosophy and the Mirror of Nature*, Blackwell, Oxford, 1980.
Rosales, A., *Sein und Subjektivität*, Walter de Gruyter, Berlin, 2000.
Rosen, St., 'Phronesis or Ontology: Aristotle and Heidegger', in Pozzo, R. (ed.), *The Impact of Aristotelianism on Modern Philosohpy*, The Catholic University of America Press, Washington, 2004, 248–265.
Roy, J.-M., 'Le 'Dreyfus Bridge': Husserlianisme et Fodorisme', *Archives de Philosophie* 58 (1995), 533–548.

Ruff, G., *Am Ursprung der Zeit. Studie zu Martin Heideggers phänomenologischem Zugang zur christlichen Religion in den ersten 'Freiburger Vorlesungen'*, Duncker & Humblot, Berlin, 1997.

Ruggenini, M., 'La finitude de l'existence et la question de la vérité: Heidegger 1925-1929', in Courtine, J.-F., *Heidegger 1919-1929. De l'herméneutique à la métaphysique du* Dasein, Jean Vrin, Paris, 1996, 153-178.

Sadler, T., *Heidegger and Aristotle. The Question of Being*, Athlone, London, 1996.

Safranski, R., *Ein Meister aus Deutschland. Heidegger und seine Zeit*, Carl Hanser, Munich, 2000 (Trad. cast. de Raúl Gabás, *Un maestro de Alemania. Heidegger and su tiempo*, Tusquets, Barcelona, 1997).

Sallis, J. (ed.), *Heidegger and the Path of Thinking*, Duquesne University Press, Pittsburgh, 1970.

Schaber, J., 'Martin Heideggers 'Herkunft' im Spiegel der Theologie- und Kirchengeschichte des 19. und beginnenden 20. Jahrhunderts', in Denker, A., Gander, H.-H. and Zaborowski, H. (eds), *Heidegger-Jahrbuch 1: Heidegger und die Anfänge seines Denkens*, Karl Alber, Freiburg and Munich, 2004, 159-184.

Schacht, R., 'Husserlian and Heideggerian Phenomenology', *Philosophical Studies* 23 (1972), 293-314.

Schaeffler, R., *Frömmigkeit des Denkens. Martin Heidegger und die katholische Theologie*, Wissenschaftliche Buchgesellschaft, Darmstadt, 1978.

——, 'Heidegger und die Theologie', in Gethmann-Siefert, A. and Pöggeler, O. (eds), *Heidegger und die praktische Philosophie*, Suhrkamp, Frankfurt au Mein, 1989, 286-312.

Schalow, F., *The Renewal of the Heidegger-Kant Dialogue: Action, Thought, Responsibility*, State University of New York Press, Albany, 1992.

——, 'Freedom, Finitude, and the Practical Self. The Other Side of Heidegger's Appropiation of Kant', in Pelligrew, D. and Raffoul, F. (eds), *Heidegger and Practical Philosophy*, State University of New York Press, Albany, 2002, 29-42.

Schulz, W., 'Über den philosophiegeschichtlichen Ort Martin Heideggers', *Philosophische Rundschau* 1 (1953-1954), 65-93.

Schüßler, I., 'Le *Sophiste* de Platon dans l'interprétation de Heidegger', in Courtine, J.-F., *Heidegger 1919-1929. De l'herméneutique à la métaphysique du* Dasein, Jean Vrin, Paris, 1996, 91-112.

Segura, C., *Hermenéutica de la vida fáctica: in torno al Informe Natorp*, Trotta, Madrid, 1999.

Sheehan, Th., 'The original form of *Sein und Zeit*: Heidegger's *Begriff der Zeit*', *Journal of the British Society for Phenomenology* 10 (1979), 78-83.

——, 'Heidegger's 'Introduction to the Phenomenology of Religion' (1920-21)', *The Personalist* 56 (1979/80), 312-324.

——, 'Caveat Lector. The New Heidegger', *The New York Review of Books*, vol. 27, no. 19, 1980, 39-41.

——, 'Heidegger's Early Years: Fragments for a Philosophical Biography', in Sheehan, Th. (ed.), *The Man and the Thinker*, Precedent, Chicago, 1981, 3-19.

——, 'Heideggers Lehrjahre', in Sallis, J. et al. (eds.), *The Collegium Phaenomenologicum*, Kluwer Academic Publisher, Dordrecht, 1988, 16-17.

Sherover, H., *Heidegger, Kant, and Time*, Indiana University Press, Bloomington and Indianápolis, 1971.

Smith, P. Ch., 'The Uses and Abuses of Aristotle's Rhetoric in Heidegger's Fundamental Ontology: The Lecture Course, Summer, 1924', in Babich, B. E. (ed.), *From Phenomenology to Thought. Errancy and Desire*, Kluwer Academic Publisher, Dordrecht, 1995, 315-333.

Sokolowski, R., *Introduction to Phenomenology*, Cambridge University Press, Cambridge, 2000.
Sommer, Ch., *Heidegger, Aristote, Luther. Les sources aristotéliciennes et néo-testamentaires d'*Être et Temps, PUF, Paris, 2005.
Spiegelberg, H., *The phenomenological movement. A historical introduction*, Kluwer Academic Publisher, Dordrecht, 1983.
Steinbock, A. J., *Home and Beyond. Generative Phenomenology after Husserl*, Northwestern University Press, Evanston, 1995.
——, 'Translator's Introduction', in Husserl, E., *Analyses Concerning Passive and Active Synthesis. Lectures on Transcendental Logic,* Kluwer Academic Publisher, Dordrecht, 2001, xv–xvii.
Steinmann, M., 'Die echte Ferne des Ursprungs. Martin Heideggers Konzeption der Philosophie zur Zeit der frühen Freiburger Vorlesungen', in Barbaric, D. and Koch, D. (eds), *Denkwege*, J. C. B. Mohr, Tubinga, 2001, 77–105.
——, 'Der frühe Heidegger und sein Verhältnis zum Neukantianismus', in Denker, A., Gander, H.-H. and Zaborowski, H. (eds), *Heidegger-Jahrbuch 1: Heidegger und die Anfänge seines Denkens*, Karl Alber, Freiburg and Munich, 2004, 259–293.
Stewart, R., 'Signification and Radical Subjectivity in Heidegger's *Habilitationsschrift*', *Man and World* 12 (1979), 360–86.
Stolzenberg, J., *Ursprung und System: Probleme der Begründung systematischer Philosophie beim frühen Heidegger,* Vandenhoeck & Ruprecht, Gotinga, 1995.
Storck, J. W. and Kisiel, Th., 'Martin Heidegger und die Anfänge der *Deutschen Vierteljahresschrift für Literaturwissenschaft und Geistesgeschichte*. Eine Dokumentation', *Dilthey-Jahrbuch für Philosophie und Geschichte der Geisteswissenschaften* 8 (1992–1993), 181–225.
Streeter, R., 'Heidegger's formal indication: A question of method in *Being and Time*', *Man and World* 30 (1997), 413–430.
Strube, C., *Zur Vorgeschichte der hermeneutischen Phänomenologie*, Königshausen & Neumann, Würzburg, 1993.
Taminiaux, J., 'Heidegger and Husserl's *Logical Investigations*', in Sallis, J. (ed.), *Radical Phenomenology. Essays in Honor of Martin Heidegger*, Atlantic Highlands Humanities Press, New Jersey, 1978, 58–83.
——, 'La réappropriation de l'*Éthique à Nicomaque: poíesis* et *prâxis* dans l'articulation de l'ontologie fondamentale', in *Lectures de l'ontologie fondamentale. Essais sur Heidegger*, Jérôme Millon, Grenoble, 1989, 149–189.
——, *Heidegger and the Project of Fundamental Ontology*, State University of New York Press, Albany, 1991.
Thomä, D. (ed.): *Heidegger-Handbuch: Leben – Werk – Wirkung*, Metzler, Stuttgart, 2003.
Thompson, E., *Mind in Life. Biology, Phenomenology, and the Science of Mind*, Harvard University Press, Cambridge and London, 2007.
——, Noë, A. and Cosmelli, D., 'Neurophenomenology: An Introduction for Neurophilosophers', in Akins, K. and Brook, A. (eds.), *Cognition and the Brain: The Philosophy and Neuroscience Movement*, Cambridge University Press, New York, 2005, 40–97.
Thurner, R., 'Heideggers *Sein und Zeit* als philosophisches Programm', *Allgemeine Zeitschrift für Philosophie* 11 (1986), 29–51.
——, 'Zu den Sachen selbst! Zur Bestimmung der phänomenologischen Grundmaxime bei Husserl und Heidegger', in Schramm, A. (ed.), *Philosophie in Österreich*, Hölder-Picheler-Tempsky, Viena, 1996, 261–271.

——, *Wandlungen der Seinsfrage. Zur Krisis im Denken Heideggers nach* Sein und Zeit, Attempto, Tubinga, 1997.
Troeltsch, E., 'Ein Apfel vom Baume Kierkegaards', in Moltmann, J. (ed.), *Anfänge der dialektischen Theologie*, Kaiser, Munich, 1977, 132-143.
Tugendhat, E., *Der Wahrheitsbegriff bei Husserl und Heidegger*, Walter de Gruyter, Berlin, 1967.
——, 'Heideggers Idee der Wahrheit', in Pöggeler, O. (ed.), *Heidegger*, Kiepenheuer & Witsch, Cologne and Berlin, 1969, 286-297.
——, *Selbstbewußtsein und Selbstbestimmung. Sprachanalytische Interpretationen*, Suhrkamp, Frankfurt au Mein, 1993.
Varela, F. J., 'Neurophenomenology: A Methodological Remedy for the Hard Problem', *Journal of Consciousness Studies* 3 (1996), 330-350.
——, Thompson, E. and Rosch, E., *The Embodied Mind: Cognitive Science and Human Experience*, MIT Press, Cambridge, 1991.
Vattimo, G., *Introduzione a Heidegger*, Laterza, Roma, 2009 (Trad. cast. de Alfredo Báez, *Introducción a Heidegger*, Gedisa, Barcelona, 1986).
Vedder, B., 'Die Faktizität der Hermeneutik', *Heidegger Studien* 12 (1996), 95-108.
Vigo, A., 'Wahrheit, *Logos* und *Praxis*. Die Transformation der aristotelischen Wahrheitskonzeption durch Heidegger', *Internationale Zeitschrift für Philosophie* (1994), 73-95.
——, 'Heidegger: Phänomenologie und Hermeneutik in den frühen Freiburger Vorlesungen (1919-1921)', in Flatscher, M. and Vetter, H. (eds.), *Hermeneutische Phänomenologie – Phänomenologische Hermeneutik*, Peter Lang, Frankfurt au Mein, 2005, 241-269.
Vollrath, E., *Die These der Metaphysik. Zur Gestalt der Metaphysik bei Aristoteles, Kant und Hegel*, Henn, Wuppertal, 1969.
Volpi, F., *Heidegger e Brentano: l'aristotelismo e il problema dell'univocità dell'essere nella formazione filosofica del giovane Martin Heidegger*, Daphne, Pádova, 1976.
——, 'Heideggers Verhältnis zu Brentanos Aristoteles-Interpretation', *Zeitschrift für philosophische Forschung* 32 (1978), 254-265.
——, 'Dasein comme *praxis*. L'assimilation et la radicalisation heideggerienne de la philosophie pratique d'Aristote', in Volpi, F. *et al.* (eds), *Heidegger et l'idée de la phénoménologie*, Kluwer Academic Publisher, Dordrecht, 1988, 1-44.
——, *Heidegger e Aristotele*, Daphne, Pádova, 1984.
——, '*Sein und Zeit*. Homologien zur *Nikomachischen Ethik*', *Philosophisches Jahrbuch* 96 (1989), 225-40.
——, 'Dasein as *praxis*: The Heideggerian Assimilation and the Radicalization of the Practical Philosophy of Aristotle', in Macann, Ch. (ed.), *Martin Heidegger. Critical Assessments* II, Routledge, London and New York, 1992, 91-129.
——, '*Being and Time*: A Translation of the *Nichomachean Ethics*?', in Buren, J. and Kisiel, Th. (eds), *Reading Heidegger from the Start: Essays in his Earliest Thought*, State University of New York Press, Albany, 1994, 195-212.
——, 'La question du *lógos* dans l'articulation de la facticité chez le jeune Heidegger lecteur d'Aristote', in Courtine, J.-F., *Heidegger 1919-1929. De l'herméneutique à la métaphysique du* Dasein, Jean Vrin, Paris, 1996, 33-65.
——, 'Le fonti del problema dell'essere nel giovane Heidegger: Franz Brentano e Carl Braig', in Esposito, C. and Porro, P. (eds), *Heidegger e i medievali*, Brepols, Turnhout, 2001, 39-52.

——, 'Der Rückgang auf die Griechen in den zwanziger Jahren. Eine hermeneutische Perspektive auf Aristoteles, Platon und die Vorsokratiker im Dienste der Seinsfrage', in Thomä, D. (ed.), *Heidegger-Handbuch. Leben – Werk – Wirkung*, Metzler, Stuttgart and Weimar, 2003, 26–36.

——, 'Brentanos Interpretation der aristotelischen Seinslehre und ihr Einfluß auf Heidegger', in Denker, A., Gander, H.-H. and Zaborowski, H. (eds), *Heidegger-Jahrbuch 1: Heidegger und die Anfänge seines Denkens*, Karl Alber, Freiburg and Munich, 2004, 226–242.

——, 'Bibliografía', in Heidegger, M., *Essere e tempo*, Longanesi, Milán, 2005, 557–578.

——, '*Ser and tiempo*: ¿una versión moderna de la *Ética a Nicómáco*'?, in Rocha, A. (ed.), *Martin Heidegger. La experiencia del camino*, Uninorte, Barranquilla, 2009, 3–31.

——, 'Heidegger und der Neoaristotelismus', in Denker, A., Figal, G., Volpi, F. and Zaborowski, H. (eds.), *Heidegger-Jahrbuch 3: Heidegger und Aristoteles*, Karl Alber, Freiburg and Munich, 2007, 221–236.

—— (ed.), *Heidegger*, Laterza, Roma, 1997.

Watanabe, J., 'Categorial Intuition and the Understanding of Being in Husserl and Heidegger', in Sallis, J. (ed.), *Reading Heidegger. Commemorations*, Indiana University Press, Bloomington and Indianápolis, 1993, 109–117.

Watson, P., *Historia intelectual del siglo xx*, Crítica, Barcelona, 2002.

Weigelt, Ch., *The Logic of Life. Heidegger's Retrieval of Aristotle's Concept of Logos*, Coronet Books, Estocolmo, 2002.

——, '*Logos* as *kinesis*. Heidegger's Interpretation of the *Physics* in *Grundbegriffe der aristotelischen Philosophie*', *Epoche* 9/1 (2004), 101–116.

Welte, B., 'Erinnerungen an ein spätes Gespräch', in Heidegger, M. and Welte, B., *Briefe und Begegnungen*, Klett-Cotta, Stuttgart, 2003, 147–150.

Welton, D., *The Other Husserl. The Horizons of Transcendental Phenomenology*, Indiana University Press, Bloomington and Indianápolis, 2000.

——, 'The Systematicity of Husserl's Transcendental Philosophy: From Static to Genetic Method', in Welton, D. (ed.), *The New Husserl. A Critical Reader*, Indiana University Press, Bloomington and Indianápolis, 2003, 255–289.

Wetz, F. J., 'Wege – nicht Werke', *Zeitschrift für philosophische Forschung* 41 (1987), 444–455.

Wolzogen, Ch., 'Es gibt„: Heidegger und Natorps "Praktische Philosophie" ', in Gethmann-Siefert, A. and Pöggeler, O. (eds., *Heidegger und die praktische Philosophie*, Suhrkamp, Frankfurt au Mein, 1989, 313–336.

Wucherer-Huldenfeld, K., 'Zu Heideggers Verständnis des Seins bei Johannes Duns Scotus und im Skotismus sowie im Thomismus und bei Thomas von Aquin', in Vetter, H. (ed.), *Heidegger und das Mittelalter*, Suhrkamp, Frankfurt au Mein, 1999, 41–59.

Xolocotzi, Á., *Der Umgang als Zugang. Der hermeneutisch-phänomenologische Zugang zum faktischen Leben in den frühen Freiburger Vorlesungen Martin Heideggers*, Duncker & Humblot, Berlin, 2002.

——, 'En torno a Heidegger. Diálogo con Friedrich-Wilhelm von Herrmann', *Revista de Filosofía* 108 (2003), 35–44.

——, *Fenomenología de la vida fáctica and su camino a Ser and tiempo*, Plaza and Valdés, Mexico, 2004.

——, *Subjetividad radical and comprensión afectiva. El rompimiento de la representación in Rickert, Dilthey, Husserl and Heidegger*, Plaza and Valdés, Mexico, 2007.

——, *Facetas heideggerianas*, Los Libros de Homero, Mexico D. F., 2009.

Yfantis, D., *Die Auseinandersetzung des frühen Heidegger mit Aristoteles. Ihre Entstehung und Entfaltung sowie ihre Bedeutung für die Entwicklung der frühen Philosophie Martin Heideggers (1919-1927)*, Duncker & Humblot, Berlin, 2009.

Zaborowski, H., 'Besinnung, Gelassenheit und das Geschenk der Heimat. Zum Verhältnis zwischen Martin Heidegger und Bernhard Welte', *Meßkircher Heimathefte* 10 (2003), 111-120.

——, ' "Herkunft aber bleibt stets Zukunft". Anmerkungen zur religiösen und theologischen Dimension des Denkweges Martin Heideggers bis 1919', in Denker, A., Gander, H.-H. and Zaborowski, H. (eds), *Heidegger-Jahrbuch* 1: *Heidegger und die Anfänge seines Denkens*, Karl Alber, Freiburg and Munich, 2004, 123-158.

Zahavi, D., 'Merleau-Ponty on Husserl: A Reappraisal', in Embree, L. and Toadvine, T. (eds), *Merleau-Ponty's Reading of Husserl*, Kluwer Academic Publisher, Dordrecht, 2002, 3-29.

——, *Husserl's Phenomenology*, Stanford University Press, Stanford, 2003.

——, 'Husserl's Noema and the Internalism-Externalism Debate', *Inquiry* 47 (2004), 42-66.

INDEX

Abgeschiedenheit (seclusion) 50
absolute being 125
abstraction 37
actualization 78–9, 98, 116
affective state 118
Der Akademiker 42, 43
anxiety 116–19, 121
appropriation 114–15, 120
Arendt, Hannah 73, 80
Aristotle 2, 60–80
   Nichomachean Ethics 61, 62, 66, 67–70, 76, 79
   Physics 77, 78, 79
Augustine of Hippo, St 60
authenticity 55, 71, 142
Authority and Freedom (Förster) 44

The Basic Problems of Phenomenology (Heidegger) 2–3, 111
being
   Dasein 4, 71–2, 148
   meaning of 2, 103, 146–7
   pre-understanding 4
   question of 124–32
Being and Time (Heidegger)
   hermeneutic phenomenology 133
   intellectual foundation of 7
   logic 24
   ontology in 141
   as philosophical novel 15
   questions addressed in 5–6
being-in-the-world 65, 98, 128–32, 143
Bismarck, Otto von 13
Blochmann, Elisabeth 16, 43, 81
Braig, Carl 47
Brentano, Franz 61

capitalism 13
care 72–6, 121
Cartesianism 119–24, 134–7
categorical intuition 34, 37, 99–103

categorical objects 130
categories doctrine 31–2
Catholicism 43, 44, 46, 47
Christianity
   degreekanizing of Christian experience 50–2
   historical conscience 48
   phenomenon of life 50–60
   primordial temporality 58
   religious experience 40–1
   see also Jesus Christ
comportment modes 122
The Concept of Time in the Science of History (Heidegger) 37
Confessions (Augustine) 60
conscience 48, 55–6
consciousness 27, 28, 72, 118, 122–4
   being of 126–7
   intentionality 128–32
   lived experience 123
   natural attitude 127
   ontological features 125–7
   pure consciousness 129
constitution process 136–7
construction, phenomenological 134
context of signification 145
Corinthians, Epistles to 54
Courtine, J.-F. 23, 118
Critique of Pure Reason (Kant) 81, 82

Dasein (existence)
   anxiety 119
   and Aristotelian *praxis* 70–2
   authenticity 71, 142
   being of 3–4, 18, 71–2, 148
   being-in-the-world 131, 143
   concept of 130, 132–4
   conscience 56
   disclosedness 66
   ontological difference 148
   ontological role 147

possibility and necessity 75
practical wisdom 73–4, 76
as protagonist of narrative 15
relation with itself 74–5
self-actualization 78–9
self-realization 71
self-understanding 96, 146
temporality 59–60
and time 84–5
de-vivification 120
death, anticipation of 59–60
The Decline of the West (Spengler) 15
Der Akademiker 42, 43
Descartes, René 119–24, 134–7
description 68
destruction, phenomenological 134
destructuring of tradition 95–6
Dilthey, Wilhelm 42, 103
doctoral dissertation, Heidegger's 10, 27, 28, 38
doctrine of the categories 31–2
Duns Scotus, John 8, 9, 32, 35–7, 49–50

Eckhart, Johannes 50
encountering 114, 120
episteme (theoretical knowledge) 72
ethical knowledge 73
ethics 61, 62, 66, 67–70, 135
  see also praxis
evaluative neutrality principle 94
existence *see* Dasein
existentialist view 112
experience
  concept of 100
  consciousness 123
  process versus appropriation 114–15
  see also lived experience
explanation 121

factical life/facticity 120
  categorical intuition 99–103
  concept of 78
  experience of life 52
  formal indicators 96–9
  hermeneutics of 93–103, 142
  intentionality 88
  kairological features 56–60
  meaning of 19
  origin of term 53

pre-theoretical structure 31
problem of 9
question of being 2–6
self-interpretation 93–6
structures of 19–20
see also life
false propositions 65–6
forgetfulness of being 62
formal indicators 96–9
forms, material determination 30–4
Förster, Friedrich Wilhelm 44, 45
foundationalism 134, 135
Freiburg lecture course 6–11, 17–18, 19, 35
The Fundamental Concepts of Metaphysics. World - Finitude - Solitude (Heidegger) 98

Gadamer, H.-G. 9
generalizations 97
genetic phenomenology 137–9
German history 13–14
Gethmann, C.-F. 148
givenness 64, 112, 113–14, 120
Greek metaphysics 51
Greekanizing process, Christian theology 50–2
Grimm brothers 144

Habilitationsschrifft, The Theory of Categories and Meaning in Duns Scotus (Heidegger) 8, 10, 22, 30, 31, 34, 40
haecceitas (singularity of things) 36–8, 49
happiness requirements 71
Heidegger, Martin
  Aristotle's practical philosophy 60–80
  Cartesianism critique 119–24
  interpretations of Husserl's phenomenology 88–90, 134–9
  and Kant 80–5
  marriage 16
  philosophical itinerary 17–20
  and psychologism 26–30
  'hermeneutic idealism' 146
  hermeneutic phenomenology 86–148
    anxiety 116–19
    appropriation 114–15
    Cartesianism critique 119–24
    caveats 105

Dasein concept 132–4
  development of 106–34
  experience of surrounding world 109–14
  of facticity 93–103
  lectern example 109–11, 113
  meaning of 103–34
  need for 104–6
  phenomenology critique 124–32
  pre-predicative seeing 65
  pre-theoretical sphere 106–8
  process versus appropriation 114–15
  purpose of 4
  question of being 124–32
  reduction versus anxiety 116–19
  reflexive phenomenology comparison 120–2
  theoretical attitude 107–8
  transcendental phenomenology comparison 140–2
'hermeneutic situation' 94
Herrmann, F.W. 132
historical conscience 48
history 13–14, 47, 49, 52
History of the Concept of Time (Heidegger) 102, 125, 126
holding 116
how 120
human beings
  conceptions of 3, 64, 75
  pre-understanding of being 146
human nature 73
Husserl, Edmund
  Cartesianism 119–24, 134–7
  categorical intuition 99–103
  consciousness 125–7, 131
  evaluative neutrality principle 94
  genetic phenomenology 137–9
  Heidegger's interpretation of 88–90, 134–9
  on Heidegger's phenomenology 117
  idealism 135
  importance to Heidegger 67
  intentionality 129, 130
  Logical Investigations 22–3, 25–6, 63
  meaning of being 103
  natural attitude 127–8
  phenomenology 1, 60, 134–9
  psychologism refutation 25–6
  reflection 131
  reflexive phenomenology 104
  transcendental idealism 134–7
  worldview problem 88–90

The Idea of Philosophy and the Problem of Worldview (Heidegger) 5
idealism 25, 31, 135
immersion 115, 121
individuality, *haecceitas* doctrine 36–8
individuation principle 32–3
intellectual context 14–17
intentionality
  being-in-the-world 128–32, 148
  co-belonging 131
  factical life 88
  reflexive phenomenology 121
  transcendence comparison 132
interpersonal relations 144
irrationality 30–1

Jaspers, Karl 16, 80
Jesus Christ 48, 55, 57
  see also Christianity
judgement, theory of 24, 27, 28, 29, 30–4
Junkers 13

kairological features of factical life 56–60
Kant, Immanuel 47, 80–5
Kehre ('the turn') 6, 145
Kierkegaard, Søren 56
Kiseil, Th. 8
knowledge
  ethical 73
  forms of 68
  mathematical 123
  perception and 111
  pre-theoretical 108
  scientific 124
  theoretical 72
  theories of 33, 35, 40
kosmos concept 144
Krebs, Engelbert 46

Lafont, C. 146
language 38
Lask, Emil 30–4
lectern example, experience of seeing 109–11, 113

lecture courses 6–11, 17–18, 19, 23, 35, 81–2
life
    categories 99
    phenomenon of 50–60
    problem of 49–50
    reality of 18–19
    self-sufficiency 112
    see also factical life/facticity
lifeworld 29
lived experience
    absolute being 125
    consciousness 123
    hermeneutic phenomenology 120
    process versus appropriation 114–15
    scientific treatment of 124
living spirit 35–6, 38
logic
    definition/domain 22–4
    judgements 35
    mathematical 29
    nature of 22–30
    philosophical 24, 30–9
    universal laws 23
Logic. The Question of Truth (Heidegger) 23, 63, 64, 83
Logical Investigations (Husserl) 22–3, 25–6, 63
logos concept 64, 70
Löwith, Karl 9, 16–17, 48
Luther, Martin 56, 59, 87

manuscripts, textual basis 6–11
Marburg lecture course 6–11, 17, 19, 81–2
material determination of form 30–4
mathematical knowledge 123, 124
mathematical logic 29
mathematics 26, 29, 72, 123, 124
meaningfulness, perception and 111
medieval scholasticism 49, 52–3
Merleau-Ponty, Maurice 137
metaphysics 34, 51
militarism 13
mineness 72
modernism 44
movedness/movement 76–80
My Path Up to the Present (Heidegger) 6

My Way to Phenomenology (Heidegger) 7–8, 17–18
'Mystery of the Church Tower' (Heidegger) 43
mysticism 50

Natorp-report (Heidegger) 5, 48, 53, 60–1, 141
natural attitude 127–8
natural sciences 25, 122
naturalism 25
neo-Kantianism 42, 89, 140
'New Research on Logic' (Heidegger) 27
Nichomachean Ethics (Aristotle) 61, 62, 66, 67–70, 76, 79
Nietzsche, Friedrich 14–15
nothingness 28–9, 117

object/subject relation 36, 110, 147
objects
    perception of 101, 102, 130
    production of 68–9, 77
observation 68, 121
On the Soul (Aristotle) 79
On the Way to Language (Heidegger) 7
ontology
    consciousness 125–7
    of human life 6
    logical beings/psychic beings 24–30
    ontological difference 142–8
    unveilment modes 67–70
Ontology. The Hermeneutics of Facticity (Heidegger) 87, 95

parousia (Second Coming) 54, 55, 58
Pascendi dominici gregis encyclical 44
Pauline literature 50, 51, 52–6, 57, 59
perception
    and experience 113
    and knowledge 111
    meaningfulness 111
    reflexive phenomenology 120
    subject/object relation 110
    and understanding 143
perceptual intuition 100, 101
perceptual objects 130
Phenomenological Interpretations of Aristotle (Heidegger) 5, 48, 53, 60–1, 141

phenomenology
    analytical method 133–4
    of association 139
    chronology 82–5
    construction 133–4
    critique of 124–32
    destruction 134
    genetic phenomenology 137–9
    Heidegger's approach 39, 106
    Husserl's approach 1, 60, 134–9
    reductions, limit of 127–8
    reflexive phenomenology 104, 108
    transcendental phenomenology 1, 139, 140–2
    transcendental subjectivity 134–7
    truth as unconcealment 63–7
    validity of judgements 32
    see also hermeneutic phenomenology
The Phenomenology of Religious Life (Heidegger) 40, 42–60
philosophical itinerary, Heidegger's 17–20
philosophical logic 24, 30–9
philosophy
    meaning of 92–3
    pre-theoretical sphere 90–1
    as primordial science 87–93
    tradition 2, 3
Philosophy as Rigorous Science (Husserl) 89
phronesis (practical wisdom) 60–80
physicists 21
Physics (Aristotle) 77, 78, 79
Plato's Sophist (Heidegger) 67
poems 43
Pöggeler, O. 52
poiesis (production of objects) 68–9, 77
positivist optimism 13, 14
practical philosophy/wisdom, Aristotelian 60–80
praxis (ethical and political action) 68–9, 70–2, 75–6
pre-theoretical sphere 34, 90–1, 106–8, 132–3
primordial science 87–93, 121
primordial temporality 58
process 114–15, 120
production of objects 68–9, 77
propositions, analysis of 65–6, 84
Protestantism 47

psychic phenomena 24–30
psychologism 24–30
pure consciousness 129

reality 38, 135
reduction 116–19, 121, 127–8
reflection 115, 118, 119, 121, 122, 131
reflexive phenomenology 90, 104, 108, 120–2
relational sense 116
religion
    actualization process 56–7
    phenomenology of 40, 42–60
    primitive Christianity 52–6
    temporality 58
    see also Christianity; Jesus Christ
repetition 121
Richardson, William 5
Rickert, Heinrich 31, 47, 80, 140
Romans, Epistle to 59

St Paul's epistles 50, 51, 52–6, 57, 59
salvation 58
Schleiermacher, Friedrich 47
science 21–2, 24, 25, 121, 147
    limits of 45
    meaning and object of 91–2
    philosophy comparison 92–3
    see also primordial science
scientific knowledge 22, 124
scientific method 111, 122, 141
scientificity criterion 123–4
seclusion 50
Second Coming of Christ 54, 55, 58
the self 138, 139
self-actualization 78–9, 98, 116
self-consciousness 72
self-determination 74
self-interpretation 93–6
self-realization 71
self-reference 97–8
self-sufficiency 112
self-understanding 146
'significance' 9
signification 120, 143, 145
singularity of things (*haecceitas*) 36–8, 49
Socrates 135
Spengler, Oswald 15
the spirit 35–6, 38

spoken language 38
subject/object relation 36, 110, 147
subjectivity 67, 116, 120, 131, 134–7, 148
sunrise example, process/appropriation of lived experience 114–15

techne (technological knowledge) 69–70
temporality *see* time
theology 42, 43–9
   see also Christianity
theoretical attitude 107–8, 113
theoretical knowledge 72
'theoretical', meaning of 90–1
theoria (observation and description) 68
Thessalonians, Epistle to 53–4, 58
thinking/thought dichotomy 26
time
   anticipation of death 59–60
   movedness of human life 76–80
   phenomenological chronology 82–5
   problem of 80–5
   religious temporality 58
'to world' expression 53
totality of signification 143
transcendence 44, 49, 128–9, 132
transcendental aesthetics 82, 83
transcendental idealism 134–7
transcendental logic 137–8
transcendental phenomenology 1, 139, 140–2
transcendental reflection 118
transcendental subjectivity 67, 116, 120, 131, 134–7
truth
   Aristotelian modes 67–70
   and disclosedness 66
   phenomenon of 63–7
   types of 61
   as unconcealment 63–7
Tugendhat, E. 66
'the turn' (*Kehre*) 6, 145

understanding 121, 143, 147
Untimely Meditations (Nietzsche) 15
unveilment modes 67–70

Volpi, F. 61

Weimar Republic 13–14
Welt concept 144
Welte, Bernhard 43
what 120
the world
   essence of 130
   experience of 109–14
   hermeneutic concept 143–5
'to world' expression 53
worldviews, philosophy of 5, 88–90

Xolocotzi, Ángel 18